T0276425

MUSIC TITANS

250 GREATEST RECORDING ARTISTS
of the Past 100 Years

STEVE WILLIAMS

ISBN: 979-8-35093-374-1 paperback
ISBN: 979-8-35093-375-8 ebook

"If I were not a physicist, I would probably be a musician. I often think in music. I live my daydreams in music. I see my life in terms of music."

Albert Einstein

"Without music to decorate it, time is just a bunch of boring production deadlines or dates by which bills must be paid."

Frank Zappa

"I merely took the energy it takes to pout and wrote some blues."

Duke Ellington

"Musicians want to be the loud voice for so many quiet hearts."

Billy Joel

"Music gives a soul to the universe, wings to the mind, flight to the imagination, and life to everything."

Plato

"Country music is three chords and the truth."

Harlan Howard

CONTENTS

MUSIC TITANS

250 GREATEST RECORDING ARTISTS
of the Past 100 Years

INTRODUCTION

There are not a lot of universals in this fractured world. Certainly we are divided by politics, religion, class, and, all too often still, by race. One universal bonding element, however, is music. Music is found in all cultures, and even the most hardened or stoic individual can be moved by a song, a melody, a chord, a lyric, a beat.

Not that we all love the same songs or the same styles of music. As a child, all too often, I heard my father hollering to "turn that noise down," while I often looked to flee the room to avoid having to hear his melancholy tunes. Still, I think it is safe to say that virtually all human beings can be stirred, at times, by some form of music.

This book is an attempt to honor that universal grace that we call music. I am not a professor of music and I don't purport to know much about Indian or Chinese or Middle Eastern music. I may speak a little Spanish, but I am not qualified to write about Mexican ranchera or mariachi styles. What I have been doing, ever since I was a little boy in the mid-'50s, is listening to music—religiously, fanatically, constantly. In countless ways, music has colored, even defined and given meaning to my life. I bought my first 45s at age seven, made weekly lists of my favorite songs when I was 11 or 12, sang in choirs and choruses and informal doo-wop gatherings with friends as I grew into adolescence. As I said, I didn't listen to mariachi or Indian music because it wasn't readily available, but I consumed everything within my grasp. When I bought my first $8 guitar from Woolworth's, I learned to play (badly) and in no time I was singing and strumming in a teenage band, then later in parks, on beaches, and street corners, caring not for the coins or occasional bills that came my way but only for the love of singing and sharing song. Never parlaying the occasional coffee house, recording session, or church gig into a career, I grew instead into a teacher but never left the world of music behind.

This book, then, is a labor of love. Whenever I watch or read about the latest Rock & Roll Hall of Fame inductees, or check out someone's list of the greatest this or that, or listen to a trendy artist picking up a handful of Grammys, I am always intrigued and sometimes ready to differ. That's what this book is about—it seeks to answer the question, just who are the greatest recording artists of the past century?

Why the past 100 years? We could go back to the late 1800s, to people like Alexander Graham Bell, Thomas Edison, and Emile Berliner, when the first recording devices were invented. By the early 20th century, the old Victrolas were playing the scratchy band marches of John Philip Sousa, pieces by classical artists such as the hugely popular Enrico Caruso, esteemed vocalists like Billy Murray, the syncopated ragtime of Scott Joplin, and the patriotic martial music of World War I. By 1920, the phonograph was ubiquitous and millions of records were being sold; however, it wasn't until the mid-1920s, when electrical recording methods replaced the traditional acoustic approach that had required musicians to position themselves close to the open end of a giant funnel, that the sound quality was drastically improved and the modern-day recording industry really began to soar. This new, recorded music boom, however, soon had to face and overcome three existential crises in three successive decades: the rise of radio in the '20s, seen initially as a threat, but ultimately a boon to the recording industry; the Great Depression in the 1930s, which severely ate into record sales; and, in the early '40s, a musicians' union strike that put a halt to the recording of most new music in the U.S. Nevertheless, in the 1920s the sale of records increasingly replaced the sale of sheet music, a new market culture was exploding, and the sonic quality of records was vastly improved; so I take as my starting point the decade of the 1920s as I seek to answer the question: Who exactly are the greatest artists of recorded music of the past 100 years?

Criteria
To be considered for this list, all artists needed to be **recording artists.** There have been many brilliant composers, songwriters, producers,

arrangers, and executives who assisted greatly in bringing wonderful music to our ears. My focus, however, is on the singers and the musicians whose voices, notes, and rhythms we hear when we listen to our favorite songs.

Also, the main body of work of each recording artist needs to be in English (if, indeed, their music has lyrics) to be eligible; they may also record in Spanish, French, or any other tongue, but more than half their recorded output needs to be based in English.

That still begs the question: Greatest in what sense?

Well, we could make a list based strictly on **Popularity**. Simply counting the number of records each artist sold and then listing the artists in order, it might be argued, could do that. That's not as easy as it sounds, however. After researching the topic, I discovered that not all such best-selling lists yield the same results and for a variety of reasons. Record sales were not always carefully counted. This was much more haphazard in the United States before the late '50s, for instance. Counting methodologies improved significantly in the 1990s. Also, counting methods differed and still differ country to country. Some best-seller lists use what are known as "Certified Sales," as determined by the RIAA (Recording Industry Association of America), and while there is an international certifying body, there is sometimes a lack of uniformity in the counting process. Most lists also include "Claimed Sales" which are supposed to be carefully checked to see if the source of the claim is reliable. It's not a pure science. Exaggeration, faulty sources, shipped records that were never actually purchased, even fraud, can all color the results. Nevertheless, an analysis of a number of these best-seller lists will yield a reasonably accurate understanding of just who are the best-selling artists. For example, few people dispute that the Beatles, Elvis Presley, and Michael Jackson are at the top; but where, for example, should Bing Crosby be listed since counting was much more slipshod in his era? Even if you create your list based on records sold, is that the ultimate gauge of popularity? Joe Smith, and millions like him, might have bought Album X and played it 1000 times while his neighbor Jenny Jones, and those like her who bought the same album, played it once and never again. How would we know? That won't show up in the data. Radio airplay can also be factored in to measure popularity, and today, with the rise of streaming services and digital downloads, that too is considered. However, to be clear, popularity, as measured by record sales, is based on *estimated* numbers of records sold, and that estimate was derived after studying a variety of lists of best-selling artists.

Another gauge of popularity can be how many people pay to see the artist perform in person. Are they a huge concert draw? It's hard to come by all those numbers for the past century; we are again forced to *estimate*. I also considered the artist's reputation as a live performer.

A third component of popularity relates to longevity. For how many years, for how many decades or generations, has the artist's music been selling? Is it still played or remembered today? Suffice it to say that popularity is but **one** important metric to determine who is the greatest of all time, but I think more factors need to be considered.

A second category that I used to determine this list is what I call **Impact or Influence**. Did the artist have a significant impact on the music of their day? Did they impact other musicians? Did they change the listening habits of the general public? And what about future generations of musicians and listeners? Was music enriched, influenced, or altered because of the music of a particular artist? In addition, I considered how the greater culture or society was impacted by the artist under consideration. Were language, fashion, other arts, commerce, symbols, attitudes, ways of being in the world in some way impacted by the work of the artist? Did they have an impact on the day's politics, for example? Was there an uptick in a certain type of youth behavior, for another? And what about long term? Were the social or cultural impacts of a certain artist ephemeral or longer lasting, affecting later generations as well? Obviously it is difficult, if not impossible, to assess the impact and influence of a musical artist in a scientifically rigorous way, and I don't pretend to have done so, but through careful analysis it is obvious that many music critics and cultural observers have written perceptively on these issues, and, therefore, some conclusions can be drawn. In assessing an artist's musical and cultural influence, I read many articles and critiques from a variety of books, periodicals, web sites, and other sources. I also consulted a number of compilations such as the

Library of Congress *National Recording Registry*, the RIAA Songs of the Century, the various *Rolling Stone* lists, and a number of other such collections, *none* of which limited their selections to simply American artists. Needless to say, this category is the most difficult to measure, but it still feels important enough to try. Here is an example: It is obvious to me and many other observers that Elvis Presley had a significantly greater impact on the listening habits and social attitudes of teenagers worldwide than, say, Pat Boone. We may differ on *how* to quantify that difference, but I have made an attempt to do so under the two sub-categories, **musical influence** and **cultural influence**.

The third category I used to formulate my list was **Honors and Awards**. I looked at the type and the number of awards and honors won by each artist in their lifetime and posthumously. Not every award was considered as every school, town, city, and trade organization bestows awards, but I looked at such major recognition as Grammys; musical Oscars; Rock, Blues, Jazz, Country, R&B, and Songwriters Halls of Fame; national and international honors such as Kennedy Center Honors and Presidential Medals of Freedom and their overseas counterparts; Pulitzer Prizes and the like. I deemed some awards more prestigious than others. For example, a Nobel Prize for Literature awarded to Bob Dylan for his lifetime contributions to song counts for more, in my mind, than an MTV Video Music Award from 1996, simply because it is so much more rare.

Why not just make the "greatest" synonymous with the "best"—such that the Greatest Recording Artists of the Past 100 Years would be ranked according to who is the best, who is second-best, and so forth? Does anybody care whom *I* deem best? Wouldn't that simply be a list of my personal tastes? Well, suppose we research what the chief music critics of *Rolling Stone*, or *DownBeat*, or *Country Music People*, or *The New Yorker* have to say? Wouldn't we then just get a list of their favorite rock, jazz, country artists, or an eclectic mix of their personal tastes, no matter how well supported with argument and explanation? In fact, there have been many of these sorts of lists and books published. What I propose is something else. What I have done is to devise a complex point system, an algorithm, using the three basic categories explained above:

Popularity - This is a combination of *estimated* total records sold; their fame as a concert attraction as defined by *estimated* ticket grosses *and* artistic reputation as a live artist; and their longevity as a popular artist as shown by how long their records sold and how long they were a major live attraction.

Impact or Influence - Two sub-categories were considered in awarding points to each artist: How did the artist influence the musical artists and musical tastes of their day and of future generations? How did the artist influence the larger culture of their day and of future generations? Quite subjective, I know, but I've done extensive reading and research from various music and social critics from dozens and dozens of books and publications, both print and online sources, in awarding points.

Honors and Awards - These included Halls of Fame (e.g., Rock & Roll; Country; Blues, Jazz, R&B, Songwriters); national awards such as Kennedy Center Honors, national medals, etc.; and important awards such as Grammys, Oscars, American Music, and Peoples' Choice prizes.

In cases of ties, I considered whether the artist was also a songwriter.

I tried very hard **not** to allow my personal tastes to color these results. For that reason you will find artists of all **genres** and **generations** included here. If I did my job well, my personal favorites will not be glaringly obvious. Indeed, there are artists listed throughout whose music I ordinarily would not seek out, but my idea is to make this list, consistent with the algorithm, as inclusive as possible, and not about my personal favorites. So, here you will find a wide range of **rock** (embracing such subgenres as early rock & roll, hard rock, metal, progressive, punk, New Wave) and **pop** artists of differing styles and sensibilities; there are also **R&B** artists, **country** artists, and **jazz** greats from different eras. In addition you will find assorted **hip-hop/rap** artists; and those primarily noted for the **blues, folk, contemporary classical, electronic, gospel, disco, dance,** and **reggae.**

Many, if not most, of these artists recorded across several genres, and it is not always easy or even possible to list all their genres; I have, however, capitalized the genres for which they are best known.

Artists' peak years of creativity and popularity are noted, as well as when they began recording. You will find recording artists from every decade, but the greatest number were active in the 1950s, '60s, '70s, '80s, '90s, and 2000s. No doubt, in five years this list will shift significantly as many of today's recording stars will have more hits, greater longevity, and more pronounced impact; and some of them will be tomorrow's legends.

In addition, I have listed several songs for each artist. These are not necessarily their most popular (though they often are) or most honored (though they could be) songs. They are offered as representative songs that I found interesting, an opening to the artist's musical world. You could make a playlist from this list, as I did, if you are so inclined, or you could make your own.

You will also find mini-biographies/musical commentaries for each artist, written in the two-fold hope that I make the case as to why the artist is on the list, and that they spark your interest to explore their music for yourself.

I have listed the artists in reverse order, from #250 to #1 to increase the suspense and the drama. Of course, you can cheat and look ahead, but what's the fun in that?

You will notice immediately that many hugely successful recording artists did not make the list of the 250 greatest. This is not to disparage their music or their careers. In fact, a few of my all-time favorite artists did not make the cut-off, and it caused me a great deal of angst and second-guessing to have to leave various artists off. We simply have had many more than 250 great artists. To reiterate, there have been many brilliant, influential, popular, and honored recording artists in the past century, **a lot** more than 250!

So what, exactly, is the point of this book? I wanted to start an argument—more precisely, a conversation. As I was working on the commentaries, I shared copies of my list with family members and friends, and, unsurprisingly, they aroused strong and differing reactions: "Where is so-and-so?" "Why is this artist so high?" "Why is this one so low?" "Are you kidding me? She's only #_?" You get the picture. **I don't pretend that my list or ranking is scientific or definitive**, as it is based on estimates in Category 1 and my reading of musical and cultural impact in Category 2. Still, I really did **try** to be fair and objective, using the criteria and formula I devised. No doubt, using my same criteria and formula, others would come up with a different ranking, though I like to think not *so* different. This list, this book, ultimately, is meant to provoke conversation, debate, argument, and interest in music and musicians. But, also, I found in doing this that it opened up for me a whole new world of music. I confess that my musical world had narrowed, had shrunk considerably over the years. In doing this project, I spent hundreds and hundreds of hours with what for me was new music and I have been greatly enriched in the process, for that is what music ultimately does—it enriches our lives; so my hope is that it does the same thing for you—that it inspires you to seek out and listen to music you might otherwise never have been inclined to sample. I hope that it brings you as much joy as it has brought me.

On the following pages you will discover the Music Titans, the 250 greatest recording artists of the past 100 years.

ARTIST PROFILES

#250 Tom Waits (1949 - present)
Began Recording: 1971
Peak: 1976 - 1987; 1999
Genres: Jazz; Blues; Experimental Singer/Songwriter/Instrumentalist

Too quirky for mainstream success, Tom Waits is an acquired taste; yet he has won two Grammys, is a member of the Rock & Roll Hall of Fame, and he has legions of fiercely loyal fans.

As a Southern California middle class kid, Tom was exposed to a wide variety of musical forms—R&B, country, folk, rock, show tunes, jazz, mariachi. Attracted to Kerouac and Bob Dylan, Waits began playing folk and jazz wherever he could, finally landing a gig at L.A.'s Troubadour, which led to a recording contract. "Ol' '55" is representative of his very early style—the seemingly simple piano ballad may just be a song about visiting his girl, but there are hints, too, that he may be singing of death. Morphing from his folky debut to a more jazzy style, Tom became the poet-laureate of the lost, forgotten, beaten down, drunken, and despairing—society's under-class. With each album, his voice took on a harsher, raspier, even spooky affect. Patrick Humphries reports that Waits was fond of a particular description: "Louis Armstrong and Ethel Merman meeting in hell."

His early works through about 1982, featuring "Bones" Howe as his usual producer, stayed pretty consistently in the jazz lane, with blues, rock, folk, strings, and beat poetry inflections. Outstanding examples include the deeply moving "Tom Traubert's Blues" and "Christmas Card from a Hooker in Minneapolis." Then, in 1980, Waits met Kathleen Brennan who became his wife (43 years and counting) and new collaborator, and since 1983 Tom has moved in a decidedly more experimental direction, featuring new rhythms, odd, ambient sounds, and experimental instruments, interspersed all the while with throwback tunes of brilliant poetry and memorable melodies. The LPs *Swordfishtrombones*, *Rain Dogs*, *Franks Wild Years*, and *Mule Variations* are worth a listen to hear his newer work.

Suggested Songs:

Tom Traubert's Blues (Four Sheets to the Wind in Copenhagen) (1976)
Christmas Card from a Hooker in Minneapolis (1978)
Time (1985)
Come on Up to the House (1999)

#249 John Legend (1978 - present)

Began Recording: 2004
Peak: 2005 - 2015
Genres: R&B; Pop Singer/Songwriter/Pianist

Turning 45 at the end of 2023, John Legend is one of a handful of artists to have earned an EGOT—an Emmy (he's got two); a Grammy (12 actually); an Oscar; and a Tony.

Born John Stephens to working class, but musical, parents in Ohio, as a young child he learned piano and sang in his church choir. A superb student, John turned down a chance to attend Harvard and graduated magna cum laude from the University of Pennsylvania where he was deeply involved with music. After graduating in 1999, he took a job as a management consultant by day and worked at night on writing, performing, and self-producing his music, even as he made time to work in the background for the likes of Lauryn Hill, Alicia Keys, and Kanye West, who, ultimately, signed him and helped produce his debut LP, *Get Lifted*. Now using the stage name John Legend, the album, still his most celebrated and best selling, established him as a star. It was the first of three Legend LPs to take home a Grammy for Best R&B album, the other two being 2010's *Wake Up!*, a collaboration with The Roots, and 2020's *Bigger Love*.

Legend's music has been described as "old-school" R&B, as neo-soul, as smooth and elegant. He has a warm, calm demeanor and vocal style, rarely flashy, quite polished, most effective with a simple piano accompaniment. Two of his best-loved songs are piano ballads—'05's "Ordinary People," which reflects on the ups and downs in a mature love relationship, and 2013's "All of Me," a massive world-wide chart-topper that finds John swooning in his love for his fiancée. Another award winning record (a Grammy, Golden Globe, and an Oscar), "Glory," is a song of uplift for the movie *Selma*, done in collaboration with the rapper Common.

Politically outspoken and ubiquitous in the media, it will be fun to watch and listen to Legend as he develops in the coming years.

Suggested Songs:

Ordinary People (2005)
Green Light (w. André 3000) (2008)
All of Me (2013)
Glory (w. Common) (2014)

#248 Leon Russell (1942 - 2016)

Began Recording: 1968 (w. Marc Benno); 1970 (solo)
Peak: 1970 - 1973; 1975
Genres: Rock; Country; R&B; gospel; blues Singer/Songwriter/Instrumentalist

Known as a "musician's musician," Leon Russell was a legendary session man, songwriter, arranger, and pianist who had a brief moment of fame in the early '70s.

Born Claude Russell Bridges in Oklahoma, he was taking classical piano lessons by four and playing in Tulsa-area clubs by 14. Moving to L.A. in 1958, he changed his name to Leon Russell, learned guitar, and was soon one of the most sought-after session musicians in the business, usually, though not always, on piano. He also found time to write, arrange, produce, and play in various bands. Over his 60-year career, Leon worked with Jerry Lee Lewis, Ricky Nelson, Phil Spector, the Beach Boys, Frank Sinatra, Glen Campbell, Herb Alpert, the Byrds, Eric Clapton, the Rolling Stones, Bob Dylan, and scores more.

In 1969, Joe Cocker had a hit with his "Delta Lady," and the following year Leon was leading Cocker's sprawling, celebrated *Mad Dogs & Englishmen* tour. Soon Russell, with his sophisticated mix of rock & roll, country, R&B, and gospel, was an in-demand headliner. With a loose, drawn-out southern drawl of a vocal style, his '72 release, *Carney*, reached #2 on the *Billboard* 200. "A Song for You," not a hit when released on his first LP, has since become his best-loved piece, covered by over 200 artists, most notably by Ray Charles, Willie Nelson, and Whitney Houston. Other signature Russell tunes include "Tight Rope," with its circus imagery and sound; "This Masquerade," a Grammy winner when George Benson covered it; and "Lady Blue," his 1975 love pledge.

Though he continued working steadily, Russell fell out of commercial favor from 1980 to 2010 when Elton John, noting that Russell had been his "biggest influence as a piano player, a singer, and a songwriter," pulled him back into the spotlight with their collaborative effort, *The Union*. "The

Master of Space and Time," as he was known, died peacefully at 74. He's a member of the Rock and Songwriters Halls of Fame.

Suggested Songs:

A Song for You (1970)
Tight Rope (1972)
This Masquerade (1972)
Lady Blue (1975)

#247 Frank Ocean (1987 - present)

Began Recording: 2011
Peak: 2012 - 2013; 2016 - 2017
Genres: R&B; hip-hop; Avant-garde Soul Singer/Songwriter

Frank Ocean is one of the most groundbreaking R&B artists in decades. People have heard echoes of Marvin Gaye, Prince, Brian Eno, Drake, Stevie Wonder, Brian Wilson, and Depeche Mode in his music; and that's just for starters.

Born Christopher Breaux, his family moved to New Orleans when he was five. Christopher left university and headed to L.A. shortly after Hurricane Katrina to break into the music business. His initial success came as a songwriter for the likes of Brandy, Beyoncé, and Justin Bieber. He signed with Def Jam in 2009, but with things moving too slowly for Frank Ocean, as he had begun calling himself, he self-released a mixtape, *Nostalgia, Ultra*, featuring the lead track "Novacane," a surreal tale of the ways in which we numb ourselves. His label and the industry took notice, and in 2012 he dropped *Channel Orange*, his debut album, which mixes jazz, funk, and electronic elements into an underlying soulful R&B groove. Lyrically he explores unrequited love, heartache, sex, lust, empty materialism, and the search for connection and meaning, often utilizing wildly inventive narrative. "Pyramid" is a case in point as it flies from ancient Egypt to a modern strip club while exploring prostitution, pimping, and a deep yearning for love, all the while floating on an arresting 10-minute musical suite. Ocean's voice is a wonder, as well, as he weaves from rap to his singing tenor, regularly jumping in and out of a high falsetto.

Frank virtually disappeared after that, only to reemerge in 2016 with a visual album, followed the next day by his second LP, the even more sonically adventurous *Blonde*. *Pitchfork* simply called it the best album of the 2010s.

Suggested Songs:

Thinkin Bout You (2012)
Pyramids (2012)
Nights (2016)
Pink + White (2016)

#246 Joe Cocker (1944 - 2014)

Began Recording: 1964 (as Vance Arnold & the Avengers); 1968 (as Joe Cocker)
Peak: 1969 - 1971; 1982 - 1983
Genres: Rock; Blues; pop Singer/songwriter

One of the great blues-rock interpreters, sometimes compared with Ray Charles, Joe Cocker had his own distinctive, soulful vocal and performing style.

Born John Cocker near the end of World War II in Sheffield, England, Cocker appeared headed for a career as a gas fitter, even as he sang with various bands in local pubs. His incarnation as Vance Arnold didn't pan out, but, in 1968, he had a #1 hit in Britain with his wildly different take on the Beatles' Ringo sung tune, "With a Little Help from My Friends." Turning it into a slow burning soul-rock affair, Cocker became an international star when his performance was captured at Woodstock for the subsequent film. With arms flailing, fingers chording an air guitar, Cocker grimacing and gyrating, he roared out his heart with total abandon. Though the gestures were toned down some over the years, this became Joe's signature mode—audacious, raspy, sometimes whispered, sometimes screamed, heart and soul vocals. To the very end of his performing days in 2013, he left nothing in reserve.

There were bumps along the way; for much of the '70s he had a major problem with drugs and alcohol. It was feared he may end up like Janis or Jimi, but, by the '80s and thereafter, he seemed to stay clean. Career highlights include his first three albums, *With a Little Help from My Friends*, *Joe Cocker!* and *Mad Dogs and Englishmen*; his covers of Dave Mason's "Feeling Alright" and the Box Tops' "The Letter," his first American Top 10 hit; his fragile, yet stirring take on "You Are So Beautiful;" and his moving 1982 duet with Jennifer Warnes, "Up Where We Belong," which topped the *Billboard* Hot 100, won a Grammy, an Oscar, and a place in the RIAA Songs of the Century.

Cocker recorded and remained a much loved, major concert draw 'til the end; he succumbed to lung cancer at the age of 70.

Suggested Songs:

With a Little Help from My Friends (1968)
The Moon Is a Harsh Mistress (1974)
You Are So Beautiful (1975)
Up Where We Belong (w. Jennifer Warnes) (1982)

#245 John Prine (1946 - 2020)

Began Recording: 1971
Peak: 1971 - 1972; 1991; 2005; 2018 - 2020
Genres: Country Folk; Americana Singer/Songwriter

He was called a musical Mark Twain, a master storyteller able to inhabit the lives of ordinary Americans and comment with wry humor and compassion on life's fragile beauty and painful absurdity, often within the same verse.

John Prine grew up in a working class Chicago suburb. He learned guitar from an older brother and was soon writing his own songs, afraid he'd forget the words of other people. After high school he became a mailman before he was drafted and sent to West Germany. Upon his release, he returned to mail delivery by day and singing in the evenings. A late-night visit from Kris Kristofferson led to a record contract, and, in 1971, Prine released his eponymous debut LP, widely considered a classic, featuring such standouts as "Hello in There," a plea by an old person to be seen; "Sam Stone," about a war vet coming home with a killing drug addiction; "Paradise," which laments the destruction of his parents' Kentucky town at the hands of strip miners; and "Angel of Montgomery," told movingly from the point of view of an unhappy aging woman. All the songs were bigger hits as covers by other artists, a recurring theme throughout Prine's career. With a ragged, everyman's voice, Prine delivered his poignant, often irreverent tales in a country-flavored folky style, sometimes dipping into other genres. When hit records didn't come his way, he formed his own label. He loved Johnny Cash and Bob Dylan, and they returned the compliment, as did artists as diverse as Bette Midler, Roger Waters, and Bonnie Raitt.

Prine was never afraid to push the envelope—give a listen to the irreverent "Jesus, the Missing Years" or his plea for a kinder world, "Some Humans Ain't Human." With a Lifetime Grammy and a spot in the Songwriters Hall of Fame, Prine died of COVID-19 in 2020, just two years after releasing his highest charting LP, *The Tree of Forgiveness*.

Suggested Songs:

Hello In There (1971)
Sam Stone (1971)
Jesus, the Missing Years (1991)
I Remember Everything (2020)

#244 Depeche Mode

Began Recording: 1981
Peak: 1984 - 1993
Genres: Synth Pop; New Wave/Alternative Rock Band

The quintessential English synth-based rock band, Depeche Mode became one of the world's most popular musical acts in the late '80s and early '90s.

In 1980, Vince Clarke helped his rocking mates, Andy Fletcher, Martin Gore, and Dave Gahan, to move in a more electronic direction. Knocking on London label doors, they got a deal and released their debut LP, *Speak & Spell*, in 1981. The album reached #10 in Britain, and the Clarke-composed "Just Can't Get Enough," a light, catchy dance number, became a hit. And then Clarke quit. Alan Wilder took his place, and Depeche Mode, named for a French fashion magazine, began moving, little by little, into slightly darker territory. With moody, yet melodic, layered musical textures, Gore's ruminative lyrics about solitude, politics, avarice, religion, sex, and personal demons, and Gahan's seductive, insinuating baritone vocals, Depeche Mode was poised to take off, beginning with "Everything Counts," a 1983 anti-greed track. Other celebrated work includes 1984's "People to People," a rhythmic soundscape that sounds like gunfire and reached #1 in West Germany while also breaking through in the U.S., and three consecutive strong albums: *Black Celebration*, featuring "Stripped," a "get away from the fumes and toxic technology" track; *Music for the Masses*, featuring "Strangelove;" and their best-loved *Violator*, with the anti-idolatry "Personal Jesus;" Gore favorite, "Policy of Truth;" and "Enjoy the Silence," perhaps their best-known single.

At the height of their fame in the early '90s, Gore and Gahan struggled with substance abuse, Fletcher was battling depression and suffering a nervous breakdown, and Wilder quit in 1995. The Hall of Fame band would be back with more great music, however, notably 1997's *Ultra* and the singles, "Barrel of a Gun" and 2005's "Precious." In 2022, Andy Fletcher died suddenly of an aortic dissection, or tear. Gore and Gahan carry on.

Suggested Songs:

Stripped (1986)
Enjoy the Silence (1990)
Policy of Truth (1990)
Precious (w. Steve Fitzmaurice) (2005)

#243 Nas (1973 - present)

Began Recording: 1992 (as Nasty Nas); 1994 (as Nas)
Peak: 1994 - 1999; 2002 - 2008; 2012
Genres: Hip-Hop Rapper/Songwriter

Widely acclaimed as one of the great rap lyricists of all-time, Nas reached an artistic and critical peak at the age of 20 and, fairly or not, has taken heat ever since for never quite achieving the same level of sustained brilliance.

Born Nasir Jones in Brooklyn, Nas grew up in the notorious Queensbridge housing project in Queens, New York, raised by his mother after his jazz musician father, Olu Dara, and she divorced. A school dropout after eighth grade, Nas largely educated himself thereafter, while absorbing the heartbreaking, yet eye-opening, effects of the drugs, violence, and poverty he witnessed all around him. It was this world that is masterfully reflected in his 1994 debut LP, *Illmatic*, which has been praised for its complex wordplay, internal rhyme scheme, and poetic mixture of first person narrative, hope, and despair. Routinely listed among hip-hop's greatest albums, it's been included in the Library of Congress *National Recording Registry*. Among the acclaimed tracks are—"Life Is a Bitch," a 20-year-old's embrace of cash and getting high, because life holds no certainties, least of all long-term survival; "The World Is Yours," ultimately a life-affirming ode for all those who come from hard places; and "N.Y. State of Mind," with its hard-boiled, matter-of-fact depiction of urban alienation and violence.

Subsequent releases have found Nas ruminating on a variety of topics, from the "thug life" ("The Message") to braggadocio ("Got Urself a Gun"), from empowerment anthems ("I Can") to fatherhood ("Daughters"). A Grammy winner as recently as 2021, in his own words—"I see myself as a musician who raps...It's important that I make something that touches people."

Suggested Songs:

The World Is Yours (1994)
N.Y. State of Mind (1994)
I Can (2003)
Daughters (2012)

#242 Four Tops
Began Recording: 1956
Peak: 1964 - 1968
Genres: Soul; R&B; Pop Vocal Group

Lawrence, Obie, Duke, and Levi met while they were high school students in Detroit in 1953, first singing together at a birthday party. They began practicing and performing locally, calling themselves the Four Aims. By 1956, they had a recording contract with Chess and had changed their name to the Four Tops, but seven years and four record labels later they still had no hits, though they had a wealth of live experience, working with the likes of Billy Eckstine and developing a repertoire of R&B, jazz, and traditional pop standards.

In 1963, they joined Berry Gordy, Jr.'s Motown family, and the following year the crack songwriting-production team of Holland-Dozier-Holland gave them their first hit, "Baby I Need Your Loving," a lonely, pleading, soulful single that set the template for the next few years of Four Tops' success. They were Lawrence Payton Jr., who usually worked out the vocal harmony parts; Obie Benson, who sang bass; Duke Fakir, tenor; and Levi Stubbs, their lead singer, noted for his powerful, dramatic, emotionally charged baritone. In an age of "me-first," the Tops were unusual in that they stayed together as an unbroken unit for 44 years until Payton's death in 1997. Stubbs, who refused to place himself above his mates though frequently lauded for possessing "one of the great soul voices of the last 50 years," quit in 2000 after a stroke. Only Fakir, the lone surviving member, continues to perform with today's Four Tops.

Members of the Rock, Vocal Group, and R&B Halls of Fame, between 1965 and 1967 they were an unstoppable force with such gritty, soul-pop hits as "Ask the Lonely;" "I Can't Help Myself," their first #1; "It's the Same Old Song;" "Reach Out I'll Be There," a *National Recording Registry* selection; "Standing in the Shadows of Love;" and "Bernadette." Even after

Holland-Dozier-Holland, and the Four Tops themselves, left Motown, they still had the occasional hit, right up to 1988.

Suggested Songs:

Baby I Need Your Loving (1964)
Ask the Lonely (1965)
Reach Out I'll Be There (1966)
Walk Away Renee (1968)

#241 Howlin' Wolf (1910 - 1976)

Began Recording: 1951
Peak: 1951; 1956 - 1965
Genres: Blues Singer/songwriter/instrumentalist

He was large and larger than life, with a roaring, force-of-nature voice married to raw, Chicago-style blues. He learned from the best—from Charlie Patton, who taught him guitar licks and much about singing and showmanship; and from Sonny Boy Williamson he learned to blow harmonica. He idolized Jimmie Rodgers, but soon enough discovered he couldn't yodel.

Born Chester Arthur Burnett on a cotton plantation in rural Mississippi, he was called Wolf from an early age. He had no formal education and an insecure childhood, bouncing from his mother to an abusive uncle to his father. He was 17 when he got his first guitar, and, though he farmed 'til the late '40s, he also played the Delta blues wherever and with whomever he could. By 1948, he had a band and a West Memphis radio gig. A young Ike Turner brought him to the attention of Sam Phillips, later of Sun Records fame, and, in 1951, Howlin' Wolf, as he now called himself, recorded the double sided, R&B hit, the bluesy "Moanin' at Midnight" and the rock & roll-flavored "How Many More Years." A year later he was under contract with Chess, and he relocated to Chicago. Never a big hit maker, there was a relatively friendly competition between Wolf and Muddy Waters, with Willie Dixon penning for both. Howlin' Wolf's most iconic tracks include "Smokestack Lightning," with what's been termed its "hypnotic" riff and Wolf's signature, ferocious growl punctuated by his high pitched keening; "Spoonful," later made famous by Cream's 1966 version; "The Red Rooster," faithfully covered as "Little Red Rooster" by the Rolling Stones; and "Killing Floor," with its slaughterhouse metaphor for damaged relationships.

Like Waters and B.B. King, Howlin' Wolf was celebrated by blues rockers and their fans and found entry into both the Rock and Blues Halls of Fame. Very disciplined in his personal life, he had a long and happy marriage, earned a GED diploma, and never ceased educating himself. Wolf was noted for paying his musicians a fair wage. He died two months after giving his final, highly acclaimed show.

Suggested Songs:

How Many More Years (1951)
Smokestack Lightning (1956)
Spoonful (1960)
Killing Floor (1964)

#240 Nina Simone (1933 - 2003)

Began Recording: 1959
Peak: 1964 - 1969
Genres: Classical/Jazz/Blues/Gospel/Soul Singer/Pianist/songwriter

Born Eunice Waymon, one of eight children in rural North Carolina, by the age of four she was playing piano at the Methodist Church where her mother preached. She was a high school valedictorian and hoped to study classical music at Philadelphia's prestigious Curtis Institute of Music but was rejected, a slight that Waymon took to be racially motivated. Needing to earn a living, she found a gig in 1954 in Atlantic City, where she was required to sing as well as play piano. Calling herself Nina Simone to hide from her mother the fact that she was playing "devil's music," she gained a following with a varied mix of blues, jazz, gospel, classical, and pop. In addition, she had a deep, soulful, idiosyncratic vocal style and, in 1959, a recording contract.

The Gershwin classic "I Loves You, Porgy" was an early hit, and Nina was soon a major concert and club draw. In 1964, in the wake of the murder of Civil Rights activist Medgar Evers, Nina wrote and recorded her first "movement" song, the lyrically powerful and heavily censored "Mississippi Goddam." Never a best-selling artist, she was, nonetheless, praised by such greats as Miles Davis, Mary J. Blige, Lauryn Hill, and David Bowie.

Nina suffered from bipolar disorder, took antipsychotic medicine, and was known to scold an inattentive audience, but she was a virtuoso, eclectic performer. Some of her best-loved recordings include "Don't Let Me Be Misunderstood," later covered by the Animals; her smooth take on Screamin' Jay Hawkins' "I Put a Spell on You;" and "Four Women," her portrait of four suffering but strong women of color. "My Baby Just Cares for Me" and "Feeling Good" were hits some three decades after she recorded them.

Nina is a member of the R&B and Rock & Roll Halls of Fame, and, two days before she died, she was awarded an honorary doctorate from the Curtis Institute, the music school that had rejected her a half century earlier.

Suggested Songs:

Mississippi Goddam (1964)
Don't Let Me Be Misunderstood (1964)
I Put a Spell on You (1965)
Four Women (1966)

#239 Carpenters

Began Recording: 1966 (as Karen Carpenter); 1969 (as Carpenters)
Peak: 1970 - 1975
Genres: Pop; Soft Rock Vocal/Instrumental Duo

They were brother and sister and very close. Richard Carpenter, born in 1946, was the quiet one, a musical prodigy taking lessons at Yale School of Music at 14; sister Karen, born in 1950, was more outgoing, happy playing outside, when she wasn't tagging after Richard. Their parents moved to California in 1963 so Richard could be closer to the music business. In high school, Karen began playing the drums and Richard, already a gifted pianist and arranger, discovered his sister could sing. Inspired by Les Paul and Mary Ford's "vocal overdubs and layered harmonies," they began to cut demos and enter various contests. In 1969, they were signed to A&M by Herb Alpert. Their debut single, a melancholy take on the Beatles' "Ticket to Ride," was a minor hit, but it was the Bacharach-David composition "Close to You" that made them overnight international stars, followed by a second signature song, "We've Only Just Begun." Suddenly they were Grammy and Oscar winners ("For All We Know"), and the Carpenter sound, light, soft, lush, and layered, though against the musical grain of its day, was everywhere. "Rainy Days and Mondays," "Superstar," "Hurting Each Other," "Sing," "Yesterday Once More," "Top of the World," "Please Mr. Postman"—giant hits all.

Karen, a superb drummer, was coaxed out front where she could be seen as well as heard, as her voice was a revelation—deep, calm, pitch perfect, with just a hint of sadness. Paul McCartney said she had "the best female voice in the world," but by the late '70s there were few hits, Richard had developed a pill addiction for which he successfully sought treatment, and Karen was losing weight at an alarming rate. Her disastrous, rushed marriage only made matters worse. Finally admitting she had a problem, she sought treatment for her eating disorder, but she struggled to recover fully. In 1983 she died of heart failure, her body mortally weakened by anorexia nervosa.

Considered "uncool" by many in their day, the Carpenters' reputation has greatly risen with time, and they remain commercially popular to this day.

Suggested Songs:

(They Long to Be) Close to You (1970)
We've Only Just Begun (1970)
Rainy Days and Mondays (1971)
I Need to Be in Love (1976)

#238 Smokey Robinson (1940 - present)
Began Recording: 1958 (w. the Miracles); 1973 (solo)
Peak: 1975 - 1976; 1981; 1987 - 1988
Genres: R&B; Soul Singer/Songwriter

His legacy is secure as the lead singer and chief songwriter for the Miracles, but he left them 50 years ago and continues performing to this day.

William Robinson Jr. was born in a poor section of North Detroit. A favorite uncle gifted him with the nickname Smokey, and it stuck. By his mid-teens, Smokey and some friends formed the Five Chimes who went on to become the Miracles, one of the first and most successful acts at Motown.

Aside from fronting his group, Smokey was a prolific and talented songwriter, penning such hits for his label mates as "My Guy" for Mary Wells, "My Girl" for the Temptations, "Ain't That Peculiar" for Marvin Gaye, and scores more. In a fit of hyperbole, perhaps, Bob Dylan once called him "America's greatest poet."

By the late '60s, Smokey was Motown's vice president, a position he held 'til the late '80s. He finally left the Miracles in 1972, but in 1973 he launched his solo career. His 1975 LP *A Quiet Storm* was a celebrated mix of laid back, smooth, jazz-inflected soul, a subgenre of music that stayed popular for about two decades, taking its name from Smokey's album title. In 1979, his string-laden, mid-tempo cooing romancer "Cruisin'" was a hit on both the pop and R&B charts. In 1981, his infectious "Being With You" reached #2 in the U.S. and #1 in Britain. The mid-'80s saw Smokey battle substance abuse, only to emerge clean in '87 with "One Heartbeat" and the Grammy winning "Just to See Her."

A word about his voice: Ron Rosenbaum called it an "eerie, insinuating male soprano." Not exactly a falsetto, for he stays in that range, it is easily one of the most recognizable in all of popular music. Robinson has won too many awards to list them all, from Kennedy Center honors to the Gershwin Prize to a handful of Halls of Fame inductions; yet, he's still, somehow, under-appreciated.

Suggested Songs:

Just My Soul Responding (1973)
Cruisin' (1979)
Being With You (1981)
Just To See Her (1987)

#237 Peggy Lee (1920 - 2002)

Began Recording: 1941
Peak: 1943; 1947 - 1949; 1952 - 1959; 1969 - 1970
Genres: Swing/Jazz; Pop Singer/Songwriter

Tony Bennett called her "the female Frank Sinatra," while jazz critic Peter Clayton deemed her "the finest singer in the history of popular music." Peggy Lee was comfortable singing jazz, blues, Latin, traditional pop, even light rock tunes, but she was devoted to minimalism, commenting once that she prefers to "leave out all but the essentials." With a voice described as sultry but cool, bewitching but sad, there was an underlying melancholy that filtered through her artistry, perhaps reflective of her painful childhood.

Born Norma Egstrom in North Dakota, her mother died when she was four, and her alcoholic dad's new wife physically and emotionally abused Norma who sought escape in music. Singing on the radio as a teenager, she left home at 17, was discovered by bandleader Benny Goodman in 1941, and quickly scored two breakout hits with his band– "Somebody Else Is Taking My Place" and "Why Don't You Do Right?" After marrying guitarist Dave Barbour and giving birth to her only child, she was ready to quit music, but her husband, recognizing her twin gifts for singing and songwriting, convinced her to return to the spotlight.

In all, Peggy made over 1,000 recordings, wrote or co-wrote over 270 songs, and had huge smashes at the ends of the '40s ("Mañana," #1 for nine weeks in 1948), '50s ("Fever," her 1958 sultry signature song), and '60s ("Is That All There Is?" which some hear as nihilistic, while Peggy found it life affirming). One of her proudest accomplishments was co-writing the songs for Disney's *Lady and the Tramp* with Sonny Burke, then singing and taking on four roles for the film.

Quitting only when her health gave out, Lee won a Lifetime Grammy and is a member of the Songwriters and Big Band Jazz Halls of Fame.

Suggested Songs:

Why Don't You Do Right? (w. Benny Goodman) (1943)
The Folks Who Live on the Hill (1957)
Fever (1958)
Is That All There Is? (1969)

#236 Frank Zappa (1940 - 1993)

Began Recording: 1963 (as sideman); 1966 (as band leader)
Peak: 1966 - 1968; 1974 - 1979
Genres: Rock; Jazz-fusion; Experimental/Avant-garde; R&B; Classical
Bandleader/Guitarist/Songwriter/Composer

Frank Zappa was an iconoclast; many would say a genius. The middle-of-the-road was not for him. Critics, listeners, other musicians loved him or hated him. An outstanding rock guitarist, he was also adept at composing complex, avant-garde orchestral and chamber works. He loved doo-wop and jazz-fusion. A brilliant satirist, he pilloried society's foibles, offending those on the left as well as those on the right. He had little time for hippies and the drug culture, though many thought, wrongly, that he was a prime export of that late '60s scene. With over 100 albums, and counting, to choose from, it's hard to know where to begin if one wants to sample his oeuvre.

He was born in Baltimore, of Italian descent. His dad was a chemist involved in classified defense work; there's some evidence that young Frank's early exposure to toxic materials may have contributed to his early demise by cancer. Drawn at a young age to music, by high school graduation he was playing drums, guitar, singing doo-wop, and composing orchestral pieces. A police sting operation busted him, unfairly, in the early '60s for pornography, and he remained a lifelong foe of censorship, even testifying before Congress.

From 1966 to 1968, he released three groundbreaking, experimental rock LPs with his backing band, the Mothers of Invention, skewering American culture and mindless conformity. "Brown Shoes Don't Make It" is a well-known track from this era. By the '70s, Zappa had moved on from his original band. Acclaimed albums from this period include '74's *Apostrophe (')* and '79's *Sheik Yerbouti* and the two *Joe's Garage* LPs. His most celebrated tracks from this time include "Don't Eat the Yellow Snow," "Cosmik Debris," "Joe's Garage," and "Dancing Fool."

A legendary workaholic, Zappa's been recognized in death by the Rock & Roll Hall of Fame as well as by many esteemed jazz and classical artists.

Suggested Songs:

Peaches en Regalia (1969)
Watermelon in Easter Hay (1979)
Valley Girl (w. Moon Zappa) (1982)
Uncle Meat (from The Yellow Shark) (1993)

#235 Carly Simon (1945 - present)
Began Recording: 1964 (w. Simon Sisters); 1971 (solo)
Peak: 1971 - 1978
Genres: Soft Rock; traditional pop Singer/Songwriter

On paper, she seemed to have all the advantages—a wealthy New York upbringing, her dad a powerful publishing baron, a musically gifted family. Yet, Carly Simon was sexually abused at seven, only to have it swept under the rug; her father was depressed, distant, and dead before she was 16; and she stuttered, learning to overcome it by singing. In 1964, she began performing professionally with older sister Lucy, calling themselves the Simon Sisters, but Lucy bowed out at the end of the decade. Signed to Elektra in 1970, Carly released her eponymous debut LP the following year. Buoyed by the haunting lead single, "That's the Way I've Always Heard It Should Be," drawing perhaps from her parents' troubled marriage, Simon was acclaimed as an introspective, confessional singer/songwriter, in the mold of Carole King and Joni Mitchell. She was awarded the coveted Best New Artist Grammy.

Later in '71, she followed up with *Anticipation*, noteworthy for the title track, written by a teenage Carly awaiting her date with Cat Stevens, and the moving "Legend in Your Own Time," a look at the double edged sword that is fame. However, it was 1972's "You're So Vain," from her best-loved *No Secrets* LP, that has made Carly an immortal. An RIAA Song of the Century, the song has produced endless speculation about just who is the narcissistic lover. Warren Beatty was sure it was he, while Simon's been coy over the years.

From 1972 to 1983, Simon was married to James Taylor, making them, in effect, the first couple of rock. Their 1974 duet cover of "Mockingbird" seemed to signal all was well, but it was a troubled union as Taylor wrestled with a heroin addiction.

Carly's 1977 "Nobody Does It Better" is one of the best-loved James Bond themes, and she's had some success with her releases from the Great

American Songbook, especially 2005's *Moonlight Serenade*. Simon is a member of both the Songwriters and Rock & Roll Halls of Fame.

Suggested Songs:

That's the Way I've Always Heard It Should Be (1971)
Legend in Your Own Time (1972)
You're So Vain (1972)
Coming Around Again (1986)

#234 Barry Manilow (1943 - present)

Began Recording: 1971 (w. Featherbed); 1973 (solo)
Peak: 1974 - 1978
Genres: Pop Ballads; Adult Contemporary Singer/Songwriter

In the mid-'70s, Barry Manilow, with his lush, fully orchestrated, theatrical ballads, was a dominant force on the pop charts, and, even when those hits dried up, he was a mainstay on Adult Contemporary radio throughout the '80s.

Born in a poor Brooklyn neighborhood, he was raised by his mother and grandparents after his father left when he was two. A grandfather and his stepdad helped steer the shy boy into music; he learned to play the accordion and piano and was drawn to jazz and Broadway tunes. He got into Juilliard and found work in the '60s writing and producing advertising jingles. A big break came when Bette Midler hired him to be her pianist, and, subsequently, her arranger, musical director, and producer. With dreams of writing and arranging, he turned reluctantly to performing, which he still claims he never enjoyed, in order to get his songs heard. Ironically, some of his biggest hits were penned by others.

Beginning in 1974, with the emotionally charged "Mandy" (originally entitled "Brandy"), in quick succession he also scored with "I Write the Songs," which he feared sounded too egotistical; "Could It Be Magic," based on a Chopin piece; "Weekend in New England," with its hint of forbidden love; "Looks Like We Made It;" "Can't Smile Without You;" and the musically upbeat, yet lyrically dark "Copacabana."

Critics have been harsh, terming his music melodramatic, saccharine, bland, sentimental, even schlock. Manilow himself once told an *L.A. Times* writer, "I'm good, not great. Sinatra is great, Judy (Garland) is great, Tony Bennett is great. I'm pretty good." Yet, as recently as 2005, he had a #1 album on the *Billboard* 200; he's had at least one Top 40 album for six straight decades; he's won a Grammy, a Tony, and an Emmy; and, at the age of 79, he still draws large, adoring crowds whenever he performs.

Suggested Songs:

Could It Be Magic (1973 and 1975)
Mandy (1974)
Can't Smile Without You (1978)
When October Goes (1984)

#233 Daft Punk
Began Recording: 1994
Peak: 1997; 2001; 2005 - 2016
Genres: Electronic; EDM Duo

Dismissed by those who never listened to their music as those silly guys in robot helmets who play electronic disco, Daft Punk, in the words of *The Guardian*'s Alexis Petridis, are the "most influential pop musicians of the 21st century." Their reach can be heard in the work of such giants as Madonna, Ye, the Weeknd, and countless other artists.

They are Guy-Manuel de Homem-Christo and Thomas Bangalter, two French lads who met in a Parisian secondary school in 1987. Along with a third friend, they formed a short-lived rock band, Darlin', recorded a couple of tracks, and received a negative press review from Dave Jennings of *Melody Maker* calling them "daft punky." They took the moniker Daft Punk, cut a couple of electronic dance numbers, and scored a hit in 1995 with "Da Funk." A label bidding war ensued, and they signed with *Virgin Records,* citing the opportunity to be "musically free."

Releasing four studio LPs in 16 years, they were restless innovators blending "Chicago house and Detroit techno with pop, funk, indie rock and hip-hop into nostalgic yet futuristic forms," in the words of *AllMusic*'s Heather Phares. Each album, though, is different, even if all are under-pinned by electronica and dance. 1997's *Homework* is funky, as can be heard in the club hit, "Around the World." From 2001's *Discovery*, hear the joyful instrumental and vocal textures masking a rather dispiriting dystopian lyric on "Harder, Better, Faster, Stronger." *Human after All* is darker still, while 2013's *Random Access Memories*, winner of five Grammys and #1 in much of the world, looks back to '70s and '80s pop, prog, and R&B, even as it gives us something new and timeless, such as the ambitious ode to love, "Touch" or their guitar driven, world-wide hit, "Get Lucky."

Yes, they guarded their privacy and created a mystique behind the helmets, and in 2021, they cryptically signaled they were no more, but their legacy appears secure.

Suggested Songs:

Harder, Better, Faster, Stronger (2001)
Something About Us (2003)
Get Lucky (w. Pharrell Williams & Nile Rodgers) (2013)
Touch (w. Paul Williams) (2013)

#232 Chris Brown (1989 - present)

Began Recording: 2005
Peak: 2005 - 2008; 2011 - 2012
Genres: R&B; hip-hop; pop; dance Singer/Songwriter

At 34, Chris Brown has already established himself as one of the best selling recording artists of all-time and one of the most popular R&B vocalists of the past two decades.

He was born in a tiny Virginia town and, like so many artists, sang in his church choir as a child. Inspired by Michael Jackson and Usher, he threw himself into dancing and singing and was discovered at the age of 13. Moving to New York, he had a number of label offers and signed with Jive Records in 2004. He was just 16 when he released his eponymous LP, which debuted at #2 on the *Billboard* 200 chart. His first single, the dance-flavored "Run It," with its MJ echoes, reached #1 in the U.S. and several other countries. Four more hit singles followed, then the equally successful *Exclusive*, which featured the chart topping "Kiss Kiss."

With his dancing prowess and smooth voice, variously described as light, soulful, versatile, and emotional, Chris, sporting a "squeaky-clean" image, seemed poised for greatness; then came the shocking news that he had beat up his girlfriend, the hugely popular singer Rihanna. The images were gruesome, and Brown was charged with two felonies. He escaped jail time and apologized repeatedly, but he has not managed to stay out of trouble. Fights, other assault accusations, jail time for a parole violation; and yet Brown continues to release music that people love and purchase– 2011's *F.A.M.E.*, which took home a Grammy; several more best-selling albums; and hugely successful collaborative hits, such as "No Guidance" with Drake, and "Go Crazy" with Young Thug.

Given Brown's relative youth, it may be too early to say what will be his lasting legacy.

Suggested Songs:

Run It (w. Juelz Santana) (2005)
 With You (2007)
No Air (w. Jordin Sparks) (2008)
Go Crazy (w. Young Thug) (2020)

#231 Sammy Davis Jr. (1925 - 1990)
Began Recording: 1946 (pseudonyms); 1950 (solo)
Peak: 1955 - 1969; 1972 - 1976
Genres: Traditional Pop; swing; Show Tunes Singer

In his day, Sammy Davis Jr. was often called "the world's greatest living entertainer." A remarkably gifted singer, dancer, actor, and impressionist, even Michael Jackson paid tribute. His parents were both vaudeville dancers; they split up when Sammy was three, so his dad took him on the road. He quickly became part of the Will Mastin Gang, even appearing in film when he was seven. What little formal education he received came from backstage tutors.

Drafted into the army in 1943, Davis was repeatedly brutalized by racist conscripts. After the war he rejoined his father and Mastin; their 1951 show at Hollywood's famed Ciro's was a sensation. In 1954, Davis lost an eye in a car accident, but he also scored his first hit single, "Hey There." His debut album, 1955's *Starring Sammy Davis Jr.*, went to #1, a first for a Black solo artist. Soon he was everywhere– nightclubs, on records, on Broadway, and in film. By 1959 he was an integral member of Sinatra's Rat Pack. When he married Swedish actress May Britt in 1960, racism again reared its ugly head, and when he converted to Judaism a year later, many scratched their heads. His music was out of step with '60s trends, but he had hits with Anthony Newley's "What kind of Fool Am I?," his stirring rendition of "I've Gotta Be Me," and the chart topping "The Candy Man," a song he greatly disliked.

Sadly, Davis came to be seen as a "hipster caricature" and an "Uncle Tom" by some, but he helped force Miami and Las Vegas to integrate, paid the dues that helped countless artists of color who came after him, and was embraced by Dr. King and Jesse Jackson.

Suggested Songs:

Something's Gotta Give (1955)

What kind of Fool Am I? (1962)

I've Gotta Be Me (1968)

Mr. Bojangles (1972)

#230 Etta James (1938 - 2012)
Began Recording: 1955
Peak: 1960 - 1964; 1967 - 1968
Genres: R&B; Jazz/Soul/Blues Singer/songwriter

Hers was not a pretty life. Born to a 14-year-old mom who had no clue how to care for her, Jamesetta Hawkins never knew her father and was raised by foster parents. Physically abused and forced to sing, she was a natural, first in church, then, after joining her mother in San Francisco, in a doo-wop group, the Creolettes. Musician Johnny Otis discovered the young teen, changed her name and the group's to Etta James and the Peaches, helping her record the sexually suggestive "Roll with Me Henry," changing the title to "The Wallflower" and bringing Etta a #1 R&B single at the age of 17.

Over time, her doo-wop R&B style morphed into a more jazzy, tougher blues-based sound, but what remained a constant was her inimitable ability to sing. Jon Pareles of *The New York Times* wrote that she had "one of the great voices in American popular music." Blessed with a powerful contralto, she communicated honesty and raw emotion. Janis Joplin was a huge fan, and, in 2008, Beyoncé played her in the film *Cadillac Records*.

The hard to categorize James never enjoyed much mainstream success. Her 1961 powerhouse, love-affirming version of "At Last," once a hit for Glenn Miller, has become a signature tune. In 1967, she had her biggest hit on the pop charts with "Tell Mama," driven by a crack Muscle Shoals band; the B-side, "I'd Rather Go Blind," with her soulful, bluesy vocal, has become even better known.

Sadly, Etta's longtime struggle with heroin undercut what might have been a more successful career. Still, she continued recording and perform-ing 'til late in her life, recognized in time by the Rock, Blues, and Rockabilly Halls of Fame. "A lot of people think the blues is depressing," said Etta. "When I'm singing blues, I'm singing life."

Suggested Songs:

All I Could Do Was Cry (1960)
At Last (1961)
Something's Got a Hold on Me (1962)
I'd Rather Go Blind (1967)

#229 Dizzy Gillespie (1917 - 1993)
Began Recording: 1937
Peak: 1942 - 1960
Genres: Jazz - Bebop; Afro-Cuban Trumpeter/Composer/Bandleader

Dizzy Gillespie is widely considered one of the two finest trumpet players (with Louis Armstrong) in jazz history and, along with Charlie Parker, was one of the leading developers of bebop.

Born in South Carolina, John Gillespie was the youngest of nine children. His father, a bricklayer, was also a part-time musician and bandleader. When his father died, the family fell on hard times. Boyhood stints picking cotton and digging ditches convinced the young Gillespie that he was meant for bigger things. Learning piano, trombone, and trumpet, he parlayed a music scholarship into paying gigs by 1935 with the likes of Teddy Hill and Cab Calloway, who fired him after he and Cab brawled. His clowning ways and audacious playing style earned him the nickname Dizzy. By 1943, working with Earl Hines, Gillespie was playing with sax innovator Charlie Parker. By 1944-45, their style, with its speed, complex rhythms and chords, was being touted as bebop. Many found it too fast, dissonant rather than melodic, and not danceable, though Gillespie pointed out that he regularly danced to it. Never completely embraced by the public, out of bebop grew modern jazz.

Noted for his trumpet, angled upward at 45 degrees, and his horn rim glasses, Gillespie's best-known works include the racing "Salt Peanuts," "Woody 'n You," the now classic "Groovin 'High," "A Night in Tunisia," and the Latin rhythms of "Manteca."

An international jazz ambassador in his later years, Gillespie, cited by Wynton Marsalis for his "rhythmic sophistication" and being a "master of harmony," has been awarded Kennedy Center Honors, a Lifetime Grammy, and is a member of the Jazz Hall of Fame.

Suggested Songs:

Woody 'n You (w. Coleman Hawkins) (1944)
Salt Peanuts (1945)
Groovin' High (1945)
Manteca (1946)

#228 Philip Glass (1937 - present)
Began Recording: 1971
Peak: 1976 - 2002
Genres: Contemporary Classical Composer/ pianist

Love him or hate him, Philip Glass is, without doubt, one of the best-known and most influential creators of modern "classical" music. Known for minimalism, a term he does not favor, Glass describes his work as reliant on "repetitive musical structures." His melodies tend to repeat over and over with subtle variation and nuanced layering, creating an effect that legions of supporters call "mesmerizing," "sublime," or "transcendent," while detractors deem them "boring," "simplistic," or "numbing." No matter, he's hugely prolific and highly popular, having created scores of operas, symphonies, concertos, soundtracks, and more. His Philip Glass Ensemble, with Glass playing keyboards, has recorded and performed for over 50 years.

His father owned a record store in Baltimore and introduced his son to music. By age 15, Philip was enrolled at the University of Chicago, studying piano and beginning to compose. A student of the famed Nadia Boulanger in Paris, his first famous work was the 1976 five-hour, unconventional opera *Einstein on the Beach*. 1982 saw Glass collaborate with filmmaker Godfrey Reggio in *Koyaanisqatsi*, the groundbreaking visual and musical meditation on modern life out of balance. 1982 also saw the release of the more accessible *Glassworks*. Other well-known creations include 1989's *Metamorphosis*, a solo piano LP; Symphonies #1 and #4, based on David Bowie's *Low* and *"Heroes"* albums; and the celebrated film scores for *The Hours* and *The Truman Show*.

Glass has been honored with the Glenn Gould Prize, a National Medal of Arts, and by the Kennedy Center.

Suggested Songs:

Glassworks: I. Opening (1982)
Cloudscape (from Koyaanisqatsi) (1982)
Metamorphosis: One (1989)
Symphony No. 4, Movement I: "Heroes" (1996)

#227 Bob Seger (1945 - present)
Began Recording: 1965
Peak: 1976 - 1983; 1986 - 1987
Genres: Rock Singer/Songwriter

Kid Rock said it best, calling him "underrated" at the 2004 Rock Hall induction ceremony. A gritty, soulful vocalist, Bob Seger composes memorable melodies with thoughtful, often profound, lyrics that look backward and forward at the same time, and has turned out more than a handful of musically arresting records, yet he is rarely mentioned among the pantheon of great rockers.

A Michigan kid, by his mid-teens he had begun his rock & roll odyssey playing in or fronting a series of bands, singing, playing guitar or keyboards, and making a name for himself in and around Detroit. Ten years after his first local hit, Seger broke through nationally in 1976 with the Silver Bullet Band. His *Live Bullet* demonstrated to the rest of the country what he was about with his R&B tinged hard driving rock and wistful ballads, perfectly encapsulated in his musician's life on the road saga, "Turn the Page." Later that year, *Night Moves* took him to the Top 10; the title track was a mid-tempo elegiac recollection of an adolescent affair, surprisingly still wounding and present after all these years. Over the next six years, there were more standouts: from 1978's *Stranger in Town*, "Still the Same," a character sketch of a gambler or, perhaps, an ex-lover, and "Old Time Rock and Roll," immortalized a few years later by Tom Cruise dancing in his underwear to the track in *Risky Business*, and said to be the #2 jukebox selection in history; "Against the Wind," from the 1980 album of the same name, a classic rumination on growing up, for good and ill; and from 1982's *The Distance*, "Roll Me Away," a roaring, double-edged ode to the wide open possibilities of taking a chopper to the highway.

Bob's 78 now and has talked about bowing out for decades, but as recently as 2019, bad back and all, he was still on the road.

Suggested Songs:

Night Moves (1976)
Old Time Rock and Roll (1979)
Against the Wind (1980)
Roll Me Away (1983)

#226 Genesis
Began Recording: 1968
Peak: 1973 - 1978; 1980 - 1983; 1986 - 1987; 1991 - 1992
Genres: Progressive Rock; Pop Rock Band

Poor Genesis– like Rodney Dangerfield, they just "don't get no respect." From 1969 to 1975 led by flamboyant frontman Peter Gabriel, they mixed folk, classical, psychedelic, and blues, producing a body of progressive rock that explored fantasy, mythology, and modern society, and they were often pilloried for it by the critics who found it "middle class" and pretentious. When Gabriel left and drummer and vocalist Phil Collins stepped to the fore, Genesis became a massively successful pop rock band and were slammed for "selling out."

Formed at England's exclusive Charterhouse School in 1967 by Gabriel, their lead singer; Mike Rutherford, bass and guitar player; Tony Banks, keyboardist; and a couple of mates who didn't stay; they added the jazzy drummer, Collins, in 1970, and guitarist Steve Hackett in 1971. This iteration of Genesis can be, perhaps, best understood with a listen to 1972's 23 minute, 7-part, musically adventurous, if lyrically obscure, song suite, "Supper's Ready," from the LP *Foxtrot*. With Gabriel's penchant for dressing up on stage in elaborate masks and costumes, by 1975 he was overshadowing the rest of the band. After Peter's departure for a solo career, Collins stepped forward as a very capable vocalist, and Genesis grew more and more popular. Best-loved songs from the Collins era include 1978's romantic pop "Follow You Follow Me;" the strangely obsessive, synth driven "Mama" from 1983; and the melodic, catchy "That's All."

In 1996, Collins departed, by then a huge solo star, and in 2000, Genesis dissolved, only to reform several more times up to this very day. One of the best selling bands of all time, they were inducted into the Rock & Roll Hall of Fame in 2010.

Suggested Songs:

Supper's Ready (1972)
The Carpet Crawlers (1974)
Follow You Follow Me (1978)
That's All (1983)

#225 Sarah Vaughan (1924 - 1990)

Began Recording: 1944 (w. Billy Eckstine); 1946 (solo)
Peak: 1947 - 1952; 1955 - 1959
Genres: Jazz; Traditional Pop Singer

Nicknamed "Sassy" and "The Divine One," Sarah Vaughan, as a singer, was admired by the likes of Frank Sinatra and Mel Torme. Jazz critic Scott Yanow said she had "one of the most wondrous voices of the 20th century."

Born in Newark to working class musical parents, Sarah played piano and sang in church as a child. By her teens, she was more interested in popular music and began sneaking into local clubs to play and sing. In 1942, she won a talent contest at Harlem's famed Apollo Theater and got herself hired as a pianist for the Earl Hines Band. Soon, however, she was singing. In 1944, she joined Billy Eckstine and recorded for the first time, but by 1945 she was freelancing, singing with a variety of orchestras and musicians. Her solo debut, "If You Could See Me Now," a pop-flavored jazz standard, was soon followed by a number of hits between 1947 and 1959: "Tenderly," which shows off her remarkable voice; an a cappella version of "Nature Boy;" the Sonny Burke/Paul Webster bluesy classic "Black Coffee," perhaps her signature song; the magnificent lamentation of "That Lucky Old Sun;" and, finally, "Whatever Lola Wants" and "Broken Hearted Melody," her two highest charting singles, if not her favorites.

Critics say Sarah was blessed with an operatic voice, expressive and rich, with great pitch, control, and a wide range from soprano to contralto. With age and too many cigarettes her instrument deepened, as can be heard on her powerful version of "Send in the Clowns." A Lifetime Grammy winner and a member of the Jazz Hall of Fame, Vaughan is generally termed a jazz singer, but she resisted such pigeon holing, preferring instead to simply be recognized as a versatile singer.

Suggested Songs:

Tenderly (1947)
Black Coffee (1949)
That Lucky Old Sun (1949)
Send in the Clowns (1974) (1981 w. Count Basie)

#224 Dionne Warwick (1940 - present)

Began Recording: 1959 (w. Gospelaires); 1962 (solo)
Peak: 1964 - 1970; 1985 - 1986
Genres: R&B; Pop Singer

Between 1955 and 1999, only Aretha Franklin, among female artists, had more records on the charts; yet Dionne Warwick is strangely underappreciated.

Born into a gospel music family, Marie Dionne Warrick, called by her middle name since childhood, was singing in church by the age of six. As a teenager, she sometimes filled in for one of the Drinkard Sisters and formed her own vocal group, the Gospelaires, with her sister Dee Dee and her aunt Cissy Houston, mother of Whitney. By 1960, they were in-demand session backing singers, even as Dionne studied music at college. At a session with the Drifters, Dionne was noticed by Brill Building songwriter Burt Bacharach. Soon Burt and his lyricist partner Hal David were writing songs for the young woman.

Her 1962 soulful debut single, "Don't Make Me Over," reached #21 on the *Billboard* Hot 100, and a label spelling error led to a change in her surname. Eight times in the '60s she reached the Top 10, seven with Bacharach-David tunes: the yearning "Anyone Who Had a Heart;" the heartbreaking "Walk On By," perhaps her most celebrated track; "Message to Michael," a plea for her lover to return; "I Say a Little Prayer," later a hit for Aretha; "Do You Know the Way to San Jose," with its upbeat music and lyrics chronicling show biz failure; "This Girl's in Love with You," a huge hit for Herb Alpert as "This Guy's...;" and "I'll Never Fall in Love Again."

In 1972, Dionne stopped working with Bacharach-David. She only reached the Top 10 four more times, with two reaching #1—"Then Came You" with the Spinners in 1974 and 1985's "That's What Friends are For," a collaboration with Elton John, Stevie Wonder, and Gladys Knight to raise funds for AIDS research.

An underrated vocalist with exquisite phrasing and emotional range, Warwick has a singing voice that's been described with words like elegant, sophisticated, soothing, and sensual. She's won five Grammys, as well as one for her lifetime of work, and she's a member of the Rhythm & Blues Music Hall of Fame.

Suggested Songs:

Don't Make Me Over (1962)
Walk On By (1964)
Heartbreaker (1982)
That's What Friends Are For (w. E. John, G. Knight, S. Wonder) (1985)

#223 Outkast

Began Recording; 1993
Peak: 1994 - 2004
Genres: Hip-Hop; Progressive Rap Duo

Andre Benjamin and Antwan Patton got together to rap as Atlanta high school students and were signed to LaFace Records before their graduation. Calling themselves Outkast, the duo, Dre and Big Boi, released their initial LP, *Southernplayalisticadillacmuzic*, in 1994 to positive reviews and modest commercial success. The hip-hop establishment didn't know what to make of it; it wasn't east coast, nor was it west coast rap.

With *ATLiens*, their 1996 second album, it was clear that Outkast was a unique and talented entity blending laid back funk with tinges of reggae, gospel, and psychedelic rock; the lyrics, too, varied from typical urban concerns to introspective looks at fame, the treatment of women, and questions about drugs. The reflective "Elevators" got the most attention. The next two releases, *Aquemini* and *Stankonia*, were both praised for continued musical development and willingness to experiment, but also for their philosophical maturity, intricate wordplay and positivity, without whitewashing the pain and complexity of modern life. Standout tracks from this period include "Da Art of Storytellin' (Part 1)" with its surprising swerve into tragedy; "B.O.B.," a much misunderstood sonic masterwork; and the movingly complex address to a baby's grandmother, "Ms. Jackson." In 2003, Outkast released the monster hit *Speakerboxxx/The Love Below*, a two album LP featuring Big Boi on the first disc and Andre 3000, as Dre now called himself, on the latter. Hailed as a masterpiece, it took home the Grammy award for Album of the Year.

In 2007, Outkast disbanded with the two artists pursuing solo careers, but they reunited in 2014 for a series of shows.

Suggested Songs:

Elevators (Me and You) (1996)
Da Art of Storytellin' (Part 1) (1999)
B.O.B. - Bombs Over Baghdad (2000)
Ms. Jackson (2000)

#222 Tammy Wynette (1942 - 1998)

Began Recording: 1966
Peak: 1967 - 1976
Genres: Country Singer/Songwriter

Tammy Wynette was known as the "First Lady of Country," though "Heroine of Heartbreak" was an equally fitting moniker. Virginia Wynette Pugh grew up picking cotton in rural Mississippi. Escaping into music, she was soon playing piano and the guitar her father left her when he died before her first birthday. Married at 17 and divorced at 23 with three children, she'd go on to marry four more times, though never very happily. Her third marriage to fellow country star George Jones was marred by his raging alcoholism. From others she also suffered abuse, even once having her house set on fire, apparently in a failed attempt to kill her. A 1970 hysterectomy led to numerous and repeated health complications. She tried to cope using pain medication and grew increasingly addicted, suffering further health issues, and finally died, curled up on her couch at 55.

An exceptional singer whose distinctive voice has been described as emotional, tearful, and vulnerable, she was, for three consecutive years, the CMA Female Vocalist of the Year. With the lush, string-laden Nashville Sound behind her, Wynette sang of a woman's dignified, determined forbearance, often in the midst of sadness, loneliness, and duty. "I Don't Wanna Play House," "D-I-V-O-R-C-E," and "'Til I Can Make It on My Own" never sounded like mere performances coming from Tammy. 1969's "Stand By Your Man" is unquestionably her best-known song. Though hated by many feminists, it was chosen as the #1 country song of all-time by the CMT network and is included in the *National Recording Registry*. She was inducted into the Country Music Hall of Fame shortly after her death.

Suggested Songs:

D-I-V-O-R-C-E (1968)
Stand By Your Man (1969)
Golden Ring (w. George Jones) (1976)
'Til I Can Make It on My Own (1976)

#221 Iron Maiden
Began Recording: 1979
Peak: 1982 - 1988; 2010 - 2019
Genres: Heavy Metal Band

Conservative Christians called them satanic, but then, as their leader and songwriter Steve Harris pointed out, "They obviously hadn't read the lyrics." Harris, famous for his "galloping" bass style and songs that draw from dreams, literature, history, and religion, founded Iron Maiden in London in late 1975, and he remains with the band to this day. While membership has been fluid, key contributors have included stellar guitarists, Dave Murray, Adrian Smith, and Janick Gers; lead vocalist, Bruce Dickinson; and drummer, Nicko McBrain.

Their heavy metal style is informed with virtuoso, interweaving guitar playing; interesting, often melodic riffs; racing, high energy speed; Dickinson's impassioned, high pitched vocals; and, often, extraordinary story songs. Never as popular in the U.S. as in their native England, their third LP, 1982's *The Number of the Beast*, has, nonetheless, sold over 19 million copies and is considered one of the finest metal albums ever, with standout cuts "Run to the Hills," an exploration of American Manifest Destiny's effect on the Native Americans, and "Hallowed Be Thy Name," the iconic, powerhouse track that takes the point of view of a man about to be hung. 1983's *Piece of Mind* features "The Trooper," based on the classic poem "The Charge of the Light Brigade," while "2 Minutes to Midnight," from *Powerslave*, considers the horrific effects of war. As Harris said, listen to the songs before destroying the records and besmirching the band's name.

Artists as diverse as Metallica, Kurt Cobain, and Lady Gaga have praised Iron Maiden, and their music is frequently heard in video games, TV shows, and movies.

Suggested Songs:

Run to the Hills (1982)
Hallowed Be Thy Name (1982)
The Trooper (1983)
2 Minutes to Midnight (1984)

#220 Alan Jackson (1958 - present)

Began Recording: 1987
Peak: 1991 - 2008
Genres: Neotraditional Country; gospel Singer/Songwriter

65-year-old Alan Jackson was born 40 miles southwest of Atlanta, the youngest of five children. His first musical love was gospel, but as a teen he began singing country. Married to his high school sweetheart for 44 years, Jackson was late getting into music professionally. He caught a break when his wife met Glen Campbell around the same time Alan was working at the Nashville Network mailroom. That chance meeting led in time to a record deal with the new label Arista Nashville, and, in 1990, Jackson had his first hit with the neotraditional "Here in the Real World," with its "life is not like the movies" lyrics.

Though he later had crossover success on the pop charts, Jackson has been a "keep it country" type of performer with sporadic forays into gospel and bluegrass. Three times he was the Country Music Association Entertainer of the Year; he has had 26 #1 singles on the country charts, is a member of the Grand Ole Opry, and was inducted into the Country Music Hall of Fame.

Up-tempo, honky tonk hits have been a big part of Jackson's repertoire with "Don't Rock the Jukebox" and "Chattahoochie" two notable examples, but, oozing sincerity, Jackson has that uncanny ability to touch hearts with emotionally weighted works like 2003's love ode to his wife, "Remember When," and the Grammy winning "Where Were You (When the World Stopped Turning)," which managed to capture some of the feelings experienced by many on 9/11 without succumbing to maudlin exploitation.

Coping with a hereditary neurological condition, Jackson is expected to wrap up his Last Call Tour in 2024.

Suggested Songs:

Don't Rock the Jukebox (1991)
Gone Country (1994)
Where Were You (When the World Stopped Turning) (2001)
Remember When (2003)

#219 Aaron Copland (1900 - 1990)

Began Composing: 1920; Began Recording: 1951 (?)
Peak: 1936 - 1949; 1960 - 1990
Genres: Classical; popular Composer/conductor/pianist

AllMusic put it succinctly– the music of Aaron Copland "has transcended the concert hall and entered the popular consciousness."

Copland was the Brooklyn born son of Lithuanian Jewish immigrants. His mother and older sister introduced him to music and he was already writing as a pre-teen. Playing and studying in New York after high school, he moved to Paris in the early 1920s and studied for three years with famed music teacher Nadia Boulanger. Determined to evoke the particularly American experience and to compose in a style accessible to the average person, he developed an optimistic musical language drawing from the classics, as well as American jazz and folk. Sometimes attacked by critics for pandering or "dumbing down" so-called "serious music," Copland's been, nonetheless, hailed as the "Dean of American Composers" and lauded by such greats as Leonard Bernstein.

Producing works for piano, ensembles, and orchestras, as well as ballets, operas, theater, and film scores, his best-loved compositions include "El Salon Mexico," inspired by his visit to a Mexico City dance hall; the western ballets, "Billy the Kid" and "Rodeo;" the pioneer ode, "Appalachian Spring," a ballet later turned into an orchestral suite; and the iconic "Fanfare to the Common Man," certainly his most recognizable piece.

Winner of an Oscar, a Grammy, a Pulitzer, a Presidential Medal of Freedom, and a Kennedy Center inductee, Copland did less and less composing by the 1960s and turned, increasingly, to conducting and recording his vast work, which is readily available in a variety of formats.

Suggested Songs:

El Salon Mexico (1936; 1975 recording)

Rodeo: Hoe Down (1942; 1963 recording)

Fanfare to the Common Man (1942; 1960 recording)

Appalachian Spring: VII. Doppio movimento (Shaker Hymn) (1944; 1963 recording)

#218 Alabama
Began Recording: 1976
Peak: 1980 - 1993
Genres: Country; Country Rock; Country Pop; bluegrass Band

For decades charismatic lead vocalists dominated country music, while the bands stayed in the background. That all changed in the 1980s with the emergence of Alabama. Formed in 1969 by cousins Randy Owen, Teddy Gentry, and Jeff Cook, they were an on and off outfit for several years while they finished up their schooling, but, by 1973, they were committed to the music, living in their native Alabama, gigging at the Myrtle Beach Bowery, running through a couple of name changes and several drummers. Early attempts to record cost them more money than they made, but, in 1980, signing with RCA, they hit pay dirt, going on to score 21 consecutive #1 country singles.

With Owen singing lead and playing rhythm guitar, Gentry added bass while Cook handled lead guitar, fiddle, and keyboards; all three were involved in the songwriting. Known for their tight, clean harmonies and Bakersfield (Merle Haggard) and Nashville (strings and pop accents) flavored country, they also incorporated a rock element, by this time adding Mark Herndon on drums. Among their best-loved chart toppers are "Tennessee River," the one that got things rolling; "Feels So Right" and "Love in the First Degree," two '81 singles that became pop crossover successes as well; "Mountain Music," a song that features tasteful guitar and a fiddle outro, from their best selling studio LP of the same name; '83's "Dixieland Delight;" "Lady Down on Love," a story ballad that tells of a divorce from both the woman's and the man's point of view; "If You're Gonna Play in Texas," which makes clear you need a fiddle; and their 1988 look back at Depression era poverty in "Song of the South."

CMA Entertainers of the Year from 1982 to 1984, they were inducted into the Country Music Hall of Fame in 2005.

Suggested Songs:

Mountain Music (1982)
Dixieland Delight (1983)
Lady Down on Love (1983)
Song of the South (1988)

#217 Harry Styles (1994 - present)

Began Recording: 2011 (w. One Direction); 2017 (solo)
Peak: 2017 - 2023
Genres: Pop Rock; Soft Rock Singer/Songwriter

He came roaring out of the acclaimed boy band One Direction, going solo in 2017, and, in the ensuing half decade, Harry Styles has been as successful as anyone in music.

British born and raised, at 16 Styles used a third place finish on TV's *The X Factor* as a springboard to stardom in the hugely popular One Direction, who had five best-selling albums between 2011 and 2015. When they disbanded in 2016, Styles signed with Columbia and surprised the world the following year with his debut single, the stunning, Bowie-tinged "Sign of the Times." Widely acclaimed, the soft rock anthemic ballad hits powerful notes of both despair and hope. #1 in the U.K., it highlighted his eponymous first LP, a giant hit in Mexico, Brazil, and Poland, as well as in the U.S. and U.K. *Fine Line*, his 2019 follow-up LP, featured the upbeat pop hits, "Adore You" and "Watermelon Sugar, while the title track, with its moody musical texture and cryptic lyric, goes in a wholly different direction. 2022 saw his third album, *Harry's House*, drop and reach #1 throughout much of the world. The lead single, "As It Was," which spent 15 weeks atop the *Billboard* Hot 100, is a driving, danceable track that carries a marked aura of sadness. "Late Night Talking" and the funky "Music for a Sushi Restaurant" are two other featured singles. In 2023, the LP won the coveted Album of the Year Grammy against stiff competition.

Styles has mentioned Joni Mitchell, Van Morrison, Harry Nilsson, and Shania Twain as important influences. Blessed with a charismatic, dynamic stage presence, people have seen a bit of Freddie Mercury and Mick Jagger in the way he owns the stage and plays to the crowd. A fashion icon, known for his gender fluid, flamboyant style, Harry has pointedly refused to define his sexuality, arguing that he wants all people to be OK with who they are and to feel accepted. In 2022, he headlined at Coachella and played 15 sold-out shows at Madison Square Garden. At 29, it would seem he's just getting started.

Suggested Songs:

Sign of the Times (2017)
Fine Line (2019)
As It Was (2022)
Music for a Sushi Restaurant (2022)

#216 Dire Straits

Began Recording: 1978
Peak: 1979 - 1986
Genres: Rock Band

At a time when disco and punk were ascendant, a London based pub rock band with blues and jazz flavors emerged in 1977 and became, arguably, the most popular '80s band in the U.K., with a huge international following to boot. Scottish born Mark Knopfler was the clear leader of Dire Straits—chief songwriter, singer, and lead guitarist; brother David played rhythm guitar and stuck around for three years before leaving; John Illsley, on bass, stayed for the duration. Other key members included Pick Withers, drummer, and Alan Clark and Guy Fletcher, keyboard players.

Their debut single, "Sultans of Swing," from the eponymous first album, set the template—arresting, story-song lyrics; a Dylan-like voice; a rhythmic, tight band; and a phenomenal, new guitar talent who was fluid, intricate, and melodic. In all, Dire Straits released six albums in the 15 years they were together, all commercially successful, with three of them topping British charts. Their fifth release, 1985's *Brothers in Arms*, was #1 in much of the world and has sold in the neighborhood of 30 million copies. Two of their best-known singles, "Money for Nothing," a hilarious send-up of a rock musician's life, and "Walk of Life" are exuberant rockers, but Knopfler and Dire Straits also feature ambitious operatic numbers like the first love, neon-lit rush of "Tunnel of Love;" the lovesick, unrequited "Romeo and Juliet;" the 14-minute opus to the rise and possibly falling of America, "Telegraph Road;" and the understated swell of the anti-war "Brothers in Arms."

In 1995, an exhausted Knopfler, overwhelmed by rock star status, dissolved the band for the second and final time, choosing to pursue a more low-key solo career. Dire Straits, winner of four Grammys and three Brits, was inducted into the Rock & Roll Hall of Fame in 2018.

Suggested Songs:

Sultans of Swing (1978)
Romeo and Juliet (1980)
Telegraph Road (1982)
Brothers in Arms (1985)

#215 Amy Winehouse (1983 - 2011)
Began Recording: 2003
Peak: 2004 - 2008
Genres: R&B/Soul; jazz Singer/Songwriter

Gary Mulholland deemed her "the pre-eminent vocal talent of her generation." Tragically, though, she was gone at 27.

Born and reared in a Jewish family in North London, Amy Winehouse was early on exposed to jazz, adding hip-hop, R&B, and pop influences as a teen. Her vocal talents were recognized by several labels, and she recorded her first LP, the jazz-soul-pop hybrid *Frank*, before she was 20. A hit in Britain, "Stronger Than Me," with its swipe at an older, weaker boyfriend, and "Pumps," a satirical jibe at lonely, money grubbing ladies, got the most attention.

Celebrated for her pained, deeply expressive contralto and jazzy, idiosyncratic phrasing, Amy's public image began to morph between the success of her debut and her celebrated 2006 follow-up LP. Outwardly it manifested in her beehive hair-do, winged eyeliner, pin-up girl tattoo, short dresses and the rest, but her relationship with her boyfriend coincided with a dangerous pattern of public alcohol and drug abuse, mutual physical abuse, weight loss, and run-ins with the law. A temporary break from the boyfriend and a period of sobriety was accompanied by the creation of her celebrated *Back to Black*, winner of five Grammys, with sales of over 16 million, and a coveted place on several "Best" lists. Featured tracks include "Rehab," a tough listen in light of Amy's future demise; "You Know I'm No Good," in which a cheating Amy reiterates that she always said she was trouble; and her girl-groups inspired signature song, the magnificently performed "Back to Black."

At the pinnacle of success, Winehouse then spiraled downward, succumbing to an alcohol overdose in 2011. The Janis Joplin of her generation, her musical legacy is assured.

Suggested Songs:

Intro/Stronger Than Me (2003)
Rehab (2006)
You Know I'm No Good (2007)
Back to Black (2007)

#214 Kate Bush (1958 - present)

Began Recording: 1978
Peak: 1978 - 1982; 1985 - 1986; 2005 - 2006; 2022 - 2023
Genres: Art & Progressive Pop/Rock Singer/Songwriter

It took 44 years, but the U.S. is finally catching on to what Britain, and much of the rest of the world, has known for decades—Kate Bush is one of the great musical auteurs in recording history.

Born southeast of London to a comfortable, middle class, musical family, Kate learned to play piano by 11 and was soon writing her own songs. When she was 15, a family friend connected her to Pink Floyd's David Gilmour who helped her record "proper demos" and introduce "The Man with the Child in His Eyes" to EMI Records; she was signed at 16. Given a couple of years to continue her studies, take dance and mime lessons, and work on her debut LP, she was 19 when "Wuthering Heights," her first single, dropped. The song was a sensation, musically and lyrically sophisticated, with Bush taking the role of the ghost Cathy pleading in her hysterical high soprano for Heathcliff to open the window and let her in. #1 in the U.K. for four weeks, it was the first time a woman in Britain had topped the charts with her own composition. The album, *The Kick Inside*, was also a huge hit, but barely registered in the U.S.

Over the next four plus decades, Kate has become legendary, releasing 10 LPs, all hits throughout much of the world, though less successful in America. By her second LP, she was co-producing; by her fourth, the experimental *The Dreaming*, she was fully in charge. 1985's *Hounds of Love* is her best-known album and features "Running Up That Hill" in which the singer imagines a man and woman trading places. In 2022, the song was featured in the Netflix series *Stranger Things* and raced again up the charts, hitting #3 on the U.S. *Billboard* Hot 100.

Kate Bush sounds like no one else; musically she draws from everywhere, even mixing in ambient sounds. In her inimitable, dramatic soprano voices, she sings stories taken from literature, mythology, history, the newspaper, and her own fearless imagination. In performance (and she has only done two brief runs of shows), she mixes song, theater, dance, and magic. She's been extolled by artists as diverse as Prince, Johnny Rotten, Big Boi, and Adele. In 2023, she was finally inducted into the Rock & Roll Hall of Fame.

Suggested Songs:

Wuthering Heights (1978)
Running Up That Hill (1985)
Cloudbusting (1985)
This Woman's Work (1989)

#213 Backstreet Boys

Began Recording: 1995
Peak: 1996 - 2001
Genres: Pop; R&B; Dance Pop; Vocal Harmony Group

The Backstreet Boys were the quintessential turn of the millennium boy band, no disrespect to their talented contemporaries, NSYNC, intended. Blending pop, R&B, rock, and dance elements over the years, they see themselves more as a vocal harmony group, à la Boyz II Men. Put together in Orlando by would-be mogul Lou Pearlman in 1993, they are AJ McLean, or "Johnny No Name," the group's "bad boy" and often cited as the strongest vocalist; quiet, earnest, underappreciated Howie Dorough; Nick Carter, the good looking, but talented, baby of the band; Brian Littrell, who survived open heart surgery in the midst of their peak years; and oldster Kevin Richardson, who took a hiatus from BSB from 2006 to 2012.

Their 1999 album, *Millennium*, is among the best-selling LPs of all-time, and the Backstreet Boys have placed albums at the top of U.S. charts in three decades. Among their best-loved songs are the smooth, R&B flavored "Quit Playing Games;" the catchy, dance pop energy of "Everybody (Backstreet's Back);" the sweet, melodic we love each other number "As Long as You Love Me;" their signature song, "I Want It That Way," a fixture on many "bests" lists; "Larger Than Life," a refreshing pop rock ode to their fans; the mid-tempo love song "Shape of My Heart;" and the power ballad "Incomplete," from their 2005 comeback album, *Never Gone*.

The Backstreet Boys, still active, have received eight Grammy nominations and a host of *Billboard*, MTV, Peoples' Choice, and American and World Music awards. They are currently in the midst of a world tour.

Suggested Songs:

As Long as You Love Me (1997)
I Want It That Way (1999)
Larger Than Life (1999)
Incomplete (2005)

#212 Johnny Mathis (1935 - present)
Began Recording: 1956
Peak: 1957 - 1963
Genres: Traditional Pop; Pop Singer

It was the rock & roll era, the age of Chuck Berry and Elvis; yet, for a few brief years in the late '50s, Johnny Mathis was *the* American romantic balladeer. Then came the Beatles and popular music shifted; still, over the course of 67 years, Mathis has sold millions of records, appeared hundreds of times on TV, and, at 88, is still performing.

Born in Texas, raised in San Francisco, Mathis, an African-American of mixed race heritage, had a father who recognized his musical interest and ability and, though he couldn't afford it, took him to an opera teacher with whom he studied for six years in exchange for doing odd jobs. A gifted athlete with Olympic track and field potential, he gave that up when he was discovered at 19 singing jazz in a local club. Signing with Columbia, where he remained for all but four years, his jazz debut flopped, but he broke through nationally after moving in a more romantic pop direction, especially after his appearance on *The Ed Sullivan Show* in 1957. "It's Not for Me to Say;" "Chances Are," his first #1; "The Twelfth of Never;" "Wild Is the Wind" are all hyper romantic, big orchestra, lush arrangements from '57. In fact, in the two year '57 through '58 period, Johnny had four charting albums reach the numbers 4, 3, 2, and top *Billboard* spots with *Johnny's Greatest Hits* staying on the chart for 490 weeks, nearly 10 years, a record finally broken by Pink Floyd's *Dark Side of the Moon*.

1959's "Misty"—his favorite single—, "Gina," and "What Will Mary Say," in the early '60s, were also hits, and though he stayed afloat with albums full of Beatles or Broadway, Duke Ellington or Christmas tunes, his moment had passed, save for a second trip atop the charts in '78 with his "Too Much, Too Little, Too Late" duet. What has remained though, remarkably, is the voice—the precise enunciation, the rich, rounded tones, the vibrato, and the velvet, immaculate, polished, athlete's operatic tenor. Check the paper; he may be performing near you.

Suggested Songs:

It's Not for Me to Say (1957)
The Twelfth of Never (1957)
Misty (1959)
Too Much, Too Little, Too Late (w. Deniece Williams) (1978)

#211 Nine Inch Nails

Began Recording: 1989
Peak: 1994 - 1995; 1999 - 2000; 2005 - 2007
Genres: Industrial Rock/Alternative Rock Band

Nine Inch Nails is the brainchild of Trent Reznor who has been the only permanent member since it formed in 1988. Reznor grew up in rural western Pennsylvania and was raised by his grandparents. He is a multi-instrumentalist who learned piano, sax, and tuba as a child and has since added guitar, bass, other keyboards, and synthesizers. Working at a Cleveland recording studio, he put together demos in his free time and soon got a record deal.

Inspired by The Clash, Pink Floyd, and David Bowie, Reznor, with a rotating array of studio and touring musicians and producers, has created a body of work that mixes industrial sounds, heavy metal, rock, punk, and electronic music into an arresting, driving, dark soundscape that touches lyrically on themes of isolation, alienation, depression, addiction, obsession, self-hatred, sex, and violence; over time, Reznor and Nine Inch Nails have increasing channeled that rage toward our world's unjust social structures, movers, and shakers.

The band's first three albums are best known—1989's *Pretty Hate Machine*, which features the powerful rhythmic industrial rock of "Head Like a Hole;" '94's masterpiece, *The Downward Spiral*, which culminates in the classic, "Hurt," traces a character's descent into madness and possible suicide; and 1999's *The Fragile*, which reached the top of the *Billboard* 200, is over 100 minutes long, and features the single "The Day the World Went Away."

Oft criticized for excessively graphic lyrics, as heard on 1994's brutal "Closer," Reznor may not be advocating so much as detailing a character's reality, an argument often made by gangsta rappers. In 2020, Nine Inch Nails was inducted into the Rock & Roll Hall of Fame.

Suggested Songs:

Head Like a Hole (1989)
Terrible Lie (1989)
Hurt (1994)
The Hand That Feeds (2005)

#210 Randy Newman (1943 - present)

Began Recording: 1962
Peak: 1972 - 1978; 1996 - 2008
Genres: Pop; Rock; Americana; Film Scores Singer/Songwriter/
Composer/Pianist

With three uncles and four cousins celebrated for composing film scores, perhaps it was inevitable that Randy Newman would join the family business, but not before establishing himself as one of the most idiosyncratic and talented singer-songwriters in the world. By 17, he was a professional songwriter, and, though he first recorded in 1962, it would be another decade before the public began to know his "everyman's" voice. Before that time, his songs were covered by the likes of Judy Collins, Harry Nilsson, Three Dog Night, and a host of others.

1972's *Sail Away*, while not a hit, was a breakthrough of sorts. A critical darling, it featured two classics—the searing, ironic, slave-trade title track ("Like a vision of heaven superimposed on hell," noted Greil Marcus) and "Political Science," a satire that dares imagine the U.S. again dropping the atom bomb. In 1974, *Good Old Boys* took an American southerner's point-of-view; "Rednecks" was the hit, a song that skewered southern racism *and* northern hypocrisy. The song was misunderstood by some, as was 1977's "Short People," an obvious swipe at those with inane prejudices. Even with 1983's "I Love L.A.," celebrated as an anthem, many missed Newman's double-edged portrait of his hometown. Eschewing the typical confessional style of most singer-songwriters, Newman instead wrote from his songs' characters' perspectives, be they racist or lonely, money grubbing or charlatans; again and again, the satire was lost on many.

Beginning in the 1980s, Newman turned increasingly to writing scores and songs for films. Nominated for 22 Oscars, he has won twice. His most celebrated works were the Disney/Pixar movies, beginning with *Toy Story*, which features the oft-heard "You've Got a Friend in Me."

Newman is a member of the Songwriters and Rock Halls of Fame.

Suggested Songs:

I Think It's Going to Rain Today (1968)
Sail Away (1972)
I Love L.A. (1983)
Feels Like Home (2008)

#209 Foo Fighters

Began Recording: 1995
Peak: 1996 - 2008; 2011 - 2015; 2017 - 2022
Genres: Alternative Rock; Hard Rock; post-Grunge Band

When Kurt Cobain died by his own hand in 1994, Nirvana drummer Dave Grohl, as much for therapy as anything else, put together a tape of songs he'd written over the years and passed the demo to friends with the idea of a limited release album. Playing virtually all the instruments himself, he used the moniker Foo Fighters, a World War II-era term for UFOs. Capitol Records bid for a chance to release the songs, the album became a major hit, and Grohl decided to create a band to play the songs live.

Grohl stated in a 2021 *NY Times* article that he sees Foo Fighters as "a continuation of life," and they have been relentlessly busy, remarkably consistent, and one of rock's most successful and honored bands for a quarter of a century. Nine of their ten LPs have reached at least Platinum status, with five—*There Is Nothing Left to Lose; One by One; Echoes, Silence, Patience & Grace; Wasting Light;* and *Medicine at Midnight*—winning Grammys for Best Rock Album.

1997's *The Colour and the Shape*, perhaps their best-loved collection, features three iconic Foo Fighter tracks—"Monkey Wrench," a punk-flavored rocker that posits leaving an unhealthy relationship; the thrashing but highly melodic "Everlong," arguably their best-known song; and "My Hero," the drum heavy track with a nod toward the ordinary. Utilizing a heavy, guitar driven sound, reminiscent of punk, grunge, and arena-style hard rock, Foo Fighter songs also tend toward the melodic. Other favorites include 1999's "Learn to Fly," a straight ahead rocker with cryptic lyrics; the hard driving "All My Life" from 2002; the hopeful "Times Like These" from '03; and "Best of You," their highest charting single from 2005.

In 2021, Dave Grohl and Foo Fighter bandmates, Nate Mendel, Taylor Hawkins, Chris Shiflett, Pat Smear, and Rami Jaffee were inducted into the Rock & Roll Hall of Fame; tragically, Hawkins, their 50-year-old star drummer, was found dead in 2022 before a show in Colombia. The official report cited cardiac arrest as the cause of death; however, it was known that Hawkins had an enlarged heart, and a number of controlled substances were noted in his toxicology report. Josh Freese has stepped in as the new drummer.

Suggested Songs:

Everlong (1997)
My Hero (1998)
Aurora (1999)
The Pretender (2007)

#208 Jackson Browne (1948 - present)
Began Recording: 1972
Peak: 1974 - 1983
Genres: Soft Rock; rock; country rock Singer/Songwriter

Perhaps the quintessential male singer-songwriter of the 1970s (though a case can also be made for James Taylor), Jackson Browne was born in Germany as his dad was in the U.S. military, but by age three was living in the L.A. suburbs. A songwriting prodigy, while still in his teens Browne had a professional songwriting gig, composing for the likes of the Nitty Gritty Dirt Band, Nico, the Byrds, Linda Ronstadt, and the Eagles, before ever recording his own music. That changed in 1972 when he had a hit with "Doctor, My Eyes." His first two LPs failed to catch on but yielded such gems as the arresting but harrowing "Song for Adam;" "Take It Easy," the Eagles' first hit; and "These Days," a signature tune he wrote at 16.

The next three albums represented popular and critical break-throughs—the acclaimed, reflective *Late for the Sky*, with its philosophic ode to a dead friend, "To a Dancer," and "Fountain of Sorrow," a beautifully poetic exploration of relationships and meaning; *The Pretender*, released in 1976 after the tragic suicide death of his wife, featured the title track, a rumination on giving up on one's dreams; and Browne's highly creative ode to the musician's road, *Running on Empty*, his commercial apex.

Browne's intensely personal explorations, though always mixed with concern for the wider world, turned more overtly political in time, best exemplified with his 1986 *Lives in the Balance*, a blistering attack on U.S. foreign policy in Central America. Deeply involved in social justice issues, Browne has continued to probe the personal, the social, and the political realms in his music, and has been honored by both the Rock and Songwriters Halls of Fame.

Suggested Songs:

For a Dancer (1974)
The Pretender (1977)
Lawyers in Love (1983)
Sky Blue and Black (1994)

#207 Fats Domino (1928 - 2017)

Began Recording: 1949
Peak: 1950; 1955 - 1961
Genres: R&B; Rock & Roll Singer/Songwriter/Pianist

Elvis once called him "the real king of rock & roll." The Beatles considered him a major influence. Born Antoine Domino Jr., the youngest of eight children in New Orleans, his first language was French Creole. An in-law taught him piano while he was a child, and, by 14, he had quit school and was playing and singing locally. Bandleader, and later road manager, Billy Diamond, nicknamed him "Fats," and in 1949, working with longtime collaborator Dave Bartholomew, Domino released "The Fat Man," which soared to #2 on the R&B chart. With Fat's distinctive, barreling piano and prominent backbeat, the track has been called, by some, the first million selling rock & roll record.

Domino played a propulsive blend of New Orleans-flavored boogie-woogie and rock & roll; he simply deemed it rhythm and blues. His cheery, upbeat vocal style was a constant, whether singing of innocent love or heartbreak. With 37 Top 40 singles, Domino was popular with Black and white audiences; his best-known successes include 1955's crossover smash "Ain't That a Shame," which was successfully covered by Pat Boone; "Blueberry Hill," an oft recorded song by the likes of Glenn Miller and Louis Armstrong, though the definitive version belongs to Domino; "I'm Walkin'," which Ricky Nelson later covered; and 1960's "Walking to New Orleans," unusual for Bartholomew's added strings.

A shy, humble man who stayed married to the same woman for sixty years, Domino, the New Orleans legend, was still living in his childhood neighborhood when Hurricane Katrina struck in 2005 and needed to be rescued. He was a member of the 1986 inaugural class of the Rock & Roll Hall of Fame.

Suggested Songs:

The Fat Man (1949)
Ain't That a Shame (1955)
Blueberry Hill (1956)
I'm Walkin' (1957)

#206 Roxy Music
Began Recording: 1972
Peak: 1972 - 1976; 1980 - 1983
Genres: Avant-garde/Art Rock; Pop Rock; New Wave Band

They've been called the best British art rock band since the Beatles and second only to David Bowie, who loved them, as a creative force in '70s British music. Brian Ferry, son of working class parents, loved American jazz and R&B, and, drawing from his art school background, formed Roxy Music in 1971 with sax-oboe player Andy MacKay, techie Brian Eno, and several others who failed to stick; guitarist Phil Manzanera joined them in 1972, and they recorded *Roxy Music*, a wildly eclectic blend of all-out rock, wailing synth, and Ferry's odd, impressionistic lyrics delivered in his semi-deranged vocal style. Somehow, it worked and became a hit in Britain. Mixing quirky fashion and pop art that was both retro and futuristic, early standout tracks include the wild "Re-make/Re-model;" "Virginia Plain," their breakout single; "In Every Dream Home a Heartbreak," Ferry's sad ode to an inflatable sex companion; the aggressive "Street Life;" the wonderfully ambivalent rocker, "The Thrill of It All;" and the American breakout hit, "Love Is the Drug."

Such a creative brew wouldn't last, of course. Eno split in '73 over differing creative visions. After a mid-'70s hiatus, Roxy Music regrouped in 1979 with a newer, smoother, yet still sophisticated, melodic sound. Their final LP, 1982's *Avalon*, became their best seller and features the ethereal soft croon of "More Than This." Ferry and Eno went on to highly successful solo careers, but the off-kilter, Hall of Fame innovators, Roxy Music, influenced the likes of Talking Heads and Duran Duran, and have reformed several times in the 21st century.

Suggested Songs:

Editions of You (1973)
The Thrill of It All (1974)
Love Is the Drug (1975)
More Than This (1982)

#205 John Denver (1943 - 1997)
Began Recording: 1965 (w. The Mitchell Trio); 1969 (solo)
Peak: 1971 - 1977
Genres: Pop-Country-Folk; Soft Rock Singer/Songwriter

Critics never took to him. They called him sentimental, saccharine, and lightweight; yet, for a time in the mid-'70s, John Denver was the most popular singer-songwriter in the United States. He was everywhere, with best-selling, genre-crossing records and top-rated TV shows, concerts, and movies. And then he seemed to disappear 'til we heard he was dead at 53.

Henry John Deutschendorf, Jr. was an Air Force brat, constantly moving as a child. His grandmother's gift of a vintage Gibson guitar got him into music, and, in 1963, he quit college to try and make it as a folk singer. Changing his name to John Denver he joined The Mitchell Trio, an established folk act, in 1965. In 1969, Peter, Paul, and Mary had a #1 hit with his "Leaving On a Jet Plane," establishing Denver's name. His initial solo records didn't sell, but he broke through in 1971 with "Take Me Home, Country Roads." After that, the hits kept coming with singles like the celebratory ode to his beloved Colorado, "Rocky Mountain High;" "Sunshine on My Shoulders," his paean to the healing power of the sun; "Annie's Song," a melodic declaration of love to his wife; and the unabashed, bluegrass flavored "Thank God I'm a Country Boy."

With a pure, sweet, heartfelt tenor, and an acoustic style that betrayed easy categorization, was he folk? country? pop? Clearly he touched a nerve and he used his newfound fame to promote causes dear to his heart such as environmentalism, feeding the hungry, and thawing the Cold War. An intrepid adventurer, he perished in a plane crash off the coast of Monterey in 1997. John Denver is the first person since Stephen Foster to have written two official state songs.

Suggested Songs:

Take Me Home, Country Roads (1971)
Rocky Mountain High (1972)
Sunshine on My Shoulders (1973)
Annie's Song (1974)

#204 Pink (1979 - present)
Began Recording: 2000
Peak: 2001 - 2002; 2006 - 2013; 2017 - 2019
Genres: Pop Rock; R&B; Pop Singer/Songwriter

She's been around for over two decades, "never as big as Britney or Christina," in her own words, but she has quietly sold over 100 million records and gained a reputation for artistic integrity. Born Alecia Beth Moore just north of Philadelphia, by the age of 14 she was singing publicly and going by the name of Pink. After a couple of stints in two local R&B female vocal groups, Pink made her solo debut in 2000 with *Can't Take Me Home*, a modest R&B-flavored hit featuring "There You Go." Wresting creative control for her next project, she moved in a more pop rock direction with 2001's *Missundaztood*, the best selling LP of her career. While "Get the Party Started" was the big hit, it was the more personal numbers, "Don't Let Me Get Me;" "Just Like a Pill;" and the naked depiction of her own childhood, "Family Portrait," that spoke loudest.

With seven more studio albums, all of which reached #1 status in one country or another (she is especially popular in the U.K.), Pink's best-loved singles include "Who Knew," a moving ode to a deceased friend; the tongue-in-cheek, I don't need my husband, I'm still a rock star, "So What;" her party beat salute to underdogs everywhere, "Raise Your Glass;" the let's work it out, love duet, "Just Give Me a Reason;" and the political anthem, "What About Us."

Known for her live aerial acrobatics and her quirky hair and fashion sense, Pink is a powerful, gifted vocalist, pure and clear, with just a hint of a rasp, emotionally expressive and honest. Inspired by Madonna and Janis Joplin, she, in turn, has been extolled by the likes of Kelly Clarkson and Adele.

Suggested Songs:

Family Portrait (2002)
Raise Your Glass (2010)
Just Give Me a Reason (w. Nate Ruess) (2013)
What About Us (2017)

#203 Bill Haley (1925 - 1981)

Began Recording: 1948 (w. 4 Aces of Western Swing)
Peak: 1954 - 1957
Genres: Rock & Roll; Western swing; rockabilly Singer/songwriter/
Bandleader

They were all there, the pioneers, the founding fathers, in the 1986 inaugural class of the Rock & Roll Hall of Fame—Little Richard, Chuck Berry, Fats Domino, Elvis, Jerry Lee, the Everlys, Buddy Holly, and several others—but there was one glaring omission: Bill Haley, though that would be rectified a year later.

Blind in one eye, William Haley had working class, yet musical, parents; his dad gave him a guitar, and, as a teenager growing up in Pennsylvania, Bill played, sang, and yodeled in a series of bands. Working as a DJ, by 1950, dressed in full western regalia, he was leading a group known as the Saddlemen. Though Haley and his band didn't really invent rock & roll, they did begin mixing elements of R&B and Dixieland jazz with their country & western sounds, experimenting quite freely, borrowing from "race records," and, in 1951, released a cover of "Rocket 88," which some have termed the first rock & roll record. 1952's "Rock the Joint" was played by Cleveland DJ Alan Freed, who was calling it rock & roll. Haley and his band dropped the western garb, donned a new moniker, Bill Haley & His Comets, and released the first rock & roll song to hit the pop charts, "Crazy Man, Crazy," in 1953. "Rock Around the Clock," released in '54, was a moderate hit, but superseded by the suggestive "Shake, Rattle and Roll." When "Rock Around the Clock" was inserted in 1955 into the film *Blackboard Jungle*, the song exploded, becoming one of the top-selling singles of all time; the Rock & Roll Era was on.

Haley was soon eclipsed by Elvis and the rest, though he remained popular in Europe for a short time and, oddly, made a splash in Mexico with the Twist. By the late '60s, he was a nostalgia act and he died young, addled by alcohol and mental illness. Somewhat overlooked, Haley was, indisputably, one of the greats.

Suggested Songs:

Crazy Man Crazy (as Bill Haley & His Comets) (1953)
Rock Around the Clock (as Bill Haley & His Comets) (1954; 1955)
Shake, Rattle and Roll (as Bill Haley & His Comets) (1954)
Rip It Up (as Bill Haley & His Comets) (1956)

#202 Alanis Morissette (1974 - present)

Began Recording: 1991
Peak: 1995 - 2002
Genres: Alternative Rock; Pop Rock Singer/Songwriter

She was 21 years old and, quite overnight, the most talked about artist in the world. Alanis Morissette was born in Canada, daughter of two teachers. She learned piano as a young child, was writing songs by 10, appeared briefly on children's TV, and recorded two dance pop albums before she was out of high school. Dropped by her label, she made her way to L.A. where she connected with producer Glen Ballard, creating a demo album that was rejected by a dozen companies before Maverick Records released it as *Jagged Little Pill*.

The alternative-rock-flavored *Jagged Little Pill* went on to top the charts in 13 different countries, sell over 30 million copies, and win five Grammys, including Album of the Year. Hailed for its confessional, raw, transparent lyrics, some critics trashed it as overwrought, but it struck a chord with a generation of young people who, 27 years on, still revere it as a touchstone. The post punk anthem "You Oughta Know," performed by Alanis on *Letterman* with Patti Smith-like abandon, was a bitter swipe at an ex-love; "Hand in My Pocket," a mid-tempo rocker, expresses a young person's complexity of conflicting emotions; while "Ironic" triggered widespread discussion about the true meaning of the word.

Morissette has released more strong work, notably the dramatic, Grammy-winning "Uninvited;" the LPs *Supposed Former Infatuation Junkie* and *Under Rug Swept*; and such tracks as "Thank U," the rare song that recognizes growth through hardship; and "Hands Clean," her unvarnished look at an age-inappropriate relationship. But it's her 1995 masterwork, later made into a Broadway musical, for which she is truly celebrated.

Suggested Songs:

Hand in My Pocket (1995)
Uninvited (1998)
Thank U (1998)
Hands Clean (2002)

#201 Duran Duran

Began Recording: 1981
Peak: 1981 - 1985; 1993 - 1994
Genres: New Wave; Synth-Pop Band

They came out of Birmingham, England, in the late '70s, part of what was termed the "new romantic" movement. Duran Duran's original lineup of five included Nick Rhodes, keyboardist; John Taylor on bass; Simon Le Bon, lead vocalist; Roger Taylor on drums; and Andy Taylor, guitarist who left in 2006. Warren Cuccurullo, likewise a guitarist, was with the band for over 12 years.

Upon their 2022 induction into the Rock & Roll Hall of Fame, it was noted that Duran Duran played "infectious pop melodies concealing complicated musical arrangements; pioneering synthesizers combined with distorted glam rock guitars." They called the music new wave, and Duran Duran debuted just as MTV was beginning to air. With the song "Rio" going in the background, the image of the band on a Caribbean beach and sailboat with a swim-suited model prancing about has become iconic. Their catchy music and ubiquitous video presence in the early '80s made them global superstars. Critics were less than overwhelmed, perhaps because their biggest fan base, early on, seemed to be teenage girls, but that negative assessment has changed with time.

Among their best-loved works are the eponymous 1981 debut album with the single "Planet Earth" carrying an ominous sci-fi lyric; 1982's *Rio*, their most acclaimed LP, featuring the appealing title track; the driving synth-rock of "Hungry Like the Wolf;" and the romantic hook-up song, "Save a Prayer;" 1984's funky dance-pop, "The Reflex;" the sophisticated James Bond theme, "A View to a Kill;" and the 1993 comeback LP, *The Wedding Album*, with the beloved ballad, "Ordinary World."

Suggested Songs:

Rio (1982)
A View to a Kill (1985)
Ordinary World (1993)
Come Undone (1993)

#200 Kraftwerk

Began Recording: 1970
Peak: 1974 - 1987
Genres: Electronic/Avant-garde; Electropop Band

Ralf Hutter and Florian Schneider were two post-war German university music students who formed in the late '60s the groundbreaking, experimental band Kraftwerk.

Early on they used mostly traditional instruments, often distorted in post-production, to produce an avant-garde form of rock, but they soon came to rely on the latest in recording technology, from synthesizers, to the vocoder, to software, and the recording studio itself as musical instruments. Their musical purpose was twofold—to discover the unique sound of modern Germany, in the wake of World War II and its cultural destruction, and to explore the "human machine," as they saw us all becoming, with the ubiquitous incursion of modern technology into human life. The result has been a stunning body of work, beginning with the 1974 international 22 minute hit, "Autobahn," with its hypnotic electronic simulated ride. With minimalist lyrics and music that varies from ultra-simple to melancholic to humorous to dance pop friendly, Kraftwerk songs both celebrate and warn about the brave new world we all inhabit.

1977's *Trans-Europe Express* is an ode to Europe, but it also seems to examine reality and illusion. *The L.A. Times*, in 2014, called it "the most important pop album of the last 40 years." Never a big commercial success, Kraftwerk's influence, nevertheless, has been huge in synthpop, disco, EDM, new wave, and hip-hop; they've been extolled by David Bowie to Neil Young to Depeche Mode. Critics have termed them unfeeling, antiseptic, and inhuman, but fans point out that they are mirroring where we already are and where we are heading.

Suggested Songs:

Radioactivity (1975) (2005, live)
Trans-Europe Express (1977)
The Model (1978)
Computer Love (1981)

#199 Nicki Minaj (1982 - present)

Began Recording: 2007
Peak: 2010 - 2022
Genres: Hip-Hop; Pop Rapper/Singer/Songwriter

Born Onika Tanya Maraj in Trinidad, Nicki Minaj, as she calls herself professionally, moved to Queens with her older brother and mother when she was five. Nicki attended a Manhattan performing arts high school and struggled to get into acting before moving to hip-hop. Her Myspace demos got her signed to a local record label, but Lil Wayne soon discovered and signed her to Young Money and became an important mentor. She then released her third mixtape, *Beam Me Up Scotty*, featuring "I Get Crazy" and "Itty Bitty Piggy;" brandishing a street-tough persona, Minaj became a star.

In 2010, Nicki created a sensation with her appearance on Ye's "Monster;" released her debut LP, *Pink Friday*; and scored with the R&B-flavored "Your Love." Since then she's been a consistent presence on both the hip-hop and pop charts with four best-selling albums and strong performing singles such as the upbeat pop rap "Super Bass;" techno pop dance track "Starships;" sex-drenched rap "Anaconda;" and her remix of Doja Cat's "Say So."

Many publications have deemed her the "Queen of hip-hop" or "rap." *PopMatters* called her the finest rapper, male or female, of the 2010s. Known for her alter egos, or characters, Minaj has been extolled for her incisive wordplay, her exceptional flow, her theatricality, and her pop crossover appeal. Sassy, ferocious, and profane, she can also be emotionally vulnerable, with tracks like "I Lied" and "All Things Go." Now that she's a mom, she has talked of backing away from the overly sexual raps, but 2022's "Super Freaky Girl" might indicate otherwise.

Suggested Songs:

Super Bass (2011)
Starships (2012)
All Things Go (2014)
Say So (w. Doja Cat) (2020)

#198 Tim McGraw (1967 - present)

Began Recording: 1991
Peak: 1994 - 2016
Genres: Country; country rock; country pop Singer

With 13 studio LPs and over two dozen singles that have topped the country charts, Tim McGraw is one of the most popular artists of the past three decades.

He grew up with the surname Smith, thinking his stepdad was his biological father, but, at age 11, he found out he was the son of Major League Baseball pitcher Tug McGraw. When Tug got involved in his life seven years later, Tim changed his name. He began playing guitar and singing during his college years, and he dropped out and moved to Nashville in 1989. Signing with Curb Records, he had little success until 1994's *Not a Moment Too Soon*, a huge bestseller that featured "Indian Outlaw," a song that's been skewered for its racial stereotypes, and "Don't Take the Girl," a three scene, tear-jerking, story song.

McGraw has not really had a dry patch since his breakout. His voice may carry a bit less Louisiana twang, and one hears more rock and pop elements in his music, but he's been remarkably consistent. Married to fellow artist Faith Hill, with whom he's shared three daughters and two Grammys, he no longer drinks to get onstage where he's still a bit of a sex-god under a trademark black straw cowboy hat. With so many songs to choose from, three favored tracks are "I Like It, I Love It," which showcases rock & roll Tim; "2004's "Live Like You Were Dying," advice from one facing mortality, which won him a Grammy for his vocals; and 2016's sweet, counsel laden "Humble and Kind." Tim has won a boatload of country related awards, and has been praised, as well, for his acting roles.

Suggested Songs:

Don't Take the Girl (1994)
I Like It, I Love It (1995)
Live Like You Were Dying (2004)
Humble and Kind (2016)

#197 Ariana Grande (1993 - present)
Began Recording: 2011
Peak: 2013 - 2022
Genres: Pop; R&B; rap Singer/songwriter

It's only been a single decade, but Ariana Grande's musical footprint is already huge—among the 100 top-selling artists of all time, one of the most streamed and social-media-followed singers of her time, and a voice that has been compared to the greats.

Born in Florida to two successful parents, from a young age she sang and did children's theater, landing a Broadway role in 2008. From 2010 to 2014, she was a fixture on Nickelodeon as the slow-witted but sweet sitcom character Cat Valentine. Ariana released her first single in 2011, "Put Your Hands Up," which she later described as "bubblegum pop" and not representative of what she hoped to do. Since 2013, she has released six studio albums, five reaching the top spot on pop charts, with the one that missed hitting #2.

Her musical style has been described as R&B-flavored pop, though she has mixed in various dance, EDM, and hip-hop elements, as well, singing of the push-pull of relationships, sexual desire, self and female empowerment, material wealth, and moving on in the face of loss. It is Ariana's voice, however, that has garnered most of the attention. With a four-octave range, the ability to reach the whistle or highest register, and wonderful control, she has been compared endlessly to Mariah Carey.

Her most talked about songs include 2013's "The Way," a pop/hip-hop duet with troubled rapper Mac Miller; "One Last Time," a love loss mid-tempo ballad that took on new meaning in 2017 after a bombing at her Manchester Arena concert that killed 22 people, as the song became a loving send off to the victims; "No Tears Left to Cry," Ariana's positivity response in the face of tragedy; "God Is a Woman," a song of seduction and self-assertion; and the giant "Thank U, Next," which celebrates all that we can learn from past loves.

She is only 30; we can only guess at what she will accomplish in a full career.

Suggested Songs:

One Last Time (2015)
No Tears Left to Cry (2018)
God Is a Woman (2018)
Thank U, Next (2019)

#196 The Everly Brothers
Began Recording: 1956
Peak: 1957 - 1960
Genres: Rock & Roll; Country; pop; country rock Duo

Noted for their close harmony singing, Don and Phil, The Everly Brothers, had a string of hits from 1957 to 1960 that made them one of the foundation acts of rock & roll. As preteens in Iowa, they sang locally with their parents as The Everly Family. After graduating from high school in Tennessee, the brothers focused on starting a music career in Nashville. Chet Atkins helped get them connected, and, though Columbia dropped them after one record, they signed with Cadence Records, breaking through internationally with "Bye Bye Love," a song that's been covered by both the Beatles and Simon and Garfunkel. Both groups, in fact, have cited the Everlys as huge influences.

Accompanying themselves on acoustic steel-string guitars, The Everly Brothers produced a clean, melodic, sweet blend of rock & roll, country, and pop, singing mostly of young love and teenage angst, but it was their intricate, interweaving harmonies that set them apart. The hits came one after another—"Wake Up Little Suzie," "All I Have to Do Is Dream," "Bird Dog," "Let It Be Me." Switching labels, they scored their biggest success in 1960 with "Cathy's Clown," but by 1963 the hits had dried up. There was conflict with their publisher, new music from across the ocean was filling the airwaves, Don developed a serious pill problem, a stylistic switch to a more country rock sound didn't seem to help, and, in 1973, there was a painful breakup. A decade later, the brothers reunited and played together 'til Phil's death in 2014; Don died in 2021. Indicative of the esteem in which they are held, The Everly Brothers are members of the Rock, Country, and Vocal Group Halls of Fame.

Suggested Songs:

Bye Bye Love (1957)
Wake Up Little Suzie (1957)
All I Have to Do Is Dream (1958)
Cathy's Clown (1960)

#195 Talking Heads

Began Recording: 1977
Peak: 1978 - 1981; 1983 - 1985
Genres: New Wave Band

They were new wave pioneers, three art school students who came together in the New York punk scene in the mid-'70s but forged their own path, experimenting, and adding funk and African rhythms over time into the mix, producing a truly idiosyncratic body of work.

David Byrne was born in Scotland, but was a U.S. resident before he was out of elementary school. Teaming up with drummer Chris Frantz and Chris's future wife of 45 years and counting, Tina Weymouth, the three took a loft in the Lower East Side. With Tina working on learning to play bass, and David writing the songs, playing guitar, and singing, they added Jerry Harrison on keyboards. Their initial album was only a hit in New Zealand, but the single "Psycho Killer" contained all the iconic Talking Heads elements—off-kilter lyrics (including a bit of French), a minimalist, edgy sound featuring Tina's now famous bass line, and Byrne's unhinged, but totally captivating vocal style.

From 1978 to 1980, they worked with Brian Eno to produce their next three LPs, culminating in the classic *Remain in Light*. Standout tracks from this period include "Take Me to the River," an Al Green cover; the "apocalyptic punk/funk" (as *AllMusic* put it) of "Life During Wartime," which features lyrics that are both frightening and funny at the same time; acclaimed, existentially questioning "Once in a Lifetime."

Jonathan Demme's arresting *Stop Making Sense*, a 1984 concert film of the band, has found its way into the Library of Congress. Byrne left the band in 1991 for a brilliant, eclectic solo career, and there had been some "bad blood" ever since, but a recent rerelease of Demme's classic seems to have healed whatever wounds still remained. Talking Heads reunited only once to play, at their 2002 Rock & Roll Hall of Fame induction.

Suggested Songs:

Psycho Killer (1977)
Life During Wartime (1979 or 1984 live)
Once in a Lifetime (1981)
This Must Be the Place (Naive Melody) (1983)

#194 Blondie
Began Recording: 1976
Peak: 1978 - 1981
Genres: New Wave; Rock; Pop; punk; disco Band

They saw themselves as a new wave band, but they've been called everything from punk to art-rock to disco sellouts. Perhaps *AllMusic* said it best— Blondie "brought underground sounds into the mainstream." Debbie Harry and Chris Stein were two former art students who connected in the New York punk scene, became lovers, then formed Blondie in 1974. Platinum blonde Harry was the lead vocalist while Stein played lead guitar. Clem Burke, longtime drummer, joined a year later; while Jimmy Destri, Frank Infante, Nigel Harrison, and Gary Valentine all played key roles.

Blondie was wildly experimental, breaking through in Australia with their first LP and internationally with 1978's *Parallel Lines* which contains two classics: the controversial, synth driven, new wave-disco mix, "Heart of Glass," their first #1 on *Billboard's* Hot 100; and the driving rhythm of "One Way or Another," inspired by an ex-boyfriend stalking Harry, and featuring her brilliant, manic vocals. In 1980, Blondie had two more #1s: the disco-rock-flavored "Call Me" and the reggae cover "The Tide Is High." A year later their radically diverse *Autoamerican* produced a fourth chart topper, "Rapture," which was the first rap style song in the U.S. to reach #1 on *Billboard's* mainstream chart. As the band reached the pinnacle of its commercial success, the media's focus increasingly was on the strikingly attractive and sensual Harry whom some saw as a latter day Marilyn Monroe. Harry herself said it was all a role, "the same thing David Bowie did."

By 1982, Stein was deathly ill with an autoimmune disease; in addition, there were infighting and drug issues in the band, and they broke up, only to regroup in 1997, performing to this very day. In 2006, Blondie was inducted into the Rock & Roll Hall of Fame.

Suggested Songs:

Heart of Glass (1979)
One Way or Another (1979)
Call Me (1980)
Maria (1999)

#193 Bryan Adams (1959 - present)
Began Recording: 1976 (w. Sweeny Todd); 1978 (solo)
Peak: 1983 - 1996
Genres: Rock; Pop Rock Singer/Songwriter

One of Canada's best selling artists of all-time, Bryan Adams, as a child, attended schools in Portugal, Austria, and Israel as his father had a career in the military and later in the diplomatic corps. To escape his parents' fighting, he took refuge in music, laser focused on mastering the guitar. A fan of hard rock, he quit high school to play in a series of bands. Determined to make a career in music, he signed a record deal in 1978 with A&M for $1.

Bryan's third LP, *Cuts Like a Knife*, proved to be the breakthrough he was looking for. The pop-flavored ballad "Straight from the Heart" and the hard rocking title cut were the biggest hits, but it was the follow-up album, 1984's *Reckless*, that made him an international superstar. Widely considered his best and, with sales of over 12 million, his most successful, the cheating rocker "Run to You;" the forever love power ballad "Heaven;" and the anthemic "Summer of 69," arguably his best-loved number, are the featured tracks.

Adams has had a Canadian chart topper as recently as 2019, but '91's *Waking Up the Neighbors* and the huge international hit "(Everything I Do) I Do It for You" are the most celebrated. He has had his detractors. He's been called, by some, a generic version of Springsteen, given to clichéd rock anthems and power ballads, but there's no denying his massive, sustained popularity throughout the globe. He's a music giant in India and has played such off-the-beaten-path locations as Turkey, Vietnam, Nepal, and Bangladesh. In addition, Bryan has participated in countless benefits over the years and he is an accomplished, world-recognized photographer.

Suggested Songs:

Cuts Like a Knife (1983)
Heaven (1985)
Summer of '69 (1985)
(Everything I Do) I Do It for You (1991)

#192 Crosby, Stills, Nash & Young

Began Recording: 1969
Peak: 1969 - 1970
Genres: Folk Rock; Country Rock Band

One of rock's early supergroups, Crosby, Stills, Nash & Young (CSNY) are a tantalizing example of "if only." Each member was a musically gifted alum of a Hall of Fame band. David Crosby, fired from the Byrds, had a sweet voice, ideal for harmony, and played rhythm guitar; Stephen Stills, late of Buffalo Springfield, is a driven multi-instrumentalist, with a throaty vocal style; England's Graham Nash, originally with the Hollies, sings as a soft or light tenor and plays guitar; while Neil Young, Stills' Buffalo Springfield bandmate, plays a ferocious lead guitar and sings with a distinctive, plaintive high pitch. All four shared the writing chores.

Crosby, Stills, and Nash began singing at an L.A. party, liked the sound of their shared vocals, and decided to form a band, cutting their eponymous debut LP in early '69. With a soft rock, acoustic folk feel, featuring their complex harmonies, best heard on Stephen's 4-part "Suite: Judy Blue Eyes," they struck a nerve. Inviting Neil Young, who was just launching a solo career, to join them, they played their second ever live gig in front of half a million people at Woodstock. With the release of the festival film and CSNY's *Deja Vu* in early 1970, they were suddenly the face of the counterculture. Their version of Joni Mitchell's "Woodstock" and Nash's "Teach Your Children" became anthems. When National Guardsmen shot down four college students at Kent State during an antiwar rally in May, they responded within weeks with Neil's powerful protest "Ohio."

In the end, three dominating egos, and Graham Nash, just didn't gel. Six more studio LPs followed over the next three decades, some with Neil, some without, as each also pursued solo projects. Limitless potential, for a brief moment realized, but they are today mostly a memory. In January 2023, the prickly David Crosby passed away.

Suggested Songs:

Suite: Judy Blue Eyes (CSN) (1969)
Wooden Ships (CSN) (1969)
Teach Your Children (CSNY) (1970)
Ohio (CSNY) (1970)

#191 Christina Aguilera (1980 - present)

Began Recording: 1997
Peak: 1999 - 2003; 2006 - 2008; 2010 - 2011
Genres: Pop; R&B; Dance Pop Singer/Songwriter

She came out of *The All New Mickey Mouse Club* in the early '90s along with Britney Spears and Justin Timberlake, but her early life was no TV sitcom as she had to cope with an abusive household and, later, bullying peers that led to homeschooling.

New York born Christina Aguilera's recording of "Reflection" for the *Mulan* soundtrack, led to a contract with RCA. Her 1999 eponymous debut LP, on the heels of the Britney explosion, was a teen pop sensation, earning Aguilera a Best New Artist Grammy at the age of 19, and featured four smash singles—the suggestive "Genie in a Bottle;" the R&B-flavored "What a Girl Wants;" "I Turn to You," which shows off her vocal prowess; and the sexy "Come On Over Baby." Fighting for greater artistic control, Aguilera, in 2002, released *Stripped* which added R&B, hip-hop, and rock elements to her pop sound and veered strongly toward a more adult, sexualized image. "Dirrty," with Redman, was the polarizing single, but the giant hit "Beautiful" was a Grammy-winning self-love ballad. *Back to Basics*, from 2006, found Aguilera swerving again, this time reappearing as an Old Hollywood platinum blonde and seeking to pay homage to her idols, Etta James, Billie Holiday, and the like. The regret-tinged ballad "Hurt" garnered the most attention.

Christina Aguilera has been called a modern day sex symbol, but her voice has drawn great acclaim; she is a powerful four-octave soprano, sometimes compared to Mariah Carey and Whitney Houston, and sometimes taken to task for over-singing, but more than capable of emoting in multiple genres. The list of singers she has influenced is too long to include.

Suggested Songs:

Genie in a Bottle (1999)
Beautiful (2002)
Hurt (2006)
Say Something (w. A Great Big World) (2013)

#190 The Mills Brothers
Began Recording: 1931
Peak: 1931 - 1939; 1943 - 1954
Genres: Jazz; Traditional Pop Vocal Quartet

They began as a novelty act but wound up smashing color lines, winning the admiration of the likes of Bing Crosby, arguably recording more records than anyone in history, and staying in the public eye for over half a century.

Their dad was an Ohio-based barber who sang in a quartet. The four boys, John Jr., Herbert, Harry, and Donald Mills, learned from their dad how to harmonize and sang in church. John Jr. played guitar, and the brothers learned to blend the sounds of trumpets, trombone, and tuba using just their voices. A 1928 radio gig brought them to the attention of Duke Ellington who introduced them to a New York recording company. Soon they had a regular national CBS radio program, a first for black artists, and a #1 song, their jazzy debut, "Tiger Rag." Listeners found it hard to believe that the horns were coming not from musical instruments but from The Mills Brothers, "Four Boys and a Guitar," as they were also known.

More hits followed– "You Rascal You," "Good-bye Blues," "Bugle Call Rag," and many others. They made movies and became stars in Europe. Still, the novelty of their vocal gymnastics began to wear off, brother John died suddenly (to be replaced by their father), and World War II arrived. But in 1943, they launched a comeback with "Paper Doll" which spent 12 weeks atop the charts and became an all-time best-selling single. By the late '40s, the full transition away from their earlier style can be heard with songs like "Glow-Worm" which features full orchestration. With the rise of rock & roll, their popularity declined, but they continued to perform until, one by one, death came calling. The Mills Brothers have been honored with a Lifetime Grammy and membership in the Vocal Group Hall of Fame.

Suggested Songs:

Tiger Rag (1931)
Paper Doll (1943)
I'll Be Around (1943; 1958)
You Always Hurt the One You Love (1944)

#189 Bjork (1964 - present)

Began Recording: 1977
Peak: 1993 - 2015
Genres: Experimental/Avant-Garde/Electronica Pop Singer/Songwriter

Musician Taylor Ho Bynum put it like this: "No contemporary artist so gracefully bridges the divide between music experimentalist and pop celebrity." Bjork Guomundsdottir, known around the world simply as Bjork, grew up in a commune in Iceland with her mom and musical stepfather. She studied classical piano and flute as a child, and cut her first album, largely in her native tongue, when she was 11. Over the next 16 years, she was in and out of various bands, experimenting with punk, jazz-fusion, and alt-rock. Moving to London, she released *Debut*, her first solo LP. Surprising her fans, who knew her primarily as a rocker, the album featured forward-looking electronic dance music, including two of her best-loved songs, the sexy, catchy "Venus as a Boy" and "Big Time Sensuality," highlighted by Bjork's trademark vocal gyrations.

Her voice has been called dynamic, elastic, quirky, and she uses swoops and shrieks and howls to express the most intimate of emotions. Musically, Bjork is a restless boundary pusher; she draws from every imaginable source, with influences as diverse as German electronic composer Stockhausen, female giants Kate Bush and Joni Mitchell, electronic pioneers Kraftwerk, and from jazz, hip-hop, and whatever else catches her ear. She then turns it all into truly original, adventurous, emotional pieces that are somehow natural, organic and romantic, but at the same time cool, technological, even cybernetic. She loves to create whole new worlds with each LP– *Post*, with its diversity of styles; *Homogenic*, her ode to Iceland; the erotic, moody *Vespertine*; and *Vulnicura*, which has been called particularly honest and personal. Great songs? Try "Hyperballad," with its bizarre dream imagery married to an evolving musical score; the sonically rich, thrilling "Joga;" or the truly strange "It's Oh So Quiet," her hilarious cover of a 1951 song.

Bjork is an original, said to be the greatest musical artist Iceland has ever produced.

Suggested Songs:

Venus as a Boy (1993)
It's Oh So Quiet (1995)
Hyperballad (1996)
Joga (1997)

#188 Henry Mancini (1924 - 1994)

Began Recording: 1957
Peak: 1958 - 1973
Genres: Film Scores; Jazz; Pop Composer/Conductor/pianist

Henry Mancini, the son of Italian immigrants, grew up in a small town outside Pittsburgh. Already a multi-instrumentalist as a boy, he had a keen interest in jazz, arranging, and composing. A scholarship to Juilliard was interrupted by World War II and Henry's stint in the U.S. Army Air Forces. After the war, he played piano and arranged for the reconstituted Glenn Miller Orchestra while he studied composition. In 1952, Mancini landed a job at Universal-International, contributing, in various capacities, to the music for over 100 films. His big break came in 1958 when he was assigned to do the score for Orson Welles' *A Touch of Evil*.

Henry then left Universal to freelance and hooked up with Blake Edwards, the creator of TV's *Peter Gunn*. Mancini's rock-jazz score was a sensation, earning the first ever Album of the Year Grammy. Over the next few decades, Henry would collaborate regularly with director Edwards, producing his most iconic compositions– 1961's *Breakfast at Tiffany's*, which earned Mancini his first Oscar for best score. "Moon River," from the same film, gave him a second Oscar and became his signature song; a pop clas-sic, it's been covered over 500 times. "The Days of Wine and Roses," now considered a light jazz standard, brought him yet another Academy Award, as did his score for Edwards' '82 film *Victor/Victoria*. Mancini's work on the *Pink Panther* franchise is also considered groundbreaking.

Mancini was prolific, releasing over 90 LPs, and finding time to give hundreds of concerts, often playing the piano, or leading a world-class symphony orchestra. Winner of 20 Grammys, Mancini was still creating when he passed away in 1994.

Suggested Songs:

Peter Gunn Theme (1958)
Moon River (1961)
The Pink Panther Theme (1963)
Love Theme from Romeo and Juliet (1969)

#187 The Byrds

Began Recording: 1964
Peak: 1965 - 1968
Genres: Rock- Folk Rock; Psychedelic Rock; country rock Band

The Byrds certainly don't rank among the all-time best selling artists, but they had a hand in pioneering three subgenres of music, and, for a time, were mentioned in the same breath as the Beatles, the Rolling Stones, and Bob Dylan.

Jim McGuinn, Gene Clark, and David Crosby all came out of the early '60s folk scene. Drawn to the music of the Beatles, in 1964 they formed a band in L.A. and began working toward bridging the gap between folk and rock. McGuinn, who later changed his name to Roger, was a talented guitarist and turned to a 12-string electric; Clark was a gifted songwriter; while Crosby played rhythm; and all three shared the vocals. Adding Michael Clarke on drums and Chris Hillman, a mandolin player who switched to bass, in 1965 the Byrds blasted into musical history with their stunning cover of Bob Dylan's "Mr. Tambourine Man." With its bright, jangly guitar tones and intricate, gorgeous harmony, the single was a #1 smash in the U.S and the U.K. Critics had a name for the new sound– folk rock. The album of the same name followed with three more Dylan covers and five originals, and soon critics were gushing over the "American Beatles." When the Beatles later that year released *Rubber Soul*, people were sure they heard Byrd-like echoes in several tunes.

In October 1965, the Byrds released "Turn! Turn! Turn!," a Pete Seeger song taken almost entirely from the Bible's Book of Ecclesiastes. Again, the beautiful, interwoven harmonies, McGuinn's ringing 12-string guitar, and the song's plea for peace produced their second, and last, #1 single, but with 1966's controversial "Eight Miles High," the Byrds helped usher in what was soon known as psychedelic rock.

By 1968 only McGuinn and Hillman remained of the original Byrds; yet, recorded in Nashville, their *Sweetheart of the Rodeo* is recognized today as one of the first examples of country rock. Though their moment is gone, the influence of the Byrds can be heard in the music of the Eagles, Tom Petty, R.E.M., and countless others.

Suggested Songs:

Mr. Tambourine Man (1965)
I'll Feel a Whole Lot Better (1965)
Turn! Turn! Turn! (To Everything There Is a Season) (1965)
Eight Miles High (1966)

#186 Kris Kristofferson (1936 - present)

Began Recording: 1967
Peak: 1970 - 1975; 1985
Genres: Country; country rock Singer/Songwriter

One of country music's great songwriters, Kris Kristofferson was surprised when offered a recording deal because he thought he couldn't sing.

Born in Texas and son of an Air Force major general, Kris moved frequently before settling in California as a teen. A multi-sport, gifted athlete and brilliant student, he was a Rhodes scholar at Oxford where he studied English literature, hoping to make it as a novelist. He also loved playing and writing music, but in 1961 he married and joined the army, becoming a helicopter pilot. Assigned to teach at West Point in 1965, Kris instead quit the army and moved to Nashville to try his hand professionally at music; his family disowned him.

Struggling to make ends meet as his family life was crumbling, Kris was a janitor at a recording studio, drove a helicopter for an oil company, and plugged away at writing songs. In the late '60s he began to get some traction as a songwriter, but determined to get a demo to Johnny Cash, he audaciously piloted his chopper onto Cash's property. In 1969, the two met and Cash invited Kristofferson to the stage at Newport, and doors began to open.

Writing deeply personal tales of brokenness, alienation, love, sex, and freedom, Kris' 1970 eponymous debut LP failed to sell initially, but four of the tracks, covered by other artists, reached #1 on various charts and are today recognized as classics– "Help Me make It Through the Night" is a lonely yearning-for-intimacy song that became a #1 country hit for Sammi Smith; "For the Good Times," a sad "end of love" song, gave Ray Price a #1 country hit; "Sunday Mornin' Comin' Down" was a country chart topper for Cash and movingly details a lonely, stumbling, hungover morning; while "Me and Bobby McGee," a tale of regretful lost love, gave Janis Joplin a posthumous *Billboard* Hot 100 #1 record. Kris' biggest personal chart hits include "Lovin' Her Was Easier," from his second album, and the humble country gospel of "Why Me." A hugely successful Hollywood actor and later a member of the famed supergroup The Highwaymen, Kristofferson is a member of the Country Music Hall of Fame.

Suggested Songs:

Help Me Make It Through the Night (1970)
For the Good Times (1970)
Sunday Mornin' Comin' Down (1970)
Why Me (1973)

#185 Journey

Began Recording: 1975
Peak: 1978 - 1983
Genres: Rock Band

Formed in 1973, San Francisco's Journey remains one of the best-selling bands of all time. Highly acclaimed guitarist Neal Schon was playing with Santana at the age of 17 and is the only current member of Journey who was there at the start. Key bandmates included Gregg Rolie, keyboard player who left without rancor in 1980 to be replaced by Jonathan Cain; Steve Perry, gifted lead singer during their peak years; Ross Valory, longtime bassist; and drummer Aynsley Dunbar who was succeeded by Steve Smith.

Originally a prog-rock and jazz-rock collective, they changed their sound when Columbia threatened to drop them for underperforming; soon Perry joined, they had their first hit LP, *Infinity*, and Dunbar departed, unhappy with the new mainstream rock direction. For about a decade, beginning in 1978, they were a dominant force on radio, records, and in concert. 1981's "Don't Stop Believin'," from their best selling LP, *Escape*, has been called by critic Kelefa Sanneh, "a masterpiece of hard-rock melancholy that endures as perhaps the most beloved power ballad ever recorded." Indeed, the anthem, which tells of two lonely seekers making a connection, reached new heights as it played through the closing scene of the iconic TV series *The Sopranos*. It is said to be the best-selling digital song that comes from the 20th century. Other Journey classics include 1982's "Open Arms," a much covered love ballad, and 1983's "Faithfully," a road musician's pledge of fidelity to a waiting wife.

Journey was inducted into the Rock & Roll Hall of Fame in 2017, but, sadly, their legacy has been marred by animosity and a series of firings, suits, and countersuits over song trademarks and the band's name.

Suggested Songs:

Wheel in the Sky (1978)
Don't Stop Believin' (1981)
Open Arms (1982)
Faithfully (1983)

#184 Olivia Newton-John (1948 - 2022)

Began Recording: 1966
Peak: 1974 - 1975; 1978 - 1982
Genres: Pop; country pop; pop rock Singer/songwriter

A descendent of Martin Luther and granddaughter of Nobel physicist Max Born, Olivia Newton-John was pop royalty. Born in Cambridge but raised in Australia, Olivia returned to England in 1965 after winning a TV talent contest and recorded a one-off single as her prize. She sang in several vocal groups with little traction before breaking through in 1971 with "If Not for You," a Dylan cover, gaining a sizable British following. "Let Me Be There," an American country hit, won her a Grammy, but 1974's "I Honestly Love You" made her an international pop star and earned two more Grammys. "Have You Never Been Mellow" was a huge crossover follow-up, but it was her 1978 role as Sandy, alongside John Travolta in the beloved musical *Grease*, that took her to another level. The soundtrack, one of the best selling albums of all time, features her iconic, electric duet with Travolta, "You're the One That I Want," and her Oscar-nominated "Hopelessly Devoted to You."

Olivia scored again in 1980 with the catchy soft rock "Magic" and the disco flavored "Xanadu" from the failed fantasy movie of the same name. An underrated vocalist, blessed with a high, clear voice, she shed the virginal, girl-next-door image with 1981's "Physical," a dance pop number with suggestive lyrics that stayed atop *Billboard*'s Hot 100 for 10 weeks. The international hits dried up soon after.

In 1992, Newton-John was diagnosed with breast cancer. She became a strong anti-cancer advocate and activist, raising awareness and funds to help others fight and deal with the illness, even as she continued to record, perform, and act. She succumbed in 2022 to her illness, with eulogies underscoring how much she was loved.

Suggested Songs:

I Honestly Love You (1974)
You're the One That I Want (w. John Travolta) (1978)
Magic (1980)
Physical (1981)

#183 Bonnie Raitt (1949 - present)

Began Recording: 1971

Peak: 1989 - 1994

Genres: Blues Rock; Rock; Blues; R&B; folk rock Singer/Guitarist/songwriter

Her dad was a well-known Broadway musical actor, her mom a gifted pianist. Bonnie Raitt picked up the guitar, as much to forge her own path, at a young age, drawn to blues and folk. She dropped out of Radcliffe to pursue a musical career and released her first album in 1971. From the start her guitar work opened eyes and ears, and she was a frequent session player. Raitt's own releases, from 1971 to 1983, were mostly covers of blues, folk, and pop artists, usually critically lauded but not big sellers. 1977's *Sweet Forgiveness* was her highest charting LP, reaching #25 on *Billboard*'s Top LPs while her best-known songs from this era were a striking blues rock version of Del Shannon's "Runaway" and her moving cover of John Prine's regret filled "Angel from Montgomery."

In 1983, her record label dropped her for underperforming commercially. She had to fire her band, and, drinking heavily, she fell into a depression. Bonnie credits AA with helping her regain sobriety in 1987. Connecting with producer Don Was, she created a demo that was repeatedly turned down 'til Capitol Records took a chance. The aptly named LP *Nick of Time* soared to #1 and won the coveted Grammy Album of the Year, making Raitt a superstar at 40, unheard of in the music business. The self-penned title track affectingly deals with aging, and the album, a *National Recording Registry* selection, seems to speak to baby boomers. Her follow-up LP, *Luck of the Draw*, sold even better and features the hauntingly sad but achingly beautiful "I Can't Make You Love Me." A soulful, bluesy, husky voice singer, Raitt has won 11 Grammys and is a member of the Rock & Roll Hall of Fame.

Suggested Songs:

Angel From Montgomery (1974)
Nick of Time (1989)
Something to Talk About (1991)
I Can't Make You Love Me (1991)

#182 Rush

Began Recording: 1973
Peak: 1976 - 1997
Genres: Progressive Rock; Hard Rock; Heavy Metal Band

One of the finest groups of brilliant instrumentalists in rock history is Rush, a Canadian trio that formed in Toronto in 1968. Alex Lifeson was the wonderfully imaginative lead and rhythm guitarist who drew from blues rock greats, later incorporating classical elements and a whole lot of heart and spontaneity; Geddy Lee was the outstanding bass and synthesizer player, as well as the oft-criticized high pitched vocal frontman; the original drummer left before Rush became stars to be replaced by Neil Peart, one of rock's most esteemed percussionists, and the band's lyricist.

Rush's origins as a metal/ hard rock outfit in the mold of Cream and Led Zeppelin can be heard on "Fly By Night," their first minor hit. By 1976, with *2112* they had fully embraced progressive rock; the LP's title track is a 20-minute, 7-part, sci-fi song suite that tells the story of a planet that has banned music. 1977's "Closer to the Heart" got them radio airplay; 1980's "The Spirit of Radio" took aim at music radio's tendency to pander; "Limelight" expressed how it feels for an introvert like Peart to live in a luxurious fishbowl; while "Tom Sawyer," a paean to integrity, features the band firing on all cylinders and has become their signature tune.

A great touring collective that built a loyal following in that way, Rush has also been polarizing, both loved and loathed. Still, even the detractors have come to appreciate the superb musicianship. In the '80s they moved toward synth-driven new wave, as heard on "New World Man," but later returned to a hard rock sound. Members of the Rock and Canadian Music Halls of Fame, Rush disbanded in 2015; the great Neil Peart succumbed to cancer in 2020.

Suggested Songs:

The Spirit of Radio (1980)
Tom Sawyer (1981)
Red Barchetta (1981)
New World Man (1982)

#181 The Miracles
Began Recording: 1958
Peak: 1960 - 1971
Genres: R&B; Pop; Soul Vocal Group

The Miracles were the breakout act for Berry Gordy's massively influential Motown Records. The Miracles were formed in 1955 as a Detroit high school doo-wop group by boyhood friends William "Smokey" Robinson, Ronnie White, and Pete Moore; cousins Bobby Rogers and Claudette Rogers soon joined the trio while Marv Tarplin added guitar. They initially went by the 5 Chimes, then the Matadors, before settling on the Miracles. Auditioning for singer Jackie Wilson's management team, they were rejected but caught the ear of songwriter Berry Gordy, Jr. who offered to work with them, but with little initial success. When Gordy formed his own label, Tamla, which morphed into Motown, the Miracles and Motown in 1960 had their first million seller, the lively, R&B-flavored "Shop Around."

As the decade progressed, the quintet, more and more going by their frontman's moniker, Smokey Robinson & the Miracles, until it became official in 1965, were a steady presence on the R&B and pop charts– "You've Really Got a Hold on Me," a soulful ballad later covered by the Beatles; "Mickey's Monkey," which helped ignite a dance craze; "Ooo Baby Baby," arguably *the* romantic slow dance song at high school hops from around '65 to '68; "The Tracks of My Tears," ranked an all-time great by the Library of Congress, *Rolling Stone*, *Mojo*, and the RIAA; '67's "I Second That Emotion;" and 1970's calliope-accented "The Tears of a Clown."

The Miracles were particularly noteworthy for several reasons: Smokey Robinson was a prolific and gifted songwriter, so there was no need for outside writers, and Robinson's high tenor-falsetto vocal style was instantly recognizable and effective. There was an outcry when the Rock & Roll Hall of Fame inducted Smokey, without the Miracles, in 1987, but after years of furious lobbying from many quarters, this was rectified when the rest of the Miracles were admitted in 2012. The entire group is also included in the Rhythm & Blues Music Hall of Fame.

Suggested Songs:

Shop Around (1960)
You've Really Got a Hold on Me (1962)
Ooo Baby Baby (1965)
The Tracks of My Tears (1965)

#180 The Kinks
Began Recording: 1964
Peak: 1964 - 1971
Genres: Rock; Pop Band

U.K.'s *Express* called the Kinks "the most underrated rock & roll band of all time." North Londoners Ray Davies and younger brother Dave were the mainstays for the group's nearly 35 years together. Ray was the songwriter and lead singer, while Dave played lead guitar. The original lineup featured Pete Quaife on bass and Mick Avory on drums.

In 1964, they broke through with two hard hitting rockers, "You Really Got Me" and "All Day and All of the Night," two records heard today as proto-punk and metal, featuring simple power chords, ferocious guitar solos by the 17-year-old Dave, and Ray's uninhibited vocals. As charter members of the '64 British musical invasion, the sky was the limit, but in 1965 they were banned from performing in the U.S. for four years (various reasons have been given for why). The effect was telling. Ray turned inward and began exploring his British heritage with a sophisticated mixture of English music hall, folk, and baroque pop, alternately extolling and lampooning traditional English values with a series of wonderfully insightful themed albums– *Face to Face*, *Something Else*, *The Village Green Preservation Society*, and *Arthur*. Highlight tracks from this '66 to '69 era include the tax-burdened aristocrat's lament, "Sunny Afternoon;" the highly acclaimed meditation "Waterloo Sunset;" the ambivalent ode to the queen, "Victoria;" and the British class satire "Shangri-La." In 1970, the Kinks had a huge hit with an early trans anthem, "Lola." Increasingly, though, hits were harder to come by; still, today the Kinks are recognized as a seminal '60s band, helping to pioneer both heavy rock and delightfully witty concept albums.

Suggested Songs:

Waterloo Sunset (1967)
Shangri-La (1969)
Lola (1970)
Celluloid Heroes (1972)

#179 Alice Cooper

Began Recording: 1969 (as group); 1975 (solo)
Peak: 1971 - 1973; 1975 - 1976
Genres: Hard Rock; Heavy Metal Band and Singer/Songwriter

Alice Cooper was a hugely popular hard rock band in the early 1970s that essentially "invented the rock show," as Rob Zombie put it; when they broke up in 1974, their lead singer and frontman legally took the name and carried on as a solo act to this very day.

Inspired by the Beatles, Vince Furnier, Glen Buxton, Michael Bruce, Dennis Dunaway and Neal Smith formed in Phoenix; were signed by Frank Zappa; persisted through two failed LPs; and broke through with their neither-a-boy-nor-a-man anthem "I'm Eighteen" in 1970, which was followed by the "shock rock" album, *Love It to Death*.

With dark, often bloody, costumes and elaborate stage shows featuring, at times, live snakes, a straight jacket, electrocution, and a guillotine, Vince/Alice became a rock & roll villain, outraging many a parent and politician. The music, though, was hard, heavy, and gritty; Alice was an arresting vocalist, and many of the songs featured memorable hooks and lyrics– the fast, driving "Under My Wheels;" the student dream "School's Out;" the clever "No More Mr. Nice Guy." With *Billion Dollar Babies* in 1973, they had a #1 album in the U.S. and the U.K. The band was burned out, though, and went on hiatus in 1974, but Alice continued as a soloist, sometimes evincing a softer side with tracks like "Only Women Bleed," "You and Me," and "I Never Cry," which was, in fact, a naked confession that Alice's alcoholism was out of control. Sober now nearly 40 years, Alice credits his 46-year marriage, his family life (two children have followed him into the business), his Christian faith, and his substitute addiction, golf.

Alice Cooper, the band, was inducted into the Rock & Roll Hall of Fame in 2011.

Suggested Songs:

I'm Eighteen (1970)
Ballad of Dwight Fry (1970)
School's Out (1972)
No More Mr. Nice Guy (1973)

#178 Carrie Underwood (1983 - present)

Began Recording: 2005
Peak: 2005 - 2023
Genres: Country Pop; Country Rock; gospel Singer/songwriter

Without a doubt, Carrie Underwood is one of the most successful musical artists of the past two decades as measured by records sold, concert receipts, and honors bestowed.

Born in Muskogee, Oklahoma, a town once celebrated by Merle Haggard, like so many other great vocalists, Carrie was singing in church at a young age. She nearly had a recording contract at 14, only to have it snatched away, and began to think a singing career was not to be. While at a state university, she auditioned for *American Idol*, winning the competition in 2005 and signing with Arista Nashville. In less than a month Carrie had the #1 single in the U.S. and Canada, the country pop ballad "Inside Your Heaven." Several months later, she released her debut LP, *Some Hearts*, the first of eight consecutive #1 country albums. Four of her LPs have also topped the pop charts.

Drawing on rock, country, and her Christian faith for inspiration, Carrie has cited both Freddie Mercury and Martina McBride as particular influences. With an incredibly powerful, wide ranging voice, she's been described as very versatile in her ability to move comfortably between genres, though she seems to favor up-tempo country-rock-pop story songs of adversity which end, typically, in triumph. With 14 singles reaching #1 on the country charts, some award-winning favorites include "Jesus, Take the Wheel," about a young mother who reaches out to her Lord after surviving a car accident; "Before He Cheats," a revenge fantasy fan favorite among wronged ladies and perhaps her biggest seller; "Last Name," about a drunken Vegas marriage; "Blown Away," a sublime example of Underwood's vocal chops on an edgy track that hints at a father's abuse; and her faith affirming crowd pleaser, "Something in the Water."

Carrie is 40 and has already won eight Grammys and four CMA Female Vocalist of the Year awards; it would seem that the sky is the limit.

Suggested Songs:

Jesus, Take the Wheel (2005)
Before He Cheats (2006)
Blown Away (2012)
Something in the Water (2014)

#177 Joan Baez (1941 - present)
Began Recording: 1959
Peak: 1960 - 1965; 1971; 1975
Genres: Folk; Folk Rock; Country Folk; Latina Singer/songwriter

In a career that spanned 60 years, she had only one Top 10 single and a handful of albums that were moderate hits; yet, who else can claim to have played at 1963's March on Washington, at Woodstock in 1969, and at 1985's Live Aid benefit?

Joan Baez is the daughter of a Scottish mother and a Mexican born, prominent physicist father. Raised a Quaker, from an early age she was drawn to its social justice traditions. Pete Seeger was an early musical inspiration, and, by the late '50s, Joan was playing folk music in and around Boston and Cambridge. In 1959, the 18-year-old played the Newport Folk Festival and was dubbed the "barefoot Madonna." Soon she was recording, with her first few albums going gold. In 1962, she was on the cover of *Time* Magazine, as the "Queen of the Folk Singers." In 1963, she began introducing the world to a scruffy, baby faced folkie by the name of Bob Dylan who would soon eclipse her in fame and influence, but Joan's early support played a crucial role in his acceptance in the folk world.

At 82 her voice is not what it once was, but in her prime she had a clear, crystalline, soaring soprano with a very pronounced vibrato. Lana del Rey called it "ethereal and heavenly." An elegant, fingerpicking guitarist, Joan is a gifted cover artist, drawing from traditional sources as well as from Dylan, Guthrie, Phil Ochs, Paul Simon, the Beatles, and a host of others. Her biggest hit, "The Night They Drove Old Dixie Down," is a Civil War lament taken from The Band; her most beautiful might be her own bittersweet, autobiographical look back at a '60s love affair with Dylan, "Diamonds and Rust." But music has always been secondary to Baez. Working tirelessly for a more just and peaceful world has been her life's focus since she was first arrested as a teen for civil disobedience. Known as a beautiful, dignified, down to earth woman, nobody has ever married justice seeking and music so fully as Joan Baez, and her work has been recognized with countless honors.

Suggested Songs:

There But for Fortune (1965)
The Night They Drove Old Dixie Down (1971)
Diamonds and Rust (1975)
Brothers in Arms (1987)

#176 Dave Brubeck (1920 - 2012)

Began Recording: 1948
Peak: 1954 - 1963
Genres: Jazz Pianist/Composer/Bandleader

Beginning in the mid-'50s, rock & roll began to eclipse jazz as a cultural force. Ellington and Armstrong were still around, but the biggest new names in the popular imagination were Presley, Berry, and Richard; in jazz circles it was Miles Davis and Dave Brubeck.

Dave Brubeck grew up in the San Francisco Bay Area, the son of a cattle rancher and a piano teacher. Planning to follow his father into ranching, his teachers divined where his heart truly lay. In World War II his superiors had him form a jazz band; studying music on the GI Bill, by 1946 Dave formed his first outfit, an octet.

He is best-known for the Dave Brubeck Quartet featuring himself on piano and, for about 27 years, Paul Desmond on tenor sax, with a number of rhythm players, most prominently Eugene Wright on bass and Joe Morello on drums. A freak diving accident left Brubeck unable to play speedy right hand runs; so he compensated with dense, complex chords. Desmond's sax, described as "ethereal," was the perfect complement. Brubeck was famous for his unusual time signatures and his polytonality, or the playing of two or more keys simultaneously. He became a huge hit in the 1950s on college campuses playing cool jazz, but it was his 1959 LP, *Time Out*, that made him a huge star; it was the first jazz album to ever sell a million copies, and it featured the Desmond composed international hit "Take Five," said to be the best selling jazz single of all-time.

Known as a gentle, humble man, when *Time* Magazine did a cover feature on him in 1954, he felt Duke Ellington was much more deserving; the following year he recorded his tribute, "The Duke." When clubs or TV shows balked at presenting his integrated quartet (Wright was Black), Brubeck canceled. Brubeck was married for 70 years to his wife, Iola, his sometime collaborator and manager, and four of their six children followed him into music and frequently played with him. Winner of a Lifetime Grammy and Kennedy Center honors, Dave once remarked, "One of the reasons I believe in jazz is that the oneness of man can come through the rhythm of your heart."

Suggested Songs:

Take Five (1959)
Blue Rondo a la Turk (1959)
Unsquare Dance (1961)
It's a Raggy Waltz (1961)

#175 The Allman Brothers Band

Began Recording: 1969
Peak: 1970 - 1974
Genres: Blues/Country Rock Band

The tragic story of The Allman Brothers Band is in stark contrast to their singular musical brilliance. Nashville-born brothers Duane and Gregg lost their father to murder while they were still toddlers. In high school they began playing in various R&B and rock bands. Duane, a guitar genius, tired of session work, put together a band in 1969 with fellow premier guitarist Dickey Betts; bassist Berry Oakley; drummers Butch Trucks and Jaimoe; and Gregg, a gifted, soulful vocalist, organ player, and songwriter, the final piece.

Relocating from Florida to Macon, Georgia, the band lived together and practiced relentlessly, becoming a superb blues-rock-country ensemble with distinctive R&B, jazz, and even classical elements. Their first two albums were not hits, but as a remarkable live act they decided in 1971 to record three New York shows. The result, *At Fillmore East*, became a huge, double-album smash with extended jams like Gregg's "Whipping Post." Considered an all-time great live LP, as it reached gold status, Duane, the band's undisputed leader, was killed in a Macon motorcycle crash. He was 24. The band, numb with grief and an excess of drugs, carried on, releasing the celebrated *Eat a Peach*, the final studio LP featuring Duane. Just a year after Duane's death, Oakley, also 24, was similarly killed on a motorcycle, three blocks from Duane's demise. Though more popular than ever, internal strife and drugs fractured the group in 1976, even as their friend Jimmy Carter was winning the presidency. There'd be reunions, new members, and recordings up to 2014, but they never recaptured their legendary, groundbreaking magic.

Suggested Songs:

Midnight Rider (1970)
In Memory of Elizabeth Reed (live) (1971)
Blue Sky (1972)
Ramblin' Man (1973)

#174 Elvis Costello (1954 - present)

Began Recording: 1977
Peak: 1977 - 1983
Genres: New Wave; Punk; Rock & Roll; Pop; country; jazz Singer/Songwriter

Declan Patrick MacManus figured he'd skip the family business. His grandfather played trumpet; his dad was a respected jazz performer; even his mom, who ran a record shop, had an encyclopedic knowledge of music. Declan figured he couldn't carry a tune, but by his teenage years he was playing guitar and singing, first in Liverpool, then back to his native London. Supporting himself with data entry work, his demo tapes got him signed as a solo artist in 1977.

Now going by Elvis Costello, he released *My Aim Is True*, his highly lauded debut LP, mixing punk, new wave, and rock & roll with "revenge and guilt" lyrics, as he put it, and it reached #14 on the U.K. charts. Two of the tracks have become classics– "Alison," a song Costello says is about a "disappointing somebody," is given life by his empathetic vocals, while "Watching the Detectives" seems to skewer escapist TV viewing with its wildly cryptic, reggae flavored lyrics.

Costello's next two albums are also deeply loved– 1978's *This Year's Model* and 1979's *Armed Forces*. "Oliver's Army" is a much-celebrated favorite, reaching #2 in Britain and, behind a catchy pop melody, is a blistering critique of occupational armies, specifically England in Northern Ireland.

AllMusic called Costello the "most evocative, innovative, and gifted songwriter since Bob Dylan." Dylan, in his new book on songwriting, has praised him as well. Costello's lyrics are sophisticated and clever; early on he did have an angry, hurt take on life, and political and social satire was always close at hand, but he has lightened some over time. Costello is also noted for his adventurous exploration of genres– he's not just a Buddy Holly look alike punk rocker; he's also new wave and rock and pop, and country and jazz and even a little bit classical. With his distinctive nasal voice, he can deliver tender and scathing. He has played with everybody, from his crack backing band, the Attractions, to Paul McCartney to George Jones. Costello is a member of the Rock & Roll Hall of Fame.

Suggested Songs:

Alison (1977)
Watching the Detectives (1977)
Oliver's Army (w. the Attractions) (1979)
Man Out of Time (w. the Attractions) (1982)

#173 Ramones
Began Recording: 1976
Peak: 1976 - 1980
Genres: Punk Rock; pop punk Band

Never as popular or famous as the Sex Pistols, The Clash, or Patti Smith, *AllMusic*'s Stephen Erlewine called them "the most important band in punk history." Drawing on sources as diverse as Iggy and the Stooges and the Who, New York Dolls, and '60s bubblegum, New York's Ramones ignited a movement in the mid-'70s, taking rock back to its high-energy, raw basics. Playing fast, loud, pounding, short songs laced with dark and comic images, the Ramones are today recognized for their influence on artists such as Green Day, Metallica, Pearl Jam, and countless others; but in their day, they couldn't buy a hit.

Formed in Forest Hills, Queens, in 1974, they were lead singer Joey (Jeffrey Hyman); bass player Dee Dee (Douglas Colvin); guitar wizard Johnny (John Cummings); and drummer Tommy (Thomas Erdelyi), replaced in 1978. Though unrelated, all decided to go by the surname Ramone. Their regular gigs at the East Village CBGB created word-of-mouth enthusiasm and they released their debut LP, *Ramones*, in 1976 to laudatory reviews and commercial failure. Today it's a recognized classic in the *National Recording Registry*. The lead track, "Blitzkrieg Bop," with its call-out refrain and notorious Nazi references, is their signature song. 1977's *Rocket to Russia* did a little better and features a Beach Boys pop sheen overlaid on the elemental punk. "Rockaway Beach," an ode to Dee Dee's boyhood, and "Sheena Is a Punk Rocker" are the best-known tracks. *Road to Ruin* in '78 found the Ramones adding guitar solos and ballads but also features a second signature track, "I Wanna Be Sedated."

The four original Ramones all died young, three to cancer, Dee Dee to heroin, but they were honored in 2002 with induction into the Rock & Roll Hall of Fame.

Suggested Songs:

Blitzkrieg Bop (1976)

Sheena Is a Punk Rocker (1977)

Rockaway Beach (1977)

I Wanna Be Sedated (1978)

#172 Usher (1978 - present)
Began Recording: 1991 (w. NuBeginnings); 1993 (solo)
Peak: 1997 - 2012
Genres: R&B; soul; pop; dance; hip-hop Singer/Songwriter

One name is sufficient to identify a few of the giants– Elvis, Adele, Madonna, Bowie; we can add Usher to that list. Born Usher Raymond IV in Dallas, he was raised in Tennessee where he began singing in church. By 12 he was part of an R&B quintet, the NuBeginnings, even cutting a mail order LP. Relocating to Atlanta, Usher signed a record deal with LaFace Records and released his first single at 14. His first major label album, *Usher*, was not a big hit, but got him noticed. His sophomore effort, *My Way*, was a well-received multi-platinum success with three giant singles– "You Make Me Wanna...," a love triangle musing; "Nice & Slow," a sexy, romancing ballad; and the title track.

The early Usher sound featured melodic, sensual ballads sung in a fluid, easy style, his voice effortlessly gliding from tenor to falsetto and back. People heard echoes of Michael Jackson, who Usher freely acknowledged as an influence, also citing Prince. *8701* produced two Grammy-winning tracks, "U remind Me" and "U Don't Have to Call," won for his R&B vocals, but it was 2004's giant selling *Confessions* that brought Usher acclaim as one of the world's biggest artists. Four singles hit the top of the pop charts– the hip-hop-flavored R&B track "Yeah!" with Lil Jon & Ludacris; the break-up ballad "Burn;" the controversial "Confessions Part II," which Usher explained was a character song, not an autobiography; and his duet with Alicia Keys, "My Boo." Three more subsequent albums have reached #1 as have the singles "Love in This Club," a mid-tempo number showcasing Usher's vocals, and the critically panned, auto-tuned "OMG" with will.i.am.

Frequently acknowledged as one of the finest and most honored R&B artists of the last three decades, Usher is a mere 45 years old.

Suggested Songs:

U Remind Me (2001)
U Got It Bad (2001)
Burn (2004)
Love in This Club (w. Young Jeezy) (2008)

#171 LL Cool J (1968 - present)
Began Recording: 1984
Peak: 1987 - 2002
Genres: Hip-Hop Rapper/Songwriter

A best-selling, groundbreaking rapper, in-demand TV and film star, successful author and businessman, generous philanthropist, and married for over 25 years, by any measure LL Cool J has had an extraordinary life; when his traumatic childhood is taken into consideration, it is down-right miraculous.

Born James Todd Smith and raised in Queens, he was just four when his distraught father shot and nearly killed both his mother and his grand-father. A few years later, his mom's drug addicted boyfriend used to strip him naked and beat him with little or no provocation. James coped by living in his imagination and learning to compose rhymes. Away from his abuser and with the support of his mother and grandfather, James began to rap, making demos by age 14. Signed to the new Russell Simmons-Rick Rubin label, Def Jam, at 16, LL Cool J (or Ladies Love Cool James), as he now called himself, released the aggressive, minimalist "I Need a Beat," followed by his debut LP, *Radio*, in 1985. With Rubin's help, LL was helping to usher in a New School of rap, based less on funk and disco and more hard hitting, drum machine driven, street savvy and boastful, with just a hint of rock. With his subsequent releases, *Bigger and Deffer* and *Mama Said Knock You Out*, LL became, arguably, rap's first superstar, and, along with Run-DMC, the Beastie Boys, and others, helped usher in hip-hop's golden age.

Sometimes there was pushback in the hip-hop community against LL because he often favored R&B, even pop-flavored, crossover romancers, songs like "I Need Love;" his third LP, *Walking with a Panther*, was especially derided in some circles, but, for the most part, LL Cool J is highly respected as a rap pioneer who helped bring hip-hop to the mainstream and for his longevity. In 2002, he was still releasing chart-topping albums (*10* was #1 on *Billboard*'s R&B/Hip-Hop chart) and singles ("Luv U Better"). The first rapper to win Kennedy Center Honors, LL Cool J is also a Rock & Roll Hall of Fame inductee.

Suggested Songs:

I Can't Live Without My Radio (1985)
I Need Love (1987)
Mama Said Knock You Out (1990)
Hey Lover (w. Boyz II Men) (1995)

#170 Pearl Jam

Began Recording: 1991
Peak: 1992 - 1996
Genres: Rock - Alternative Rock; Grunge Band

They came out of Seattle, part of the grunge movement that took over popular music in the early '90s. Born of the ashes of several different bands, Pearl Jam are Mike McCready on lead guitar; Stone Gossard, rhythm guitar; Jeff Ament on bass; and San Diego recruit Eddie Vedder, lead singer and chief lyricist; at least five different drummers have backed them through the years.

Drawing equally on post punk and classic rock, the still active Pearl Jam has had a knack for writing melodic hooks, anthemic arena rockers, and arresting story songs that touch on personal struggle and social issues, with an always sympathetic eye and ear on the underdog.

Their 1991 debut album, *Ten*, broke slowly at a time when Nirvana's *Nevermind* was taking the world by storm, but it stayed around for years and has since surpassed it in sales, if not fame, certified 13x Platinum by the RIAA. Though considered a grunge classic, *AllMusic's* Steve Huey has also heard echoes of Hendrix and Zeppelin. Four of Pearl Jam's best-loved tracks are found on *Ten*– the heavy rocking look at homelessness, "Even Flow;" Vedder's semi-autobiographical "Alive," with its memorable McCready solo; the difficult look at a teenage school site suicide, "Jeremy;" and the pained, but melodic, soaringly beautiful "Black."

Known as well for their principled stands against ticket price gouging and for environmental and other liberal causes, Pearl Jam has released five #1 albums, *Vs.*, *Vitality*, *No Code*, *Backspacer*, and *Lightning Bolt*. In 2017, Pearl Jam was inducted into the Rock & Roll Hall of Fame.

Suggested Songs:

Alive (1991)
Black (1991)
Daughter (1993)
Just Breathe (2009)

#169 Katy Perry (1984 - present)

Began Recording: 2001 (as Katy Hudson); 2007 (as Katy Perry)
Peak: 2008 - 2014
Genres: Pop; Dance Pop; Pop Rock Singer/Songwriter

A pop star's window of notice and acclaim can be very small; for a time, Katy Perry was as big as any recording artist in the world. Time will tell if she will experience a second or third wave of massive popularity.

Born Katheryn Hudson to strict Pentecostal parents in California, Katy was raised on gospel music. At 16, she released a Christian rock album, *Katy Hudson*, on a small label that soon folded. Turning to secular music, she struggled to find a major label before signing with Capitol, taking her mother's maiden name, Perry. *One of the Boys*, her secular debut, was a breakout hit, and featured the controversial EDM-flavored "I Kissed a Girl." The religious right hated it for promoting homosexuality, while many in the LGBTQ+ community felt the song was using bisexuality to garner attention. The song was a worldwide smash, followed by her dance-pop "Hot n Cold." In 2010, Katy released one of the most successful albums of all time, *Teenage Dream*, an album notable for sending five singles to the top of the *Billboard* Hot 100, something only Michael Jackson had done– "California Gurls," with Snoop Dogg, lauding the sexy women of the West Coast; "Teenage Dream," quintessential Katy, a big pop celebration of first love; "Firework," one of Perry's best-loved empowerment anthems; "E.T.," with Kanye West, featuring odd lyrics extolling an alien lover; and "Last Friday Night," which celebrates mindless, drunken teenage partying. *Prism*, the 2013 follow-up LP, offers up the massively successful "Roar," her arena-sized ode to self-assertion, and "Dark Horse," with Juicy J, weaving a bewitching tale.

The "Queen of Pop," as she's been called, was also termed the "Queen of Camp" by *Vogue*, and, indeed, Katy favors a sort of psychedelic cartoon vibe in her theatrical presentations. Already among the all-time best sellers, Katy has fallen into disfavor among some critics and fans who have questioned her authenticity. Still, at 39, it would be foolish to think her moment can't come around once again.

Suggested Songs:

I Kissed a Girl (2008)
Teenage Dream (2010)
Firework (2010)
Roar (2013)

#168 Tom Jones (1940 - present)
Began Recording: 1964
Peak: 1965 - 1972
Genres: Pop; R&B; Country; dance; gospel; rock Singer

From the mid-1960s through the early '70s, Welsh-born Tom Jones was arguably the most prominent male pop vocalist in the world. Born Thomas Woodward, a coal miner's son, he has been singing since childhood, influenced by R&B and early rock & roll. Laid low by TB for two years, Tom was married with a child before he was 17. The marriage was to last, despite Tom's well-known dalliances, for 59 years.

He began singing professionally in 1963 as Tom Scott and the Senators with little more than local success, but Tom found a new manager, moved to London, and changed his name to Tom Jones. Signing with Decca, Tom's second single, 1965's "It's Not Unusual," was his breakthrough, reaching #1 in the U.K. and #10 in the U.S.

From the start, Tom's voice was a revelation. Stephen Erlewine described him as "a full-throated, robust baritone," while others have noted his power, his unique, operatic tone, and his crying, emotional style. Standout singles from his early years include the country pop styling of "Green, Green Grass of Home," that moves from an idyllic dream to the waking realization that the narrator is a prisoner who will only return home to be buried, and the dramatic, flamenco-flavored murder ballad, "Delilah." Capitalizing on his recording popularity and his sex appeal, from 1969 to 1971 Jones was big enough to host his own weekly TV show, popular in both the U.K. and the U.S. When the hits began to dry up toward the mid-'70s, Jones turned to Las Vegas and then, in the early '80s, to country music. He continued to find periodic chart success in the U.K. from 1988 through the next two decades, experimenting with a variety of styles and collaborators. In 2021, he released the highly acclaimed UK #1 LP *Surrounded by Time* which features the stunningly resonant "I'm Growing Old." *The Guardian* opined, "Time has neither dimmed Jones' lustre nor tamed his ferocious vocal cords...the power and precision of Jones' stentorian baritone remain staggering."

Suggested Songs:

It's Not Unusual (1965)
Delilah (1968)
I (Who Have Nothing) (1970)
I'm Growing Old (2021)

#167 Alison Krauss (1971 - present)

Began Recording: 1986
Peak: 1990 - 2011; 2017 - 2022
Genres: Bluegrass; Country; folk Singer/Instrumentalist

With 27 Grammy wins, Alison Krauss ranks fourth all time behind only Beyoncé, Quincy Jones, and conductor Gorg Solti. Alison grew up with folk and rock music, while studying classical violin from the age of five; drawn to bluegrass, she taught herself to play fiddle music by ear and was soon entering and winning contests. Recognized early on as a virtuoso, she recorded an album of traditional fiddle tunes at the age of 14. She was but 19 when she won the Best Bluegrass Album Grammy for *I've Got That Old Feeling*. By this time she was alternating between so-called solo releases and collaborations with her crack band, Union Station.

Krauss has been credited with doing more to extend the reach of traditional bluegrass music than any other modern artist; she has, in fact, been embraced by the country music establishment and has not been afraid to reach into the worlds of folk, rock, and pop without compromising her singular artistic vision. In part, this is because she is an exquisite vocalist. A soprano, her voice has been variously described as sweet, angelic, silky, haunting, breathy, and spellbinding. Her collaborations have often been award-winning, if not legendary: "Whiskey Lullaby," with Brad Paisley, is a haunting, if melodramatic, tale of a broken couple's demise; "How's the World Treating You," with James Taylor, doesn't end with drunkenness and death, but it too is a heartbreaker. Then, in 2007, the music world was shocked to see Alison pairing with ex-Led Zeppelin frontman Robert Plant. The result, *Raising Sand*, was stunning as the duo swept the Grammys with such standouts as "Gone, Gone, Gone," "Please Read the Letter," and "Killing the Blues."

2021 saw Krauss and Plant release a new album, *Raise the Roof*, with a tour in 2022.

Suggested Songs:

Endless Highway (1990)
Gravity (w. Union Station) (2004)
Whiskey Lullaby (w. Brad Paisley) (2004)
Killing the Blues (w. Robert Plant) (2007)

#166 Creedence Clearwater Revival

Began Recording: 1968
Peak: 1969 - 1970
Genres: Blues, R&B, Country inflected Rock & Roll Band

They seemed to come out of nowhere in 1968, but, by 1970, with the breakup of the Beatles, a case could be made that Creedence Clearwater Revival was the world's most popular band.

Doug Clifford, Stu Cook, and John Fogarty were junior high students in 1959 in El Cerrito, California, who formed a band, the Blue Velvets. Soon they were backing John's older brother Tom, who sang lead, even cutting a few records. Signing with local label Fantasy, they were renamed the Golliwogs, a moniker they hated. By 1968, they renamed themselves Creedence Clearwater Revival and had a modest hit with their cover of "Suzie Q."

With John now firmly in control as songwriter, lead vocalist, and lead guitarist, they made a pact to stay drug free and focus on the music. Tom played rhythm, Doug, the drums, and Stu, bass. In 1969, they exploded with three hit albums– *Bayou Country*, *Green River*, and *Willy and the Poor Boys*. Mixing blues, rockabilly, Louisiana-flavored R&B, hints of country, and good old-fashioned rock & roll, critics called it swamp rock. No matter, the music was tight, driving, and deeply American. Singing of a South they'd never visited, CCR gave us "Proud Mary" and "Born on the Bayou;" socially conscious works, like the fiercely anti-war "Fortunate Son" were also part of the mix; as were songs taken from personal experience ("Green River" and "Travelin' Band") or things read or simply imagined ("Bad Moon Rising" and "Down on the Corner").

In 1971, Tom left the group, tired of what he saw as John's iron fisted control and dominance; by late '72, Creedence was no more. There were bitter feelings, even lawsuits with Fantasy. Tom died in 1990, and even a Rock & Roll Hall of Fame induction failed to reunite the remaining three. CCR's music, though, lives on 50 years later, a staple of classic rock radio.

Suggested Songs:

Proud Mary (1969)
Bad Moon Rising (1969)
Fortunate Son (1969)
Who'll Stop the Rain (1970)

#165 Steely Dan
Began Recording: 1972
Peak: 1973 - 1980; 2000 - 2001
Genres: Jazz-Pop-Rock Fusion Band

Walter Becker and Donald Fagen met in college in the late '60s. Drawn to similar music, they began playing in local bands and writing songs together. For a while they toured as backing musicians for Jay and the Americans. Moving to California to be staff writers for ABC Records, they decided to form their own band, Steely Dan, to get their compositions recorded.

From 1972 to 1974 they were a real band with a full lineup, LP and single releases, and a touring schedule, but, in '74, Becker and Fagen decided to drop the live act and focus on the crafts of writing and recording. Their bandmates drifted away, and, thereafter, Steely Dan was Walter, a guitar and bass player, and Donald, on keyboard and lead vocals, with a host of studio collaborators.

Steely Dan draws from jazz, blues, R&B, and pop as much as they do from rock; horns are always in the mix along with guitars, often with brilliant solos, and keyboards. Studio perfectionists, the playing and production is always complex, harmonic, and impeccable. They've been called cold, cryptic, obscure, and perverse by those who don't get or like their lyrics, but repeated listening usually opens up the songs. "My Old School" and "Kid Charlemagne" are classic story-songs: the former about a college drug bust, the latter about famed LSD chemist, Owsley Stanley. "Do It Again" seems to muse at the ways we repeat the same futile patterns, while the majestic "Deacon Blues" may be an autobiographical take on the duo's early years. There's not a bad album in their discography, but 1977's *Aja* has been deemed, by many, a masterpiece.

After a 20-year studio hiatus, in 2000 they released *Two Against Nature*, which went on to win the Best Album Grammy. In 2001, they were inducted into the Rock & Roll Hall of Fame. Walter Becker died of cancer in 2017.

Suggested Songs:

My Old School (1973)
Rikki Don't Lose That Number (1974)
Haitian Divorce (1976)
Deacon Blues (1978)

#164 Patti Smith (1946 - present)
Began Recording: 1974
Peak: 1975 - 1979
Genres: Punk Rock Singer/Songwriter

She said she was on a mission—a mission to blend poetry with rock & roll, but, more importantly, to reach out to all the people who were seen as weird or different, the disenfranchised and persecuted.

Patti Smith grew up feeling that way. Raised in Philadelphia and South Jersey, she was poor, tall and gangly, a tomboy, part of a strict Jehovah's Witnesses household– not unhappy, but different. Drawn to art, she studied to be a teacher, got pregnant, had the baby, and put her up for adoption. Moving to Manhattan in 1967, she got romantically involved with photographer Robert Mapplethorpe. She broke off their sexual relationship when he realized he was gay, but they remained the best of friends. Smith's memoir, *Just Kids*, written decades later about those New York years, won the coveted National Book Award. In those early years, Patti, living hand to mouth, painted, wrote plays and acted, but mostly she composed poetry, which she'd recite wherever they'd have her. She invited a friend, guitarist Lenny Kaye, to play behind her. Soon she had a pianist, Richard Sohl, and a full band. Reciting and singing at the East Village club CBGB, she attracted Arista Records. Her 1975 debut album, *Horses*, though it barely cracked the Top 50, is considered today one of the seminal works of punk rock. The ambivalent opening line of the first track, "Gloria," about Jesus' salvation and Patti's sins is one of the most iconic in music history; she is then off for 43 minutes of brilliant sung poetry, touching on such diverse and difficult themes as bullying and victimization, lust and sexual predation, alienation and escapism, surrender and defiance, suicide and survival, intolerable pain, death, and transcendence. The music is all over the place, three-chord garage rock to reggae to aching, melodic ballads, while Patti's vocals plead, pout, cry, and burn with raw emotion. *Horses* has been called an all-time great by *Time*, *Rolling Stone*, and the Library of Congress.

In the '80s, Smith mostly retired to raise a family, but she's been back since the mid-'90s and continues to astonish. Most people know her hit "Because the Night," but listen, as well, to "People Have the Power" or "Paths That Cross." She's an original!

Suggested Songs:

Gloria: In Excelsis Deo (1975)
Birdland (1975)
Because the Night (1978)
People Have the Power (1988)

#163 Chicago
Began Recording: 1969
Peak: 1970 - 1977
Genres: Rock; Jazz Rock; Soft/Pop Rock Band

They described themselves as a "rock & roll band with horns." They formed in the city from whence they derived their name in 1967 with music students Lee Loughnane on trumpet, James Pankow on trombone, and Walter Parazaider on woodwinds. Connecting with Terry Kath on guitar, Danny Seraphine on drums, and Robert Lamm on keyboards, they each downed a shot of whiskey and made a pact to dedicate themselves to becoming a new kind of rock band. Adding bass player Peter Cetera to the mix, Robert, Terry, and tenor Peter handled the vocals, while they shared the task of songwriting. They began as a cover band, partial to James Brown and R&B. At the behest of manager/producer James Guercio, they moved to L.A. in 1968 and signed with Columbia Records.

Their debut LP, *Chicago Transit Authority*, moved languidly up the charts, staying there for three years. It was an unusual double album, with a soulful, jazzy rock feel. The hit singles came slowly—"Beginnings" and the philosophical "Does Anybody Really Know What Time It Is?" By 1970, they had settled on the moniker Chicago as the band's name and released their second LP. The middle of the night musing of "25 or 6 to 4" shows off many of the band's strengths as it is a Lamm composition with Cetera's soaring vocals, but it's Kath's stunning guitar work that has made the song a Chicago classic. The LP also features the classical-tinged 7-part rock suite, "Ballet for a Girl in Buchannon," composed by Pankow.

Between 1972 and 1975, Chicago charted five consecutive #1 albums, and, in 1976, they had their first #1 single, Peter Cetera's "If You Leave Me Now." Then, in 1978, Terry Kath, often called the soul of Chicago, accidently shot and killed himself. Though the band carried on and had popular success in the '80s, they were, increasingly, a pop rock outfit, quite different from their roots. They are today members of the Rock & Roll Hall of Fame and winners of a Lifetime Grammy.

Suggested Songs:

25 or 6 to 4 (1970)
Colour My World (1971)
Feeling Stronger Every Day (1973)
If You Leave Me Now (1976)

#162 Lionel Richie (1949 - present)
Began Recording: 1974 (w. Commodores); 1982 (solo)
Peak: 1981 - 1987
Genres: R&B; Pop; Soul Singer/Songwriter

One of the most popular balladeers of the past 50 years is Lionel Richie, a name synonymous with "smooth" and "romance."

Richie came from a musical family, as his grandmother played classical piano and his uncle was a big band artist who introduced Lionel to the saxophone. He considered becoming an Episcopal priest and rode a tennis scholarship back to Tuskegee Institute where he had spent his childhood. At Tuskegee, he, along with several classmates, formed an R&B/funk/soul band, which became known as the Commodores. Lionel shared songwriting and lead-vocal tasks with Clyde Orange. Three Richie penned hits were "Easy," "Three Times a Lady," and "Still." While still with the Commodores, in 1981 he teamed with Diana Ross on a movie ballad "Endless Love," one of the most celebrated duets of all-time.

In 1982, Lionel, already an accomplished composer for other artists (The Temptations and Kenny Rogers both had #1 hits with Richie tunes), left the Commodores to pursue a solo career; he was stunningly successful. His three '80s LPs charted nationally at #s 3, 2, and 1 on *Billboard*'s Top Pop Albums, with the second entry, *Can't Slow Down*, earning the coveted Grammy Album of the Year award and selling over 20 million copies. He was so big that he was chosen to sing at the closing ceremony of the 1984 Olympics to its billion TV viewers. Memorable songs from that era include "Truly," a beloved wedding ballad; "You Are," a more upbeat proclamation of love; "All Night Long," with a Caribbean dance groove; "Hello," with its yearning lyric; "Stuck on You," a coming back to you number with a country flavor; and "Say You, Say Me," another endless love pledge than won an Oscar.

Richie virtually disappeared from '87 to '96, never regaining the same level of success when he did return, but he's been honored extensively by the Kennedy Center, the Rock and Songwriters Halls of Fame, and the prestigious Gershwin Prize.

Suggested Songs:

Easy (w. Commodores) (1977)
All Night Long (1983)
Stuck on You (1984)
Say You, Say Me (1985)

#161 Buddy Holly (1936 - 1959)
Began Recording: 1956
Peak: 1957 - 1959
Genres: Rock & Roll; Rockabilly; pop Singer/Songwriter

AllMusic deemed him "the single most creative force in early rock & roll." Born Charles Holley in Depression-era Lubbock, Texas, he was called Buddy from childhood. One older brother gave him a guitar while his other brother taught him to play. Influenced by the country & western and R&B he was listening to, after graduation he threw himself whole-heartedly into music and the new sounds of rock & roll, especially after seeing a live Elvis show. With Jerry Allison on drums, Larry Welborn on bass, and Buddy on electric guitar, they scored a couple of gigs opening for Presley in 1955 and later for Bill Haley, and that got them signed to Decca. Initial recording sessions did not go well, so Buddy and his band, now calling themselves the Crickets, found their own studio and producer and, in the spring of 1957, released their first classic, "That'll Be the Day," which became a #1 hit in both the U.S. and U.K. Contractual issues forced them to use the moniker Crickets rather than Buddy Holly (his surname misspelled at signing), and for the rest of his life, some of his releases were credited to him and others to the Crickets.

"Peggy Sue" was another giant hit and featured Allison's wonderful drumming, a new bass player, Joe Mauldin, and a ringing Holly guitar solo. Holly's vocal style was unusual, regularly swinging from his normal register into falsetto and punctuated with singing hiccups. An early example of a singer-songwriter, much more common after the arrival of Dylan and the Beatles, Holly also was open to experimentation—his last recording session featured an 18-piece orchestra, as heard on the lovely, string-laden "True Love Ways."

Holly died in a tragic plane crash in February of 1959, along with Richie Valens, the Big Bopper, and a 21-year-old contracted pilot. Over time, Holly's legacy has grown with posthumous releases; extensive covers by the likes of the Beatles, the Rolling Stones, and Linda Ronstadt; a biopic; a Broadway play; and Don Mclean's "American Pie." Buddy Holly is part of the Rock & Roll Hall of Fame's inaugural class.

Suggested Songs:

That'll Be the Day (as The Crickets) (1957)
Peggy Sue (as Buddy Holly) (1957)
Everyday (as Buddy Holly) (1957)
True Love Ways (as Buddy Holly) (1960)

#160 Charlie Parker (1920 - 1955)
Began Recording: 1940
Peak: 1945 - 1950
Genres: Jazz/Bebop Saxophonist/Composer

Widely recognized as one of the "fathers" of modern jazz, Charlie "Bird" Parker was a brilliant saxophone master, a troubled soul, and a musical genius who was gone before he was 35.

Born in Kansas City, his mom bought him a sax when he was 11. Enthralled by the local jazz scene, he quit school at 15 and, after a humiliating jam session with some of Count Basie's Band, was soon practicing from 10 to 15 hours a day. From 1935 to '39, he played locally where he could and soon got a gig with Jay McShann's band. A serious car accident nearly killed him and, it's believed, introduced him to painkillers and opioids, which would haunt him for the rest of his life.

In 1939, he began experimenting with new chord changes to "Cherokee" and, over the next six years, was in the forefront, along with trumpeters Dizzy Gillespie and Miles Davis, pianists Bud Powell and Thelonious Monk, guitarist Charlie Christian, and drummers Max Roach and Kenny Clarke, of the development of bebop, a new jazz style distinguished by its fast tempos, innovative improvisation, more complex chordal harmonies, and rapid chord changes. Much of this evolution took place during the Musicians' Union Strike of 1942 - '44, which essentially shut down record production; so when recording resumed in 1945, many were astonished at the new modern jazz style. Critics and the public were divided, but Parker has become legendary for his role in the change. Songs like "Koko," "Billie's Bounce," "Ornithology," and "Yardbird Suite" have become classics, and his *Jazz at Massey Hall* and *Charley Parker with Strings* have been inducted into the Grammy Hall of Fame.

Sadly, heroin and alcohol destroyed his body and played havoc with his mind. When his three-year-old daughter died in 1954, the unstable Parker tried to end his own life. A year later he was dead, a combination of pneumonia, a bleeding ulcer, cirrhosis, and heart attack—the results of a lifetime of abuse that left him with the body of a 50- or 60-year-old man, according to the coroner. Musically, though, he's an immortal.

Suggested Songs:

Koko (1945)
Ornithology (1946)
Summertime (1950)
A Night in Tunisia (1953, live)

#159 N.W.A

Began Recording: 1987
Peak: 1988 - 1991
Genres: Hip-Hop; Gangsta Rap Group

N.W.A, or "N***** Wit Attitudes," was a wildly controversial hip-hop group out of what used to be known as South Central Los Angeles that is generally credited with popularizing the hardcore sub genre known as gangsta rap.

Eric Wright was a Compton street-level drug dealer who got out of that scene when his cousin was shot and killed and began self-recording, soon co-founding Ruthless Records. Calling himself Eazy-E, in 1987, he teamed with Andre Young, aka Dr. Dre; O'Shea Jackson, or Ice Cube; Antoine Carraby, aka DJ Yella; and Kim Nazel, or Arabian Prince. A year later, Lorenzo Patterson, MC Ren, joined them.

Their first few 1987 tracks were more party jams than anything else, but their 1988 debut LP, *Straight Outta Compton*, was anything but. Musically arresting, thanks to the talents of Dr. Dre and DJ Yella, the raps were incendiary, confrontational, and violent. The album's first three tracks are case in point—the title track tells us what we are about to hear; then the verses follow with graphic, explicit depictions of the young, Black male experience. But it was the second track that really raised hackles. "Fuck tha Police" took on racial profiling and police brutality, with Ice Cube, MC Ren, and Eazy-E testifying before Judge Dre, making it clear that they would fight back. "Gangsta Gangsta," track three, lays gang life out there vividly. "Revolutionary or perverse?" asked the *L.A. Times*, calling N.W.A a "sonic Molotov cocktail." They got virtually no radio airplay, yet the more taboo they were deemed, the more records they sold. The three biggest outcries were that they glorified the violent gangster lifestyle, that they promoted the violent exploitation of women, and that they were a danger to law enforcement. Ice Cube later explained that it was "reality rap," like a music documentary, not picking sides, just showing what life was like for young, urban

Black men. By 1992 they were over, broken apart in a blaze of animosity, but their long-term impact on the genre has been profound.

Suggested Songs:

Straight Outta Compton (1988)
Fuck tha Police (1988)
Gangsta Gangsta (1988)
Express Yourself (1988)

#158 Diana Ross (1944 - present)

Began Recording: 1960 (w. The Primettes/Supremes); 1970 (solo)
Peak: 1970 - 1976; 1979 - 1982
Genres: R&B/Soul; Pop; Dance Singer

Billboard, in 1976, called her the "female entertainer of the century." She is among the best-selling recording artists of all-time.

Diana Ross grew up in Detroit, a neighbor of Smokey Robinson. She began singing publicly in a Baptist church choir and, in her teens, joined the Primettes, later known as the Supremes, the best selling female group in history. In 1970, Diana left the Supremes to begin her solo career; 53 years later, she continues to perform.

Her debut LP features the gospel soul social uplift of "Reach Out and Touch (Somebody's Hand)" and her first solo, the *Billboard* Hot 100 and R&B #1 "Ain't No Mountain High Enough," which was a radically different version of the Marvin Gaye/Tammi Terrell 1967 hit. In '71, she had a breakthrough #1 single in the U.K., where she has been hugely popular, with "I'm Still Waiting." 1972 saw Ross make her acting debut playing Billie Holiday in *Lady Sings the Blues*, and her soundtrack LP reached #1 on the pop chart. Diana's "Touch Me in the Morning," with its soaring, honest vocals, brought her still another #1, and she was back on top, again, two years later with the theme song from her second movie, *Mahogany*. In the mid-1970s, Diana's music began to morph toward a sleeker, dance-disco sound as heard on her giant hits, "Love Hangover," which changes tempo mid-song, and "Upside Down," from her celebrated 1980 album *Diana*. From that same album comes the popular LGBTQ+ anthem, "I'm Coming Out." In 1981, she scored a huge international duet hit, "Endless Love," with Lionel Richie.

Diana Ross is known for her stunning sartorial presence, favoring floor-length, often sequined gowns, and for her bright, sweet, light lyric soprano vocals. Her impact on other artists' ability to carve out a path for themselves has been huge, and her influence has been cited by such artists as Michael Jackson, Beyoncé, and JAY-Z. She is the recipient of Kennedy Center honors and a Presidential Medal of Freedom.

Suggested Songs:

Ain't No Mountain High Enough (1970)
Touch Me in the Morning (1973)
Love Hangover (1976)
Chain Reaction (1985)

#157 Dr. Dre (1965 - present)

Began Recording: 1985 (w. World Class Wreckin' Cru); 1992 (solo)
Peak: 1992 - 1993; 1999 - 2000; 2015
Genres: Hip-Hop Rapper/Producer

As a rapper, producer, and business mogul, nobody did more in the early '90s to set the direction of the entire hip-hop genre than Dr. Dre.

A product of Compton, California, Andre Young was first drawn to rap by Grandmaster Flash. His mid-'80s meeting with Eric Wright, aka Eazy-E, helped bring about N.W.A and the birth of gangsta rap.

In 1991, Young, calling himself Dr. Dre, wanted out of N.W.A and Ruthless Records, feeling he was underpaid. Co-founding his own label, Death Row, Dre released his solo debut, *The Chronic*, in 1992. Drawing on his experience as one of the principal producers for N.W.A, Dr. Dre created a new sub-genre, known as G-funk, pulling from the Parliament-Funkadelic style and featuring slow, heavy beats, high end synthesizer, backing vocals, and live instruments; graphic, violent, street-gang lyrics and imagery were also a major part of the mix. The album was a triple-platinum sensation, recognized today by the Library of Congress for its significance. "Nuthin' but a 'G' Thang," the laconic lead single, helped make Snoop Dogg, who is featured on the record, a star.

Dr. Dre has released three albums with heavy collaboration, but it is hard to overstate his impact on the industry. His Death Row label introduced Snoop and gave 2Pac his biggest hit. When Dre realized that his partner, Suge Knight, was a loose cannon, he abandoned his own label and helped form Aftermath, bringing the world Eminem, 50 Cent, and Kendrick Lamar. With his perfectionist tendencies given full reign in the studio, it is no exaggeration to say that Dr. Dre, more than anyone, helped bring the pristine sound and controversial subject matter of gangsta rap to the suburbs. "Escapist fantasy," he deemed it, but not everyone is a fan. Civil Rights activist C. Delores Tucker campaigned tirelessly against "gangsta rap and misogynist lyrics." Then, in 2015, there was a great deal of media attention paid to the four women who, over the years, had accused Dre of physically assaulting them, prompting Dre to tell the *New York Times*, "I apologize to the women I've hurt. I deeply regret what I did." Still, his 2022 appearance at the Super Bowl halftime show demonstrates just how fully he has entered the mainstream.

Suggested Songs:

Nuthin' but a 'G' Thang (w. Snoop Dogg) (1992)
Still D.R.E. (w. Snoop Dogg) (1999)
Forget About Dre (w. Eminem) (2000)
Talking to My Diary (2015)

#156 Roy Orbison (1936 - 1988)

Began Recording: 1956 (w. Teen Kings); 1957 (solo)
Peak: 1960 - 1964; 1988 - 1989
Genres: Pop Rock Ballads; Rock & Roll; country; rockabilly Singer/Songwriter

Elvis said it was the greatest voice he'd ever heard; k.d. lang commented that it was the juxtaposition of the beautiful voice with the dark vision. Roy Orbison was an American original who wrote unusual story-songs about vulnerable, lonely, yearning, insecure men and married these to grand, musically complex, structurally odd arrangements, lush with strings, that tended to build and build before climaxing in often surprising ways. On top of all this was Roy's melancholic, three-octave, operatic voice that welled and soared with conviction and passion.

Raised in Texas, he fell in love with music at six when his dad gave him a guitar. He was there at Sun Records in the late '50s with Presley and Cash. He had little success with rockabilly and longed to do ballads. In 1960, he got his chance at Monument Records beginning with "Only the Lonely." "Running Scared," with its Bolero-style, paranoid build and Roy's triumphant crescendo was a revelation. The magnificent country-flavored, pain drenched ballad "Crying" followed; then came "Dream Baby;" "In Dreams," with its unforgettable, visually evocative opening verse; "Blue Bayou;" "It's Over;" and the biggest-seller of them all, the rocking "Oh, Pretty Woman."

Then Roy changed labels, the hits stopped coming, and tragedy struck, twice. In 1966, his wife Claudette was killed in a motorcycle accident; two years later, two of their three sons died in a house fire while Roy was touring. Roy doubled down on touring to cope with his grief; he remarried. Covers of his songs by the likes of Linda Ronstadt, Don McLean, and Van Halen kept him alive in the public imagination. In 1987, the Rock & Roll Hall of Fame honored Roy, and a year later he was asked to join George Harrison, Tom Petty, Jeff Lynne, and Bob Dylan in the Traveling Wilburys. His star was again ascendant when his heart gave out while visiting his mother. He was 52, and one of rock & roll's sweetest, gentlest men was gone. His post-humous LP, *Mystery Girl*, was the biggest of his career.

Suggested Songs:

Running Scared (1961)
Crying (1961)
In Dreams (1963)
Not Alone Any More (w. Traveling Wilburys) (1988)

#155 Pete Seeger (1919 - 2014)
Began Recording: 1941
Peak: 1950 - 1952; 1963 - 1969
Genres: American Folk; Protest Singer/Songwriter

Pete Seeger was born into a blue blood musical family—his father, Charles, was a famed musicologist; his mother, Constance, was a concert violinist; while his stepmom, Ruth Crawford Seeger, was a renowned modernist composer. Two half siblings, Mike and Peggy, both became award winning folk artists. No surprise, then, when Pete dropped out of Harvard to devote himself to a career in folk music. Working with Library of Congress folk archivist and family friend Alan Lomax, Pete met legendary artists Lead Belly, Burl Ives, and Woody Guthrie, and was soon performing alongside them. With an interest in social justice and radical change, from the start Pete was doing benefits for migrant and workers' rights.

In 1940, he formed the Almanac Singers with Guthrie and several friends. Their 1941 LP, *Songs for John Doe*, took a strong anti-war stance and was seen in some quarters as subversive. It didn't help that Seeger joined the Communist Party in 1942 and the group was hounded out of existence. Though Pete did a World War II stint in the U.S. Army and quit the party in 1949, his radical past would catch up to him during the McCarthy era. First, though, came mainstream fame with the folk quartet The Weavers. Their cover of Lead Belly's "Goodnight, Irene" topped the pop charts for 13 weeks and was the biggest single of 1950. "Tzena, Tzena, Tzena," originally a Hebrew song, and the traditional "On Top of Old Smoky" were also huge hits. But then came Congressional investigations, a Contempt of Congress conviction, and Seeger was blacklisted. With the folk revival of the early '60s, Seeger came to be seen as a wise folk elder who paved the way for the likes of Baez, Dylan, and Springsteen. His compositions "If I Had a Hammer," "Where Have All the Flowers Gone?" and "Turn, Turn, Turn" became hits for others, while he is also credited for helping to make "We Shall Overcome" *the* Civil Rights anthem. For Seeger, it was never about fame and success; music was always about growing conscience and moving society forward.

Suggested Songs:

If I Had a Hammer (w. the Weavers) (1949; 1997)
Goodnight, Irene (w. the Weavers) (1950)
Where Have All the Flowers Gone? (1955)
Little Boxes (1963)

#154 Curtis Mayfield (1942 - 1999)

Began Recording: 1958 (w. the Impressions); 1970 (solo)
Peak: 1963 - 1967; 1972 - 1973
Genres: R&B/ Soul; Gospel; Psychedelic Soul/Funk Singer/ Songwriter/
Guitarist

Like so many greats, Curtis Mayfield got his start singing gospel as a child in church. Growing up in Chicago public housing, he learned piano from his mom, but he fell in love with the guitar. At 14, he joined a group known as the Roosters which was led by his older church friend, Jerry Butler. In 1958, they renamed themselves the Impressions. When Butler left two years later for a solo career, Curtis took over as lead singer and composer, and, in 1961, the Mayfield led Impressions scored an R&B hit with "Gypsy Woman."

Between 1963 and 1970, the Impressions were a musical force, repeatedly on Top 40 radio with their gospel-flavored Chicago soul sound featuring strong melodies, horns, strings, and bright harmonies led by Curtis' trademark high tenor which seemed to climb effortlessly into a falsetto. His voice was sweet, gentle, and approachable, and his songs were aspirational and inspirational, stressing, "It's All Right;" cajoling folks to "Keep On Pushing;" and, using train imagery to speak of the spiritual journey, reminding "People Get Ready." This 1965 iconic song was embraced by Dr. King and used at his marches, has been covered by such luminaries as Bob Dylan, Aretha Franklin, and Rod Stewart, and is on a slew of all-time best lists. "We're a Winner," two years later, became an early Black pride anthem.

In 1970, Curtis decided to go solo. Perhaps reflecting the times, his music got funkier and the lyrics darker, noting the state of racial strife, social injustice, and urban poverty. His 1972 soundtrack, *Super Fly*, has been hailed as a landmark LP for its unflinching portrayal of the ugly side of drug dealing, addiction, and death. "Freddy's Dead," "Super Fly," and "Pusherman" still sound timely and fresh today.

In 1990, Mayfield suffered a freak onstage accident that left him paralyzed below the neck; yet he continued to record, lying on his back to sing.

He died in 1999, the same year he was inducted for the second time, as a solo artist, into the Rock & Roll Hall of Fame; he was already there for his work with the Impressions.

Suggested Songs:

It's All Right (w. the Impressions) (1963)
People Get Ready (w. the Impressions) (1965)
Freddy's Dead (1972)
Pusherman (1972)

#153 Green Day

Began Recording: 1989
Peak: 1994 - 1998; 2004 - 2005; 2009 - 2010
Genres: Punk; Alternative Rock Band

They called themselves Green Day and came roaring out of the East Bay
in Northern California with a driving punk sound, loud, fast, and loaded
with angry, lost attitude. They were frontman Billie Joe Armstrong, lead
singer, guitarist, and chief lyricist; friend and bassist, Mike Dirnt; and
Frank Wright, who went by Tre Cool and joined a few years later, on drums.
Compared to the Ramones and the Clash, they drew inspiration from the
Replacements and released two early LPs on a small, local label, building a
following around Berkeley. Moving to the Reprise label, their 1994 release,
Dookie, is an acclaimed punk Grammy winner and the best seller of their
career at nearly 20 million copies worldwide. Celebrated tracks include
"Longview," with its arresting drum and bass intro and Armstrong's angsty
vocal bemoaning his boredom in a particularly masturbatory way and
"Basket Case," a punk driven look at anxiety and panic attacks.

Their fifth LP, *Nimrod*, produced the iconic, out of left field single loved
by millions who otherwise know nothing of Green Day, "Good Riddance
(Time of Your Life)," with its nasal-voiced, glancing back lyric that has made
it a surprise staple of countless proms and graduations. It is, however, their
2004 socio-politically charged, punk rock opera masterwork, *American
Idiot*, that truly sets them apart. It's a modern day coming of age story set in
the time of 9/11, the War on Terror, and the 2nd Bush presidency, featuring
such tracks as "American Idiot," which skewers media brainwashing and
sheep-like response; "Jesus of Suburbia," the five-part song suite that has
been compared to Queen's "Bohemian Rhapsody" and tells of the opera's
central character who doesn't seem to fit in anywhere; and "Boulevard of
Broken Dreams," the Grammy-winning cry of alienation. The album was
such a breakthrough that it became a successful Broadway show in 2010.

Green Day has had more success, notably 2009's *21st Century Breakdown*. They were inducted into the Rock & Roll Hall of Fame in their first year of eligibility in 2015.

Suggested Songs:

Basket Case (1994)
Good Riddance (Time of Your Life) (1997)
Jesus of Suburbia (2004)
Holiday/Boulevard of Broken Dreams (2004)

#152 Beastie Boys
Began Recording: 1982
Peak: 1987 - 2005
Genres: Hip-Hop; Rap Rock Band

Initially disparaged as a mindless, hedonistic "party band," the Beastie Boys, in time, came to be seen as one of the most creative, one-of-a-kind outfits in recording history.

They were three young Jewish boys from well-to-do homes in New York City, drawn to hardcore punk as the 1980s began. Michael Diamond, a drummer, and Adam Yauch, a bassist, found themselves in the same band in 1981. When they lost their guitar player, Adam Horowitz stepped in. In 1982, they created a prank rap song that got some traction in local clubs, and they were soon signed to Rick Rubin and Russell Simmons' new label, Def Jam. Calling themselves the Beastie Boys, they released their debut LP in 1986, *Licensed to Ill*, a hard-hitting rap rock album that rose to the top of the pop charts, eventually selling over 10 million copies in the U.S. alone. Disparaged by the hip-hop community and blasted by the right for stirring up hormone raging, partying teenagers, their anthemic "Fight For Your Right" was held up as a prime example of their brainless, riotous influence, totally missing the point that the song was an ironic satire. Over time, it has become clear that this is what Beastie Boys do. "Hey Ladies," from their now acknowledged classic (it wasn't always seen as such) *Paul's Boutique*, is a veritable cornucopia of sampled snippets and humorous cultural references. Their best-loved "Sabotage," from 1994's *Ill Communication*, is a hard galloping goof on their producer who is supposedly pushing them too hard. "Intergalactic," from the best selling *Hello Nasty*, might be a spoof of braggadocio rap (MCs boasting about themselves), but instead of waving a glock, the Beasties have another clever rhyme in store for us. Far from a dull-witted bunch of screamers, the Beasties were musically inventive, mashing together rap, punk, metal, and a little jazz, laden with sharp, sophisticated, often laugh out loud lyrics.

When "MCA" Yauch passed away of cancer in 2012 at the age of 47, the other two Beasties decided to call it quits, but they are today recognized by artists like Eminem and institutions like the Rock & Roll Hall of Fame for their groundbreaking brilliance.

Suggested Songs:

Fight for Your Right (1987)
Hey Ladies (1989)
Sabotage (1994)
Intergalactic (1998)

#151 Justin Timberlake (1981 - present)

Began Recording: 1996 (w. NSYNC); 2002 (solo)
Peak: 2002 - 2003; 2006 - 2007; 2013 - 2018
Genres: Pop; R&B; Dance Singer/Songwriter

Recognized as a consummate showman, Justin Timberlake has spent the better part of his life performing. At 12, he won a spot on *The All-New Mickey Mouse Club* alongside Britney Spears, Christina Aguilera, and Ryan Gosling. Starting in 1995, along with fellow Mouseketeer JC Chasez and three others, he was part of the popular boy band NSYNC. In 2002, he began his successful solo career with the debut single "Like I Love You," an R&B/hip-hop hybrid. Months later, his award winning LP *Justified* dropped, presenting to the world a more mature, complex Timberlake than his boy band fans had grown to know. The featured track was "Cry Me a River," a somewhat spiteful break-up song that nonetheless garnered critical acclaim and a Grammy, his first of 10.

In February of 2004, Timberlake was involved in the infamous "wardrobe malfunction" Super Bowl incident with Janet Jackson, baring her breast as he reached a crucial line in his song "Rock Your Body." Quick to apologize, in the aftermath, while her career suffered, his did not.

His follow-up LP, *Future Sex/Love Sounds*, a more musically diverse offering than *Justified*, with rock, rap, and dance touches added to the usual R&B and pop, included the #1 hits, "SexyBack," "My Love," and "What Goes Around... Comes Around." The album is widely considered his best. Timberlake has frequently interrupted his recording career with acting roles, gaining notice in such films as *The Social Network*, but he returns time and again to song; two notable hits this past decade are the upbeat love song "Mirrors" and the Oscar-nominated "Can't Stop the Feeling." At 42, he already ranks among the best sellers in history.

Suggested Songs:

Cry Me a River (2002)
My Love (w. T.I.) (2006)
Mirrors (2013)
Can't Stop the Feeling (from *Trolls*) (2016)

#150 The Notorious B.I.G. (1972 - 1997)

Began Recording: 1993
Peak: 1994 - 1997
Genres: Hip-Hop Rapper/Songwriter

He released one album in his lifetime, yet sources as diverse as MTV, *Rolling Stone*, and *The Source* have called him one of the greatest rappers of all time.

Christopher Wallace was born to a Jamaican immigrant mother who worked as a preschool teacher, making sure her son received a Catholic school education. He never knew his dad. He gained the nickname Big for being overweight. Chris was a skilled teenage rapper, doing it for fun, but he slowly was lured into the life of a street hustler, selling drugs on Fulton Street, blocks from his home. When a 1991 demo tape was sent to *The Source*, the hip-hop bible ran a feature on Biggie Smalls, as he was then calling himself; that caught the attention of Sean "Puffy" Combs who signed and began working with him.

It was "Juicy," the lead single off his 1994 album, *Ready to Die*, that turned The Notorious B.I.G., as he was now known, into a major hip-hop star. "Juicy" begins with a dedication to the various teachers who let him know he'd be a nobody and is a humorous, slightly exaggerated, autobiographical romp through Biggie's life, growing up poor, slinging drugs, and, ultimately, holding out hope that one can rise above it all. The single and the album are both considered among hip-hop's finest. The LP, and Biggie's work in general, have been praised for his easy, laid-back flow, and his honest, balanced, cinematic storytelling approach to showing both sides of the street hustler's (and later, successful criminal kingpin's) life, with its material rewards and adrenaline highs, but also the terrible insecurity, fear, stress, and paranoia that goes with it. Just listen to the album's final track, "Suicidal Thoughts," to hear the harrowing underbelly.

Less than three years later, Wallace was dead, killed in a drive-by in L.A., six months after the similar murder of ex-friend and later bitter enemy, Tupac Shakur. A product of the senseless East Coast-West Coast rivalry or not, both murders remained unsolved for 26 years (In September 2023, an arrest was finally made in the Shakur case). Four LPs have been released posthumously, and, in 2020, The Notorious B.I.G. was inducted into the Rock & Roll Hall of Fame.

Suggested Songs:

Juicy (1994)
Big Poppa (1994)
Suicidal Thoughts (1994)
One More Chance (Stay With Me remix) (1995)

#149 Lil Wayne (1982 - present)
Began Recording: 1995 (w. B.G.'z); 1999 (solo)
Peak: 2004 - 2012
Genres: Hip-Hop Rapper/Songwriter

He was born Dwayne Carter Jr. and grew up without his father in one of the most dangerous neighborhoods of New Orleans. A gifted honors student, he was rapping at the age of eight, got noticed soon after, and began actively pursuing a record deal for himself. At 12, afraid his mom was going to deny him the chance to pursue his dream, he took her gun and shot himself in the chest. Years later, he spoke openly about his struggles with mental illness and extolled "Uncle Bob," the police officer who saved his life. Soon after his brush with mortality, he released a rap duo LP, *True Story*, which went nowhere, but two years later, now calling himself Lil Wayne, he was part of a group called the Hot Boys who had some moderate success. In 1999, Lil Wayne made his solo debut with *The Block Is Hot*; he was 17 and a star.

2004 saw Lil Wayne release the first of his five *Tha Carter* LPs, which are among the most celebrated in all of rap. His 2008 *Tha Carter III* captured the best Rap Album Grammy, while two of its tracks, "A Milli" and "Lollipop," were also Grammy winners.

Weezy, as he is sometimes called, has cited JAY-Z, Missy Elliott, and Nirvana as important influences. He is known for his voluminous, aggressively explicit, inventive, often offensive lyrics; his smooth, skillful flow; a bit of a croak in his voice; and his heavily tattooed face and body. Kendrick Lamar has said of Wayne, "I was influenced by a certain sound and flow and cadence that he brung to the game."

There have been concerns in the past about Lil Wayne's drug use, even referenced in his famous underground track, "I Feel Like Dying," the hope is that that has abated in recent years. A record company executive, as well as a recording star, Wayne's most recent LPs, *Tha Carter V* and *Funeral*, were well received and topped the rap and pop charts. He talks of retiring to focus on his kids, but there are no signs that he has, in fact, slowed down.

Suggested Songs:

Dr. Carter (2008)
I Feel Like Dying (2011)
Mirror (w. Bruno Mars) (2011)
Can't Be Broken (2018)

#148 Reba McEntire (1955 - present)
Began Recording: 1971 (w. siblings); 1976 (solo)
Peak: 1984 - 1998
Genres: Country; country pop Singer

She's been called the "Queen of Country," with 24 chart topping singles, 11 #1 studio albums, and four straight decades at the top of the country charts.

Born and raised on an 8,000-acre Oklahoma cattle ranch, rodeo came naturally to the young Reba McEntire as both her father and grandfather were world champions. Her mother encouraged her singing, and, as a teenager she was, along with her siblings, part of The Singing McEntires. She was discovered while performing the national anthem at the 1974 National Rodeo Finals and signed with Mercury. Her career started slowly, but, in 1982, she scored her first #1 country hit, "Can't Even Get the Blues." Unhappy with the direction of her career, she changed labels and released her breakout LP, *My Kind of Country*, in 1984, a back-to-basics album that featured two #1 singles, "How Blue" and "Somebody Should Leave." Two years later she released perhaps her most celebrated work, *Whoever's in New England*, with a title track that won her a Grammy telling the story of a housewife holding on while she watches her husband slipping away. Reba's 1990 cover of Bobbie Gentry's "Fancy" was controversial as the song and the video portrays a woman who, with the push of her mother, does what she must to escape grinding poverty; the song has become one of Reba's signature tunes. In 1991, a small plane carrying eight members of her touring band crashed, killing all onboard. Her subsequent release, *For My Broken Heart*, was dedicated to the deceased and features songs of loss, sorrow, and grief. One track, "Is There Life Out There," which featured another mini-movie video, a Reba specialty, later became a TV film.

Reba took a musical hiatus for a few years in the early 2000s and became a TV sitcom star with the fictional *Reba*. Though not as prolific musically as she was in the '80s and '90s, she continues to release successful records and garner awards.

Suggested Songs:

Whoever's in New England (1986)

Fancy (1990)

The Greatest Man I Never Knew (1992)

Does He Love You (w. Linda Davis) (1993)

#147 Bette Midler (1945 - present)

Began Recording: 1972
Peak: 1972 - 1974; 1980; 1989 - 1991
Genres: Pop; Traditional Pop Singer

For the past 50 years, Bette Midler has been a giant of stage, screen, and recording, and she has won an armful of Tonys, Emmys, Golden Globes, and Grammys. Born into and raised in a working class family in Honolulu, Bette relocated to New York to pursue her dream of performing. A role on Broadway was followed by a stint at Manhattan's Continental Baths, a gay hotspot, beginning in 1970 where, working with pianist-arranger Barry Manilow, she honed her stage persona as The Divine Miss M, mixing torch ballads, up-tempo jazz and pop, with outrageous bawdy humor. Signed to Atlantic Records, word of mouth had already made her a sensation when *The Divine Miss M* debut album dropped in late '72. With a strong, clear, soaring voice, she had "the vocal resources to sing in the style of any woman vocalist of the past 30 years," said the *New Republic*'s Richard Poirier.

Her slow and sexy cover of Bobby Freeman's "Do You Want to Dance?" was an early highlight, as was her faithful rerecording of the Andrews Sisters' World War II classic "Boogie Woogie Bugle Boy." Bette was a huge Hollywood presence as well, appearing in over three dozen films, most notably *The Rose, Beaches, For the Boys*, and *Hocus Pocus*. Two of her biggest albums were, in fact, the soundtracks of the first two above-mentioned films, and her two best-known singles were taken from those movies. 1979's "The Rose" is a hopeful ballad encouraging a lonely, doubting pilgrim to persevere through the dark night in the belief that love will bloom in its time. "Wind Beneath My Wings," appearing a decade later, is a Grammy-winning ode to a friend or lover, acknowledging the singer's deep debt and gratitude.

In 2021, the hard driving Midler won a Kennedy Center honor and hinted that it may be time to start slowing down, but she continues to work and speak her mind with abandon.

Suggested Songs:

Do You Want to Dance? (1972)
Friends (1973)
The Rose (1979)
Wind Beneath My Wings (1989)

#146 Lena Horne (1917 - 2010)
Began Recording: 1936
Peak: 1955 - 1962; 1981 - 1983
Genres: Traditional Pop; Jazz; R&B Singer

Brooklyn-born Lena Horne, one of the 20th century's most popular Black entertainers, was a star of nightclubs, theater, movies, radio, TV, and recording. Her mixed-race family was upper middle class, but her parents' divorce left her shuttling back and forth between her traveling actress mother, her grandparents, an uncle, and her gambling, hotelier father.

At 16, though limited as a singer and dancer, the beautiful Lena was hired as a chorus girl at Harlem's famed Cotton Club where Black entertainers performed for a mostly white clientele. Lena moved quickly, and, with mentors like white bandleader and racial pioneer Charlie Barnet and Duke Ellington sidekick Billy Strayhorn who taught her to sing, Horne was soon dividing time between a Broadway revue, clubs like the Cafe Society, radio, recording, and low-budget films. Her seven-year mid-'40s stint with MGM made her a movie star, but her progressive push for racial change got her blacklisted in the early '50s. Indeed, Lena was in the forefront of the fight for racial justice throughout her career: her movie contract stipulated that she not have to play stereotypical Black roles such as maids and nannies; she sued a number of restaurants and hotels for discrimination; when entertaining troops, she pointedly played to the Black soldiers; she steadfastly refused to pass as white; and she was an active member of the NAACP and other Civil Rights organizations.

As a recording artist, she released several landmark albums—1957's *Lena Horne at the Waldorf Astoria* was a huge seller for its time, while 1981's *Lena Horne: the Lady and Her Music*, taken from her 13-month, historic, one-woman Broadway show, is a legendary Grammy winner. "Stormy Weather," from her best-known film, is her signature song, while "Believe in Yourself," from the all-Black musical *The Wiz*, is a late career highlight. Lena holds a Lifetime Grammy, a special Tony award, and Kennedy Center Honors.

Suggested Songs:

Stormy Weather (1941, 1957)
Someone to Watch Over Me (1962)
Softly as I Leave You (1967)
Yesterday, When I Was Young (1981)

#145 Britney Spears (1981 - present)
Began Recording: 1998
Peak: 1999 - 2004; 2008 - 2012
Genres: Pop; Dance Pop Singer

Steve Huey of *AllMusic* called her, "the defining figure of the Y2K era." Since her recording debut in 1998, Britney Spears has been one of the world's best-selling artists; her first two LPs alone have reportedly sold more than 45 million copies.

From an early age she took voice and dance lessons, gearing up for stardom. At the age of 11, she secured a spot on the *All New Mickey Mouse Club*; at 15, she signed a record deal and was soon opening for NSYNC. Before her 17th birthday, her first single, "... Baby One More Time," dropped, followed several months later by her debut album of the same name. Both became worldwide teen pop sensations. The ubiquitous title cut finds the school age singer missing her boyfriend, and the song stirred a bit of controversy for what some thought was an odd, ambivalent word choice. Indeed, from the start, many found a disturbing undercurrent of adult sexuality beneath the childlike innocence. The follow-up LP and single, *Oops!... I Did It Again*, seem to play with the same formula, but with equally successful results. The music was pure pop, danceable, and spectacularly produced. Britney's voice was childlike but suggestive, innocent but knowing, perhaps over-processed but technically proficient, chirpy but strangely compelling.

Before too long, Britney dispensed with the childhood motif and embraced more clearly adult themes, with unambiguously erotic costumes and dance routines. Most of the songs were catchy, high energy dance pop numbers—2003's "Toxic" was a particular standout, while "Everytime" highlighted Britney's vulnerability with a rare, wistful ballad.

Britney's all too public struggles with her personal demons have frequently overshadowed the music, but her now well-known and successful attempts to free herself from her father's conservatorship have won her sympathy. Her fans, who are legion, hope she has found a measure of peace and await new music (she has released two recent collaborative singles, one with Elton John, and a second with will.i.am). Many artists, such as Miley Cyrus and Selena Gomez who followed the trail she blazed, have expressed their gratitude to Spears.

Suggested Songs:

...Baby One More Time (1998)
Stronger (2000)
Toxic (2003)
Everytime (2004)

#144 Jerry Lee Lewis (1935 - 2022)

Began Recording: 1956
Peak: 1957 - 1958; 1968 - 1973
Genres: Rock & Roll; rockabilly; Country; Gospel Singer/Pianist/songwriter

It's been said that Jerry Lee Lewis had one foot in heaven and one foot in hell. Born dirt poor in Eastern, rural Louisiana, his parents literally mortgaged the farm to buy him a piano, which he'd mastered by 14. He was expelled from a Texas Bible College for playing a gospel hymn boogie-woogie style. Shunned by Nashville, he made his way to Sam Phillips' Sun Records in 1956, early home to Elvis, Johnny Cash, and Carl Perkins. His 1957 rock & roll cover of an R&B song, "Whole Lot of Shakin' Going On," made him an overnight international star. Six months later he was back with his second classic, "Great Balls of Fire." In the Bible Belt, where Lewis grew up, the music was deemed risqué at best or devil's music at worst, and Jerry Lee himself was unsure. But suddenly he was seen as a contender for Elvis' crown when a British tabloid told the world of Lewis' 13-year-old child bride, his own cousin, no less. His career plummeted, going from $10,000 a night gigs to $250, if he could find work at all. He carried on, eventually finding a second musical life as a country and sometimes gospel artist, in effect, returning to his roots.

Whether pounding out his early rockers or gliding soulfully through a country tune, Lewis was a compelling performer. A highly gifted pianist, the "killer," as he was known, could slay his audience with his ecstatic, blues-based boogie-woogie, replete with kicking over his stool and using fists, chops, elbows, and feet, without missing a note or the beat; or he could glide over the keys with astonishing, virtuoso country, gospel, or jazz motifs, all informed by his emotionally charged vocals. His 1964 *Live at the Star Club, Hamburg* is said to be one of the all-time great live LPs.

A truly wild character, Lewis married seven times and once drunkenly crashed his Lincoln into Presley's Graceland gates, a loaded pistol on the dashboard. He outlived all his Sun mates and is a member of both the Rock and Country Halls of Fame.

Suggested Songs:

Whole Lot of Shakin' Going On (1957)
Great Balls of Fire (1957)
Your Cheating Heart (live) (1964)
Middle Age Crazy (1977)

#143 Sly and the Family Stone

Began Recording: 1967
Peak: 1968 - 1972
Genres: Funk; R&B/Soul; Rock Band

One of the best and most influential hybrid bands of the late '60s-early '70s was San Francisco's Sly and the Family Stone. An amalgam of brothers Sylvester and Freddie Stewart's bands, it was led by older brother Sly (Sylvester) who had grown up a musical prodigy, proficient on keyboards, guitar, bass, and drums before he was a teen. When he and his brother merged, they were not an immediate hit, but one soulful party track, "Dance to the Music," proved to be their breakthrough. However, with the release of 1969's *Stand!* they were arguably pop music's most important and groundbreaking act. *Stand!* is representative of the unique blend of R&B, soul, rock, gospel, pop, and funk that Sly and the Family Stone were creating. Not only that, the band was a mix of Black and white, male and female musicians, unheard of in those days. The songs, such as the captivating title track and the peace and equality anthem "Everyday People," were positive uplifting messages of hope.

With a singular shared vocal approach featuring Sly, guitarist Freddie, sister Rose, and bassist Larry Graham, the Family also included Cynthia Robinson and Jerry Martini on horns, and Greg Errico on drums. In 1969, they played a fiery set at Woodstock, beautifully captured on film and forever cementing their legacy as a brilliant live band, as well. 1969 later saw the release of their iconic "Thank You (Falettinme Be Mice Elf Again)," with the stunning flip side "Everybody Is a Star."

By 1970, with more arresting music still to come, away from public view things were quickly deteriorating. Excessive drug use and internal conflict were tearing the band apart. 1971's *There's a Riot Goin' On* captured the dark moment perfectly, but by 1975 the band, then infamous for missing shows, was done. Sly, himself, wound up a paranoid, broken addict, living, at times, in a camper van and reappearing about once a decade; however, phoenix like, Sly has been sober the past four years and recently released his memoir. Without a doubt, their musical legacy is enormous, influencing such stars as the latter-day Temptations, Miles Davis, George Clinton, Michael Jackson, Prince, and a generation of hip-hop artists.

Suggested Songs:

Everyday People (1968)
Thank You (Falettinme Be Mice Elf Again) (1969)
Everybody Is a Star (1969)
Family Affair (1971)

#142 The Police
Began Recording: 1977
Peak: 1979 - 1984
Genres: Reggae Rock; New Wave Band

According to BMI, "Every Breath You Take" is the "most played song in radio history." Formed in 1977 London, The Police were Sting (born Gordon Sumner), a former schoolteacher and jazz musician, their principal songwriter, vocalist, and bass player; Stewart Copeland, their gifted drummer; and Andy Summers, a former session guitarist who replaced Henry Padovani after their first unsuccessful single.

Stewart's brother Miles agreed to manage the band and got them a deal with A&M. From 1978 to 1983 The Police released five LPs, each one more successful than the previous, and, by '83, they were the biggest band in the world. *Outlandos d'Amour* peaked at #6 in Britain and featured the now classic, "Roxanne," a simple love song to a prostitute which many hear as reggae rock, though Sting insists it's a tango. A year later they released *Regatta de Blanc*, which topped British charts and reached #25 in the U.S. "Message in a Bottle" was the best-loved track, a reggae-flavored song about human isolation. 1980's *Zenyatta Mondatta* featured the *Lolita*-themed sketch about a teacher and a young female student, "Don't Stand So Close to Me." *Ghost in the Machine*, with a more layered sound, reached #2 in the U.S. as The Police were becoming a worldwide sensation; "Every Little Thing She Does Is Magic" was the favored track. 1983's *Synchronicity* was simpler, less reggae-flavored, and a best-selling phenomenon pushed by the massive success of "Every Breath You Take," essentially a sinister, if catchy, stalker song.

By 1984, The Police were a fractured unit, but a 2007-'08 reunion tour for the Rock & Roll Hall of Fame band was one of the most successful in history. Sting, also a member of the Songwriters Hall of Fame, has gone on to have a highly successful solo career.

Suggested Songs:

Roxanne (1978; 1979)
Message in a Bottle (1979)
Every Little Thing She Does Is Magic (1981)
Every Breath You Take (1983)

#141 Van Halen

Began Recording: 1978
Peak: 1978 - 1995
Genres: Hard Rock; heavy metal Band

From the late '70s through at least the mid-'80s, Van Halen was the premier American hard rock band. Formed by brothers Alex and Eddie Van Halen, Amsterdam transplants to California as young children, they were making music together before reaching their teens. By 1974, the four initial core members were in place—Eddie, lead guitarist extraordinaire; Alex on drums; Michael Anthony on bass; and lead singer David Lee Roth.

With help from Gene Simmons and Doug Messenger, the L.A. club band secured a contract with Warner Bros. in 1977 and released their eponymous debut LP in '78. Today *Van Halen* is considered one of the best debut albums in history and introduced the world to one of the great guitar masters of all-time. Eddie's playing has been described as "jaw dropping," "blindingly fast," spontaneous, innovative, and fluid, yet also melodic and precise, incorporating two-handed finger taps, hammer-ons, and pull-offs to produce a dizzying array of sounds. Compared to Hendrix and Clapton, both of whom he admired, his short track "Eruption" serves as a primer on what Eddie could do. The LP also highlights the importance of vocal frontman Roth and his charismatic talent. "Runnin' with the Devil," perhaps an ode to a band's life, became a signature tune.

1984, their fourth LP, made them superstars of the highest order, while "Jump," built around Eddie's recognizable synth riff and Roth's expressive delivery, gave them their lone #1 single. Differences between Eddie and Roth in 1985 led to David Lee's departure, to be replaced by Sammy Hagar. Despite a bevy of doubters, Van Halen responded with four straight #1 albums.

Eddie died of cancer in 2020, and Van Halen disbanded. They were recognized with induction into the Rock & Roll Hall of Fame in 2007.

Suggested Songs:

Eruption (1978)
Ain't Talkin' 'Bout Love (1978)
Jump (1983)
Hot for Teacher (1984)

#140 KISS
Began Recording: 1974
Peak: 1975 - 1979
Genres: Hard Rock; Heavy Metal Band

The brainchild of Paul Stanley and Gene Simmons, the hard rock band KISS was formed in New York City some 50 years ago and is currently in the midst of its long, final tour. The original lineup consisted of Stanley who plays rhythm guitar and handles many lead vocals; Simmons, bass player and co-lead vocalist; Ace Frehley, who played lead guitar from 1973 to 1982 and again from '96 to 2002; while Peter Criss was the drummer from '73 to 1980, and later returned for two more stints.

From the start, KISS was a theatrical band, drawing inspiration from Alice Cooper and the New York Dolls as well as British blues-based bands. Noted for their comic book costumes and makeup and over-the-top live shows that featured blood spitting, fire breathing, dry ice, smoke bombs, and more, KISS has been dismissed by a number of rock & roll critics as derivative, mediocre musicians whose songs tend to sound the same. KISS, though, has had 30 gold albums, more than any other American band, and their fans are legion.

Releasing their first LP in 1974, they caught on slowly, but *Alive*, released in late 1975, provided the breakthrough spark, highlighted by their signature anthem, "Rock and Roll All Nite." With 1976's *Destroyer*, KISS hit the big time and for the rest of the '70s they were ubiquitously popular. Some of the best-loved early KISS songs include "Strutter," from their first LP, with its catchy, opening Rolling Stones-like riff; the driving "Detroit Rock City;" and "Beth," a piano and strings ballad that began its life as a B-side but became their highest charting single. With the 1979 release *Dynasty*, their sound was changing as evidenced by Stanley's hard rock/disco-like offering, "I Was Made for Loving You." Their last major hit single was the power ballad "Forever."

From 1983 through 1996, KISS performed without their traditional makeup before reforming in 1996 with the band's original members and their old costumes. In 2014, they were inducted into the Rock & Roll Hall of Fame.

Suggested Songs:

Strutter (1974)
Rock and Roll All Nite (1975)
Beth (1976)
I Was Made for Loving You (1979)

#139 Waylon Jennings (1937 - 2002)
Began Recording: 1959
Peak: 1973 - 1982; 1985
Genres: Country; Country-Rock Singer/Songwriter

February 2, 1959 has been sadly immortalized by Don McLean in his giant hit "American Pie," for at one in the morning a plane carrying Buddy Holly, Ritchie Valens, and the Big Bopper crashed in Iowa. Two members of Holly's backing band were supposed to be on that plane, but a coin flip gave Valens a seat and Waylon Jennings willingly gave up his seat to the sick Bopper, J.P. Richardson, to instead board the ice-cold tour bus. Before takeoff, Holly jokingly remarked to Waylon that he hoped their bus froze; Jennings retorted that he hoped their plane crashed; and, of course, it did! According to Waylon, he never got over the guilt and responsibility that he felt, and that it played a part in his 21 years of drug abuse.

Jennings learned guitar as a child and was a teenage DJ and singer in his native Texas when he befriended Holly who became his mentor, produced his first single, and hired him to play bass. After the crash, a dazed and grieving Jennings went back to working the radio before making his way first as a folk-pop artist and then returning to country. In the early '70s, fed up with the Nashville country establishment trying to mold him, he rebelled and returned to his hard edge, electric guitar-driven, country-rock roots, put on the black cowboy hat and leather vest, grew out his hair and beard, and, along with Willie Nelson, invented the outlaw country sub-genre. He was a sensation, with his deep, rich, guileless baritone, and simple, direct, honest songs, his singles hitting county's #1 spot 16 times from 1974 to 1987. In a five-year stretch, five of his studio albums topped the *Billboard* Country chart. He was a giant collaborator with Willie; later, Nelson, Johnny Cash, Kris Kristofferson, and Waylon sang together as the Highwaymen. *Wanted! The Outlaws*, his joint effort with Willie, Tompall Glaser, and Jessi Colter, was the first country LP ever to sell a million copies.

Among Waylon's best-loved tracks are "This Time," a gently assertive ballad; "Luckenbach, Texas," a song he grew to hate; "Mammas Don't Let Your Babies Grow Up to Be Cowboys," or musicians; and the self-referential "I've Always Been Crazy." Hard living and diabetes took his life at 64, but his music remains timeless.

Suggested Songs:

I'm a Ramblin' Man (1974)
Are You Sure Hank Done It This Way (1975)
Mammas Don't Let Your Babies Grow Up to Be Cowboys (w. Willie Nelson) (1975)
I've Always Been Crazy (1978)

#138 Sex Pistols

Began Recording: 1976
Peak: 1976 - 1978
Genres: Punk Rock Band

In the mid-1970s, England was a country divided, economically and socially. Out of this milieu, from the country's disaffected youth, rose a new musical and social movement known as punk. At the forefront were the Sex Pistols. They were four lads—working class guitarist Steve Jones and his friend, Paul Cook, a drummer, who were in a band called The Strand; they added bass player Glen Matlock and then non-singing John Lydon to the mix. Lydon, with green hair, bad teeth, plenty of attitude, and a sharp intellect, changed his name to Johnny Rotten, took over as lead vocalist and lyricist, and the band began to practice. By late '75 they were playing live gigs and soon had a following. They were loud, raw, radical, and rebellious, and in October 1976, they signed with EMI. Their first single, "Anarchy in the U.K.," featured Jones' grinding, basic guitar and Rotten's angry, braying vocal, with provocative, nihilistic, in-your-face lyrics. The song, a U.K. hit, got them a last minute TV interview in London during which Jones, egged on by the host, called him a "dirty bastard... fucker" and "rotter." Suddenly the Sex Pistols were headline news, not for their music but for being "dangerous," "nihilistic," "filth."

They were dropped by EMI, Matlock quit the band, and Rotten recruited his friend Sid Vicious (John Ritchie) to take his place, though Sid could barely play. In May 1977, the Pistols released their controversial single "God Save the Queen," a blazing guitar driven attack on a Britain that cares not for the Pistols nor for the Pistols' audience, which leaves them, in the end, with nothing. The most heavily censored song in British history, it was, nonetheless, a sensation and rose to #2 on the UK's Official Singles Chart. Later that year, they released their lone album, the celebrated *Never Mind the Bollocks, Here's the Sex Pistols*, rated by various publications among the greatest LPs ever. By early 1978 it was all over: Rotten quit the band;

Vicious overdosed on heroin. In 2006, the Sex Pistols were inducted into the Rock & Roll Hall of Fame, recognizing the impact they had on such acts as the Clash, Guns N' Roses, and Green Day. True to form, the Sex Pistols failed to attend.

Suggested Songs:

Anarchy in the U.K. (1976)
God Save the Queen (1977)
Pretty Vacant (1977)
Holidays in the Sun (1977)

#137 Perry Como (1912 - 2001)
Began Recording: 1936
Peak: 1943 - 1959
Genres: Pop; Easy Listening Singer

He was criticized for sounding too much like Bing Crosby, while others said he sounded too relaxed, too casual. Yet from 1944 to 1958, Perry Como had 42 Top 10 hits and at least 11 reached #1.

Born Pierino Como to Italian immigrant parents, English was his second language. Encouraged musically by his father, his ambition was to be a barber; indeed, he had his own shop at 14 and gained a reputation as a singing barber. At 21, encouraged by family, he began singing professionally; that same year he married his teenage sweetheart, Roselle. The two remained wed for 65 years.

Perry found moderate success from 1933 to '42, but tired of the road and missed his family. He considered quitting but, in 1943, was offered a radio program and a new recording contract with RCA. Resolved to stop touring, he began to find recording success. "Till the End of Time" was the #1 record of 1945, and was followed in '46 by two more chart toppers, "Prisoner of Love" and "Surrender." His 1949 rendition of Rodgers and Hammerstein's great "Some Enchanted Evening" also peaked at #1, and shows off Como's distinctive dreamy baritone, intimate and soulful at the same time.

A three-way star, Perry transitioned seamlessly from radio to TV in 1948 and was a fixture of the medium until 1967; at one time, he was the highest paid performer in television history. An uncommonly humble man, Como had a reputation for being one of the nicest men in show business, no different off air than on. His last #1 record was 1957's "Catch a Falling Star " as he began to get swept off the charts by rock & roll. However in 1970, "It's Impossible" reached the Top 10, and three years later he had another success with a Don McLean cover, "And I Love You So." In 1970, Como also returned to touring, after a 26 year hiatus, and found he enjoyed it.

Celebrated with a Lifetime Grammy, five Emmys, and Kennedy Center Honors, Mr. C died peacefully in his sleep a few days shy of his 89th birthday.

Suggested Songs:

Some Enchanted Evening (1949)
If (1951)
It's Impossible (1970)
And I Love You So (1973)

#136 Leonard Cohen (1934 - 2016)
Began Recording: 1967
Peak: 1968 - 1971; 1984 - 1992; 2001 - 2016
Genres: Folk-Rock; Folk-Pop Singer/Songwriter

Leonard Cohen was born into an English-speaking Jewish family near French-speaking Montreal. His dad died when Leonard was nine, but as a teen he developed a love of poetry, theater, and music. He had a successful first career as an author of poetry and fiction, but he was not satisfied and moved to New York in 1967 seeking to make it as a songwriter-performer. Encouraged by singer Judy Collins who introduced his first signature song "Suzanne" to the world in 1966, the ingredients of Cohen's artistry were present in this song and others from his debut LP—arresting story-songs with poetic lyrics that touch on love and desire, but also on spirituality, pain, and loss, married to simple but haunting melodies, delivered in Leonard's deep baritone that only grew deeper and darker with age.

In a career spanning nearly half a century, Cohen released 15 studio albums, 10 of which charted in Canada's Top 10 (though only two in the U.S.), but his songs of flesh and spirit, of broken societies and broken souls, of sexual longing and transcendent love made him one of the world's most admired songwriters, praised by the likes of Kurt Cobain, Patti Smith, Bono, and Bob Dylan. A song such as "Famous Blue Raincoat," poignantly addressed to a man who stole the narrator's wife, is not easily forgotten, and "Hallelujah," Cohen's hypnotic 1984 meditation on a fractured relationship, shot through with Biblical references and soaring into "dark night of the soul" territory, has been covered by over 300 artists and is one of the best-loved songs of the modern age.

Cohen withdrew from the world of music and writing in the 1990s, becoming a Zen Buddhist monk; he struggled through depression and had millions embezzled by an unscrupulous manager. Returning to the market-place in 2001, he remained musically active, recording and performing for the remainder of his life. A member of the Rock and Songwriters Halls of Fame, Cohen was also the recipient of Canada's highest civilian honor.

Suggested Songs:

Suzanne (1967)
Famous Blue Raincoat (1971)
Hallelujah (1984)
Take This Waltz (1986)

#135 Robert Johnson (1911? - 1938)

Began Recording: 1937
Peak: 1936 - 1938; posthumously in the 1960s and 1990s
Genres: Blues Singer/Songwriter/Guitarist

Without a doubt, the most mysterious figure in this compilation is Delta blues giant Robert Johnson. Many details about his life are sketchy, including the year of his birth, but it is believed that he spent his childhood shuttling between rural Mississippi and Memphis, where he likely imbibed the blues.

The popular legend surrounding Johnson is that he was a lazy womanizer who could barely play guitar, and that he went to the crossroads of Routes 49 and 61 in Mississippi where he made a pact with the devil who tuned Robert's guitar, giving him complete mastery of the instrument, in exchange for Johnson's soul. A few years later, Johnson was dead at the age of 27. It is true, apparently, that Son House, a slightly older bluesman, found Johnson a lousy guitarist when first they met, and so was surprised that two years later he'd become a master. Johnson, while away, had been mentored by guitar whiz Ike Zimmerman, who favored playing in midnight graveyards. In addition, in his late teens Robert was married to 16-year-old Virginia Travis who died, along with the baby, during childbirth. His widow's family told the devastated Johnson that this was God's punishment for Robert's playing secular, or devil's, music. The Crossroads Myth also seems to echo similar African and Haitian folktales that were prevalent in that region, and the story stuck.

Johnson became an itinerant musician, playing street corners and local gigs, scratching out a living. By the mid-'30s, he was recognized as a guitar virtuoso who played blues, jazz, country, whatever people wanted to hear. He also had a unique singing style, soaring from tenor to falsetto with masterful precision, yet expressive of an old soul's pain. It's true that Robert referenced hellhounds and crossroads in his lyrics, but he also sang of God's deliverance and earthly loves and cares. His death is a mystery;

he may or may not have been poisoned by a jealous husband. Even his gravesite is unknown. He recorded only 29 songs in two sessions, but his music inspired a generation of greats, from Eric Clapton to Keith Richards to Bob Dylan, and he's been honored by the Rock and Blues Halls of Fame.

Suggested Songs:

Terraplane Blues (1937)
Cross Road Blues (1937)
Sweet Home Chicago (1937)
Hell Hound on My Trail (1937)

#134 Bon Jovi

Began Recording: 1984
Peak: 1986 - 1990; 1992 - 1995; 2000
Genres: Hard Rock/Metal/Pop Band

They may not have the cachet of Springsteen or Sinatra, but the rock band Bon Jovi is certainly one of New Jersey's iconic musical exports. Teenagers Jon Bongiovi and David Bryan played together in the late '70s. When Jon began working at his cousin's New York recording studio, he had an opportunity to cut a demo with a group of session players. The demo, "Runaway," became a minor hit in 1983, leading to the formation of the band Bon Jovi and a recording contract.

The original band members were Jon, now calling himself Bon Jovi, on lead vocals, Bryan on keyboards, Tico Torres on drums, Alec John Such on bass, and Richie Sambora as the lead guitarist; Jon and Richie handled most of the songwriting. Their 1984 self-titled LP was a minor hard rock-metal hit with "Runaway," now re-recorded with the band, making another appearance.

Bon Jovi's 1986 third LP, *Slippery When Wet*, made them superstars on both sides of the Atlantic and featured their first #1 singles, "You Give Love a Bad Name," a driving pop rock anthem with the singer lamenting the fact that he's hopelessly addicted to a treacherous woman, and "Living on a Prayer," undoubtedly their best-loved song, introducing us to the working class travails of Tommy and Gina. The album also features "Wanted Dead or Alive," using the touring rocker as outlaw metaphor delivered as a power ballad.

Noted for their longevity and ability to change styles, adding more pop and even a country twang over time, Bon Jovi was also buoyed by Jon's cinematic good looks and raspy but strong, convincing vocals, and an exhausting touring regimen. Indeed Bon Jovi even introduced mainstream rock to the Soviet Union. Subsequent LPs contained more ballads such as "Bed of Roses," and a deeper look at the underside of the American Dream, such as "Dry County." Sambora moved on and Such passed away, but Bon Jovi, Rock Hall of Fame inductees, carry on to this day.

Suggested Songs:

Runaway (1984)
Livin' on a Prayer (1986)
Bed of Roses (1993)
Dry County (1994)

#133 Tupac Shakur (1971 - 1996)
Began Recording: 1991
Peak: 1993 - 1998
Genres: Hip-Hop Rapper/Songwriter

He was born Lesane Parish Crooks in East Harlem, but his parents, deeply into the Black Panther milieu, renamed him Tupac Amaru Shakur after an 18th century revolutionary. His dad exited his life early, and in 1986, now living in Baltimore, Tupac attended a public arts high school where he focused on acting, poetry, ballet, and rap. By 1988, he was on the west coast and soon took a job as a roadie and backup dancer for the Digital Underground rap group. Calling himself 2Pac, in 1991 he released his moderately successful debut album, *2Pacalypse Now*, with an emphasis on social commentary: from poverty, crime, and systemic racism to police brutality and teen pregnancy. Over the next four years, Tupac released two more studio LPs, each one more successful than the last, with songs of affirmation—"Keep Ya Head Up," an ode to black women; of pain, loss, fear, and self doubt—"So Many Tears;" and a tribute to his troubled but "Dear Mama."

By late 1993, Shakur was riding high, with a breakout movie career on the side. Then in November, he was charged with sexual assault. He claimed that what transpired was consensual, but he was found guilty of one charge and spent much of 1995 in prison.

In late 1994, before his incarceration, Tupac had been shot and robbed at a New York recording studio; he accused Notorious B.I.G., formerly a close friend, and Sean Combs, Biggie's manager, of somehow being complicit in the attack. This led to a heated East Coast-West Coast war of words, which only escalated over time.

Then, in 1996, Tupac's 4th LP, *All Eyez on Me*, took a decided turn toward gangsta rap and was a huge #1 hit and featured his most successful single, "California Love." In September of that year, Tupac was shot and killed in Las Vegas while riding next to Suge Knight, his boss at Death Row

Records (No arrest was made in his murder until 27 years later). Six months after Tupac's demise, his nemesis, The Notorious B.I.G., was gunned down in similar fashion. In death, the Tupac legend grew to gargantuan proportions. As BET put it, Tupac's "confounding mixture of ladies' man, thug, revolutionary, and poet has forever altered our perception of what a rapper should look like."

Suggested Songs:

Keep Ya Head Up (1993)
So Many Tears (1995)
Dear Mama (1995)
Changes (1998)

#132 The Andrews Sisters

Began Recording: 1937
Peak: 1938 - 1950
Genres: Swing; Boogie-woogie; Pop Vocal Group

The Andrews Sisters were the most successful female group of the first half of the 20th century. They were all over the charts from 1938 to 1951; perhaps only Bing Crosby, with whom they sometimes collaborated, sold more records in that era.

They were three daughters of immigrant parents, born and raised in Minnesota. Laverne was born in 1911, Maxene in 1916, while Patty came along two years later. When Patty was seven, Laverne organized them into a singing trio, and by 1932 they were singing professionally, soon touring with big bands. In late 1937, having signed with Decca, they recorded an English version of a Yiddish theater song, "Bei Mir Bist Du Schon (Means That You're Grand)." It became a giant worldwide hit, making the Andrews Sisters overnight stars. It was even loved in Nazi Germany until the song's origin was discovered; then, of course, it was banned. 26 more songs reached the Top 5 over the next 13 years, many of them in the jazzy, big band idiom known as "swing." The Andrews' style has been described as bright, upbeat, intricate, close-harmony singing, with mezzo-soprano Patty on lead, Maxene with high and middle backgrounds, and contralto Laverne on the low end.

As the U.S. entered World War II, they were at peak popularity. They devoted considerable time visiting and entertaining troops, at home and abroad, including hospital and war zone appearances. Their signature song, "Boogie Woogie Bugle Boy," was voted #6 in the RIAA's "Songs of the Century" poll and comes from this time. Their 1945 best seller "Rum and Coca Cola" introduced calypso to many and stirred up considerable controversy. Drawn to the rhythm, the sisters apparently overlooked the suggestive lyrics which sing knowingly of Trinidad women and American servicemen. Patty's departure to go solo and changing musical tastes in the '50s put an end to the Andrews Sisters' dominance, but their influence can be heard in the music of the Pointer Sisters, Bette Midler, Christina Aguilera, and many others.

Suggested Songs:

Bei Mir Bist Du Schon (Means That You're Grand) (1937)
Boogie Woogie Bugle Boy (1941)
Rum and Coca Cola (1945)
Civilization (Bongo, Bongo, Bongo) (w. Danny Kaye) (1947)

#131 Kenny Rogers (1938 - 2020)
Began Recording: 1957
Peak: 1977 - 1987
Genres: Country; Pop Singer/songwriter

Kenny Rogers grew up in a Houston housing project, attuned to gospel music and inspired by Ray Charles. He had a minor local solo hit in 1958 and played (guitar and bass) and sang in a number of groups, everything from doo-wop to rockabilly, from jazz to folk, from rock to country. With the First Edition he scored with two wildly different tracks—the psychedelic rock "Just Dropped In," which became something of a counterculture touchstone in 1967, and "Ruby, Don't Take Your Love to Town," a country flavored angry plea from a paralyzed war vet to his young wife who is all dolled up and about to go looking for love elsewhere.

When the First Edition broke up in 1974, Rogers decided to focus on a career in country. He was nearly 39 years old when he broke through with "Lucille," a cinematic, understated telling of a bar pick-up, and the narrator's reason for not following through. From 1977 to 1987, Rogers dominated the country charts and became the first such artist to fill large-scale arenas. Impressively, many of his biggest singles were huge crossover successes, scoring high on both country and pop charts. Rogers described his records as being of two types—the story songs, which often contain a strong social theme, such as "Ruby..." and "Lucille." Included in this vein are "The Gambler," perhaps his best-known song with an iconic sing-along chorus, and "Coward of the Country," which explores the "turn the other cheek" doctrine. The other type that Rogers sang was straight up love songs. In fact the two biggest hits of his career were his 1980 recording of Lionel Richie's "Lady" and his 1983 duet with Dolly Parton, "Islands in the Stream;" both singles were country and pop chart toppers.

In all, the silver bearded, husky voiced Rogers scored 20 #1 country hits and had 12 #1 albums. He is a member of the Country Music Hall of Fame.

Suggested Songs:

Lucille (1977)
The Gambler (1978)
Don't Fall in Love With a Dreamer (w. Kim Karnes) (1980)
Lady (1980)

#130 Al Green (1946 - present)
Began Recording: 1967
Peak: 1971 - 1975
Genres: Soul; R&B; Gospel Singer/Songwriter

In the first half of the 1970s, one of the sweetest voices in recorded history was all over the radio. Born Albert Greene (he later dropped the "e") into an Arkansas sharecropper family, he sang gospel as a child. In the late '50s, his family relocated to Michigan. Al was kicked out of his home by his religious father for playing a secular record by R&B artist Jackie Wilson. Free to pursue his passion and inspired by the likes of Mahalia Jackson, Wilson Pickett, and Elvis Presley, Al formed a vocal group and, in 1967, recorded "Back Up Train," a minor hit, for a local label. The following year, singing in a small Texas joint, Al met bandleader Willie Mitchell who agreed to mentor and produce him. Their first LP, though it failed to produce a breakthrough single, began to set the template for the Green-Mitchell sound, but it all came together in 1971 with "Tired of Being Alone"—that sound, said to be a cross between Motown and Memphis, was silky and sexy with a laid back but tight rhythmic groove, punctuated by horns, with Green's inimitable vocals, variously described as seductive, dreamy, and pure. *Rolling Stone*, in 1972, said, "He can croon, shout, scat, rise to the smoothest falsetto, and throw in the funkiest growls." A few months later, "Let's Stay Together," following a similar pattern, topped both the pop and R&B charts. More hits followed—"Look What You've Done For Me," "I'm Still In Love With You," "You Ought to Be with Me." When he reached back to his gospel roots with "Take Me to the River," the results were electric.

Then it began to fall apart. In late '74, his girlfriend poured a pot of boiling grits on him as he bathed and then shot and killed herself. This was followed by a series of assault charges. Green, seeing the hand of God in some of these events, did an about face, became an ordained minister, and, for much of the '80s, devoted himself to recording gospel. Though he returned, in time, to R&B, he never again quite found the old formula for success.

Suggested Songs:

Tired of Being Alone (1971)
Let's Stay Together (1971)
How Can You Mend a Broken Heart (1972)
Take Me to the River (1974)

#129 Otis Redding (1941 - 1967)
Began Recording: 1960 (w. the Shooters); 1962 (solo)
Peak: 1965 - 1968
Genres: Soul/R&B Singer/Songwriter

Born in rural Georgia, the son of sharecroppers, Otis Redding mostly grew up in a Macon housing project, singing in a Baptist Church choir from a young age. As a child, he learned to play piano, guitar, and drums. By 1958, he was singing and playing professionally, often along the southern "Chitlin' Circuit." Redding's first musical hero was Little Richard, but he also loved Sam Cooke. His big break came in 1962 when, after a recording session for blues guitarist Johnny Jenkins for whom Otis drove, Redding got into the studio and sang his soulful ballad, "These Arms of Mine." It got him a record deal, and the single became his first hit.

In 1965, he released the quintessential soul classic *Otis Blue/Redding Sings Soul*, one of the most acclaimed albums of all-time. The album features "Respect" (his self-penned version sounds like a plea for carnal love, while Aretha's chart-topper, two years later, became a feminist anthem); "I've Been Loving You Too Long," which finds him trying to hold on to a lover who seems ready to walk; and a brilliant cover of Sam Cooke's "A Change Is Gonna Come."

With a voice that's been variously described as "gritty yet tender," "strong yet sensitive," "rough yet sincere," Redding served up a heady mix of gospel, blues, and R&B, backed by the stellar Memphis Stax band known as Booker T. and the M.G.'s; it came to be known as Southern Soul. Hoping to break through to a larger, white audience as well, Otis, in 1967, played the Monterey Pop Festival and was an enormous hit. He also played England and released the moving cover ballad that turns into an unbridled R&B romp by the end, "Try a Little Tenderness."

On the cusp of superstardom and on his way to yet another show, his plane went down in Lake Monona, Wisconsin, killing Redding and six others. A month later, the sad, reflective "(Sitting On) The Dock of the Bay" was released, becoming the first posthumous #1 single ever and one of the most played records of all time. A hugely influential artist, the Rock and Songwriters Halls of Fame both include him.

Suggested Songs:

I've Been Loving You Too Long (1965)
A Change Is Gonna Come (1965)
Try a Little Tenderness (1967)
(Sittin' On) The Dock of the Bay (1968)

#128 Donna Summer (1948 - 2012)

Began Recording: 1968 (as Donna Gaines); 1974 (as Donna Summer)
Peak: 1975 - 1984
Genres: Disco; Dance; R&B; pop Singer/songwriter

Donna Summer was the unquestioned "Queen of Disco" during the second half of the 1970s with three consecutive #1 double albums and peaking with four #1 singles in 1979.

Born LaDonna Gaines in Boston, she first sang solo in church at the age of 10. After a brief stint in a New York rock band, Donna, as she called herself, relocated to Munich to take a role in a German production of *Hair*. Her first recordings were not hits and carried her original surname. She began using the name Summer after divorcing her first husband, actor Helmuth Sommer.

Working throughout the '70s with production-songwriting collaborators Giorgio Moroder and Pete Bellotte, Donna had her international breakthrough in 1975 with the risqué dance groove "Love to Love You Baby," highlighted by Summer's breathy vocals and orgasmic moans. The song turned Donna into a sex goddess, which she hated and struggled to live down, spiraling her into depression and a botched suicide attempt before she found a new lifestyle as a born-again Christian.

Summer's collaborative 1977 release, "I Feel Love," is recognized today as the birth of modern electronic dance music with its futuristic sounding, hypnotic synth and Donna's dreamy, sensual vocals. She was just getting started. In 1978, she recorded the Grammy winning "Last Dance," one of her favorites, and her remake of the Jimmy Webb classic "MacArthur Park," her first pop #1. These were followed by 1979's rock-flavored "Hot Stuff;" her sympathetic take on sex workers, "Bad Girls;" and her empowerment duet with Barbra Streisand, "No More Tears (Enough Is Enough)." Donna's music began to morph after that as disco declined in popularity. "She Works Hard for the Money," in 1983, was her last monster hit.

Donna Summer died of cancer in 2012, and though she had not been a pop presence for years, she remained on the dance charts to the very end. A gifted, underrated vocalist, Quincy Jones referred to her as "the heartbeat and soundtrack of a generation."

Suggested Songs:

I Feel Love (1977)
Last Dance (1978)
Bad Girls (1979)
She Works Hard for the Money (1983)

#127 The Clash

Began Recording: 1977
Peak: 1979 - 1982
Genres: Punk; post Punk; New Wave; Alternative Rock Band

They've been called the "thinking man's punks" and "the only band that matters" (*Far Out*). By taking the raw, raucous energy of punk rock and then fusing it with elements of reggae, dub, R&B, rockabilly, pop, and jazz, England's The Clash transcended their roots. Jim McGuinn said they wrote "human music." With socially conscious, left-leaning lyrics, they were fearless in taking on capitalist and consumer excess, racism, militarism, fascism, drug abuse, and the pop music industry, while advocating for youth, the working class, for social activism, and genuine freedom.

Inspired by the Sex Pistols and the Ramones, The Clash formed in 1976 and, for the bulk of their career, they were Joe Strummer, lead vocalist, rhythm guitarist and principal songwriter; Mick Jones who also played lead guitar and added backing vocals; Paul Simonon on bass; and Nicky Headon on the drums.

Favorite Clash songs? Their fans leave us with a dizzying array of choices: "White Riot," a 1977 oft-misunderstood anti-racist, punk call to action; "Complete Control," a raging rant against their record label; the apocalyptic "London Calling," title track from the ground breaking LP, with both often cited as among the greatest songs and albums of all-time; "Bankrobber," illustrating how the system might lead one to desperate action; and the radio hit "Should I Stay or Should I Go."

By 1982, The Clash, at the height of their popularity, began to disintegrate as a unit and by 1986 they were done. Their reputation and legacy, however, as true punks, as exponents of existential, responsible freedom, has endured, with artists as diverse as Public Enemy and Jacob Dylan singing their praise.

Suggested Songs:

(White Man) in Hammersmith Palais (1978)
London Calling (1979)
Train in Vain (1980)
Rock the Casbah (1982)

#126 Glenn Miller (1904 - 1944)

Began Recording: 1926 (as sideman); 1935 (bandleader)
Peak: 1939 - 1943
Genres: Big Band/Swing Bandleader/Trombonist/composer

He was fond of quoting from a Duke Ellington/Irving Mills song about the overarching importance of swing. From 1939 to 1942 Glenn Miller was the world's best selling recording artist and claimed a total of 16 #1 singles.

Born in Iowa, Miller had moved to Colorado with his family by the time he reached high school. His first instrument was a mandolin, but he soon moved on to trombone. Dropping out of college, he moved to L.A. and connected with the Ben Pollack Band before taking on free-lance trombone and arranging gigs.

His initial band was not successful until he hit upon a unique sound that allowed a clarinet and tenor sax to play the melody while three other saxophones played harmony. His second Glenn Miller Orchestra began to click in 1938, and, by the following year, they were playing to record-breaking audiences and beginning to dominate the charts. Among his many hits were "Moonlight Serenade," his own composition and, perhaps, best-loved piece; the upbeat "In the Mood," honored by both the *National Recording Registry* and NPR; the jazzy blues of "Tuxedo Junction;" "Pennsylvania 6-5000," in effect an ad to visit the band's New York venue; and "Chattanooga Choo Choo," RCA's first gold record.

With World War II raging, the 38-year-old Miller volunteered for service and formed the "Major Glenn Miller Army Air Forces Orchestra," which performed hundreds of times in England as well as recorded. His light plane disappeared over the English Channel on December 15, 1944, and he was never found; he was posthumously awarded a Bronze Star. Critics have not always been kind to Miller, saying his music was too commercial and lacked feeling, but Louis Armstrong and Frank Sinatra were among the millions who loved his unique sound.

Suggested Songs:

Moonlight Serenade (1939)
In the Mood (1939)
Tuxedo Junction (1940)
A String of Pearls (1942)

#125 Phil Collins (1951 - present)
Began Recording: 1971 (w. Genesis); 1981 (Solo)
Peak: 1981 - 1990
Genres: Soft Rock; Pop Singer/Songwriter/Drummer

Phil Collins is one of several artists appearing on these pages twice, once as the highly esteemed drummer and, later, lead singer of the British band Genesis, and here as, arguably, the most successful pop balladeer of the 1980s.

Collins started playing drums at five and later found some success as a child actor, notably in the role of the Artful Dodger on the London stage. In 1970, he joined the art-rock group Genesis as a replacement drummer, and, upon Peter Gabriel's 1975 departure, Collins became the new lead singer. Coming off a difficult divorce, in 1981 Collins released his first solo LP, the rather personal *Face Value*. His signature hit, "In the Air Tonight," is moody, pained, and noted for Phil's "gated reverb" drum punctuation. A big hit in the U.K., he was a bit slower to gain superstar footing in the U.S., but he broke through in 1984 with the yearning soundtrack ballad "Against All Odds (Take a Look at Me Now)." Still recording with Genesis as well, suddenly, Phil Collins was everywhere, on both sides of the Atlantic, famously illustrated by his appearing in one day at both Live Aid London and Live Aid Philadelphia. For Collins fans this was a boon as he hit the U.S. Top 10 13 times in a six-year period, but there was a sharp critical backlash as well. Some never forgave Genesis for morphing into a pop rock outfit under his leadership, while others, focusing on his solo success, found him too "everyman," in his voice, his appearance, and, most of all, in his music, deeming it "middle of the road" and "boring." He had his supporters, of course, notably Brian May of Queen, Zeppelin's Robert Plant, and the huge record-buying public. *No Jacket Required* and ... *But Seriously* were giant sellers with such monster singles as the Prince-flavored "Sussudio," the ultra smooth "One More Night," and the much maligned (unfairly?) reflection on homelessness, "Another Day in Paradise."

Health issues have taken the drumsticks out of Phil's hands in recent years, and he performs today infrequently, but there is little doubt that he is a recording legend.

Suggested Songs:

In the Air Tonight (1981)
Against All Odds (Take a Look at Me Now) (1984)
One More Night (1985)
Another Day in Paradise (1989)

#124 Ed Sheeran (1991 - present)
Began Recording: 2005 (self-recordings); 2011 (solo-label)
Peak: 2011 - 2015; 2017 - 2022
Genres: Pop; Folk/Soft Rock Singer/Songwriter

With just over a decade of recording under his belt, Ed Sheeran is already one of the best-selling artists in history.

Coming out of central England, Ed sang in a church choir and learned guitar as a young boy. Influenced by artists such as The Beatles, Dylan, and Clapton, Ed began self-recording at 13 and quit school at 16 to pursue a music career. His YouTube music gained him a following and, with help from Elton John, a record deal.

His debut single "The A Team," a sensitive, melodic portrait of a drug-addicted prostitute, became a 2011 U.K. hit and was followed by +, Sheeran's first LP. In 11 years, Ed has released five studio albums, all of which have reached the top spot in the U.K., while four were U.S. #1s. Other notable singles from Ed's career include "Sing," his first Official UK Top 40 #1, an R&B/hip-hop flavored collaboration with Pharrell Williams; "Thinking Out Loud," a hugely popular 2014 profession of undying love; "Photograph," an acoustic, folky ode to the difficulties of long distance love; the soft rock teenage nostalgia piece, "Castle on the Hill;" the sexy, tropical rhythm track, "Shape of You;" and the giant, romantic ballad from 2017, "Perfect."

Sheeran became so big, so fast, that he has plenty of detractors. Some have called his sensitive, non-threatening lyrics sappy; others have heard little growth since his promising debut with a tendency to rely on old pop formulas. On the other hand, Ed has been lauded for his sweet, authentic, unforced vocal style, his ability to incorporate multiple genres, from indie-folk, to hip-hop, to adult contemporary in his down-to-earth pop, as Alexis Petridis put it, and his ability to be himself in an age of manufactured and carefully sculpted celebrity.

Suggested Songs:

The A Team (2011)
Photograph (2014)
Perfect (2017)
Shivers (2021)

#123 Carter Family
Began Recording: 1927
Peak: 1928 - 1933; 1938 - 1942
Genres: Traditional Folk, Country, Gospel Band

The Carter Family is rightly known as the "First Family of Country Music." From 1927 through 1943, A.P. Carter, his wife Sara, and sister-in-law Maybelle sang, played, recorded, and popularized traditional English, Scottish, and Appalachian folk, country, and gospel songs and influenced generations of later artists, such as Woody Guthrie, Bill Monroe, Hank Williams, Chet Atkins, Joan Baez, Bob Dylan, Emmylou Harris, and a host of other artists across multiple genres.

Scratching out a living in an area known as Poor Valley, Virginia, A.P., who played fiddle and sang baritone, made music at church gatherings and parties with Sara, who was known for her striking vocals. When Sara's guitar playing cousin, Maybelle, married A.P.'s brother, they became a musical trio. Auditioning for Ralph Peer of the Victor Company the same week he discovered Jimmie Rodgers, the Carters cut six singles for $300, and their career was launched.

A.P. tirelessly scoured the countryside for traditional material, rearranged it, and sang backing on selected songs; Sara, whose voice deepened with age, sang lead and sometimes played autoharp; while Maybelle played both lead and rhythm guitar, fingerpicking the melody on the lower strings while strumming chords on the higher strings, a style that became known as the "Carter scratch" and which influenced countless guitarists who followed. Noted for their harmony, their simplicity, and their honest, poignant presentations, the Carters introduced such songs as the hopeful "Keep on the Sunny Side," the lost love ballad "Wildwood Flower," the Depression-era balm "Worried Man Blues," the railroad epic "Wabash Cannonball," the questioning gospel hymn "Can the Circle Be Unbroken," and nearly 300 other songs delivered in their trademark, unvarying style.

Later Carter generations would follow, but the original family became the first group inducted into the Country Music Hall of Fame in 1970.

Suggested Songs:

Keep On the Sunny Side (1928)
Wildwood Flower (1929)
Worried Man Blues (1930)
Can the Circle Be Unbroken (1935)

#122 George Jones (1931 - 2013)
Began Recording: 1954
Peak: 1959 - 1974; 1980 - 1984
Genres: Country Singer/Songwriter

He has been called the greatest country singer of all time, and, many would argue, one of the finest vocalists of any genre. George Jones was born in a log cabin and with a broken arm. His father, though an alcoholic and abusive, bought the boy a guitar when he was nine, and soon George was busking on the streets of Beaumont, Texas. Married and divorced by 18, he decided to try the Marines where his musical talent got him noticed, and, soon after his release, he was recording. In 1955, he had his first hit, the rockabilly "Why Baby Why."

Never far from a drink, alcohol was already getting him into trouble when he scored his first #1 single on the Hot C&W chart, "White Lightning." Drunk while recording, Jones recorded 83 takes before getting it right. Prone to binges, drunken fights, wrecked cars and marriages, he eventually earned the nickname "No-Show Jones" for missing so many concerts. Somehow, though, he continued to chart and grow in his ability to find and express the emotional heart of his recorded songs. Among his best-loved tracks are 1962's "She Thinks I Still Care," the heartbreaking 1974 divorce ballad "The Grand Tour," and the 1980 comeback song, "He Stopped Loving Her Today," a song George initially thought "too morbid" but has since been chosen in many polls the greatest country record ever.

It's the marvelous voice that is most recalled today. Singers as diverse as Merle Haggard, Bob Dylan, Frank Sinatra, and Robert Plant considered him a master. With the help of his fourth wife, he eventually broke free of his demon and today is remembered as one of the best loved of all country artists.

Suggested Songs:

She Thinks I Still Care (1962)
The Grand Tour (1974)
He Stopped Loving Her Today (1980)
Choices (1999)

#121 Justin Bieber (1994 - present)
Began Recording: 2009
Peak: 2010 - 2012; 2015 - 2017; 2019 - 2022
Genres: Pop; Dance Pop; R&B Singer/songwriter

If a young Sinatra caused heart palpitations among the teenage girls of the '40s, just as surely Justin Bieber engendered a similar response in the 2010s.

The young Bieber was discovered at 13 by super scout Scooter Braun and R&B vocalist Usher after Justin's mom posted his performance videos on YouTube. At 15, his debut single, "One Time," reached the Top 20 and a year later the catchy, pop confection "Baby" made him an international star. The product of a massively successful marketing push that saw him release two #1 albums and appear twice at the Obama White House before he was 18, the Canadian pop sensation had to contend with the natural change of voice that dropped him from a boyish soprano to an expressive tenor. At first, the young heartthrob seemed to handle all that came his way with aplomb, but, by 2013, there were signs of trouble as Bieber began appearing regularly in the news for increasingly boorish behavior; overnight his image had morphed into pop's "bad boy."

2015 marked his comeback, beginning with his electronic dance collaboration with Skrillex and Diplo, "Where Are U Now," featuring dynamic percussion, a mysterious Eastern-like drone, and Justin's vulnerable, searching, heavily processed vocals. This was followed by his most acclaimed LP, *Purpose*, which contains two signature songs—"Sorry," Bieber's stab at apology to an ex-love, and the pared down, melodic, lyrically clever kiss-off, "Love Yourself".

Bieber has continued remaking himself with remarkable success. His 2017 remix of "Despacito" shot to #1 internationally and earned him a Latin Grammy, while *Justice*, released in 2021, became his 6th straight studio LP to reach #1 on the Canadian and U.S. *Billboard* charts. The holder of numerous *Billboard* and Guinness world records, an unquestionable icon of internet age artists, and already among the all-time best sellers, Bieber is only 29 years old.

Suggested Songs:

Where Are U Now (w. Jack U) (2015)
Love Yourself (2015)
Despacito- Remix (w. Luis Fonsi & Daddy Yankee) (2017)
Ghost (2021)

#120 The Band

Began Recording: 1965 (as Levon & the Hawks); 1968 (as The Band)
Peak: 1968 - 1976
Genres: Rock; Roots Rock/Country Rock/ Americana Band

They honed their chops as the Hawks, a backup outfit for rockabilly artist Ronnie Hawkins. When Bob Dylan went electric in 1965, they became his backing road band, enduring nightly boos and catcalls through 1966 as Dylan was deemed by many folkies a sellout. Alighting in upstate New York in 1967, they famously recorded with Dylan the legendary bootleg collection known as *The Basement Tapes*. Determined to go solo, in 1968 and 1969 they released two storied albums, *Music from Big Pink* and *The Band* under the moniker The Band. They were an immediate sensation. The music seemed to emerge from a mythic American past, more 19th than 20th century, a weird alchemical amalgam of hill music, country fiddles, gospel and Civil War tales, Dixieland, folk, R&B, and good old electric rock & roll; decades later critics would call it Americana. Some of the songs are legendary—"Tears of Rage," with its spiritual, historical, and literary allusions; the cryptic, gospel flavored "The Weight;" "I Shall Be Released," with its prisoner/narrator yearning for freedom; and the Civil War themed "The Night They Drove Old Dixie Down."

In 1974, The Band toured once again with Dylan, this time triumphantly, but they were growing weary of the road and their subsequent LPs failed to match the brilliance of the first two. In 1976, they played a farewell concert, captured magnificently on film as *The Last Waltz*, still the gold standard of concert films. The aftermath proved both sad and ugly—in 1986, pianist and brilliant, soulful vocalist Richard Manuel hung himself; Rick Danko, celebrated bassist and the haunted vocalist of "It Makes No Difference" and "Stage Fright," died prematurely after years of struggle with alcohol and drugs; co-leaders Levon Helm, the underrated drummer and key back-woodsy vocalist, grew estranged from guitarist and lead writer Robbie Robertson over songwriting and royalty issues; while

Garth Hudson, the classically trained organist and multi-instrumentalist, carries on.

Suggested Songs:

The Weight (1968)
The Night They Drove Old Dixie Down (1969)
Bessie Smith (1975)
It Makes No Difference (1975)

#119 Run-DMC
Began Recording: 1983
Peak: 1984 - 1988
Genres: Hip-Hop; Rap Rock Fusion Rappers

More than any other rap group, Run-DMC ushered hip-hop into the mainstream and helped initiate "Rap's Golden Age." Encouraged by his up and coming, hip-hop mogul older brother Russell Simmons, Joseph Simmons (known as Run) teamed up with friend Darryl McDaniels (known as DMC) and Jason Mizell (or Jam Master Jay, the group's DJ) to form Run-DMC in 1982, releasing their debut single, the lean, social protest rap "It's Like That" the following year. The single's B-side, "Sucker M.C.'s," is recognized today as groundbreaking in its spare production of drum machine percussion, Master Jay's scratching, and the aggressive tone of its rapped vocals. In retrospect, this two-sided single has been acknowledged for moving rap away from a funky, soulful, dance oriented style, or "old school," toward a leaner, tougher, more forceful, street-oriented approach with an emphasis on heavy beats. 1984 saw the release of their self-titled debut LP, and it featured the seminal singles and the "new school" rap sound. The album also featured the song "Rock Box" which introduced rap-rock fusion, as Eddie Martinez wailed in the background on electric guitar.

Run-DMC also played a major role in introducing a new style of dress that came to dominate the hip-hop universe over the next couple of decades. With their black denim and leather jackets, gold chains, and unlaced Adidas sneakers, rap moved away from flashy disco attire and acquired new credibility among youth.

In 1986, they released *Raising Hell*, one of the most celebrated hip-hop albums of all time. Their collaboration with hard rockers Aerosmith not only helped revive the latter's career, but it brought rap into the mainstream, paving the way for hip-hop to become the dominant genre of the next several decades. Later artists, such as Public Enemy and N.W.A, owe much to Run-DMC.

Suggested Songs:

Sucker M.C.'s (1983)
Rock Box (1984)
King of Rock (1985)
Walk This Way (w. Aerosmith) (1986)

#118 Guns N' Roses
Began Recording: 1986
Peak: 1988 - 1992
Genres: Hard Rock; Heavy Metal Band

In 1988, Guns N' Roses, a band out of L.A., "brought raw, ugly, rock & roll crashing back into the charts," in the words of Stephen Erlewine. Initially disparaged for their misogynistic, cynical, dissolute, and dangerous lyrics and image, critics and the general public quickly discerned that this was a group of serious, if immature, musicians. Slash and Izzy Stradlin traded dazzling guitar licks; Duff McKagan played a superior, melodic bass; drummer Steven Adler was celebrated for his "speed, timing, and precision;" and frontman Axl Rose, lead singer, lyricist, and lightning rod for controversy, nonetheless possessed a primal, snarling, screeching voice capable of articulating the band's fiery, belligerent vision.

Their 1987 debut LP, *Appetite for Destruction,* got off to a slow start commercially, but with a push from label president David Geffen and MTV, it went on to become one of the best-selling albums of all time as well as be lauded as a hard rock masterpiece. "Welcome to the Jungle," with its aggressive, propulsive sound merged seamlessly to its uncompromising look at city life, set the template; "Paradise City" is hard driving, melodic, and offers a similar vision, if tinged with a bit more hope; "Sweet Child o' Mine," their only single to reach #1, presented a sweeter, love lyric, but married it to a masterful Slash guitar solo. Their '89 follow-up, *G N' R Lies,* was a weird hybrid of older cuts and acoustic numbers, notable for the missing-my-woman ballad "Patience" and "One in a Million," almost universally slammed for its racist, nativist, homophobic lyrics. In 1991, they released two LPs, *Use Your Illusion I* and *II* simultaneously, their last groundbreaking albums. The lovely anthemic power ballad "November Rain" is the best-loved track.

In the early '90s, band members began to leave, and, soon, only Rose, with new lineups, remained, but the original band, often compared to the early Rolling Stones, has not been forgotten. Indeed, Slash and McKagan rejoined Rose and several newer members in 2016 for a "Not in This Lifetime...Tour" and have stuck around.

Suggested Songs:

Welcome to the Jungle (1987)
Sweet Child o' Mine (1988)
Patience (1988)
November Rain (1992)

#117 George Michael (1963 - 2016)

Began Recording: 1982 (w. Wham!); 1984 (solo)
Peak: 1984 - 1992; 1996 - 2004
Genres: Pop; Dance-Pop; R&B/Soul Singer/Songwriter

A teen pop idol before the age of 21, George Michael managed the tricky transition to respected adult artist with unusual grace and style.

Born George Panaylotou, the son of a Greek émigré father and an English mother in north London, George changed his name and formed the pop duo Wham! with his friend Andrew Ridgeley in 1981. George quickly established himself as the songwriter/lead vocalist of the duo, and, between 1982 and '86, the teen pop sensations had remarkable success with such hits as "Wake Me Before You Go-Go" and the perennial holiday classic "Last Christmas," but it was 1984's "Careless Whisper," with its iconic sax line, its two-timing lyrics, and, most of all, George's impassioned, haunted vocals, that signaled that his talent would not be constrained. George left Wham! in 1986 after a groundbreaking 1985 tour of China, the first by a major western recording artist.

George's 1987 debut solo LP, *Faith*, has sold some 25 million copies and claimed the coveted Grammy Album of the Year award. The rockabilly title track, the R&B/gospel-flavored "Father Figure," and the controversial "I Want Your Sex" are the best-known numbers. Later LPs, *Listen Without Prejudice Vol. 1* and *Other*, likewise garnered high praise and highlighted a more reflective, even somber, Michael, with such songs as "Cowboys and Angels," "Jesus to a Child," and the celebrated gospel-flavored "Freedom! '90."

A brilliant producer and songwriter, George was an underrated vocalist, with a soft, breathy, elastic, highly expressive tenor. Conflicted early on about his sexuality, his songs regularly dropped hints that he was gay, but it took an unfortunate 1998 Beverly Hills sting operation to out him. After the death of his mother and a lover, George spiraled into a destructive cycle of drug abuse; he died of heart failure at the age of 53. A quietly generous philanthropist, he was the most played artist on British radio from 1984 to 2004, according to the U.K.'s Radio Academy. In 2023, he was inducted into the Rock & Roll Hall of Fame.

Suggested Songs:

Careless Whisper (w. Wham!) (1984)
Father Figure (1987)
Don't Let the Sun Go Down on Me (w. Elton John) (1991)
Jesus to a Child (1996)

#116 The Temptations
Began Recording: 1961
Peak: 1964 - 1973
Genres: R&B/Soul; Pop; Psychedelic and Funk Soul Vocal Group

In the 1960s, when the British invasion led by the Beatles and the Stones was raging, one of the most commercially successful alternatives was Berry Gordy's pop-flavored soul factory known as Motown. Featuring such Top 40 giants as the Supremes, the Four Tops, and the Miracles, perhaps the preeminent male vocal group was the Temptations. Formed from two fledgling groups and signed by Gordy in 1961, the Temptations broke through in 1964 with the upbeat, clever wordplay of "The Way You Do the Things You Do." Over the next decade they would reach the Top 10 15 times, including four singles that topped the *Billboard* Hot 100.

Their classic lineup was comprised of falsetto lead Eddie Kendricks; baritone Otis Williams (the only surviving and still performing original member); Paul Williams, baritone and sometime lead; Melvin Franklin, with his distinctive bass; and David Ruffin, a late addition whose characteristic raspy, mellow vocals fronted many of their most memorable tracks. When Ruffin was fired from the group in '68, he was replaced by new lead, Dennis Edwards.

Famed for their tight, smooth harmonies and arresting choreography, several songs stand out from their repertoire—"My Girl," their classic, signature love song co-written by Smokey Robinson; the heartbreaking "Since I Lost My Baby," featuring Ruffin's haunting vocal; 1969's "I'm Gonna Make You Love Me," when Gordy teamed his two top acts, the Supremes and the Temptations; "Cloud Nine," which, inspired by Sly and the Family Stone's musical direction, marked the Temptation's first foray into funk and psychedelia; and the majestic 12-minute saga of siblings searching for their mysterious father, "Papa Was a Rolling Stone."

Members of the Rock and R&B Halls of Fame, the Temptations' story has been dramatized in film and on Broadway, and their music is still heard regularly on classic radio.

Suggested Songs:

My Girl (1964)
Since I Lost My Baby (1965)
Just My Imagination (Running Away With Me) (1971)
Papa Was a Rolling Stone (1972)

#115 Count Basie (1904 - 1984)

Began Recording: 1937
Peak: 1938 - 1942; 1953 - 1961
Genres: Jazz - Swing, Big Band; Blues Pianist/Composer/Bandleader

Second only to the legendary Duke Ellington as a great jazz bandleader, Count Basie was noted for his economy of style and for linking jazz with the blues.

Born William Basie to working class New Jersey parents, he got his start as a teenager playing piano for silent films at a local theater and soon joined the vaudeville circuit. Stranded in Kansas City between jobs, he took in the local blues, which thereafter informed his jazz style. As a pianist, Basie was early on influenced by stride players like Fats Waller, but subsequently adopted a more minimalistic, yet still swinging, sound. In 1935, he formed his own 9-piece band, Count Basie and the Barons of Rhythm. Celebrated by music scout John Hammond as, "far and away the finest dance orchestra in the country," by 1937 Basie was recording and reaching a national audience leading the 13-member Count Basie Orchestra. Noted for his great rhythm section of Walter Page and Jo Jones, and his split tenor sax arrangement, Basie also had a reputation as a modest leader who was not afraid to let others, such as saxophonist Lester Young and trombonist Dicky Wells, shine. His signature song "One O'Clock Jump," an off-the-cuff improvised creation, was emblematic of the band, which used "head arrangements" as opposed to written sheet music.

Basie's first orchestra, sometimes called his "Old Testament," was disbanded in 1950, but, two years later, he put together a second orchestra, his "New Testament," which toured internationally, used sight reading and more complex arrangements, producing such standouts as "April in Paris," "Lil' Darling," and the much-covered "Everyday I Have the Blues."

In all, Basie and his band won nine Grammys, and he was inducted into both the Blues and Jazz Halls of Fame.

Suggested Songs:

One O'Clock Jump (1937)
Jumpin' at the Woodside (1938)
April in Paris (1955)
Everyday I Have the Blues (w. Joe Williams) (1955)

#114 Van Morrison (1945 - present)

Began Recording: 1963 (sax w. the Monarchs); 1964 (w. Them); 1967 (solo)
Peak: 1968 - 1974; 1989 - 1990
Genres: R&B/Soul; Rock; Jazz; Folk; gospel Singer/Songwriter/ Instrumentalist

Van Morrison, with Scottish and Northern Irish roots, listened to the blues and R&B music he found in his dad's massive record collection. Starting at 12, he was in a series of bands, playing guitar, saxophone, harmonica, and singing. His professional breakthrough came with the blues-rock group Them; their 1964 B-side single "Gloria" has become a rock & roll staple.

With the breakup of Them in 1966, Morrison moved to New York to pursue a solo career. His debut LP produced 1967's "Brown Eyed Girl," his ageless song about idealized young love, and said to be one of the most played songs of the '60s. In 1968, he released the unclassifiable *Astral Weeks* to little popular or critical acclaim. Some call it folk rock, others folk jazz, with blues and classical elements mixed in; Morrison calls it a collection of story songs, while others hear impressionistic, stream-of-consciousness lyrics that touch on pain, death, childhood, and spirituality. "Cypress Avenue" and "Madame George" are two of the most celebrated pieces from the LP, which today is hailed by many as a supreme work of art. Two years later, Morrison was back with a second album, which likewise has taken its place among historically great works: *Moondance*, a more accessible, upbeat work than its predecessor. The album features such classics as the jazzy, romantic title track and the sublime, ethereal ode to the spiritual quest, "Into the Mystic."

With his growling, plaintive, yearning vocals, and tight, jazzy R&B bands, some hear Morrison as the greatest of all white soul singers. With his lyrics that long for a better past that perhaps never was and look forward to mystical transcendence, often found in the everyday, mundane world and in nature, Morrison is seen today as a genuine original who has touched deeply the likes of the Doors, Bruce Springsteen, Joan Armatrading, Rickie

Lee Jones, Bob Seger, Bono, and countless others. He is a member of the Rock and Songwriters Halls of Fame.

Suggested Songs:

Brown Eyed Girl (1967)
Madame George (1968)
Into the Mystic (1970)
Bright Side of the Road (1979)

#113 George Gershwin (1898 - 1937)
Began Recording: 1916
Peak: 1924 - 1937
Genres: Popular; Classical; Jazz Composer/Pianist

George Gershwin longed to be taken seriously as a "classical" composer; Arnold Schoenberg certainly did so, while Leonard Bernstein was famously dismissive.

Born Jacob Gershwine in Brooklyn to Russian-Jewish immigrant parents, he was always called George and grew up in the Yiddish theater district. When his parents brought home a piano for older brother Ira, it was George who gravitated to it. From 1913 to 1918, he studied under composer-teacher Charles Hambitzer. Between 1916 and 1927, George produced over 140 piano rolls of mostly popular and self-composed songs for use in his day's fashionable player pianos. George was soon writing the music for Broadway musicals, collaborating with several lyricists, though his favorite partner was brother Ira.

1924 saw George compose his best-loved piece, the iconic "Rhapsody in Blue," of which there are several versions featuring George on piano. Gershwin traveled to Paris in the mid-'20s and composed his second great rhapsody, or single-movement piece, "An American in Paris." In 1935, he introduced his "folk opera" *Porgy and Bess*, the story of a Black street beggar trying to rescue his beloved Bess from a dangerous life. Gershwin insisted that the performers be Black, and the show has been controversial through the years, but it gave the world "Summertime," and the opera has been celebrated as one of his greatest triumphs.

Gershwin moved to Hollywood the following year to work on films. He soon began experiencing horrific headaches and blackouts. Rushed to the hospital when he passed out in 1937, he never regained consciousness and died two days later of a brain tumor. He was 38 years old. Today, it is recognized that the genius of Gershwin was his ability to mix jazz, pop, and classical music and create something new. That he is held in high esteem is seen by the fact that the Library of Congress named their highest musical award the Gershwin Prize, given for lifetime contributions to popular music. Among its recipients are Paul Simon, Stevie Wonder, Paul McCartney, and Carole King.

Suggested Songs:

Swanee (1919) (1993 reissue)
Rhapsody in Blue (1924) (2012 LP)
So Am I (1925) (1993 reissue)
An American in Paris (1928) (1998 reissue)

#112 Santana

Began Recording: 1969
Peak: 1969 - 1972; 1999 - 2002
Genres: Latin Rock; Jazz-Rock Fusion; psychedelic, blues, pop, Rock Band

In August 1969, a largely unknown band took the stage on day two of the Woodstock music festival and nearly stole the show. Formed in San Francisco in 1966 by Mexican emigrant Carlos Santana, that gig launched their career, and, when two weeks later their self-titled debut LP, *Santana*, dropped, it catapulted to #4 on the strength of that performance with stand-out tracks like "Evil Ways" and the Woodstock scene stealer, "Soul Sacrifice."

The band's eclectic blend of rock, blues, and jazz fused with complex Latin rhythms was first created by the classic Santana line up which featured Carlos on lead guitar. Over the next 50+ years he has developed one of the most recognizable styles in all of music with his long, sustained notes, his piercing, crying peaks with a sublime, searing, spiritual quality. Carlos was joined by Gregg Role on organ and lead vocals, Michael Carabello on congas, David Brown on bass, Chepito Areas on percussion, and the young Michael Shrieve on drums. In 1970, Santana released *Abraxas*, an album that has since been included in the *National Recording Registry*. The Fleetwood Mac/Gabor Szabo cover medley "Black Magic Woman/Gypsy Queen" and the Latin rock cha cha "Oye Como Va," were the hit tracks. A year later, they released *Santana III* before creative and personal differences led to all but Carlos departing the band. Over the years, there have been dozens of band members with Carlos the one constant.

In the '80s and '90s Santana went into a steep commercial decline before releasing their massive comeback album, *Supernatural*, in 1999, an album that went on to sell 30 million or more copies and garner an unprecedented nine Grammys, including three in Latin categories. The lead single "Smooth," featuring singer Rob Thomas, is one of the most recognizable songs of the 21st century. It is doubtful that any artist has so skillfully and successfully fused the sounds of rock, jazz, and Latin rhythms as Santana.

Suggested Songs:

Soul Sacrifice (1970)
Black Magic Woman/Gypsy Queen (1970)
Smooth (w. Rob Thomas) (1999)
Maria Maria (w. The Product G&B) (1999)

#111 Sam Cooke (1931 - 1964)

Began Recording: 1951 (w. Soul Stirrers); 1956 (solo)
Peak: 1957 - 1964
Genres: R&B/Soul; Pop; Gospel Singer/Songwriter

Born in Mississippi and raised in Chicago, Samuel Cook, son of a minister, was singing in various gospel groups from the age of six. At the age of 20, Sam became the lead singer of the longtime, popular gospel quintet the Soul Stirrers. With songs like "Peace in the Valley" and "Touch the Hem of His Garment," his popularity soared. In 1956, determined to test the pop waters but fearful of losing his gospel fans, Sam released "Lovable" under the pseudonym Dale Cook. His gospel label fired him. Sam added an "e" to his last name and, with the blessing of his father, set out to reach the larger pop and R&B audience.

Possessed of an extraordinary voice, variously described as velvet, pure, and crystalline, with just a hint of a rasp, Sam sang with ease and perfect pitch; he's been extolled by the likes of Smokey Robinson and Aretha Franklin. Atlantic Records' Jerry Wexler said simply, "Sam was the best singer who ever lived, no contest."

In 1957, Cooke had the biggest hit of his career, the dreamy, R&B-flavored pop number "You Send Me." Over the next eight years he was a constant presence on the charts with 29 Top 40 tunes, including "(I Love You) For Sentimental Reason," "Everybody Loves to Cha Cha Cha," "Wonderful World," "Chain Gang," "Cupid," "Twisting the Night Away," "Bring It On Home to Me," "Having a Party," "Another Saturday Night," and "Shake." In 1964, moved by Bob Dylan's "Blowin' In the Wind" and reflecting on his own experience as a victim of racism, Cooke wrote and recorded the iconic "A Change Is Gonna Come," now recognized as a landmark Civil Rights anthem and earning a spot in the *National Recording Registry*.

Sadly, Sam Cooke was shot and killed at a South Central L.A. motel in December of 1964. Though officially ruled a justifiable homicide, friends and family have never accepted official accounts of what happened that night; but Cooke, known as the "King of Soul," continues to live on in his peerless recordings.

Suggested Songs:

You Send Me (1957)
(What A) Wonderful World (1960)
Bring It On Home to Me (1962)
A Change Is Gonna Come (1964)

#110 Public Enemy
Began Recording: 1987
Peak: 1988 - 1992
Genres: Hip-Hop; Political Rap Group

Public Enemy is celebrated today for helping hip-hop mature into a more socially conscious art form. The group was the brainchild of lead rapper and principal lyricist Carlton Ridenhour, who goes by the name of Chuck D. He teamed with a Long Island college friend William Drayton, better known as Flavor Flav, who acted as a back-up rapper and comic foil; a crack production team known as the Bomb Squad; and two others, Professor Griff and Terminator X, who no longer are active with the group.

Signed by Rick Rubin, Public Enemy's 1987 debut album was not a hit, but they exploded into mainstream consciousness and controversy and onto the charts with their next three highly acclaimed LPs, *It Takes a Nation of Millions to Hold Us Back*, *Fear of a Black Planet*, and *Apocalypse 91… The Enemy Strikes Back*. With lyrics that eschewed the celebration of material bling, gangbanging, mindless partying, and sexual conquest, Public Enemy instead was all about examining the exploitation of Black America with a clear call for revolutionary self-empowerment. This strong socially conscious focus was wedded to a raw, dense, sonically inventive soundscape that perfectly complemented the street credibility of the group. As Chuck D put it, "Rap music is the invisible TV station that Black America never had."

Memorable Public Enemy tracks include "Don't Believe the Hype," still relevant for its prodding to look past the "fake news;" "Black Steel in the Hour of Chaos," with a narrator who says "No" to Uncle Sam's draft notice and to a prison cell; "Burn Hollywood Down" and "Who Stole the Soul?," both taking on the culture's stereotyping and exploiting Black men and women; and the iconic "Fight the Power," which contains the telling insight that Chuck D's heroes are not to be found on U.S. postage stamps.

Public Enemy, though not as high profile as they once were, continue to make relevant, conscious music, and they've been recognized by their inclusion in the Rock & Roll Hall of Fame.

Suggested Songs:

Rebel without a Pause (1987)
Black Steel in the Hour of Chaos (1989)
Fight the Power (1989)
Can't Truss It (1991)

#109 The Velvet Underground
Began Recording: 1966
Peak: 1967 - 1970
Genres: Experimental/Avant-garde Rock Band

Formed in the mid-1960s in New York City and over by the early '70s, The Velvet Underground were decidedly unsuccessful commercially, but their reach and legend has only grown since then such that revered music critic Robert Christgau has called them the "third most important band of the '60s," after the Beatles and James Brown and His Famous Flames.

They were led by former lit major Lou Reed, who was the band's primary writer, lead vocalist, and guitarist, and John Cale, a classically trained multi-instrumentalist who favored the electric viola, who helped create the experimental heft of the band's first two LPs. Cale was fired by Reed in 1968 over creative differences and was replaced by Doug Yule. Sterling Morrison and Moe Tucker added support with guitars and drums. Sponsored by pop artist Andy Warhol, the Velvets created four unique, groundbreaking, highly influential albums between 1967 and 1970, profoundly influencing a plethora of genres that followed—punk, post-punk, alternative, experimental, indie, and new wave. Artists such as David Bowie, Joy Division, the Sex Pistols, R.E.M., Talking Heads, U2, and countless others have acknowledged their debt to the Velvets.

With story songs that "humanized social underdogs," the Velvet Underground's themes of sexual deviance, drug use, and despair were too dark for their time, but their most iconic songs have only grown in stature with each passing year: the moving meditation on an empty life, Warhol's favorite, "All Tomorrow's Parties;" the gritty "mini-movie" about scoring drugs, " I'm Waiting for the Man;" the harrowing, controversial "Heroin;" the folk-rock ballad for a lost love, "Pale Blue Eyes;" the transcendent ambivalence of "Sweet Jane;" and Reed's atypical celebration of musical discovery, "Rock & Roll." In 1996, they were inducted into the Rock & Roll Hall of Fame.

Suggested Songs:

All Tomorrow's Parties (w. Nico) (1966)
I'm Waiting for the Man (1967)
Sweet Jane (1970)
Rock & Roll (1970)

#108 Marian Anderson (1897 - 1993)
Began Recording: 1923
Peak: 1935 - 1963
Genres: Classical; Spirituals; opera Singer

Best known for shattering racial barriers, Marian Anderson was also a brilliant contralto who could also sing in the soprano range, possessing a voice that appears "once in a hundred years," according to famed conductor Arturo Toscanini.

Born in Philadelphia, Marian began singing in her Baptist Church choir at the age of six, transitioning to adult choirs as she moved into her teens. She was so impressive that several organizations raised money so that she could train properly. Winning a contest brought her the opportunity to sing in 1925 with the New York Philharmonic, and, by 1928, she was performing at Carnegie Hall. Touring the United States, she regularly faced racial prejudice, denied entrance again and again to hotels and restaurants in many of the cities where she sang. She was a big hit in Europe in the 1930s, and, in 1939, she performed at the White House for the Roosevelts and the King of England.

That same year, she was barred from singing at Washington D.C.'s Constitution Hall by the Daughters of the American Revolution. The NAACP launched a protest, which was given a great boost when Eleanor Roosevelt quit the DAR, prompting many other members to follow suit. An alternative concert was arranged for Easter Sunday on the steps of the Lincoln Memorial, with 75,000 attending and millions more listening to the live radio broadcast.

Anderson sang classical and opera numbers as well as traditional African-American spirituals. As musician Rhiannon Giddens wrote, "By performing spirituals in the concert hall, Anderson linked generations of listeners to Black American history."

In 1955, at the age of 58, Marian shattered another color line by making her debut at the New York Metropolitan Opera. Honored with the

Presidential Medal of Freedom, a lifetime Grammy, and countless honorary doctorates, Anderson truly paved the way for other greats such as Leontyne Price and Jessye Norman.

Suggested Songs:

Ave Maria (1936)
Nobody Knows the Trouble I See (1948)
Crucifixion (1948)
Re dell'abisso affrettati (1955) (1989 compilation)

#107 The Supremes

Began Recording: 1960 (as Primettes); 1961 (as Supremes)
Peak: 1964 - 1969
Genres: R&B/Soul; Pop Vocal Group

They were three young teenagers from Detroit—Florence Ballard, Mary Wilson, and Diana Ross—singing late '50s R&B cover music at local dances and talent shows. When Ross' neighbor, the slightly older Smokey Robinson, began to break through at Berry Gordy's local Motown label, they pressed him for an audition. Initially turned down by Gordy, the girls were persistent and got signed, changing their name from The Primettes to The Supremes.

From 1960 to 1963 they had little success with their first seven singles, but there was something about the R&B driving, up-tempo "When the Lovelight Starts Shining Through His Eyes" that spelled hit, with the studio band, the Funk Brothers, featuring guitar, piano, sax, vibraphone, booming bass and drums and a Phil Spector-like wall-of-sound (complete with hand-claps and foot-stomps), written and produced by the crack team of Holland-Dozier-Holland, that proved to be the winning formula over the next six years, culminating in 12 *Billboard* Hot 100 #1 singles.

At first, the girls shared the leads, but with their first hit, Gordy decided to move Ross to the front with her thin, but bell-like, bright, dulcet vocals, while Ballard and Wilson ably handled the silky, elegant backgrounds, so often underappreciated. From '64 to '65, five straight melodic singles topped the charts, all using the same basic team—'Where Did Our Love Go," "Baby Love," "Come See About Me," "Stop! In the Name of Love," and "Back in My Arms Again." They retooled after a near miss, adding strings and a new, soaring arrangement with "I Hear a Symphony," then added four more in a row—"You Can't Hurry Love," "You Keep Me Hanging On," "Love Is Here and Now You're Gone," and "The Happening."

By 1967, they were being called Diana Ross & the Supremes, foreshadowing Ross's departure two years hence. Ballard was fired as she struggled with alcohol and depression and was replaced by Cindy Birdsong. The final iteration of the Supremes came to an end in 1977, but today they are recognized as the most successful female group in recording history, members of the Rock and Vocal Group Halls of Fame.

Suggested Songs:

Baby Love (1964)
Stop! In the Name of Love (1965)
I Hear a Symphony (1965)
My World Is Empty Without You (1965)

#106 Benny Goodman (1909 - 1986)
Began Recording: 1926 (as sideman); 1934 (bandleader)
Peak: 1934 - 1942
Genres: Jazz-Swing; classical Clarinetist/Bandleader

A pioneer in the racial integration of American music, Benny Goodman was also at the center of two of the storied moments in popular music history.

Benjamin Goodman was the 9th of 12 children born to Russian immigrant parents fleeing the Jewish pogroms. Desperately poor, his Chicago neighborhood, "Bloody Maxwell," was the site of regular, violent gang warfare. Benny's dad saw that he received clarinet lessons at a local synagogue, and, by 13, Benny had a musicians' union card. By 14, he was raising eyebrows for his virtuoso playing. Quitting school to join Ben Pollack's Orchestra, by 1928 Benny was rooming with Glenn Miller, and the two co-wrote and recorded "Room 1411," named for their New York apartment number. After eight years as an in-demand session player, Goodman put together his own band, The Benny Goodman Orchestra, with the help of Columbia legend John Hammond. Hired to play the NBC radio program *Let's Dance*, Benny turned to Black composer/bandleader Fletcher Henderson for help in arranging and teaching his band members the style known as swing. Their 1935 Palomar Ballroom stint in Los Angeles is considered today the start of the Swing Era. By that time, Goodman had scored a #1 hit with "Moonglow," a standard that's been covered more than 500 times, and the lively "King Porter Stomp" was rising on the charts. In 1938, Goodman became the first jazz bandleader to bring an orchestra to the white, classical music bastion, New York's Carnegie Hall. With a racially integrated band, including players from Duke Ellington and Count Basie's outfits, Benny Goodman helped, at long last, realize jazz music's full embrace by the American elite and mainstream. Critic Bruce Elder called it "the single most important jazz or popular music concert in history."

A perfectionist who practiced all his life and was very hard on those who played for him, Goodman is remembered today for his pioneering work with the likes of Henderson, Teddy Wilson, and Lionel Hampton, and "The King of Swing" is widely considered one of the great clarinetists of all-time.

Suggested Songs:

Room 1411 (1928)
King Porter Stomp (1935)
Stompin' at the Savoy (1936)
Sing, Sing, Sing (With a Swing) (1937)

#105 Muddy Waters (1915 - 1983)

Began Recording: 1941
Peak: 1950 - 1964; 1977 - 1981
Genres: Chicago Blues & Delta Blues Singer/Songwriter/Instrumentalist

Fellow blues legend B.B. King said of him, "It's going to be years and years before most people realize how greatly he contributed to American music."

Born McKinley Morganfield in rural Mississippi, he was raised by his maternal grandmother on a plantation near Clarksdale and gained his nickname by frolicking in the nearby swampy creeks. By five he was playing harmonica, and he learned to sing, like so many, in church. Working in the cotton fields, he sold a horse at 17 to buy his first guitar. Influenced by the Delta Blues style which features acoustic slide guitar and harmonica, Muddy was soon playing throughout the region. He caught the attention of Alex Lomax, who recorded Waters in his cabin for his Library of Congress project. Waters received two discs and $20.

In 1943, Muddy joined the Great Migration northward to Chicago. The following year, he got his first electric guitar, put together a band, and was soon recording. From 1948 through 1958, he was a regular on the R&B charts. Among his classic recordings are "Rolling Stone," which later inspired Brian Jones to name his new, British blues-rock band; "I'm Your Hoochie Coochie Man," with its stop-time blues feel and suggestive lyrics; "Manish Boy," featuring sexual bragging with a racial subtext asserting that the singer is a man, not a boy; and "Got My Mojo Working," a classic that has influenced countless rock & rollers.

By the late '50s and early '60s, Waters had gained an international following, especially among younger, white, blues-oriented rockers. With his profound and subtle, melodic and crying, sliding guitar sound coupled with his nuanced, passionate, soulful singing, Waters soon became a generous mentor to a generation of determined acolytes—to Eric Clapton he became an encouraging teacher and a father figure, and the Rolling Stones never forgot the debt they owed Waters for the profound ways he helped shape their music. A member of the Blues and Rock Halls of Fame, Waters is recognized today as the greatest ambassador of the Chicago Blues.

Suggested Songs:

Rolling Stone (1950)
I'm Your Hoochie Coochie Man (1954)
Manish Boy (Mannish Boy) (1955 - 1997 release)
Got My Mojo Working (1956)

#104 Alicia Keys (1981 - present)
Began Recording: 1997 (soundtrack); 2001 (solo)
Peak: 2001 - 2013
Genres: R&B; Soul Singer/Songwriter/Pianist

She was born Alicia Cook and grew up in the gritty Hell's Kitchen section of Manhattan. Her family was racially mixed and, unfortunately, ultimately fractured. Alicia began classical piano lessons at the age of seven, and her mom introduced her to jazz. She was accepted into the competitive Professional Performing Arts School at 12 and immersed herself in music—singing, playing, and composing, drawing from R&B after discovering Marvin Gaye, as well as from Beethoven, Chopin, Ellington, and Davis. By the age of 14, record companies were already after her, and at 15 she signed with Columbia. She graduated from high school at 16 as class valedictorian and enrolled in Columbia University. Trying to hone her musical vision and study full time at an Ivy League school proved to be too much, and she chose to drop school. Before long she found herself in a tug-of-war with her record label as Alicia had an artistic vision the label refused to honor. With the help of Kerry Brothers, Alicia decided to record on her own, eventually freeing herself from Columbia and going with recording legend Clive Davis' label.

In 2001, Alicia Keys, as she now called herself, was ready. Her first LP, *Songs in a Minor*, debuted at #1 on the *Billboard* 200, and featured the chart-topping "Fallin'," with its simple story of falling in and out and in and out of love, and "A Woman's Worth," which introduced the perennial Keys theme that women deserve to and can demand to be treated well. At year's end, *Songs in a Minor* took home five Grammys, with Alicia claiming the coveted Best New Artist award. Her next three albums all came in at #1. There were more Grammys to claim and memorable singles—"If I Ain't Got You," with its soulful take on what is and isn't important; "My Boo," a smash duet with R&B heartthrob, Usher; "No One," a 2007 mid-tempo love ballad; and "Superwoman," another anthem encouraging women to find their own strength.

Keys has continued to release soul/R&B gems, often with bits of classical, jazz, hip-hop, and gospel touches. "Empire State of Mind (Part II)" saw her following up on a duet that featured JAY-Z and expressed her love for her native city, while "Girl on Fire" offered another powerful pro-woman message.

Keys has found time to branch into acting, to write children's books, and for philanthropy. She has been especially involved in trying to make a difference in the lives of children and those suffering from HIV/AIDS. She continually speaks out for women, for underdogs, and for racial equality.

Alicia Keys is but 42-years-old, yet she has already won 15 Grammys and has been called the "female Stevie Wonder" for her musical prowess and artistic vision.

Suggested Songs:

If I Ain't Got You (2004)
Empire State of Mind (Part II) Broken Down (2010)
Girl on Fire (2012)
Underdog (2020)

#103 Bessie Smith (1894? - 1937)

Began Recording: 1923
Peak: 1923 - 1929
Genres: Blues; jazz Singer/songwriter

She sang with absolute authority, regardless of the fact that Bessie Smith, the "Empress of the Blues," was a Black woman plying her trade in 1920s and '30s America. Orphaned before she was 10 and left in the care of an older sister, she was soon singing on the streets of her native Tennessee for coins. At 18, she was hired as a dancer for a traveling minstrel show that featured blues legend Ma Rainey, who took young Bessie under her wing. Soon Bessie herself was singing as a soloist throughout the south and the east coast. In 1923, she began recording for Columbia Records and had a huge hit with "Downhearted Blues," in which she laments unrequited love but remains, nonetheless, hopeful that things will change. Success followed throughout the '20s with such hits as "St. Louis Blues," with a young Louis Armstrong on cornet; "Careless Love Blues;" "Empty Bed Blues;" and the Depression Era prophecy of 1929, "Nobody Knows You When You're Down and Out." By this time, Smith was the highest earning Black entertainer in America.

Singing of poverty, working class hardships, loss and grief, sex and drinking, or protesting a rigged justice system, Smith delivered in a powerful contralto with an earthy, honest, improvisational style; her "race records" resonated like no artist before her. Considered by some as "rough" or "low-class," she knew what it was like to be cheated by her record company and her husband, to face the perils of segregation, to be stabbed and arrested, to brave the difficulties of bisexuality in an intolerant age, and to struggle with alcohol and her own fierce temper. An early advocate of female empowerment and independence, Smith had a notable impact on such future artists as Billie Holiday, Mahalia Jackson, Aretha Franklin, and Janis Joplin.

Bessie's career declined in the '30s, a result of the Great Depression, and she died tragically in a car crash in 1937. The Blues, Jazz, Rock, and Women's Halls of Fame have all recognized her artistry and influence posthumously.

Suggested Songs:

Downhearted Blues (1923)
St. Louis Blues (1925)
Careless Love Blues (1925)
Nobody Knows You When You're Down and Out (1929)

#102 Bruno Mars (1985 - present)
Began Recording: 2009 (as guest vocalist); 2010 (solo)
Peak: 2010 - 2023
Genres: Pop; R&B; Funk; Soul; reggae rock Singer/Songwriter/
Instrumentalist

He's 38 years old, one of the great live performers of his generation, and he already has 30 Grammy nominations and 15 wins to his name. Born and raised into a multi-ethnic, performing, musical family in Honolulu, Peter Hernandez was given the nickname Bruno as a baby. An accomplished multi-instrumentalist, at one time Bruno performed Elvis and Michael Jackson impersonations. Drawing from a wide range of musical inspirations, from early rock & roll to doo-wop, from Motown to the Beatles, from Jimi Hendrix to Amy Winehouse, Bruno moved to L.A. in 2003 to pursue a musical career. For the next six years he slowly honed his craft as a performer, songwriter, and producer, and took on the stage name Bruno Mars.

His 2010 debut LP, *Doo-Wops & Hooligans*—a pop album with reggae, R&B, and rock flavors—became a huge best seller worldwide and produced two monster singles—"Just the Way You Are," a catchy pop ode to the woman he loves, and "Grenade," which looks at the pain of unrequited love. Mars has continued to release huge chart-toppers on both sides of the Atlantic—"Locked Out of Heaven," with its reggae-rock Police vibe; "When I Was Your Man," a confessional piano ballad that shows off his considerable vocal chops; "Uptown Funk," an inescapable and irresistible piece of funk pop with producer Mark Ronson; the Grammy-sweeping LP, *24K Magic*; and the old-school soul duet, "Leave the Door Open," with Anderson .Paak.

Bruno Mars has played the Super Bowl twice and his live shows have been thrilling audiences since his major debut over a dozen years ago with his on-stage echoes of James Brown, Michael, and Prince. Already among the best-selling artists of all time, the sky seems to be the limit for the talented Mars.

Suggested Songs:

Grenade (2010)

When I Was Your Man (2012)

Uptown Funk (w. Mark Ronson) (2014)

Leave the Door Open (w. Anderson .Paak, Silk Sonic) (2021)

#101 Jimmie Rodgers (1897 - 1933)

Began Recording: 1927

Peak: 1928 - 1932

Genres: Country; Blues; Folk Singer/songwriter

Calling him the "Father" of country music and country's first superstar does not begin to do justice to Jimmie Rodgers.

Born in rural Alabama, Jimmie lost his mom while he was still a little boy. Shuffling between various relatives and his father, he was introduced to various forms of popular music by an aunt. By the age of 13, he had twice run away from home, organizing traveling musical shows. His father, a railroad man, brought him back home both times and offered him a choice: school or work. Jimmie, at 14, decided to work with his dad on the railroad, working his way up, in time, to a brakeman, all the while absorbing the music all around him, particularly the white southern folk and "hillbilly" styles, and the work and blues idiom from Black railway workers. In 1924, Rodgers fell ill and was diagnosed with tuberculosis. Doctors warned him to slow down, but he decided to use this as an opportunity to focus on the music career he had dreamed of since childhood. He played tent shows, street corners, and formed bands.

In 1927, Jimmie landed a weekly spot on a North Carolina radio station and formed a band. When he got word that Ralph Peer of the Victor record company was looking to do "field recordings" in Tennessee, Jimmie traveled there and recorded his first two tracks as a solo guitarist and singer. They were modest hits, and Jimmie soon traveled to New York to ask for a second session. Out of that session came "T for Texas" (aka "Blue Yodel #1"). The song became a huge hit and Jimmie was an overnight star. For the next five and a half years he recorded regularly, cutting 110 tracks in all; he toured much of the country, playing theaters and halls, did radio shows, even made a prototype music video called *The Singing Brakeman*. Many of his shows and records were solo performances, with Jimmie playing rudimentary guitar accompanying his distinctive laid back singing, punctuated by his trademark yodel, his music an eclectic blend of traditional southern rural folk and African-American blues, with elements of gospel, traditional pop, and Dixieland jazz mixed in. He was unique and beloved. He sang about anything and everything—love and lust, rambling and gambling, railroads and murder. Some of his best-known titles include "In the Jailhouse Now," "Waiting for a Train," and "T.B. Blues".

By early 1933, it was clear Jimmie was dying. He traveled to New York in May to cut 24 sides; he got through 12, and two days later died of a lung hemorrhage.

Today he is a recognized giant. Artists as diverse as Johnny Cash, Bob Dylan, and Lynyrd Skynyrd have cited his influence. He is one of the few artists recognized by four major Halls of Fame—Country, Blues, Rock, and Songwriters.

Suggested Songs:

In the Jailhouse Now (1928)
Waiting for a Train (1929)
Blue Yodel #9 (aka Standing on the Corner) (1930)
I'm Free from the Chain Gang Now (1933)

#100 Janis Joplin (1943 - 1970)
Began Recording: 1966
Peak: 1968 - 1971
Genres: Rock; Blues Singer

Blazing like a meteor across the musical heavens in the late '60s, if you blinked you might have missed her, so sudden was her rise; and, just as suddenly, she was gone. Perhaps the greatest white female blues singer ever, Janis Joplin's voice was coarse and raspy, certainly not to everyone's taste. But she had no imitators; she was an original. Though she could whisper her way through a ballad, delicately, melodically, movingly, she was primarily a screamer. As a live performer she was a force of nature. Robert Christgau described how the press at the Monterey Pop Festival were "flabbergasted at how intense it was;" Jon Pareles noted that she was "overpowering and deeply vulnerable."

Out of Port Arthur, Texas, Janis found herself increasingly out of step with her peers as she grew up and moved to San Francisco to sing the blues and find acceptance. However, an early scare with heroin sent her scrambling back home. She couldn't stay away long, however, returning to California and hooking up with psychedelic rock band Big Brother and the Holding Company. With Janis on vocals, their debut LP did little commercially, but the 1967 Monterey Pop Festival, featuring Joplin's soulful rendition of Big Mama Thornton's "Ball and Chain," created tremendous word of mouth excitement, and Big Brother's follow-up album, *Cheap Thrills*, rose to #1 with "Piece of My Heart" and Gershwin's "Summertime" two of the standout tracks. The following year, Janis released a solo effort, *I Got Dem Ol' Kozmic Blues Again Mama!*. Her star could not have been brighter, but, in October 1970, Janis Joplin was found dead in her hotel room, an apparent victim of an accidental heroin overdose. She was 27 years old. Ironically, her biggest hits were released posthumously: the chart-topping album *Pearl* and her lone #1 single, "Me and Bobby McGee," penned by Kris Kristofferson. A half-century later, her charismatic performances are considered legendary.

Suggested Songs:

Summertime (w. Big Brother...) (1968)

Piece of My Heart (w. Big Brother...) (1968)

Kozmic Blues (1969)

Little Girl Blue (1969)

Me and Bobby McGee (1971)

#99 R.E.M.
Began Recording: 1981
Peak: 1988 - 1997
Genres: Alternative Rock Band

R.E.M. is said to mark the transition between post-punk and new wave to alternative rock. As such, they were one of the best-selling bands of the '90s. Formed in 1980 while its four members were students at the University of Georgia, R.E.M. began largely as a cover band. They may or may not have taken their name from the acronym for rapid eye movement, but they were Mike Mills, bassist and background singer, who was called "nerdy" and "goody-goody" by drummer Bill Berry, the self-described would-be "teen-age hoodlum;" Peter Buck, guitarist and avid musicologist; and Michael Stipe, lead vocalist and resident eccentric.

Dropping out of school to devote themselves full time to music, by 1981 they had recorded "Radio Free Europe" with its distinctive R.E.M. features: a jangly or chiming Byrds-like guitar and cryptic, mumbled lyrics. By 1982, they had signed with small label I.R.S., and, over the next six years, they wrote (all four took songwriting credits), recorded (usually an album a year), and toured, incessantly. From the start they were critical darlings, garnering raves from *Rolling Stone*, *NME*, and *The New York Times*. Albums such as *Murmur*, *Reckoning*, and *Lifes Rich Pageant* and songs like "So. Central Rain (I'm Sorry)" and "Fall on Me" made them the nation's #1 college and underground band. In 1987, they scored their first mainstream hit with "The One I Love," a barbed and ironic take on the usual love formula song. Soon they were touring stadiums and being termed "America's Best Rock & Roll Band."

Switching labels and taking a six-year hiatus from touring, they became superstars in 1991 with their biggest selling album, *Out of Time*, which hit #1 in the U.S., Britain, and Austria and featured their best-known single, the mandolin-driven "Losing My Religion," a song Stipe says has nothing to do with religion and everything to do with unrequited love. Their follow-up

LP, *Automatic for the People*, was likewise a multi-million seller and gained even greater critical praise with such featured tracks as the "take charge" anthem, "Drive;" the Andy Kaufman tribute, "Man on the Moon;" the comforting "Everybody Hurts;" and the piano-orchestra ode to memory, "Nightswimming."

In 1995, returning to the road, three of the members wound up in operating rooms—Berry, with a brain aneurysm; Mills, for abdominal surgery; and Stipes, needing emergency hernia surgery. After the 1996 worldwide chart-topping *New Adventures in Hi-Fi*, drummer Bill Berry announced he was retiring to go be a farmer. The split was amicable, and R.E.M. carried on as a threesome until 2011, when the rest decided that they too had had enough. R.E.M.'s impact has been huge on alternative rock; Nirvana, Pearl Jam, Radiohead, Coldplay, and the Pixies have all paid homage, and they remain beloved to this day.

Suggested Songs:

So. Central Rain (1984)
The One I Love (1987)
Losing My Religion (1991)
Man on the Moon (1992)
Everybody Hurts (1993)

#98 Tom Petty (1950 - 2017)
Began Recording: 1971
Peak: 1979 - 1995
Genres: Rock Singer/Songwriter/Guitarist/Bandleader

We are "just an American rock band," said Tom Petty. Inducted into the Rock & Roll Hall of Fame with his longtime group, the Heartbreakers, Petty also built a successful career as a solo artist and an in-demand collaborator.

He hailed from Gainesville, Florida, and, as a child, regularly suffered verbal and physical abuse from his father. He found refuge in music, meeting Elvis on a movie set in neighboring Ocala when he was 10 and was inspired at 13 when he watched the Beatles on *The Ed Sullivan Show*. Soon he was learning guitar and piano and making his own music. In 1970 he formed a band, Mudcrutch, which cut two singles in five years before disbanding. Signed to Leon Russell's label, he took two ex-Mudcrutch mates, Mike Campbell, a guitarist, and Benmont Tench, on keyboards, then added Ron Blair on bass and Stan Lynch, a drummer, and released the eponymous *Tom Petty and the Heartbreakers* in 1976. It was not a huge hit, but two songs in particular drew a lot of attention—"Breakdown," the initial single, and "American Girl," which is recognized today as a rock & roll classic. In many ways, the track is a perfect representation of the Petty sound— guitar driven, melodic, tight rhythm section, simple yet ambiguous lyrics, delivered in Petty's distinctive nasal twang, and completely compelling!

Over the next 41 years, Petty would release a slew of hard-edge, often anthemic, tight, memorable tunes, sometimes with the Byrds—Beatles-sounding Heartbreakers, other times as a soloist, and twice recording with the makeshift supergroup The Traveling Wilburys. Among the best-loved Petty tracks are "Refugee," from the best-selling *Damn the Torpedoes*, with Tom's typical challenge to stand tall in the face of adversity; "I Won't Back Down," with its similar ethos; "Running Down a Dream," with its blazing guitar outro; "Free Falling," with trademark ambivalent lyrics; and "Learning to Fly," another of Petty's inspirational "starting over" numbers.

Petty had a history of not backing down, famously taking on his record companies several times—once in protest to having his contract transferred without his permission, another time because the men in suits wanted to tack an extra dollar onto the price of an LP when Petty became a star. "Too much," said Petty, and the company relented. He fought the Goodrich tire company and George W. Bush over the unauthorized use of his music and won both times. When he slid into a heroin addiction, which he called an "ugly fucking thing," after the dissolution of his 22-year marriage, he licked it with rehab because he didn't want to be dependent on drugs. Sadly, he died in 2017 of an accidental toxic mix of prescription drugs. He was battling a broken hip, emphysema, depression, and sleep deprivation. A much-loved, one-of-a-kind, simple rocker who was always himself, Tom Petty is sorely missed.

Suggested Songs:

American Girl (1977)
Refugee (1980)
Running Down a Dream (1989)
I Won't Back Down (1989)
Mary Jane's Last Dance (1993)

#97 Kendrick Lamar (1987 - present)

Began Recording: 2003 (mixtape as K.Dot); 2009 (as Kendrick Lamar)
Peak: 2012 - 2023
Genres: Hip-Hop; jazz rap Rapper/Songwriter

He's been called the "new king of hip-hop" and the master of storytelling rap. Born Kendrick Lamar Duckworth and raised on the mean streets of Compton, in South Central L.A., young Kendrick imbibed the music and culture of his neighborhood for better and worse, several times witnessing shootings, but he kept gang life at arms length, becoming instead a straight-A student who loved to write stories, poems, and lyrics depicting what he saw and felt. At 16, he recorded a mixtape under the pseudonym K.Dot, and that got him signed to Top Dawg Entertainment, an independent record label. A series of increasingly successful mixtapes and the release of his critically acclaimed debut album, *Section.80,* followed and caught the attention of rap producer and star Dr. Dre, who signed him to his label. With Dre as his mentor and now calling himself Kendrick Lamar, in 2012 he released the critically acclaimed *Good Kid, M.A.A.D City*, a loose narrative rap LP about his teenage years growing up in Compton, featuring such unflinching tracks as the alcohol-soaked "Swimming Pools (Drank);" "Money Trees," with its reminiscence of young sex, deadly shootings, and ambivalent fantasies about money; and "Bitch, Don't Kill My Vibe," wherein the sinner looks for peace.

Lamar was suddenly feted for his sharp wordplay, cinematic storytelling, and harsh, but honest portrayal of life in Compton. Recurring themes in his work include sin and redemption, violence, drug abuse, and the personal costs of trying to be a better person even as the daily, sometimes spectacular, failures are displayed for all to see. Kendrick refuses to categorize his style, calling it "human music." With an adventurous musical vibe that often veers into jazz and funk, he cites Tupac, Eminem, Snoop Dogg, and Miles Davis as among his influences. At the same time, Kendrick himself has touched countless rappers, even inspiring David Bowie to dig a bit deeper.

Lamar's next three albums have continued his exploration. 2015's *To Pimp a Butterfly* includes tracks like the "Black Lives Matter" anthem, "Alright;" the self-reflective "i;" and Obama favorite "How Much a Dollar Cost" and is already legendary. 2017's *Damn* was honored with a Pulitzer Prize for music, making Kendrick the first non-jazz or classical artist to be so recognized. In 2022, he released the much anticipated *Mr. Morale & the Big Steppers* which seems to explore the dichotomy faced by both society and the individual: the toxic, cultural temptations to which we all too frequently fall prey and the clear light of conscience and striving for deliverance.

Not without his detractors, Lamar has been criticized, by some, as misogynistic and overly ambiguous about the violent, dark forces he seeks to expose, but he calls himself a committed Christian, and, as Spencer Kornhaber eloquently puts it, one, who by "speaking the unspeakable, can heal."

Suggested Songs:

Money Trees (2012)
How Much a Dollar Cost (2015)
i (2015)
DUCKWORTH (2017)
Mirror (2022)

#96 Coldplay
Began Recording: 1999
Peak: 2001 - 2016
Genres: Pop Rock; alternative rock Band

They were four London university students, each with a childhood musical background, and they have become, arguably, the most popular band of the 21st century. Chris Martin is the piano playing frontman, chief songwriter and lead vocalist, though he shares writing credits and royalties with his bandmates—Johnny Buckland, lead guitarist; Guy Berryman on bass; Will Champion, drummer.

In 1998, still students, they self-produced an EP which led to a 1999 small label debut single and second EP, which garnered just enough attention to land them at Parlophone. *Parachute* reached the top of the U.K. charts in 2000, the first of their nine consecutive albums to go to #1. "Yellow," a mid-tempo romantic track, was the breakout single. Their 2002 second LP, *A Rush of Blood to the Head*, made them international superstars and features three of their most defining singles—"In My Place," a chiming, guitar-driven regretful ballad; "The Scientist," the highly acclaimed piano ballad that achingly describes the difficulty of making love work; and "Clocks," the Grammy-winning, melodious, pop-rock ode to a lover, God, or the self.

Coldplay quickly gained a reputation as an arena filling, color-drenched live act with particularly partisan fans. The hit albums and songs kept appearing every couple of years—*X&Y* with the comforting "Fix You;" *Viva la Vida or Death and All His Friends* with the anthemic "Viva la Vida" (or "Long Live Life"), a political or personal rumination on how the mighty do fall; *Mylo Xyloto*, an electronic sci-fi rock opera featuring "Paradise," with its longing for a utopia in the midst of an often-soul crushing world. The somber-toned *Ghost Stories*, the upbeat *A Head Full of Dreams*, the politically tinged *Everyday Life*, and the space-themed *Music of the Spheres* followed in the next decade, continuing their string of chart toppers.

Critical darlings at the start of their career, Coldplay, increasingly, became polarizing in the manner of U2. Jon Pareles of *The New York Times* famously called them "the most insufferable band of the decade," complaining of Martin's straining singing style and "moping" tone. Others called them middle of the road, overly earnest, trite, sentimental, and mediocre, as though they'd hit upon a formula that worked and were afraid to deviate too far, lest they offend their followers. It became fashionable, in certain circles, to hate Coldplay. On the other hand, they are a musically sound, well-produced outfit that has a knack for writing catchy melodies with hopeful lyrics that have touched millions. They have also been more willing to experiment than often given credit for, collaborating with the likes of Brian Eno, Rihanna, and BTS. Winner of seven Grammys and nine Brit Awards, artists as diverse as JAY-Z and Ed Sheeran have praised their work.

Suggested Songs:

The Scientist (2002)
Clocks (2003)
Viva la Vida (2008)
Paradise (2011)
Coloratura (2021)

#95 John Lennon (1940 - 1980)

Began Recording: 1962 (w. Beatles); 1968 (wo. Beatles)
Peak: 1971 - 1975; 1980
Genres: Rock; Soft Rock; experimental Singer/Songwriter

John Lennon will forever be associated in the public mind with Paul McCartney and the Beatles, but as he pointed out in an interview three days before his tragic death, he was John Lennon before and John Lennon after his stint as a Beatle.

A sensitive child, he was virtually abandoned by both his parents, and though his mother Julia was around him regularly, he was raised by his aunt Mimi. At 16, he received his first guitar from his mom; a year later, she was run over on a Liverpool street, traumatizing the young Lennon, who grew increasingly rebellious and angry. Soon, however, he was world-famous as a Beatle until he had had enough, quitting the band in 1969. Lennon had become involved romantically the previous year with avant-garde, multi-media artist Yoko Ono, and the two had married.

Lennon's recorded work, apart from the Beatles, began in 1968 and '69 as he and Yoko released three collaborative albums of highly experimental music consisting of a seemingly random mix of ambient noises, vocal screams, screeches, growls, spoken phrases, and whispering, along with disparate instrumental snippets. Mostly trashed by critics and often categorized as noise, the LPs failed to sell.

Many of Lennon's more traditional releases have earned him high praise. His 1970 *John Lennon/Plastic Ono Band* is recognized today as a masterwork of highly confessional, vulnerable tracks such as the moving, abandonment snapshot "Mother;" "God," with its list of what John does not and does believe in; and the politically charged "Working Class Hero." A year later, he released his signature song "Imagine" from the LP of the same name. "Imagine," with it's gorgeous, hymn-like melody, was not only a worldwide hit, but is also one of the most celebrated and beloved songs of the 20th century with its dream of transcendent unity and peace; it is also reviled in certain circles as hippie, pie-in-the-sky, anti-religion propaganda.

As Lennon's star was ascending once again, he and Yoko moved to New York and became increasingly involved in anti-war and leftist causes, drawing the attention and the ire of the Nixon Administration. There was a four-year effort to have him deported, but it eventually failed. In 1976, after the birth of John and Yoko's son, Sean, Lennon retired from the music scene for the next four and a half years, choosing instead to be the father he never had and failed to be for his first son. In late August 1980, John and Yoko returned to the studio, releasing *Double Fantasy* in November of the same year. The album featured such warm, life-affirming tracks as "Woman" and "Watching the Wheels;" but on December 8, as John and Yoko returned to their Upper West Side apartment, John Lennon was murdered by a deranged, former fan. Lennon, the self- described irritable, selfish, would-be artist, who had finally found a measure of peace in his life and work, was gone, but it is clear his music will live on.

Suggested Songs:

God (1970)
Imagine (1971)
Jealous Guy (1971)
Woman (1980)
Watching the Wheels (1980)

#94 The Doors

Began Recording: 1967
Peak: 1967 - 1971
Genres: Rock-psychedelic, blues, jazz, hard, soft Rock Band

In 1965, two UCLA film students met on the sands of Venice Beach, agreeing to combine their talents and planting the seeds of one of the most consequential bands of the late-'60s psychedelic era. They were keyboardist Ray Manzarek and poet Jim Morrison, who, together with guitarist and sometime writer Robby Krieger and drummer John Densmore, became the Doors, taking their name from Aldous Huxley's early psychedelic classic, *The Doors of Perception*.

With one of the most auspicious debut albums in music history, the 1967 self-titled release established the Doors as a dark, dangerous, underground alternative breaking into the peace and love mainstream. "Break on Through" introduced us to Morrison's uber-masculine, deep, bellowing baritone while Manzarek's distinctive, jazz-tinged organ riffs helped propel the Krieger-penned "Light My Fire" to the top of the charts and into music history as an acknowledged classic. Morrison's Oedipal "goodbye song," "The End," later made doubly famous in the film *Apocalypse Now*, signaled that this was no ordinary pop band.

Over the next four years, the Doors released five more studio LPs, two of which, *Strange Days* and *L.A. Woman*, have likewise achieved iconic status, and such celebrated tracks as Jim's ode to alienation, "People Are Strange;" the driving pop rock of "Touch Me;" the brilliant "L.A. Woman," which, some suggest, personifies Morrison's beloved city; Krieger's obsessive tribute to his wife, "Love Her Madly;" and the jazzy, doom-freighted, philosophy of "Riders on the Storm."

By 1971, Morrison's alcoholism was getting the better of him, and, after several highly publicized on-stage meltdowns and arrests, he retired to Paris for a short break. In July of that year, he was discovered by his longtime girlfriend in his bathtub, dead at 27; the cause of death, to this day, is unclear, but Morrison passed into myth.

Oliver Stone's 1991 biopic *The Doors* brought Morrison and his bandmates to the big screen, but was blasted by many for focusing, overmuch, on Morrison's abuse of alcohol. His struggles certainly were all too real, but so was the gifted, sensitive poet, which is how he saw himself. In 1993, the Rock & Roll Hall of Fame inducted the Doors, recognizing their "fusion of jazz, psychedelic rock and blues." To this day, the Doors' music continues to be played and celebrated.

Suggested Songs:

Light My Fire (1967)
The End (1967)
Touch Me (1968)
L.A. Woman (1971)
Riders on the Storm (1971)

#93 Cher (1946 - present)
Began Recording: 1963 (backup); 1965 (w. Sonny & Solo)
Peak: 1965 - 1967; 1971 - 1975; 1998 - 2005
Genres: Pop; Rock; Dance Singer

She's been written off and come back more times than Judy Garland. Born Cherilyn Sarkisian (she legally changed her name to Cher in 1978), she was raised largely by her mother, a part-time actress. When her mom was between husbands, money was tight. Drawn to a show business career, Cher quit school at 16 and moved to Hollywood, where she met Sonny Bono, 11 years her senior and working for record producer Phil Spector. The connection led her to sing background on several Spector records. Cher moved in with Bono, and soon he was promoting her as a soloist. Stage fright led her to enlist Sonny as her singing partner, and, in 1965, the duo had a breakout hit with "I Got You Babe," today a recognized folk-rock classic. Sonny & Cher were overnight stars and suddenly fashion icons with their striped bell-bottoms and vests. Cher also released solo material, scoring in '66 with "Bang Bang (My Baby Shot Me Down)."

By the late '60s, however, they were considered passé, as rock had taken a harder turn. Their brief stint as a nightclub act led to a network TV show in 1971, *The Sonny & Cher Comedy Hour*, which ran until 1974. Behind the scenes the marriage was disintegrating, but Cher was experiencing her first recording revival with three giant hits—"Gypsies, Tramps & Thieves," a story song of an itinerant family who did whatever they could to survive; "Half-Breed," about a mixed-race girl who never knew where she fit; and "Dark Lady," with it's violent love triangle.

In the late '70s, Cher found brief success with disco, but abruptly switched, unsuccessfully, to rock. Through much of the '80s, she focused on acting, surprising many with her talent. *Silkwood*, *Mask*, and *Moonlight* brought her acclaim and a Best Actress Oscar.

1989 saw another musical comeback with the pop rock LP *Heart of Stone*, but it was the 1998 single "Believe," from the album of the same name, that became the biggest hit of her career. It was #1 internationally, a Grammy winner, and a dance pop track that introduced the world to the new voice altering technique, Auto-Tune. In the 2000s, Cher has scarcely slowed down. Her 2002 - 2005 world tour was one of the most successful in history. She has had top-rated TV shows, Vegas residencies, and more hit albums.

Today, she is recognized, by many, as a feminist empowerment icon. With her distinctive contralto and often extreme fashion sense, she's a Diva among divas and artists as diverse as Gwen Stefani, Lady Gaga, and Kanye West have acknowledged her influence on their careers. *Rolling Stone* put it this way: "Cher… the one-woman embodiment of the whole gaudy story of pop music."

Suggested Songs:

I Got You Babe (w. Sonny) (1965)
Gypsies, Tramps & Thieves (1971)
If I Could Turn Back Time (1989)
Just Like Jesse James (1989)
Believe (1998)

#92 James Taylor (1948 - present)

Began Recording: 1967 (Flying Machine); 1968 (Solo)
Peak: 1970 - 1977
Genres: Folk Rock/Soft Rock: blues; country; pop Singer/Songwriter/Guitarist

He was a son of privilege—dad a successful doctor and university dean, mom a classically trained would-be opera star. He'd had regular vacations on Martha's Vineyard, and, by 20, he'd already impressed Paul McCartney and been signed to the Beatles' fledgling record label, Apple. But underneath the dizzying success lay a tortured soul. At his prestigious boarding school, James had a breakdown so severe that he committed himself to a psychiatric hospital where he stayed for nine months. He was treated with an antipsychotic drug, and later called the experience a "lifesaver." The following year, singing in New York City's Greenwich Village neighborhood, he developed a severe heroin addiction, and it took a loving father's intervention, yet another stay in a psychiatric institution, and a fifteen-plus-year struggle to overcome it.

All the while, James Taylor was rising in the music industry, featured on the cover of *Time* Magazine, and being hailed as rock's savior. Self-revealing with "restraint and dignity," at the vanguard of the new, softer, gentler singer-songwriter movement, and blessed with a sweet, warm, non-threatening tenor, Taylor was also a master fingerpicking acoustic guitarist who wrote "songs of love, loneliness, anguish, and puzzlement," as critic Burt Korall put it. "I'm a very self-centered songwriter... It's the personal stuff I like, for better or for worse," said James. With artists like Taylor, Carole King, Joni Mitchell, Cat Stevens, and, of course, Bob Dylan, at the start of the '70s, singer-songwriters were ascendant.

Taylor's *Sweet Baby James* LP perfectly captured the zeitgeist. His classic "Fire and Rain" movingly hinted at his stays in the hospital, the suicide of a dear friend, and his attendant struggles. A few months later, his friend and neighbor Carole King answered him with her classic "You've Got a Friend." When Taylor recorded her song a year later, he had his first #1. In time, he married Carly Simon, still another singer-songwriter; they had a couple of children and sang a few songs on each other's albums, but by 1983 they were divorced, Taylor still battling his demons.

Sober by the mid-'80s, Taylor is still a formidable presence on oldies radio; his 1976 *Greatest Hits* collection has sold millions over the decades, and he regularly releases million-selling albums. In 2015, his 19th studio release, *Before the World*, became the first chart-topping LP of his career, some 47 years after he began. Today, he is a regular presence on TV specials, the concert circuit, and at progressive political events. It's heartwarming to see his ubiquitous, smiling, survivor's visage and reflect on how far he has traveled since those troubled early years.

Suggested Songs:

Sweet Baby James (1970)
Fire and Rain (1970)
You've Got a Friend (1971)
Mexico (1975)
Shower the People (1976)

#91 Red Hot Chili Peppers

Began Recording: 1984
Peak: 1991 - 1992; 1999 - 2007
Genres: Alternative Rock; Funk Rock; rap rock Band

Red Hot Chili Peppers are the best selling alternative rock band in history. Together for four decades, the founding members were classmates at Fairfax High in Los Angeles in the late '70s. Anthony Kiedis, son of a drug dealing, small time actor, has been with the band for the duration, singing lead and writing the lyrics. Michael Balzary, known professionally as Flea, plays bass and is the other mainstay of the group. In their earliest incarnation, Red Hot Chili Peppers, drawing on punk, metal, funk, and rap, had a hard driving sound that caught the attention of EMI. They also gained notoriety by sometimes performing naked save for a sock pulled over their privates.

Their first three LPs, released between 1984 and 1987, failed to gain much attention, but, in 1988, their lead guitarist Hillel Slovak died of a heroin overdose. Sadly, drug addiction was to be an ongoing struggle in the band's first two decades, as Kiedis was to frequently allude in his cryptic lyrics, which regularly hint at his own struggles with heroin and cocaine. Slovak's replacement on guitar, the inimitable John Frusciante, also nearly overdosed on heroin, and has twice taken years-long breaks before returning to the group.

In 1989, Red Hot Chili Peppers had a moderate breakthrough with *Mother's Milk*, which featured a ferocious cover of Stevie Wonder's "Higher Ground" and "Knock Me Down," a musical admission that we need our friends. Two years later, working with celebrated producer Rick Rubin, they released their first of two giant multi-million sellers, *Blood Sugar Sex Magik*. While their trademark funk, metal riffs, and sexually risqué lyrics did not disappear, they began their move into a more melodic direction along with more searching, introspective lyrical themes. "Under the Bridge," with its lonely, poignant, meditative vibe, became their biggest single, while "Breaking the Girl," a mid-tempo ballad, found Kiedis questioning himself about his treatment of women. 1999 saw the arrival of *Californication,* a giant among alt rock LPs. The title track is an arresting exploration of the reach of Hollywood in our culture, with references to movies, porn, plastic surgery, earthquakes, and Kurt Cobain. "Scar Tissue," with its catchy melody and laid back guitar, seems to deal with overcoming, drugs or otherwise, as does "Otherside." Other memorable tracks on their subsequent best-selling LPs, *By the Way,* Grammy-winning *Stadium Arcadium,* and *The Getaway* include the haunting "Venice Queen;" "Midnight," which may or may not reference the band's troubled drug history; the huge hit "Dani California," about a poor, doomed woman; and the striking "Dark Necessities."

Still going strong, and, by most accounts, settled and sober, Red Hot Chili Peppers have long made compelling, multi-genre music, and they've been recognized with entry into the Rock and Roll Hall of Fame.

Suggested Songs:

Under the Bridge (1991)
Scar Tissue (1999)
Californication (2000)
Dani California (2006)
Dark Necessities (2016)

#90 Woody Guthrie (1912 - 1967)
Began Recording: 1940
Peak: 1940 - 1945
Genres: Folk; country Singer/Songwriter

In 2022, the brand new Bob Dylan Center opened in Tulsa, Oklahoma, less than a block away from the Woody Guthrie Center. Why so close? Arguably, there would be no Dylan in the music firmament were it not for Guthrie.

He was named for the soon to be inaugurated Woodrow Wilson as Guthrie's dad was a Democratic Party Oklahoma politician. His dad was also, apparently, a KKK member. His mother was committed to a psychiatric hospital when Woody was 14, never to reemerge, and Woody began his rambling ways, doing odd jobs and playing music on street corners. He dropped out of high school, made his way to the Texas Panhandle, and married. The Great Depression was on, exacerbated by the severe drought known as the Dust Bowl. Leaving his growing family behind, Guthrie, like thousands of other desperate "Okies," made his way to California, walking, hitchhiking, and riding the rails. Playing guitar and harmonica, he sang where and when he could and tried his hand painting signs, pumping gas, and collecting junk.

He caught a break in 1937, landing a Los Angeles radio gig with a cousin. By this time he was writing songs, always focused on the plight of the common man. He began to see it as his life's mission, to give voice to the voiceless—the migrant, the disenfranchised for reasons of race, the underpaid and exploited worker. His family back together, Woody headed to New York and began, increasingly, to run in left-wing circles, having to deal with the communist label for the rest of his life. In 1940, he recorded his first and most successful commercial album, *Dust Bowl Ballads*, featuring tracks such as "Do Re Mi," which laments that California will be no Eden if you're a person without means and "Dusty Old Dust," an apocalyptic take on the Dust Bowl featuring a preacher who still has time to take the collection. 1940 also saw Woody recorded by the Library Of Congress' Alan

Lomax who was looking for authentic American voices to preserve. In 1944, Moe Asch had Guthrie record dozens of his songs including Woody's most famous, known by most school children today, "This Land Is Your Land."

By the late-'40s, Woody seemed to be losing control of his mind, his impulses, and his muscles. In 1952, he was diagnosed with Huntington's disease, which had taken his mother. He spent the last 11 years of his life in hospitals, losing the ability to play music, to talk, or to care for himself, but young folk acolytes made pilgrimages to see and sit with him. One such young man was Bob Dylan, newly arrived in New York and desperate to be like Woody---- Woody, the author of 3,000 songs and a man out to "prove to you that this is your world."

Suggested Songs:

Do Re Mi (1940)
Dusty Old Dust (aka So Long It's Been Good to Know Yuh) (1940)
I Ain't Got No Home in This World Anymore (1940)
Pastures of Plenty (1941)
This Land Is Your Land (1944)

#89 Neil Diamond (1941 - present)
Began Recording: 1962
Peak: 1969 - 1982
Genres: Soft Rock; Pop; country pop Singer/Songwriter

He has been one of the most popular recording and concert artists for over 50 years, yet he has never really been accepted by the rock crowd and he is not, strictly speaking, a cabaret, pop, or standards artist. He is simply a beloved singer.

Neil Diamond was born and grew up in Brooklyn. Shy and a bit insecure, he was drawn to music and did a stint writing songs at the Brill Building. 1966 saw a double breakthrough with his "I'm a Believer," a huge #1 hit for the Monkees, and "Solitary Man," featuring Diamond with his own single, an autobiographical song he still considers one of his best. Later in the year he hit the Top 10 with "Cherry, Cherry" and was on his way as a recording artist in his own right.

In 1969, Diamond released his signature song, the much loved "Sweet Caroline," which has since become associated, oddly enough, with a host of sporting teams around the world. Over the next several years he hit the Top 10 four times with "Holly Holy;" the up-tempo "Cracklin' Rosie," his first #1; "I Am...I Said," a musically dramatic reflection on being alone and lost; and "Song Sung Blue," a catchy chart topper that acknowledges that we all sometimes get the blues. In 1972, Diamond also made waves with his live performances, doing a series of shows at L.A.'s Greek Theater, later immortalized with his best-known LP, the live *Hot August Night*. Later that fall, Neil became the first rock era star to do a series of one-man concerts at a Broadway theater. He also continued a run of successful LPs with the 1973 soundtrack *Jonathan Livingston Seagull*, and 1974's *Serenade*, his third straight platinum album.

By the mid '80s, the hits were drying up, but Diamond, for the next couple of decades, was one of the biggest concert draws in the world. In 2011, Neil Diamond was finally inducted into the Rock & Roll Hall of Fame;

in reflecting on his career, he mused, "My music says what I am. It speaks about what I feel as a person, what I dream about, what I hope to be." Sadly, Neil has been diagnosed with Parkinson's and no longer performs, but a new musical, *A Beautiful Noise*, as well as membership in the Songwriters Hall of Fame, is helping to keep his legacy alive.

Suggested Songs:

Solitary Man (1966)
Sweet Caroline (1969)
The Last Thing on My Mind (1973)
If You know What I Mean (1976)
September Morn (1979)

#88 Glen Campbell (1936 - 2017)

Began Recording: 1958
Peak: 1967 - 1972; 1975 - 1977
Genres: Country, western; Pop; soft rock Singer/Guitarist

"Had Glen Campbell 'only' played guitar and never voiced a note, he would have spent a lifetime as one of America's most consequential recording musicians. Had he never played a guitar and 'only' sang, his voice would rank with America's most riveting, expressive, and enduring." (Country Music Hall of Fame)

Born into a poor Arkansas sharecropping family, Glen learned guitar as a child from an uncle and was soon playing in western music bands. Making his way to L.A. in 1960, he became one of the most in-demand session guitarists as a member of the Wrecking Crew, playing on records behind the likes of Elvis Presley, the Beach Boys, Frank Sinatra, Simon & Garfunkel, and countless others. In 1967, Campbell began to emerge as a recognized solo artist with his cover of a hobo's meditation, the Grammy-winning "Gentle on My Mind," but it was his synergetic teaming with songwriting great Jimmy Webb that made him a superstar. "By the Time I Get to Phoenix" is a song of leaving, another Grammy winner, and one of the most covered songs of the era. "Wichita Lineman," called by music journalist Stuart Maconie the "greatest pop song ever composed," reached #1 on the *Billboard* country chart and #3 on their pop chart in 1968 and features Glen's yearning, soulful vocal. A year later, the Campbell-Webb team scored again with "Galveston," a scared soldier's longing daydream of his woman back home.

Campbell's middle-of-the-road, crossover popularity at this time of psychedelic rock and Woodstock fever was such that he was given a weekly TV show from 1968 to 1972 and was able to feature such guests as the Beatles, Linda Ronstadt, Johnny Cash, and Willie Nelson. His hits began to dry up in the early '70s, only to come back in 1975 with his best-selling

"Rhinestone Cowboy," seemingly summarizing Glen's own life story, and, two years later, with "Southern Nights."

Listeners were acutely aware of Glen's pure, sweet voice---a' freakishly wonderful singer," said Webb. Fewer were cognizant that Campbell was one of the most gifted guitarists in the world. Everyone knew of Hendrix and Clapton, but Campbell, it's been said, could hold his own with any of them. Glen stayed on the country charts through the '80s and continued to record and tour until 2013. His final years saw him decline slowly into Alzheimer's, which he and his family shared graciously with the world through a documentary film.

About his craft, Glen once said, "Music is music. It doesn't matter if I am trying to aim at country or trying to aim at pop. I am just trying to do a song the best possible way I can."

Suggested Songs:

By the Time I Get to Phoenix (1967)
Wichita Lineman (1968)
Galveston (1969) or (live version) (2008)
Rhinestone Cowboy (1975)
Southern Nights (1977)

#87 Al Jolson (1885 or '86 - 1950)

Began Recording: 1911
Peak: 1920 - 1934; 1946 - 1950
Genres: Traditional & Musical Theater Pop; light Jazz Singer

Though he is pilloried or largely forgotten today, performers as different as Bobby Darin, Judy Garland, and Jerry Lee Lewis were moved and influenced by him. Stephen Hanan called him a "rock star before the dawn of rock music."

He was born Asa Yoelson in Lithuania around 1886. In 1894, he, his three siblings, and his beloved mother joined his father in Washington, D.C. When she died soon after, Asa was devastated. Resisting his father's life in the synagogue, the boy was soon singing on streets, in the circus, and in vaudeville theaters alongside his older brother. By this time, he was calling himself Al Jolson, and in 1904 he performed in blackface for the first time. It was to be a mainstay for the rest of his career and, to this day, a legacy of an ignorant and intolerant time.

His brother had departed by 1906, and by 1911 Jolson was a star on Broadway. For 15 years he was the leading man in musical theater and in musical revues, touring nationally as well as regularly playing New York. Al was intensely charismatic, and as music professor Stephen Banfield notes, he was "arguably the single most important factor in defining the modern musical."

In 1927, Jolson starred in the semi-autobiographical *The Jazz Singer*. With a mix of old silent technology and new sound, Jolson sang six numbers including his signature, "My Mammy," performed, as many of his works, in blackface. The movie was a sensation, effectively sounding the death knell for the silent film era and ushering in the age of "Talkies."

Though remembered more today for his work on stage and screen, Al was also a formidable presence on radio and records. Among his best-known recordings are "You Made Me Love You," "Rock-a-Bye Your Baby

With a Dixie Melody," "Swanee," "Avalon," "April Showers," and "I'm Sitting on Top of the World."

Semi-retired by the early 1940s, Jolson was roused by America's entrance into World War II. Quickly volunteering to entertain the troops, he traveled extensively to perform and lift morale. In the Pacific, he contracted malaria and needed to have a lung removed. After the war, two films about Jolson's life, starring Larry Parks, caused his popularity to again soar as Al provided all the films' vocals. When the U.S. entered war again in Korea in 1950, Jolson paid his own way to again cheer the G.I.s. Short a lung, the exertion was too much for him, and he died of a massive heart attack later that year. Tributes poured in from everywhere.

An uncomfortable historical figure, today we recognize his performances in blackface as racist, but Jolson adopted the practice because he felt it helped him better to connect with his audience. In his own time, he was reportedly embraced by many Black entertainers, who saw him trying to introduce Black music and sensibilities to white audiences that would not have given it the time of day in its original context; and though Jolson was no saint, artists like Louis Armstrong, Duke Ellington, and Cab Calloway expressed admiration for his contemporaneously atypical treatment of Black artists.

Suggested Songs:

You Made Me Love You (1913; 1946 version)
What'll I Do? (1923 song; 2018 collection)
California, Here I Come (1924; 2020 remaster)
I'm Sitting on Top of the World (1926; 1995 collection)
My Mammy (1927 ?; 2020 remaster)

#86 Radiohead

Began Recording: 1992
Peak: 1997 - 2003; 2007 - 2016
Genres: Alternative Rock; Electronic/Experimental Band

NME put it this way: "Considering the way that they have pushed music forward, you could build a case for them as the Beatles of the 21st century."

Noted for their bold, experimental style, Radiohead is an English rock band consisting of five musicians who first played together in 1985 while attending the same boarding school, only to come back together after college in 1991 when they were quickly signed by EMI. Led by lead singer and lyricist Thom Yorke, the band features brothers Colin (on bass) and Jonny (lead guitar and multi-instrumentalist) Greenwood, ambient guitarist Ed O'Brien, and drummer Philip Selway.

In 1992, they scored a surprise hit with the arresting "Creep" off their first LP, *Pablo Honey*; with incisive, pained lyrics, there is deep yearning in the melodic verses, and a screaming/scratching guitar cry underscoring the self-loathing chorus. To this day, "Creep" remains their best-known single. It was 1997, however, that saw Radiohead become an international sensation with the abstract, experimental *OK Computer*, which explores social, emotional, and political alienation, wrapped in a vibe of paranoia. It has been praised as one of the great LPs of all time by the likes of *Rolling Stone* and the Library of Congress. Key tracks include the left-field hit "Paranoid Android," "Karma Police," and the haunted ballad, "No Surprises." Their follow-up album, *Kid A*, has been similarly feted and features the track "Idioteque" with its frightening, dystopian vision of where we may all be heading. Six of their albums, in fact, have topped the charts in the U.K, with their later work, such as 2001's *Amnesiac*; the initially self-released *In Rainbows*; and, most recently, 2016's *A Moon Shaped Pool*, still drawing rave reviews from rock critics.

Culling from sources as diverse as Pink Floyd, Bob Dylan, the Pixies, and Miles Davis, Radiohead is lauded as one of the most influential bands of the 21st century. Nominated for five Mercury Prizes and winners of six Grammys, they were inducted into the Rock & Roll Hall of Fame in 2019. *AllMusic*'s Stephen Erlewine wrote that they are a "touchstone for everything fearless and adventurous in rock."

Suggested Songs:

Creep (1992)
Paranoid Android (1997)
Karma Police (1997)
No Surprises (1998)
Idioteque (2000)

#85 Janet Jackson (1966 - present)
Began Recording: 1982
Peak: 1986 - 2004
Genres: R&B; Dance; Funk; Pop Singer/Songwriter

"It's criminal that we forget the impact that Janet Jackson has had on music," says music journalist Danyel Smith.

The youngest child of the most famous of all musical families, Janet Jackson was performing on a Las Vegas stage by age seven. From 1977 to 1985 she was a regular TV actress. With encouragement from her famous brother Michael and her father, she had released two LPs by the time she was 18, but it was the four albums that followed upon which her reputation as a musical giant in her own right rests.

Working with Prince colleagues, the producer-songwriting team of Jimmy Jam and Terry Lewis, Janet's 1986 record, *Control*, asserts her newfound independence and reached the top of the *Billboard* Pop chart. Mixing R&B, funk, dance, and rap with a heavy synth overlay, the album struck a crossover chord, generating five Top 5 hits including "Nasty" and "When I Think of You."

Her 1989 follow up, *Janet Jackson's Rhythm Nation 1814*, is her most celebrated work, having sold some 14 million copies and placing seven singles in the Top 5, a feat never before accomplished. *Atlantic* called it "dark and radiant, calculated and carefree, political and playful, sensual and austere, sermonic and liberating." Indeed, the album's foci are social concerns and the power of community, and she again mixes genres: R&B, dance, and rap with pop ballads and even blazing hard rock, all enveloped in Jam and Lewis' drum heavy synth cocoon. "Miss You Much," "Escapade," "Black Cat," and "Love Will Never Do (Without You)" all reached #1 on the Hot 100, and, as the '80s turned into the '90s, Janet was as big a music star as Prince, Madonna, Whitney, or her brother.

With 1993's *Janet*, she turned toward the erotic, with catchy songs like "If" leaving little to the imagination. Both *Janet* and her follow up, *The Velvet*

Rope, were hugely successful and critical darlings, the latter taking a turn toward very adult themes, sexually and personally, as Jackson was fighting her way through a serious bout of depression.

In 2004, Jackson headlined the Super Bowl halftime show. While performing with Justin Timberlake, his hand moved over her right breast, exposing for less than a second her nipple. The uproar was furious and predictable. She was subsequently "blacklisted," and though she continued to sell records, she never reached the same level as her classics, and, for a time, it was harder to find her on radio or TV.

In a 2022 interview, Jackson allowed that her brother's infamous pedophilia charges also hurt her career as she was seen as "guilty by association." Still, in her heyday, she was a force, and, as Terry Lewis says, "fearless, relentless, beautiful."

Suggested Songs:

Nasty (1986)
Rhythm Nation (1989)
Escapade (1990)
That's the Way Love Goes (1993)
Together Again (1997)

#84 Merle Haggard (1937 - 2016)

Began Recording: 1962
Peak: 1966 - 1985
Genres: Country Singer/Songwriter/Instrumentalist

Merle Haggard was born on the outskirts of Bakersfield, California, in a converted railroad boxcar his Okie parents called home. His dad, a would-be honky-tonk fiddler, died when Merle was nine, and the young boy went off the rails. In and out of trouble over the next 12 years, frequently running away from home, and arrested for petty theft, robbery, and assault, he did several stints in juvenile facilities and by 1958 was in San Quentin Prison.

Music turned out to be his salvation. At 12 he began teaching himself guitar, listening to the records of Bob Wills, Hank Williams, Jimmie Rodgers, and Lefty Frizzell, who once invited the young Merle onstage after hearing him sing backstage. At San Quentin, Haggard was a difficult prisoner, but resolved to turn his life around after two fellow prisoners and friends were slated for death row and he heard Johnny Cash perform for the inmates. Paroled in 1960, Haggard dug ditches by day and sang locally at night, eventually landing in Wynn Stewart's band. Asking permission to record Stewart's "Sing a Sad Song" in 1963, Haggard made the song a surprise country hit. He followed it in 1964 with "(My Friends Are Gonna Be) Strangers" and was on his way to stardom. Soon he formed a backing band, the celebrated Strangers, who went on to support him on and off for over 40 years.

1966 saw Haggard reach country superstardom with his woeful drinking songs recording in the Bakersfield idiom popularized by Buck Owens and featuring a rock & roll backbeat, the pedal steel, and electric guitars. Songs of this era include "Swinging Doors," "The Bottle Let Me Down," and "I'm a Lonesome Fugitive," which seems to reference his own troubled past, though it was not a self-penned number. In 1968, he released one of his best-loved songs, "Mama Tried," a celebration of his beloved mother who tried, yet failed for a time, to keep him on the straight and narrow. The following year, his "Okie From Muskogee" became a lightning rod for those who saw young, "hippie protesters" sullying the efforts of patriotic servicemen who were dying in Vietnam. Citing illicit drugs, campus turmoil, anti-war protest, and long hair as emblematic of all that was wrong with society, Merle held up such "small town values" of flag waving, football, and moonshine as contrast; Haggard struck a national nerve. Ironically, later in life Haggard became quite renowned for his pot smoking ways, and went out of his way to defend the Dixie Chicks, who were excoriated by much of the country crowd for criticizing the George W. Bush invasion of Iraq.

Haggard, who consistently celebrated America's blue-collar workers, had a total of 38 #1 country hits and was deemed the greatest country artist of all time by *Rolling Stone*. Friend and fellow artist Kris Kristofferson agreed, saying that Haggard was "the most successfully rehabilitated prisoner in American history" and "the greatest artist in American music history."

Suggested Songs:

Mama Tried (1968)
Working Man Blues (1969)
Okie From Muskogee (1969)
If We Make It Through December (1973)
I think I'll Just Stay Here and Drink (1980)

#83 Black Sabbath
Began Recording: 1970
Peak: 1970 - 1975; 1980
Genres: Heavy Metal Band

Black Sabbath "weren't just the first but the greatest metal band," said *Rolling Stone*. They were called the Godfathers of Heavy Metal, a genre which had its earliest roots in the blues, in blues-rock bands like the Yardbirds and Cream, and in the psychedelic sounds of some Beatles, Hendrix, and early Grateful Dead tunes. Characterized by loud power chords with strong, insistent rhythm, the lyrical content of metal has often been called dark and doomy.

Black Sabbath hailed from Birmingham, England, four working class lads. Tony Iommi was the leader, so determined that he made himself one of rock's great guitarists despite losing the tips of two fingers from his fretting hand in an industrial accident; Geezer Butler played bass and wrote most of the band's lyrics; Bill Ward was their drummer; while Ozzy Osbourne was their celebrated first vocalist. Between 1970 and 1975, Black Sabbath, who took their name from an old Boris Karloff horror film, released six albums that changed rock music. Beginning with church bells, thunder, and rain, followed by Iommi's ominous three chords, and joined to Butler's dark tale of awaking to see the devil, "Black Sabbath," the opening track from the eponymous album, was truly frightening in 1970. "Oh no, please God, help me," screamed Ozzy. Later in the year they released *Paranoid*, with its celebrated title track, and "Iron Man," which featured another classic Iommi riff. *Master of Reality, Vol. 4, Sabbath Bloody Sabbath* and *Sabotage* round out the big six. By that time, though, heavy touring, increased substance abuse, and interpersonal clashes were taking their toll on the band's quality. By 1979 Iommi had had it with Ozzy and fired him. Alcohol abuse, in time, cost Ward his place in the band as well. In 2013, all but Ward came together to release *13*, their best-charting album.

When Black Sabbath first appeared, the critical reception was almost universally hostile: "Just like Cream! But worse," said Lester Bangs; "Bullshit necromancy," sneered Robert Christgau. Indeed, the sound and the stories were usually more than a little dreary, antisocial, and depressive; some even called it devil music and said that Sabbath must be satanists. Butler countered by revealing he was a practicing Catholic, and the others pointed out that they wore crosses to ward off the curses hurled at them for refusing to participate in dark rituals. Besides, a careful listening reveals that they hate war ("War Pigs") and seem to affirm Christian faith ("After Forever") and the power of love ("It's Alright"). In the end, maybe we hear what we want to hear. Van Halen, Metallica, Frank Zappa, and countless others heard the music. Rob Zombie put it like this: "Every cool riff has already been written by Black Sabbath."

Suggested Songs:

Black Sabbath (1970)
Paranoid (1970)
War Pigs (1970)
It's Alright (1976)
Heaven and Hell (1980)

#82 ABBA
Began Recording: 1972
Peak: 1976 - 1981
Genres: Pop; Pop Rock Band

Perhaps it was the garish, campy costumes or the relentlessly upbeat dance pop grooves; maybe it was their massive commercial '70s success, but critics mercilessly trashed them in their heyday. ABBA, however, has had real staying power, and they are no longer so easily dismissed.

They are four remarkable musicians—Bjorn Ulvaeus, guitarist, co-composer, co-producer, and sometime singer; Benny Andersson, keyboardist, co-composer, co-producer, and back-up vocalist; and sopranos Agnetha Faltskog and Anni-Frid Lyngstad, who shared most of the lead vocals. Each had found a measure of success in Swedish musical circles before joining forces in 1970. They released their initial recordings in 1972, calling themselves by their first names. "Too unwieldy," said manager and label owner Stig Anderson who began referring to them as ABBA, an acronym based on those first names. The new moniker stuck. When the upbeat, dance-friendly "Waterloo" won the Eurovision Song Contest in 1974, ABBA was on its way.

Over the next seven years, ABBA released seven studio albums, each one climbing to the top of the Swedish charts, but each one crossing over internationally as well to Norway and the Netherlands, to Germany, Britain and Australia. Only in the United States did they fail to dominate the album charts, but even there they were unstoppable with their string of classic singles—"SOS;" "Mama Mia" (#1 in Australia for an unheard of 10 weeks); "Fernando" and "Dancing Queen," the two biggest of all; "Money Money Money;" "Knowing Me, Knowing You;" "Take a Chance on Me;" "Chiquitita." By 1980, though, the band dynamics were changing, for Agnetha and Bjorn, who had married in 1971, were divorcing and Benny and Anni, who likewise had wed, had by then separated. Though ABBA claims the songs are not autobiographical, the pain and heartbreak of separation are evident in two of their last hits, "The Winner Takes It All" and "One of Us." In 1981, they released their final LP and soon retired to go their separate ways.

Fans, however, never let them die. In 1992, *ABBA Gold: Greatest Hits* was released and has gone on to sell some 30 million copies, making it one of the world's all-time best sellers. When *Mama Mia*, the musical, opened in 1999, few could have predicted it would still be running in 2023 or that it would become a beloved film. 2021, 40 years after their last release, saw the four reunite for *Voyage,* which has become a worldwide #1 LP, with a concert series using cutting edge, digital "ABBAtars," along with live musicians, opening to theatergoers in 2022.

Never keen on live shows, ABBA was principally a studio band that took their underrated melodic hooks, often bittersweet lyrics, and then produced a series of mini tour de force singles, layering voice over voice over voice and perfecting richly textured music that is celebrated to this day. The critics long ago ceased scoffing.

Suggested Songs:

Waterloo (1974)
Fernando (1976)
Dancing Queen (1976)
Chiquitita (1979)
The Winner Takes It All (1980)

#81 Patsy Cline (1932 - 1963)

Began Recording: 1955
Peak: 1961 - 1963
Genres: Country; traditional pop Singer

She was one of country music's first great crossover artists, and, nearly 60 years after her untimely death, she remains hugely popular.

Born Virginia Patterson Hensley in small town Virginia to a teen mother and a much older blacksmith father, she moved with her family 19 times in 15 years as her father struggled to find work. Virginia later confided to close friend Loretta Lynn that her father sexually abused her. She was 15 when he left the family, and she quit school to work. She'd begun singing after a near fatal bout of rheumatic fever two years earlier left her with a booming voice. Inspired by Helen Morgan and Kay Starr, she landed a gig playing locally with Bill Peer's country band in 1952. The following year she married Gerald Cline, a pairing that did not last, but she took his last name, modified her middle name, and began calling herself Patsy Cline.

A 1953 talent contest led to a local TV spot and caught the attention of Four Star Records. Her contract with the label tied her up for six years, leaving her virtually penniless in the end. Still, in 1957, a winning appearance on *Arthur Godfrey's Talent Scouts* led her label to release "Walkin' After Midnight," which jumped to #2 on the *Billboard* country chart and crossed over as a pop hit as well. She even got an invitation to play the Grand Ole Opry in Nashville, long her dream. Success, though, was short-lived as her label had her record substandard material, leaving her playing dive bars for the next three years.

In 1960, though, she got the call from the Opry again, this time to become a regular performer. Free of Four Star, she signed with Decca and released, in early '61, "I Fall to Pieces," which became her second country-pop crossover success. As the song was climbing, Patsy had her second brush with death as she was thrown through the windshield in a ghastly head-on car crash. While still recovering, she was offered a chance to record young songwriter Willie Nelson's "Crazy." It has subsequently become her best-known recording and a genuine country and pop classic. By 1962, Patsy was at her peak, touring, doing TV, and again at the top of the charts with "She's Got You."

On March 4, 1963, she turned down a car ride to return to Nashville from a Kansas City benefit. With her manager Randy Hughes piloting, her plane went down the next evening in bad weather and Patsy, 30 years old, was gone.

Considered by many an all-time great vocalist, regardless of genre, listeners frequently cite the emotional impact of her singing. Loretta Lynn, Dottie West, LeAnn Rimes, and many others have cited both her artistry and her influence as an empowerment pioneer. In 1973, Patsy became the first female solo artist inducted into the Country Music Hall of Fame.

Suggested Songs:

Walkin' After Midnight (1957)
I Fall to Pieces (1961)
Crazy (1961)
She's Got You (1962)
Sweet Dreams (Of You) (1963)

#80 John Williams (1932 - present)
Began Recording: 1957
Peak: 1975 - 1994
Genres: Film; Contemporary Classical Composer/Conductor/pianist

If you have been a frequent or even occasional moviegoer these past 50 years, chances are you are familiar with the music of John Williams. Prolific and accomplished, Norwegian composer Marcus Paus called him "one of the greatest composers of any century." Certainly he is the most widely known composer and conductor of film scores, with several of his themes reaching the record charts.

Born in New York, John was raised by a jazz drummer father. Relocating to Los Angeles as a teen, John studied piano and composition privately at UCLA and, later, at Juilliard. Originally a jazz pianist, Williams commented, "It became clear that I could write better than I could play." In the '50s, he went to work for the film studios and scored his first movie, *Daddy-O*, a poorly received car comedy, in 1958. From the start, Williams generally composed and conducted the projects he worked on. In the early '60s, he did TV shows like *Wagon Train* and *Lost in Space* and such films as *Because They're Young* and *Gidget Goes to Rome*. His adaptation of Jerry Bock's *Fiddler on the Roof* earned him his first Oscar in 1972.

In 1974, Steven Spielberg reached out to Williams to compose his directorial debut, *Sugarland Express*. Thus began a collaboration that has extended to 28 films including *Jaws*, which won Williams his second Academy Award, *E.T.*, which earned him his fourth, and *Schindler's List*, which netted him his fifth.

In the mid-'70s Spielberg introduced him to his friend, George Lucas, who was looking for an old-Hollywood classic, swashbuckler type score to go with his upcoming space epic, *Star Wars*. The resulting work is today recognized by countless millions around the world and has been compared to Wagner, though Williams demurs. Alex Ross of the *New Yorker* terms it neoclassical, "steeped in mid-twentieth-century influences: jazz, popular standards, Stravinsky, and Aaron Copland." Williams has been there for all nine episodes, beginning in 1977 and concluding in 2019. He stresses that his *Star Wars* themes, as he calls them, need to be succinct, and he favors bright trumpets and loud drums because there is so much else going on between the film's visuals and loud action noises.

Williams has worked with other directors, as well, from Oliver Stone to Ron Howard. He is also noted for his concertos, which he has composed for violin, for horn, and for clarinet. For 13 years he was the chief conductor of the Boston Pops Orchestra, and he has guest conducted around the world, from New York to Vienna, where musicians sometimes seek his autograph.

Winner of 25 Grammys and a Kennedy Center honoree, he's 91 years old and continues to conduct and compose.

Suggested Songs:

Main Theme from *Jaws* (1975)
Main Title from *Star Wars* (1977)
Main Theme from *Schindler's List* (1993)
Hymn to the Fallen from *Saving Private Ryan* (1998)
Across the Stars (Love Theme from *Star Wars: Attack of the Clones* (2002)

#79 John Coltrane (1926 - 1967)

Began Recording: 1949 (sideman); 1957 (leader)
Peak: 1958 - 1967
Genres: Jazz—hard bop, modal, avant-garde, free Saxophonist/ Composer/ Bandleader

Exploratory, adventurous, groundbreaking, intrepid, revolutionary are but some of the adjectives used to describe the playing, composing, and influence of John Coltrane, widely considered the greatest tenor saxophonist in jazz history.

Born and raised in North Carolina in a religious family, John lost his father, grandparents, and aunt within a few months when he was 12. He was drawn to music, first the clarinet in high school, and later the sax. Determined to play professionally after hearing Charlie Parker, he did a stint in the U.S. Navy at the end of World War II where his talent was recognized, and he spent much of his time playing in a service band. Though he studied music briefly, he learned primarily from those around him and was noted for his fierce work ethic, constantly practicing or gigging. From 1946 to 1955, he played in a series of bands, most famously with Dizzy Gillespie, drawn especially to bebop and post-bop, though he played whatever was called for. In 1955, John auditioned for Miles Davis, the celebrated trumpeter, and for much of the next four years played in his renowned group. They were an odd couple—Miles, cocky, sullen, demanding; Coltrane, quiet, self-critical, humble—but Davis, whom Coltrane called "teacher," recognized that John was the perfect intense counterpoint to his own subdued style. Twice Davis dismissed his young sax genius for allowing a heroin addiction to get the better of him, but by 1957 Coltrane had put it behind him, opening himself up to a new spiritual way of living.

The music is legendary. With the Davis sextet, Coltrane played on *Kind of Blue*, widely hailed as the greatest jazz record of all time. In 1957, Coltrane began leading his own group of generally four or five musicians, releasing 25 albums in 10 years, at least four of which have been hailed as iconic—1960's *Giant Steps* is in the *National Recording Registry* and features the culmination of John's famed cascading, high speed runs or "sheets of sound;" 1961's modal jazz masterwork, *My Favorite Things*, contains his soprano sax popular reworking of the *Sound of Music* favorite; 1964's *Live at Birdland* was hailed by *AllMusic* as "arguably" his "finest all-around album;" and his acknowledged masterpiece, 1965's *A Love Supreme*, is John's four-part "thank you to God." The album showcases his musical, universalist spirituality, as John, by this time, saw his life's mission as being part of "the force that is truly for good" and "to make people happy through music."

Coltrane died in 1967, only 40 years old, of liver cancer. He is today revered as a canonized saint by the small African Orthodox Church and is broadly lauded as one of the 20th century's great jazz masters, brooding, dense, and searching, always searching for spiritual purification and human connection.

Suggested Songs:

Blue Train (1958)
Giant Steps (1960)
My Favorite Things (1961)
Alabama (1964)
A Love Supreme, Pt. II - Resolution (1965)

#78 Carole King (1942 - present)

Began Recording: 1958
Peak: 1971 - 1975
Genres: Pop; Soft Rock; R&B Singer/Songwriter

With more than 400 of her songs recorded by 1,000 or more artists, Carole King is arguably the most successful female songwriter of the last 70 years. Moreover, she has been inducted twice into the Rock & Roll Hall of Fame, once as a songwriter and once as a performer.

Raised in Brooklyn, Carol Klein's schoolteacher mom recognized her daughter's near perfect pitch and inordinate interest in the piano and began teaching her precocious child how to play when she was four. By 15, Carole was composing and trying to sell her songs to Manhattan publishers and began calling herself Carole King. She met her husband Gerry Goffin at Queens College, and by 17 she was pregnant. The two wrote together and had their first major success in 1960 with the Shirelles' #1 hit, "Will You Love Me Tomorrow?" Working together full-time from 1650 Broadway, Goffin-King wrote smash singles for Bobby Vee ("Take Good Care of My Baby"); their babysitter, Little Eva ("The Loco-Motion"); Steve Lawrence ("Go Away Little Girl"); The Drifters ("Up on the Roof"); the Monkees ("Pleasant Valley Sunday"); even for Aretha Franklin ("Natural Woman"). In 1968, she and Goffin divorced, and Carole moved with her two daughters to Los Angeles.

Encouraged by friend James Taylor to continue writing and to perform her compositions, Carole hit gold with her second solo LP, 1971's *Tapestry*. With Carole's earthy, girl-next-door, smiling cover photo and intimate, yet accessible, piano-based songs, *Tapestry* struck a nerve, becoming the best-selling album of all time (up to that point) and sweeping the Grammys. The album stayed on the charts for six years and featured "It's Too Late," a non-blaming breakup song; "So Far Away," a meditation on distance, physical and spiritual; and "You've Got a Friend," which Taylor recorded simultaneously, scoring his first #1. Included, too, were Carole's versions of the classics she'd written for the Shirelles and Aretha.

King released more chart-topping music for the next several years, notably the albums *Music* and *Wrap Around Joy*. She even performed in front of 100,000 fans in a 1973 Central Park concert, but gradually her star began to dim. It has been revived these past two decades with a Troubadour Reunion Tour and album with James Taylor in 2010, a 2013 Broadway musical about her life, and recognition from the Kennedy Center and the Library of Congress, making her the first woman to win the coveted Gershwin Prize for Popular Song. Among the legendary artists who have recorded Carole King compositions are the Beatles, Barbra Streisand, the Carpenters, Roberta Flack and Donny Hathaway, Linda Ronstadt, Celine Dion, the Animals, the Byrds, Tony Orlando, the Righteous Brothers, and k.d. lang.

Suggested Songs:

So Far Away (1971)
It's Too Late (1971)
Will You Love Me Tomorrow? (1971)
Music (1971)
Been to Canaan (1972)

#77 Nat King Cole (1919 - 1965)
Began Recording: 1936
Peak: 1944 - 1957; 1962 - 1963
Genres: Jazz; R&B; Traditional Pop Singer/Pianist

He was a giant in two distinct musical spheres—first as a 1940s jazz pianist and sometime vocalist with the King Cole Trio; then, increasingly, in the 1950s, taking his place alongside Frank Sinatra as one of the two most important crooners of traditional pop.

Nathaniel Coles was born in Alabama, but his family relocated to Chicago when he was four. With both parents working in the Baptist church, Nat was introduced early to gospel music and then began studying classical piano at 12. He was drawn, however, to jazz and quit school at 15 to pursue a musical career. He got his start playing with older brother Eddie but soon was touring with an all-Black musical revue. Settling in L.A., by 1937 he was married and had formed the swinging King Cole Trio with Wesley Prince on bass, Oscar Moore on guitar, and Cole on piano. Vocal harmonies were a big aspect of the group. The hits began coming in 1942, first registering on the R&B (Black) charts with "That Ain't Right" and "All for You." But by 1944, the trio was also crossing over onto the white or pop charts with "Straighten Up and Fly Right" reaching #9. "(I Love You) For Sentimental Reasons" was the #1 pop single in 1946, which also saw Cole's first recording of "The Christmas Song (Merry Christmas to You)," a track that has subsequently become one of the best-loved secular carols of all time. His recording of "Nature Boy," a song that's been covered by artists as diverse as Frank Sinatra and David Bowie, brought Nat a still wider audience, and, by 1950, he was increasingly being billed as simply Nat King Cole and was less frequently behind a piano. Two of the biggest hits of the era, 1950's "Mona Lisa" and "Too Young" from the following year, seemed to signal that Cole was now a traditional crooner; jazz aficionados were not happy. Some saw Cole as a sell-out in much the same way Bob Dylan would face similar charges 15 years hence when he morphed from a folk to a rock star. Nat's "Unforgettable" was a Top 15 hit in 1951, but the song made history in 1991 when his daughter, through the miracle of recording technology, was able to sing a duet with her deceased father. In 1956, Cole also made history by being the first African-American artist to host a weekly network TV program.

In December 1964, a sickly Cole finally agreed to see a doctor and was diagnosed with lung cancer; he was dead in two months. Jazz buffs today recognize his brilliance as a master pianist, while a very distinct group of fans revere him for his rich, warm, smooth vocal style. Neither group has forgotten him.

Suggested Songs:

Straighten Up and Fly Right (1944)
Mona Lisa (1950)
Unforgettable (1951)
Smile (1954)
The Christmas Song ((Merry Christmas to You) (1962)

#76 Rod Stewart (1945 - present)
Began Recording: 1964
Peak: 1971 - 1978
Genres: Rock; Pop; blues/folk/R&B; disco; traditional pop Singer/Songwriter

London-born Rod Stewart has one of the most recognizable voices in all of music. Variously described as scratchy, hoarse, and raspy, at his best Stewart was capable of expressing aching, tender, poignant compassion, as can be heard on his 1969 moving cover of d'Abo's "Handbags and Gladrags."

He wanted to be a footballer, but by his teens was busking with his harmonica on European streets, soon making his way as a vocalist through a series of bands, most notably with Long John Baldry, the Jeff Beck Group, and Faces. From the beginning, looking to make it as a solo artist, Stewart released a couple of critically lauded LPs, *An Old Raincoat Won't Ever Let You Down* and *Gasoline Alley*, before breaking through in 1971 with the acclaimed masterwork *Every Picture Tells a Story*, which features his tale of a young man in over his head with an older, more experienced paramour, the iconic, mandolin lilting "Maggie May." Stewart followed up with four more consecutive UK chart topping LPs: *Never a Dull Moment*; *Smiler*; *Atlantic Crossing*, which, in retrospect, seemed to signal a shift to a bit more of a pop-friendly tone; and *A Night on the Town*. He was consistently high on U.S., Canadian, and European charts, as well, throughout the '70s. His 1975 recording of Gavin Sutherland's "Sailing" became a European anthem of spiritual longing, while "The Killing of Georgie" recounted the murder of a gay friend.

By the late '70s, Rod was sporting Spandex, projecting a Hollywood playboy image, and was being chided by old fans and critics as a "sell-out" for albums such as *Blondes Have More Fun* and songs like "Ain't Love a Bitch" and the disco smash "Da Ya Think I'm Sexy." Still, he was raking in millions and though he didn't seem to matter as once he did, he regularly found his way onto the charts. Between 2002 and 2005, he reinvented himself again with four Great American Songbook LPs, reaching a whole new audience, and earning a Grammy for Best Traditional Pop Vocal Album for *Volume III*. Recently, Stewart has attempted a return to his songwriting roots with the LPs *Time* and *Blood Red Roses*. Rod is a two-time member of the Rock & Roll Hall of Fame, as a soloist and as a member of Faces, and one of the 50 top selling artists of all time.

Suggested Songs:

Handbags and Gladrags (1969, 1972)
Maggie May (1971)
Mandolin Wind (1971)
Sailing (1975)
The Killing of Georgie (Part I and II) (1976)

#75 Nirvana

Began Recording: 1988
Peak: 1991 - 1994
Genres: Alternative Rock - Grunge; punk Band

Nirvana is a Buddhist concept that implies release from suffering, desire, self, and rebirth. In retrospect, perhaps Kurt Cobain was expressing his sincere longing to be released from his own personal pain.

Growing up in Aberdeen, Washington, Kurt Cobain and Krist Novoselic decided to find a drummer and form a band in 1987. Over the next three years, they cycled through five drummers before Dave Grohl stuck. From the start, Cobain was the leader; he played guitar, was the primary vocalist, wrote most of the songs, and was the artistic decision maker. Novoselic played bass. Drawing from sources as diverse as the Beatles, Queen, and Zeppelin, but also from punk artists like the Ramones and the Sex Pistols, in 1989 Nirvana cut their first LP, *Bleach*, with Sub Pop, then a small local label but now iconic for ushering in a new subgenre of music. The album sold in the thousands, not the millions, and failed to chart, but their heavy, dark, distressing sensibility was evident from the opening track, "Blew." The album generated word of mouth and the band signed with DGC, a major label.

Nevermind was released in 1991, a bit more polished than its predecessor, but still intense and raw. The lead single, "Smells Like Teen Spirit," follows a typical Nirvana pattern, alternating between melodic, softer verses and an aggressive, high decibel chorus, with Cobain screaming his evocative, yet obscure, lyrics. As it began to get massive airplay, album sales took off, and, within months, Nirvana was the hottest band on the planet. Their sound was called grunge, a melding of punk and metal and hard rock. Suddenly, Seattle was the center of the music world with bands like Pearl Jam and Alice in Chains also catapulting to international, though not equivalent, acclaim. With Cobain's loud, distorted, sludgy guitar and mumbling, growling, screaming vocals backed by Grohl's powerful drumming, the lyrics, impressionistic and often surreal, seemed to speak to a large segment of disaffected youth, capturing a sense of alienation, anger, angst, and depression. Even when the music is restrained, as in "Something In the Way," there is still a sense of foreboding, even doom, which feels imminent.

Suddenly, Cobain was being described as the voice of Gen X, and though he was not comfortable with this role, he was outspoken—"If any of you in any way hate homosexuals, people of color, or women, please do this one favor for us—leave us the fuck alone!" *In Utero*, the follow up album, was, if anything, more intense than *Nevermind*. Behind the scenes, though, Cobain was melting down. With a history of chronic depression, heavy drug use, including a severe heroin addiction, he'd nearly overdosed several times and never found rehab entirely successful. On April 8, 1994, the world learned that Kurt Cobain had shot and killed himself. Nirvana was no more, yet Cobain and Nirvana are remembered today for bringing alternative rock and grunge sensibilities into the mainstream, and *Nevermind* is recognized as one of the best-selling and most influential albums in history.

Suggested Songs:

Smells Like Teen Spirit (1991)
Something in the Way (1992)
Lithium (1992)
Heart-Shaped Box (1993)
All Apologies (1994)

#74 Judy Garland (1922 - 1969)
Began Recording: 1929 (w. Gumm Sisters); 1936 (solo)
Peak: 1939 - 1945; 1955 - 1957; 1961 - 1964
Genres: Traditional Pop & Standards; Show Tunes Singer

Author Karie Bible called her "without question the greatest entertainer who ever lived." She was born Frances Gumm, and her vaudevillian mother had her on stage and singing by the time she was two. Moving to California, she performed with her sisters and changed her name to Judy Garland when she was 12. MGM Studios offered her a movie contract in 1935, and she appeared in nearly three dozen films between 1936 and 1963. Judy has said that during this time she was made to feel like she was a fat, ugly duckling by studio execs, that she was regularly underfed, and given amphetamines (first by her mother) to keep her working insane hours, and then barbiturates to help her sleep. Nevertheless, she became a huge, girl-next-door star, most famously playing Dorothy, at the age of 16, in the 1939 classic *The Wizard of Oz*, the most watched film in movie history. Her poignant signature song, "Over the Rainbow," was nearly cut by studio head Louis B. Mayer who relented under pressure from the film's director; both the RIAA and the NEA have since acclaimed it the #1 Song of the Century.

As a vocalist, Judy was especially gifted. By all accounts, she had an uncanny ability to connect deeply with an audience, singing with a combination of "fragility and resilience," as Jonathan Riggs put it. It was as though she had lived the song, so believable was she. Even as a child she had a woman's voice, and her contralto grew deeper and richer with age. Her 1961 live recording, *Judy at Carnegie Hall*, is a landmark LP, sitting at #1 for 13 weeks and capturing for Judy the Grammy Album of the Year, the first ever awarded to a female performer. During the 1963-'64 TV season, *The Judy Garland Show* brought her into American homes every Sunday night.

Almost as famous for her demons as for her artistry, she had a lifelong struggle with depression and anxiety, drug and alcohol addictions, and an eating disorder. There were several suicide attempts, and she died at age 47 of an accidental barbiturate overdose. Yet, her gifts as an artist are today legendary. Frank Sinatra put it this way: "She will have a mystic survival. She was the greatest. The rest of us will be forgotten, but never Judy."

Suggested Songs:

Over the Rainbow (1939)
Last Night When We Were Young (1956)
The Man That Got Away (1961)
I Can't Give You Anything But Love (1961)
Old Man River (1964)

#73 B.B. King (1925 - 2015)
Began Recording: 1949
Peak: 1952- 1965; 1968 - 2005
Genres: Blues; R&B; jazz Singer/Guitarist/Songwriter

B.B. said he used to pick cotton all week and on Saturdays he'd go downtown with his guitar to sing; gospel numbers got him no tips, but he'd make a few bucks when he sang the blues—so, he became a bluesman.

Born into a sharecropping family, by his teenage years he was largely on his own. In 1946 he made his way to Memphis, sharpened his guitar skills with the help of cousin Bukka White, and was drawn to the electric guitar after hearing T-Bone Walker. He landed a DJ gig at an all-Black radio station, spinning discs and playing some of his own music live, gaining a name as the Beale Street Blues Boy, or B.B. for short. In 1949, he was given a chance to cut some records, working for a bit with Sam Phillips, who would later gain fame for discovering Johnny Cash and Elvis. His 1951 single, "3 O'clock Blues," with its forlorn, suicidal lyrics punctuated by single-note guitar accents, broke through on the R&B chart to #1. This was followed up a year later with another chart-topper, and B.B. began a lifelong, grueling regimen of constant touring, hitting the "Chitlin' Circuit" in the South and urban clubs in the north, from New York to Chicago. It's estimated that B.B. did over 15,000 shows in his lifetime, doing 342 nights in a busy 1956.

As the '50s wore on, King stayed on the R&B charts with a string of hits, and in 1962 he signed with a bigger label, ABC-Paramount. In 1965, he released his landmark LP, *Live at the Regal*, considered one of the greatest blues classics. As white, English blues-based rock by artists like Cream and the Rolling Stones gained traction, B.B. King began to get noticed by a wider audience. 1969 proved to be a breakthrough year as King got to open for the Stones and later released his iconic "The Thrill Is Gone," his highest charting, best-known song. Soon King was playing in big auditoriums and arenas, touring as far as Europe, Russia, Japan, and China, playing even for Pope John Paul II at the Vatican.

In 1971, he did a show at Cook County Jail and the experience so moved him that he continued performing for free at prisons the rest of his life. B.B. had a unique single-note, alternately warm and rounded, then sharp and stinging, signature guitar sound that alternated with his strong, melodic, confident, unfettered baritone. Eric Clapton, who recorded with him, deemed King "the most important artist the blues ever produced," while *AllMusic* called him "the single most important electric guitarist of the last half of the 20th century." A member of the Rock and Blues Halls of Fame, B.B. truly was the "King of the Blues."

Suggested Songs:

3 O'clock Blues (1951)
Every Day I Have the Blues (1955)
Why I Sing the Blues (1969)
The Thrill Is Gone (1969)
Come Rain or Come Shine (w. Eric Clapton) (2000)

#72 Grateful Dead

Began Recording: 1966
Peak: 1968 - 1974; 1977; 1987
Genres: Rock, Folk, Country. Blues, Psychedelia, Jazz Improvisational Band

They were unlike any band in history. Virtually unclassifiable, they were master musicians who could be transcendent or sloppy as hell on stage. They may have played live to more people than any artists in history, yet they never had a huge hit record. Hatched as the Warlocks in Palo Alto, California, in 1965, they shortly thereafter changed their name to the Grateful Dead. They got their start playing as the house band for the Merry Pranksters' Acid Tests which were public LSD parties organized by celebrated author Ken Kesey in California, leading directly to San Francisco's famous 1967 Summer of Love, the birth of the hippie movement.

The Grateful Dead's first eponymous LP was a folk-rock-blues amalgam that only reached #73 on *Billboard*, which was typical of their early work. Their next two, *Anthem of the Sun* and *Aoxomoxoa*, were highly experimental electronic collages mixing rock, folk, and jazz in an often spacy, surreal manner, sounding like nothing and no one else. At their heart, though, they were a jam band, taking off, like master jazzmen, into extended improv sections that drew from bluegrass as much as electronica. Best heard live, their most celebrated LP is 1969's *Live/Dead*, which features their towering, acid rock masterpiece, "Dark Star."

A cult band whose following of Deadheads grew massive, they also recorded in what today is known as "Americana," fluidly mixing folk, country, blues, and rock, most famously in their 1970 albums, *Workingman's Dead* and *American Beauty*. Some of their best-known tracks are from these two LPs—the bluegrass-flavored "Uncle John's Band;" "Casey Jones," with its double entendre anti-drug warning; "Friend of the Devil," a classic story song of a man on the run; and the loping, country, spiritual seeking anthem, "Ripple."

Legendary today for their live hours-long performances, they sometimes played for free and famously allowed fans to tape their shows. Jerry Garcia was their renowned lead guitarist, co-lead vocalist, and chief songwriter (along with non-performing lyricist Robert Hunter); classically trained Phil Lesh played bass; Bob Weir, an exceptionally versatile rhythm guitarist, shared vocals; "Pigpen" McKernan sang, played keyboards, harmonica, and percussion before his untimely death in 1973. Against custom, they employed two drummers, Bill Kreutzmann and Mickey Hart. The closest they ever got to chart topping success came in 1987 when *In the Dark* reached #6 and the survival song "Touch of Grey" hit #9.

In 1995, Garcia, long a smoker, intermittent drug abuser, and diabetic, passed away in a rehab facility; he was 53, and the Grateful Dead disbanded, only to reemerge in later years in various iterations and under different names. Their 1977 show at Cornell has taken on mythical status, but, then again, any Deadhead could cite a dozen others that were equally mind-blowing.

Suggested Songs:

Dark Star (1969)
Friend of the Devil (1970)
Ripple (1970)
Terrapin Station Medley (1977)
Touch of Grey (1987)

#71 Shania Twain (1965 - present)
Began Recording: 1993
Peak: 1995 - 2004
Genres: Country-Pop, Country-Rock Singer/Songwriter

She is the best selling female country artist ever, and if her life story were a piece of fiction, it would not be believed. Born Eilleen Edwards in Ontario, Canada, she took her Ojibwe stepdad's surname. She was poor, abused psychologically and physically, and thought her parents would one night kill each other, so she sought refuge in music. By the age of eight, she was being dragged to bars (after 1:00 AM, when alcohol could no longer be served) to sing and earn a little money to help the family. After high school she moved to Toronto and seemed primed to begin a career in country music, when she received word that both her parents had been killed in a car crash. Scrapping her plans, she moved back home to become a surrogate mom for her siblings, supporting them by singing at a local resort. Once the siblings could fend for themselves, Twain put together a demo and a show-case concert that caught the attention of Nashville. She was 27 years old.

Eilleen began calling herself Shania, an Ojibwe word, she says, for "on my way." Her first LP flopped, but it caught the attention of star hard rock producer Mutt Lange. Within a few months, the two were married and began to co-write songs for her follow-up LP. The Lange-produced *The Woman in Me* was released in 1995 and shot to the top of the U.S. and Canadian country charts, reaching #5 on the pop charts. The album had a slick, country-pop-rock sound and was heavily promoted through music videos and TV appearances. To date, it has sold over 20 million copies. Eight of the tracks became hits, including her first country chart-topper, "Any Man of Mine."

Two years later, she was back with *Come On Over*, the best-selling country album of all time. Music critic Kelefa Sanneh called it "a futuristic hybrid of pop country and bubblegum rock." Other country voices were concerned that Shania was too much a sex symbol. Still, it was becoming clear to all that she was changing country music with her huge crossover appeal into pop and rock and with her "taking no shit" empowerment ethos. She was fierce and out for a good time (just listen to her anthemic "Man! I Feel Like a Woman"), but could also be vulnerable and celebrate love ("You're Still the One").

In 2002, Twain released another worldwide LP, *Up*. Then, after a brief tour, she virtually disappeared. A bout of Lyme disease and a devastating betrayal cost Shania her voice and her marriage. She slowly worked her way back, releasing *Now* in 2017, her first studio album in 15 years. In 2023 she released *Queen of Me* and was back on tour.

They call her the "Queen of Country Pop," and that she paved the way for artists like Taylor Swift and Carrie Underwood is undeniable. That she did so in the face of such long odds is unbelievable.

Suggested Songs:

Any Man of Mine (1995)
Whose Bed Have Your Boots Been Under? (1995)
You're Still the One (1998)
Man! I Feel Like a Woman (1999)
Come On Over (1999)

#70 George Strait (1952 - present)
Began Recording: 1976
Peak: 1983 - 2014
Genres: Country-Neotraditional Country Singer/songwriter/guitarist

At a time when country music was veering more and more toward pop, George Strait came along with a clear allegiance to the pure country sounds of fiddles and steel guitars, western swing and honky-tonk influences evident. He is second only to Garth Brooks among country artists in total records sold and nobody has ever had more #1 hits in any genre.

The cowboy look is no act, as he grew up on a Texas ranch and has lived on one much of his adult life. Eloping with girlfriend Norma after high school, they remain married after 52 years. Rock was his music of choice as a teenager, but it was the country sounds of Hank and George and Merle that grabbed him while he was in the army. In the mid-'70s, while studying agriculture in college, he joined a Texas band, Ace in the Hole, the group that still often accompanies him to this day. His wife encouraged him not to give up on his musical dreams, and, in 1981, MCA recorded his single "Unwound," offering a contract when it became a hit. Strait has been a steady presence on *Billboard*'s country charts ever since with 23 studio albums reaching the top spot and several, such as 2008's *Troubadour*, having huge crossover appeal.

It's impossible, in a short space, to list all his chart topping singles, but some of his most iconic tracks include—1982's "Amarillo by Morning," about a beat up rodeo circuit rider who can still sing, affirming his freedom; 1985's "The Chair," a humorous, romantic bar pickup tale; the 1986 rousing, crowd favorite sing-a-long, "All My Ex's Live in Texas;" and "Baby Blue," the 1988 sweet, plaintive tune that many have heard as an ode to the daughter he lost to a car crash. "Heartland," his paean to traditional country values, and wedding favorite "I Cross My Heart" come from his best-selling 1992 *Pure Country* soundtrack.

Aside from his huge sales numbers, what sets Strait apart are his expressive, authentic-sounding, pure, rounded vocals. With just a bit of a Texas twang, George makes singing sound as easy and natural as breathing. Never showy, he projects honesty and confidence, and, over time, he became one of the biggest concert headliners in the world. When he announced his retirement from touring, over 104,000 turned out for his final, 2014 show, breaking a U.S. indoor concert record held for decades by the Rolling Stones. He still does a few shows a year, still fills stadiums, and has released new music as recently as 2019. George Strait, the "King of Country," is an original.

Suggested Songs:

Amarillo by Morning (1983)
The Chair (1985)
Baby Blue (1988)
Blue Clear Sky (1996)
Troubadour (2008)

#69 Earth, Wind & Fire
Began Recording: 1971
Peak: 1975 - 1982
Genres: R&B-Jazz-Soul-Pop fusion; Funk Band

Jazz legend Miles Davis called them his "all-time favorite band;" R&B songstress Dionne Warwick concurred. *Rolling Stone* said they "changed the sound of Black pop."

Between 1973 and 1981, Earth, Wind & Fire released 10 consecutive platinum albums. The brainchild of ex-Chess session drummer Maurice White, the first iteration of the band was put together in 1970 and after two 1971 Warner LPs that failed to become hits, White decided to reform the group, retaining only his brother, Verdine White, on bass. Maurice, who handled much of the songwriting, arranging, and production, also played percussion and the African kalimba. Philip Bailey, with his striking tenor and high falsetto voice, was enlisted to share the lead vocals with Maurice. Ralph Johnson, a drummer; sax artist Andrew Woolfolk; and guitarists, Al McKay and Johnny Graham, were among the additional recruits. Over time, Earth, Wind & Fire would grow bigger; including their celebrated Phoenix Horns, sometimes they employed 16 musicians for a single concert.

After Columbia bought out their contract, Earth, Wind & Fire, so named as an astrological reference to Maurice's sun sign, put out three LPs in quick succession that began to get them noticed in R&B circles, but it was their 1975 *That's the Way of the World* which proved to be their cross-over breakthrough, hitting the top of both the pop and the R&B charts. "A spiritual soul masterpiece," said the BBC. The Grammy-winning "Shining Star," with its intricate vocal harmonies and its striking, staccato bass and horn support, was the single that broke the album. Critics fell all over themselves trying to categorize their sound. Many heard echoes of Sly and the Family Stone; others referenced the Fifth Dimension. Most mentioned that this was some sort of hybrid—a tight, well-produced, new form of smooth soul and jazz-rock fusion, or was it... ? Maurice Williams explained,

"Although we were basically jazz musicians, we played soul, funk, gospel, blues, jazz, rock and dance music… which somehow ended up becoming pop." The lyrics were relentlessly upbeat, mystical in an amorphous sort of way. White, admitting to always having had a bit of the preacher in him, said as much—"I wanted… to convey messages of universal love and harmony."

With hit after hit—"Sing a Song," "Getaway," "Fantasy," "September," "Boogie Wonderland," "Let's Groove"—Earth, Wind & Fire was no longer being compared to anyone. In concert, they were described as "spectacular," "elaborate," and "dynamic." For a while, they employed magicians to levitate pianos and cause musicians to disappear and reappear.

Maurice retired from live performance in 1995 and died in 2016, a victim of Parkinson's, but to this day Earth Wind & Fire, led now by Bailey, continue to wow audiences with their precision, energy, and music of hope.

Suggested Songs:

Shining Star (1975)
Fantasy (1978)
September (1978)
Boogie Wonderland (w. The Emotions) (1979)
Let's Groove (1981)

#68 Simon & Garfunkel

Began Recording: 1957 (as Tom & Jerry); 1964 (as Simon & Garfunkel)
Peak: 1966 - 1970
Genres: Folk Rock Duo

Growing up blocks from one another in Queens, New York, Paul Simon and Art Garfunkel attended the same elementary, junior, and senior high schools. They first connected artistically in a 6th grade production of *Alice and Wonderland*, began harmonizing in a doo-wop group soon after, and, at age 15, went downtown to cut a $25 demo, "Hey, Schoolgirl," in the style of the Everly Brothers. When a small label offered to release their single under the moniker Tom & Jerry, they had a minor hit on their hands. Their follow-ups failed to chart, and in 1958 both went off to college. When Paul released a solo single, Art experienced it as an act of bad faith, the first of a lifelong series of perceived betrayals that each experienced at the hand of the other.

Reuniting in Greenwich Village in 1963 at the height of the folk boom, the duo, now calling themselves Simon & Garfunkel, were discovered by Tom Wilson, the Columbia producer instrumental in helping Dylan electrify his sound. After hearing the Simon-penned "The Sound of Silence," with its woeful vision of societal alienation, Wilson convinced his bosses to sign them. When their first LP failed to sell, the duo split again, Simon off to England to pursue a solo career, Garfunkel back to school. Unbeknownst to the two, Wilson took the original "The Sound of Silence" recording and added electric guitar, bass, and drum, releasing the song as a single and it took off, surprising both Paul and Art. Simon hurried back to the U.S. in early '66, and they rushed out a second LP, *Sounds of Silence*, to capitalize on their unexpected hit. Later in the year, they released the more polished *Parsley, Sage, Rosemary and Thyme* with the Top 10 hits, "Homeward Bound" and "I Am a Rock."

In 1967, they agreed to do the soundtrack for a Mike Nichols film. *The Graduate* became a '60s touchstone and helped push Simon & Garfunkel to the forefront of contemporary music. As the movie was exploding, their fourth LP, *Bookends*, arrived with the *Graduate*-related "Mrs. Robinson" dominating the airwaves in the summer of '68. In early 1970, Simon & Garfunkel released their fifth and, as it turned out, final studio LP, *Bridge Over Troubled Water*. The album dominated the Grammy awards and became the biggest seller of all time up to that point in history. Simon's autobiographical "The Boxer" and the title track are, to this day, included on many all-time great lists, but the tensions between the two were so profound, Art pursuing acting, Paul wanting to see what he could do as a solo artist, that, occasional reunions notwithstanding, Simon & Garfunkel were through.

Alternately criticized for the clean, polished sound and praised for the sterling harmonies and intelligent, poetic lyrics, Simon & Garfunkel's music continues to resonate with millions to this very day.

Suggested Songs:

The Sound of Silence (1965)
America (1968)
Mrs. Robinson (1968)
The Boxer (1969)
Bridge Over Troubled Water (1970)

#67 Fleetwood Mac

Began Recording: 1967
Peak: 1975 - 1987
Genres: Rock/Soft & Pop Rock; Blues Rock Band

"I don't think there's a person alive who listens to music that hasn't heard Fleetwood Mac. They're like the Beatles that way." (DJ Michael Tedesco).

Their roots were in the '60s British blues scene of bands like the Yardbirds and Cream. They took their name from drummer Mick Fleetwood and bassist John McVie (Mac), but at the start they were brilliant guitarist Peter Green's group; slide guitarist Jeremy Spencer was also part of the early mix. A hardcore blues rock band, in the late '60s they had some success in Britain, but in 1971 they lost both Green, to mental illness, and Spencer, to the religious cult, the "Children of God." With the addition of talented English singer, composer, and keyboardist Christine McVie, newly wed to John, the loss of the two guitarists, and a succession of replacements, Fleetwood Mac's sound began to morph into a more rock/soft rock direction, but by late '73 it seemed they might be through.

Lindsey Buckingham and Stevie Nicks had been romantically involved since their late teens and had formed a singer-songwriter partnership. When Mick invited the fingerpicking Buckingham to join the band in 1974, Lindsey agreed as long as they'd take Stevie as well. The classic lineup was set, and their first release, *Fleetwood Mac* (aka *The White Album*), with its soft rock sound, immediately bore fruit, climbing to the top of the U.S. charts. Four classics come out of this LP—"Over My Head," Christine's double-edged tribute to husband John; "Rhiannon," Stevie's acclaimed, spooky ode to a Welsh witch; "Say You Love Me," Christine's ambivalent celebration of her love; and Nicks' haunting meditation on change, "Landslide."

In 1976, under enormous pressure to build on what they had just created, the band gathered in northern California with their personal lives in turmoil. Christine and John, married for eight years, were in the midst of a divorce, working together but unable to talk. Lindsey and Stevie were also coming undone as a couple, and drummer Fleetwood, after learning of his wife's infidelity, had just divorced. Out of this messy brew sprang *Rumours*, rock & roll's greatest musical soap opera. "What distinguished *Rumours*," says Patrick McKay, "what makes it art—is the contradiction between its cheerful surface and its anguished heart." The songs "Go Your Own Way," Lindsey's rueful take on his separation and "Dreams," giving us Stevie's side, are matched by Christine's chipper "You Make Loving Fun;" "Don't Stop," which helped elect Bill Clinton; and the bitter "The Chain." The LP's final track muses about what is to come next. With sales of over 40 million, *Rumours* is one of the most played and celebrated LPs in recording history, cementing Fleetwood Mac's status as a truly iconic band. Interestingly, despite all the personal turmoil, the band carried on intact for another decade. There have also been reunions, but Christine McVie passed away in 2022.

Suggested Songs:

Landslide (1975)
Rhiannon (1976)
Go Your Own Way (1976)
Dreams (1977)
You Make Loving Fun (1977)

#66 Bee Gees
Began Recording: 1963
Peak: 1967 - 1971; 1975 - 1979
Genres: Soft & Pop Rock; Disco Band

Most artists are fortunate to have one chart topping stretch in their career; the Bee Gees, thanks to their often-brilliant songwriting and superlative three-part harmonies, had two. The Gibb brothers, Barry, and younger twins, Robin and Maurice, were singing together around Manchester, England, by the late '50s. Migrating to Australia in 1958, a local DJ began calling them the Bee Gees and helped them find local gigs. By 1963, they were writing and recording regularly without making a big dent in the charts. Returning to England in 1967, they broke through internationally with the haunting "New York Mining Disaster 1941," which had listeners wondering if it was a new Beatles tune. A few months later, "Massachusetts" gave them their first #1 in the U.K.

Often writing together as a trio, they drew liberally from pop, rock, R&B, even American country and drew on sources like Roy Orbison, the Everly Brothers, even Otis Redding. Barry, who later developed his trademark falsetto during their second phase, or Robin, with his more soulful, vibra-to-inflected voice, usually traded lead while the other two sang background. Barry played rhythm guitar, and Maurice was the multi-instrumentalist.

In 1968, they released two more gems: "I've Gotta Get a Message to You," a lament from a man awaiting execution and "I Started a Joke," with its gorgeous melancholic melody and cryptic lyric, yet, by 1969, they were coming apart, sniping at one another in the press. A year later, they reunited, memorializing their travails with the stirring ballad, "How Can You Mend a Broken Heart."

By the mid '70s, their records were no longer selling. Moving to Miami, they recorded an R&B-flavored dance number, "Jive Talking," which, along with the 1976 disco follow-up, "You Should Be Dancing," revitalized their career. When they were asked to record a soundtrack for a new John

Travolta film, the result was *Saturday Night Fever*, a musical, movie, and cultural phenomenon. Though late to the party, suddenly the Bee Gees were in the forefront of the disco dance craze. With songs like "Staying Alive," "How Deep Is Your Love," and "Night Fever," they were dominating the charts like nobody since the Beatles. And then it was over. Disco faded, and so did the Bee Gees. They continued recording and had the occasional European hit; they had individual successes and wrote hits for others, but suddenly, in 2003, Maurice died awaiting an operation. Nine years later, Robin was gone. Older brother Barry still carries on with the occasional record and appearance.

Their legacy? Praised by artists as diverse as Carrie Underwood, Beyoncé, and Justin Timberlake, they are today recognized as legends.

Suggested Songs:

New York Mining Disaster 1941 (1967)
I Started a Joke (1968)
How Can You Mend a Broken Heart (1971)
You Should Be Dancing (1976)
Staying Alive (1977)

#65 Lady Gaga (1986 - present)

Began Recording: 2006 (SGBand); 2008 (solo)
Peak: 2009 - 2023
Genres: Dance-Pop; Synth-Pop; Jazz Standards Singer/Songwriter

Musical giant or performance artist? She is provocative, over-the-top, and seemingly everywhere at once. She is also one of the defining recording artists of the past 15 years.

Stefani Germanotta was born 37 years ago to successful Manhattan parents who got her started on piano at four and into an elite Catholic all-girls high school. Self-described as an insecure misfit, Stefani involved herself in music and theater, gaining entry to NYU's prestigious Tisch School of the Arts at 17. She dropped out to pursue a music career, picked up the moniker Lady Gaga along the way, and after a false start with Def Jam, released a breakout debut LP in 2008, *The Fame*. With a dance-pop vibe, the album featured two singles, "Just Dance" and "Poker Face," that set the Gaga template—super catchy, highly propulsive, synth dance pop with suggestive lyrics you wouldn't want your mom to hear and even more aggressively risqué arty videos. A year later, eight more tracks were added, and the LP was reissued as *The Fame Monster* with its thrilling (or frightening, depending on your point of view) new number, the massively popular "Bad Romance."

Getting the superlatives out of the way, Lady Gaga has already won 13 Grammys, two Golden Globes, and an Oscar; six of her LPs have gone to #1 in the United States as have five of her singles, and she has been among the best-selling artists in the world since her debut; she has a monster presence as a concert draw, and there is simply nobody who has generated more buzz, for good or ill, in the realm of fashion—who else would even think of wearing a dress made of raw meat? She has proven that she has serious vocal chops too, surprising many by holding her own alongside jazz pop legend Tony Bennett.

On the other hand, there are many who see her as outrageous for the sake of being outrageous and more than a little artificial; after all, it was she who said, "People say Lady Gaga is a lie, and they are right. I am a lie… and then eventually it becomes a reality." More than a few people have seen her as recycling Bowie and Madonna, rather than giving us anything really new. And yet, she continues to turn heads and gain converts with numbers like "Born This Way," "I Can't Give You Anything but Love," and "Shallow." She has also been a tireless advocate for the LGBTQ+ community, anti-bullying campaigns, and for the promotion of mental health. No doubt, we 'll see new iterations of Lady Gaga in the coming years, and she will continue to surprise.

Suggested Songs:

Poker Face (2008)
Bad Romance (2009)
Anything Goes (w. Tony Bennett) (2014)
Million Reasons (2016)
Shallow (w. Bradley Cooper) (2018)

#64 Paul Simon (1941 - present)
Began Recording: 1957 (w. Garfunkel); 1972 (solo)
Peak: 1972 - 1976; 1986 - 1991
Genres: Folk & Pop Rock; World Music Singer/Songwriter

Paul Simon originally rose to fame as half of the '60s folk rock duo Simon & Garfunkel, celebrated for such culturally important hits as "The Sound of Silence," "Mrs. Robinson," and "Bridge Over Troubled Water."

By 1970, he was ready to move on from his partner to avoid becoming artistically stale. His solo work began in earnest with the 1972 release *Paul Simon*. It was a major success on both sides of the Atlantic and featured the reggae inflected "Mother and Child Reunion." His next two albums, *There Goes Rhymin' Simon* and *Still Crazy After All These Years*, continued his hot streak with the lively reminiscent track "Kodachrome," the gospel tinged " Loves Me Like a Rock," the meditative secular hymn to perseverance in the face of personal and national trial, "American Tune," and his humorous take on breaking up, "50 Ways to Leave Your Lover." Soon after, however, the hits began to dry up.

In 1986, at a personal and creative nadir, Simon was introduced to a mixtape of South African township music. Determined to continue his penchant for experimenting with different musical genres, he flew to Johannesburg and began working on a new album. This was a particularly controversial move since there was a cultural boycott against South Africa because of the brutal policy of racial segregation known as apartheid that was practiced there. Perhaps to offset breaking the boycott, Simon paid local musicians 12 times the going rate and, with the backing of a South African Black musicians union, proceeded despite heavy criticism and death threats. The result, *Graceland*, was an astounding blend of a capella Zulu choral music, up-tempo local street sounds, American pop, with Louisiana zydeco and Tex-Mex elements mixed in there as well. "World music," they called it, and though it remained controversial–cultural appropriation, said some; a bridge between the developed and the developing worlds, said others—it was a commercial and critical triumph, Simon's biggest seller and most critically celebrated record.

Four years later, he was back with another take on world music, this time mixing African, Brazilian, and North American sources to produce the less accessible, but still striking *The Rhythm of the Saints*. New albums have continued to appear every few years, many with great critical acclaim, his latest in 2023, but Simon is no longer a hit maker. No matter—he is the only artist to have LPs nominated for a best album Grammy in five consecutive decades, winning three times. A two-time member of the Rock Hall of Fame and a Kennedy Center honoree, Paul is also the first recipient of the coveted Library of Congress Gershwin Prize, as much for his poetic, introspective lyrics as for his groundbreaking musical exploration. To quote Simon, he writes about "hope and dread...a balance between the two, but coming down on the side of hope."

Suggested Songs:

Duncan (1972)
American Tune (1973)
Still Crazy After All These Years (1976)
Graceland (1986)
Father and Daughter (2006)

#63 Metallica

Began Recording: 1983
Peak: 1986 - 1992
Genres: Heavy Metal/Thrash Metal; Hard Rock Band

They were the masters of thrash metal, with its power chords, racing tempos, driving double bass drumming, and dark, dystopian themes—until they weren't.

Formed in 1981 by Danish transplant, drummer, and co-writer Lars Ulrich and James Hetfield, principal writer, singer, and rhythm guitarist, by 1982, Cliff Burton was on board as Metallica's bassist; Kirk Hammett joined as lead guitarist a year later, just before they cut their debut LP, *Kill 'Em All*. Their follow up, *Ride the Lightning*, in 1984 was on the same small independent label, and though neither LP was a hit, songs like the aggressive "Seek and Destroy;" "Fade to Black," with its suicidal ideation that Hetfield contends helped many who were feeling that way; the antiwar "For Whom the Bell Tolls;" and "Creeping Death," with its Biblical plague-informed lyric, generated enough excitement in metal circles that the band was signed to Elektra.

Master of Puppets was the 1986 offering on their new label. Breaking through to mainstream rock fans, but still loved by metalheads, this became the first metal LP chosen by the Library of Congress for preservation in the *National Recording Registry* for being "culturally, historically, or aesthetically significant." The title track, with its anti-drug theme and relentless guitar, has become, perhaps, Metallica's most iconic song, though "One," with its *Johnny Got His Gun* body horror and machine gun-visceral barrage from the follow up album, *And Justice for All*, may be a close second.

As Metallica was touring triumphantly in support of *Master of Puppets*, tragedy struck when their bus skidded and bass player Burton was thrown through a window and killed. With Burton's family's blessing, he was replaced, and the band carried on. 1991 saw the release of *Metallica* (aka *The Black Album*), their biggest seller ever, which marked the start of a stylistic shift away from thrash toward a slower heavy metal sound. "Nothing Else Matters" is nothing less than a love ballad. Subsequent releases have all reached the top of the charts, but they are generally less well regarded than their earlier work.

In 2000, Metallica became embroiled in controversy when they sued Napster, the online music sharing service, alleging that Napster enabled thievery and copyright infringement. People quickly took sides, some accusing Metallica of behaving like all wealthy fat cats protecting their interests and going after poor students, others noting that this new technology threatened to rob artists of their livelihood. Napster settled out of court and wound up declaring bankruptcy. As Lars put it, "If I wanna give my shit away for free, I'll give it away for free. That choice was taken away from me."

The most honored metal band in history, many have noted a return to the thrash metal sound of their early career in their recent releases. Metallica's latest LP, *72 Seasons*, dropped in 2023 to mostly positive reviews.

Suggested Songs:

For Whom the Bell Tolls (1984)
Master of Puppets (1986)
One (1989)
Nothing Else Matters (1992)
Whiskey in the Jar (1999)

#62 Mahalia Jackson (1911 - 1972)

Began Recording: 1931
Peak: 1947 - 1963
Genres: Gospel Singer

Mahalia Jackson, born in New Orleans, was raised by an aunt who was religious, strict, and physically abusive. Mahalia took refuge in the Baptist Church, though she was mesmerized with the more raucous sounds that emanated from the nearby Pentecostal Church. She was taken from grade school to be a laundress, and, in her free time, she secretly listened to Bessie Smith recordings.

As a teenager, she migrated to Chicago and began singing in a Baptist choir and a smaller church quartet, the Johnson Singers. Though her boisterous, body shaking, testifying southern style scandalized northerners at first, her natural talent was immediately obvious and she was soon soloing at various churches in the area. When she prayed that God would spare her sick grandfather's life and he recovered, Mahalia followed through on her promise to use her gift only to praise the Lord.

Upon meeting Thomas Dorsey, a seasoned blues and jazz musician intent on wedding his music to Baptist Christian lyrics, she had met her mentor, and the two began working closely, Mahalia singing, Dorsey accompanying on piano.

Jackson's first records did not sell and have been lost to time, but, in 1937, she cut four gospel singles for Decca. Sales were weak, but Decca was willing to work with Mahalia if she would sing secular music; she refused. In 1947, now recording for Apollo Records, she released "Move On Up a Little Higher." The record was a sensation, leaping to #2 on *Billboard*'s secular chart and selling in the millions, unheard of for a gospel record. It is still the best-selling gospel record ever and it made her an international star. Soon she was on radio and TV, appeared at Carnegie Hall, and toured Europe. Lucrative offers poured in for her to sing pop and jazz standards, but she continued to resist.

A racial pioneer, she repeatedly broke down walls with her media presence, her invitation to white and Black members of her concert audiences to sit together like "Christian brothers and sisters," her commitment to the Civil Rights struggle, and her willingness to move into an all-white neighborhood despite death threats. Battling a debilitating inflammatory illness, sarcoidosis, she died at the age of 60.

Recognized by many as the greatest gospel singer of them all, without Mahalia, it's doubtful we would know of Aretha Franklin, Whitney Houston, or Beyoncé. An untrained contralto, who easily slid up to soprano, a master of improvisation and melisma, she claimed she sang by feeling and by faith, an open vessel for God. The Rev. Dr. Martin Luther King Jr., her friend, summed up her gift: "A voice like hers comes along once in a millennium."

Suggested Songs:

Move On Up a Little Higher (1947)
Amazing Grace (1947)
His Eye Is On the Sparrow (1951)
Summertime/Sometimes I Feel Like a Motherless Child (1956)
Take My Hand, Precious Lord (1956)

#61 Ella Fitzgerald (1917 - 1996)
Began Recording: 1935
Peak: 1938 - 1947; 1956 - 1964
Genres: Jazz, Swing, Bebop/Scat; Traditional Standards Singer

Painfully shy offstage, she was in her element on it. Known as "America's First Lady of Song," she was the most popular female jazz singer for half a century. She lost her mother to a car crash when she was 15 and, left adrift, she strayed into illegal activities, winding up in reform school. She wanted to be a dancer, but after winning a $10 first prize at an Apollo Theater amateur night, Ella Fitzgerald had found her vocation.

Blessed with a pure, clear voice, Ella had impeccable control and could sing anything with grace and style. Originally inspired by Bing Crosby, Louis Armstrong, and Connee Boswell, in the '40s she took up bebop and became a master of scat singing, her voice expertly imitating the sounds of the band's instruments.

Bandleader Chick Webb, initially reluctant to hire her because she didn't possess the usual physical beauty of a typical female lead, relented and became her mentor. Her 1938 recording of "A-Tisket, A-Tasket," a child's nursery rhyme, became a huge bestseller and brought Ella instant fame. When Webb died in 1939, the band became Ella Fitzgerald and Her Famous Orchestra. The group disbanded in 1942, and Ella became a free-lance soloist. Her 1947 renditions of "Flying Home" and "Oh, Lady Be Good" are considered scat masterpieces.

In 1953, Ella began working with jazz producer and promoter Norman Granz, who remained her manager until her death. With his help, she began playing more upscale clubs and touring internationally. He also gently nudged her in the direction of the Great American Songbook, and from 1956 to 1964 she recorded and released a series of Song Book LPs of traditional standards composed by the likes of Cole Porter, Duke Ellington, Rodgers & Hart, Irving Berlin, and the Gershwin Brothers. This was an extraordinary cultural moment as Frank Rich of *The New York Times* noted,

"Here was a Black woman popularizing urban songs often written by immigrant Jews to a national audience of predominantly white Christians."

Ella's fame and profile soared after this. She was collaborating with her old heroes, Louis Armstrong, Duke Ellington, Count Basie, singing with Sinatra, and gaining recognition with the first of her 14 Grammy Awards. Her 1960 live *Ella in Berlin* is considered a landmark LP. She worked steadily through the 1980s, but her health began to decline. She gave the last of her 26 Carnegie Hall concerts in 1991 and died of a stroke in 1996; Ella was 79-years-old. A member of the Jazz and Women's Halls of Fame, the Grammy Museum simply calls her the "premiere American female singer."

Suggested Songs:

A-Tisket, A-Tasket (1938)
Flying Home (1947)
Dream a Little Dream of Me (w. Louis Armstrong) (1950)
Someone To Watch Over Me (1950)
Cry Me a River (1961)

#60 Billie Holiday (1915 - 1959)

Began Recording: 1934
Peak: 1939 - 1946
Genres: Jazz; blues; traditional pop Singer/songwriter

Details of her early life are fuzzy. Born Eleanora Fagan and raised in Baltimore, she had a jazz musician father, who wasn't a big part of her life. She may have been sexually abused as a child.

By age 11, she was out of school, and, in 1927, she moved with her mom to New York. She became interested in music, drawn to the "big sound" of Bessie Smith and the "feeling" of Louis Armstrong. While still a young teenager, she began to frequent Harlem nightclubs and was soon singing.

In 1933, record producer John Hammond, who would later gain fame for signing Aretha and Dylan, first heard her, and later that year the 18-year-old, now calling herself Billie Holiday, cut her first record with the up-and-coming Benny Goodman.

With Hammond producing, between 1935 and 1938 she recorded a string of hits with pianist Teddy Wilson. Billie also sang briefly with Count Basie's big band before moving on in 1938 to sing with Artie Shaw's band, unusual at the time since Holiday was Black and Shaw white.

In 1939, she released "Strange Fruit," a protest song with graphic lyrics against the practice of lynching. Despite the lack of airplay, the song sold well. In 1942, she released "God Bless the Child," one of her own compositions.

She continued to release hits through 1945, but in 1947 she was arrested for possession of heroin and received an 8-month prison sentence. Though she rebounded with several celebrated Carnegie Hall concerts, by the 1950s her use of drugs, alcohol, and a series of abusive relationships had taken their toll on her health and her voice. Arrested on her hospital deathbed, again for possession, she was gone at 44.

Billie's singing style was unusual and controversial for her time. She played with phrasing and tempo, often singing slightly offbeat. She loved to improvise, and though sponsors and promoters often protested, her vocals were always believable, usually tinged with sadness, and often heartbreaking. Hammond said she was "the first girl singer… who actually sang like an improvising jazz genius." Frank Sinatra, often touted as the century's greatest singer, called Billie "the greatest single musical influence on me." It has been said that popular singing can be divided into before and after Billie Holiday—her impact has been that profound.

"God Bless the Child" has been honored by the RIAA, the National Endowment of the Arts, and the Grammy Hall of Fame, while "Strange Fruit" was deemed the "Song of the Century" by *Time*. Billie is a member of the Jazz, Rock, R&B, and Women's Halls of Fame. With her trademark white gardenia, "Lady Day," as she was known, is a true immortal.

Suggested Songs:

Strange Fruit (1939)
God Bless the Child (1942)
I'll Be Seeing You (1944)
Lover Man (1945)
Don't Explain (1946)

#59 Mariah Carey (1969 - present)
Began Recording: 1990
Peak: 1990 - 2000; 2005 - 2006
Genres: R&B; Pop; hip-hop Singer/Songwriter

The New York Times said she had the "most impressive voice of her generation." Born into a mixed-race family in comfortable Long Island, she was raised by her opera-singing mother who began seeing that her talented daughter, Mariah, receive voice lessons from the age of four. In Mariah's telling, hers was a tumultuous childhood that included racial taunts at school and sibling abuse.

Living in Manhattan after high school, a friend slipped her demo to Columbia Records exec Tommy Mottola, and she was quickly signed. In 1990, her debut LP, *Mariah Carey*, climbed to the top of the *Billboard* pop chart as did her initial five singles, a first for any artist. Critics lauded her glorious, powerhouse voice, but were less than unanimous in their praise of her lyrics and musical production. Still, she picked up her first Grammy, for Best New Artist.

In 1993, Mariah was married to Mottola, and she launched the massive best seller *Music Box*, with the catchy dance pop "Dreamlover" and the Whitney-like anthem "Hero," her 7th and 8th chart toppers respectively. 1994 saw the release of "All I Want for Christmas Is You," which has gone on to become a bona fide holiday classic and the best-selling Christmas song by a female in history. 1995 brought *Daydream*, the best-received album of her career, up to that point, with at least three memorable tracks—"Fantasy," an up-tempo R&B groove; "One Sweet Day," a Boyz II Men collaboration about lost loved ones; and "Always Be My Baby," with the singer consoling herself that the moved-on lover will in some way return. By 1997, Mariah had split from her "suffocating" marriage and began to explore more freely her inclinations toward urban and hip-hop music with the release of *Butterfly*; "Honey" was one of the standout tracks.

By the start of the new millennium, the hit machine began to falter, and Carey suffered a much-publicized physical and emotional breakdown, revealing years later that she suffers from bipolar II. In 2005, she rebounded with her most successful work in years, *The Emancipation of Mimi*, a blend of R&B, hip-hop, and pop.

No one questions Mariah's vocal ability. With a five-octave range, she is considered technically brilliant, a master of melisma, the singing of several notes on a single syllable. Some have questioned whether her "vocalizing is all about the performance" (Jim Faber) and whether she delivers emotionally. Still, she has continued to evolve, and, in 2008, *Slate*'s Jody Rosen wrote that Carey was, "the most influential vocal stylist of the last two decades, the person who made rococo melismatic singing...the ubiquitous pop style." Love her or not, only the Beatles have had more *Billboard* Hot 100 #1 singles.

Suggested Songs:

Hero (1993)
All I Want for Christmas Is You (1994)
Without You (live) (1996)
Honey (1997)
We Belong Together (2005)

#58 Linda Ronstadt (1946 - present)

Began Recording: 1967 (Stone Poneys); 1969 (solo)
Peak: 1975 - 1979
Genres: Rock; Country Rock; folk rock; traditional pop; mariachi Singer

The "Queen of Rock" doesn't think she's a very good rock vocalist at all; she considers herself more of a balladeer.

Linda Ronstadt grew up in a musical family on a ranch near Tucson. Of German-Mexican heritage, she learned to love every kind of music and sang from an early age, inspired by the likes of her father, Mexican song-stress Lola Beltran, opera great Maria Callas, and '50s-'60s radio. At 18, she moved with a friend to Los Angeles and began recording as part of the folk rock trio, the Stone Poneys. Their single hit, 1967's "Different Drum," made her a star as her powerful voice was instantly obvious, and, in 1969, she launched her solo career.

Recording in a country rock idiom, her climb to superstardom was gradual, but there were highlights along the way. "Long, Long Time", from her second LP, *Silk Purse*, only reached #25 on the Hot 100 but is today recognized as a classic. In 1971, she was briefly backed by a group of little-known musicians who went on to become the Eagles; her cover of their "Desperado" in 1973 helped bring it to the public's attention. In 1974, she released *Heart Like a Wheel*, widely held to be her finest effort. "You're No Good" and "When Will I Be Loved" were huge hits on the pop and country charts. Her next six albums also went platinum, and, suddenly, she was filling arenas. A natural beauty, the media played up her sex appeal much to Ronstadt's chagrin, often downplaying her commanding, emotional vocals once likened to the force of a hurricane. Linda moved easily from contralto to soprano, and Christopher Loudon, a *Jazz Times* critic, remarked that she was "blessed with arguably the most sterling set of pipes of her generation."

In the 1980s, she abruptly changed direction, much to the distress of her record label. Collaborating with famed traditional pop and jazz arranger Nelson Riddle, she released three albums of standards taken from the Great American Songbook, introducing these old classics to a new generation of listeners. Then she took another turn, recording an album of traditional Mexican songs, *Canciones de Mi Padre* (*Songs of My Father*). A Grammy winner, it has become the top selling non-English language LP in U.S. history.

Sadly, Linda began noticing a decline in her abilities in 2000. She released her final LP in 2006, gave her last concert in 2009, and revealed in 2013 that she was suffering from Parkinson's. The diagnosis has since been changed to progressive supranuclear palsy, but the effect is the same—a loss of muscular control; singing is now impossible. Still, she has since then been recognized with an induction into the Rock Hall of Fame and a Kennedy Center honor, and her place in recording history is secure.

Suggested Songs:

Long, Long Time (1970)
Desperado (1973)
You're No Good (1975)
Prisoner in Disguise (1975)
La Cigarra (The Cicada) (1987)

#57 Aerosmith

Began Recording: 1973
Peak: 1975 - 1979; 1986 - 2002
Genres: Hard Rock; blues-rock; heavy metal; pop rock Band

Aerosmith is the best selling American hard rock band of all time. They formed in Boston in 1970 and paid to play at a club so that they'd be noticed by Columbia's Clive Davis; it worked, and in 1973 they released their self-titled debut LP. Compared unfavorably to the Rolling Stones, initially, the album is notable for their first single, "Dream On," a power ballad, arguably their best-known song.

Steven Tyler, lead singer, with a strong, recognizable tenor that soars upward into an other-worldly screeching falsetto, struts about the stage with Jagger-like panache, and Joe Perry is the solid lead guitarist and co-writer, along with Tyler, of many of Aerosmith's most recognizable songs. Brad Whitford plays rhythm and, sometimes, lead guitar; Joey Kramer is the bassist, and Tom Hamilton handles the drums.

Their third LP, *Toys in the Attic*, proved to be their breakthrough commercially, reaching #11 on the *Billboard* chart (it is still their bestseller), and critically, gaining them newfound respect. The album is featured among *Rolling Stone*'s greatest albums in history. Two tracks stand out—"Sweet Emotion," becoming their first Top 40 hit, and "Walk This Way" with its recognizable rock riff and sexually suggestive lyrics about a high school boy losing his innocence. The follow-up LP, *Rocks*, was also a huge commercial and critical success.

Drugs, alcohol, and debauched on-the-road living began to take their toll on Aerosmith, and, by 1981, both Perry and Whitford had left the band. When they returned in 1984, Aerosmith was a has-been act, no longer filling stadiums and arenas. When producer Rick Rubin called in '86 to suggest a crossover collaboration with up and coming rappers Run-DMC on "Walk This Way," Tyler and Perry were initially reluctant, but the huge success of the song reignited Aerosmith's career and helped bring rap to the mainstream.

While the following years saw renewed struggles with addiction, they also brought huge international success with the LPs *Permanent Vacation*, *Pump*, *Get a Grip*, and *Nine Lives,* and their first Grammys for "Janie's Got a Gun," "Livin' on the Edge," "Crazy," and "Pink." They are now members of the Rock & Roll Hall of Fame, Songwriters Hall of Fame (Tyler and Perry), and they've been immortalized in the video game universe with *Guitar Hero: Aerosmith*. Their influence can be heard in countless bands that followed, from Van Halen to Guns N' Roses, even as Aerosmith themselves continue to perform to this day.

Suggested Songs:

Dream On (1973)
Sweet Emotion (1975)
Walk This Way (1976)
Janie's Got a Gun (1989)
Crazy (1994)

#56 Drake (1986 - present)

Began Recording: 2006
Peak: 2010 - 2023
Genres: Hip-Hop; R&B; Pop Singer/Songwriter

Over the past dozen years, there may not be a more popular recording artist than Drake. The RIAA has certified him as the all-time, top-selling digital artist in the United States, and he's just 37 years old.

Born to a Canadian Jewish mother and a Black American musician father, Aubrey Drake Graham was raised mostly by his schoolteacher mom in Toronto. As a teenager, he landed a role on the Canadian TV show *Degrassi*, playing a basketball star who winds up in a wheelchair after getting shot. Eager to get into music, on the side Drake was busy recording.

A lover of melody and R&B grooves, he was also drawn to rap, to Lil Wayne, to JAY-Z, and to Kanye West. In 2006, he self-released his first mixtape which brought him little attention; his second release gained him a bit more notice in the hip-hop world, but it was the third one, 2009's *So Far Gone*, that broke through on U.S. and Canadian charts and featured his first hit, the explicit love song, "Best I Ever Had." The success of the single led to *So Far Gone* being released as an EP. Suddenly, Drake was the most sought after unsigned artist in music. He went with Lil Wayne's Young Money label and, in 2010, dropped his first LP, *Thank Me Later*, which immediately rose to #1 in both the U.S. and Canada. A year later, he was back with his most acclaimed LP, *Take Care*, with its darker, moody, sensual atmosphere, meditating in rhyme and song on the perks and burdens of fame and the joys and pains involved in relationships. The album garnered a Best Rap Grammy and was acclaimed as the LP of the year by both the *New York* and the *L.A. Times*.

Drake has released five more studio albums since *Take Care* and they all went straight to the top of the charts. Lyrically, Drake has been described as introspective. Other words that come up repeatedly in descriptors of his songwriting include honest, vulnerable, ambivalent, emotional, and melancholic. Some critics find him too self-absorbed and prone to naval gazing. Like many rappers, Drake has been accused of objectifying women, but, to be fair, sometimes the women in his songs hold the power, as in the fascinating rumination on lost love, "Marvin's Room."

Drake has changed music these past 12 years in two significant ways— he has blurred the line, more than any other artist, on how we receive our music as his mixtapes and downloads have reached as many people, if not more, than his LPs. In addition, his mixing of rap with singing has revolutionized the genre. As *The New York Times* put it, "Rappers are singers now. Thank Drake."

Suggested Songs:

Find Your Love (2010)
Marvin's Room (2011)
Hold On, We're Going Home (2013)
One Dance (2016)
Race My Mind (2021)

#55 Tony Bennett (1926 -2023)

Began Recording: 1941 (as Joe Bari); 1951 (as Tony Bennett)
Peak: 1951 - 1953; 1962 - 1963; 1992 - 2015
Genres: Traditional Pop; Jazz/Swing; show tunes Singer

Born Anthony Benedetto and raised in Queens, he was singing in public by the age of 10 and, as a teen, worked as a singing waiter. Drafted into the army in 1944, he experienced combat in France and Germany as the Allies closed in on Berlin. After the war, he studied singing on the G.I. Bill, was discovered by Pearl Bailey and Bob Hope, and shortened his name to Tony Bennett at Hope's suggestion.

Signed to Columbia in 1951, Bennett immediately had a #1 hit, "Because of You," in the popular crooner style of the day, accompanied by a lush, Percy Faith arrangement. The hits continued with Faith's arrangement of Hank Williams' "Cold, Cold Heart," followed by "Rags to Riches" and "Stranger in Paradise." By the mid-'50s, rock & roll began to take over the airways and Bennett turned toward the more jazz-oriented sound that he favored. In 1962, he released the classic for which he is still best known, "I Left My Heart in San Francisco." This was followed by a couple more hits, and then the Beatles and the Brits arrived; suddenly singers like Bennett were decidedly out of fashion.

Bennett's half-hearted attempt to do a more modern form of pop left him musically adrift and without a record label. He moved back toward jazz with pianist Bill Evans in the mid-'70s, emotionally satisfying perhaps, but no hits. Finally, at a particularly low point in his life, he turned to his son Danny Bennett for help. Danny took over as his manager and began working to expose his father to a younger audience without compromising Tony's artistic vision.

The big breakthroughs came with *Perfectly Frank*, a tribute to his friend Frank Sinatra, followed by his 1994 *MTV Unplugged* live LP, which captured the Album of the Year Grammy. These were followed by tributes to great female vocalists; to Billie Holiday; and to Duke Ellington, all hugely successful works in jazz and traditional pop circles. Then, in 2006, he released *Duets: An American Classic*, which soared to #3 on the *Billboard* 200 pop chart, and his *Duets II*, released five years later, became the first chart-topping album of his career.

In recent years, Tony formed a close friendship and singing partnership with versatile contemporary pop vocalist Lady Gaga; the two released two hit albums of jazz standards, *Cheek to Cheek* and *Love for Sale*. With the latter's release, Bennett became the oldest person ever to release an album of new material. In 2021, Bennett and his family announced that he was diagnosed with Alzheimer's disease; he did his final two shows later that year at New York's Radio City Music Hall with Gaga at his side, thus capping a 70-year career. Tony passed away in his home in 2023.

Suggested Songs:

Cold, Cold Heart (1951)
I Left My Heart in San Francisco (1962)
Who Can I Turn To (When Nobody Needs Me) (1964)
It Had to Be You (1994)
Anything Goes (w. Lady Gaga) (2014)

#54 Celine Dion (1968 - present)

Began Recording: 1981
Peak: 1992 - 1999; 2002 - 2010
Genres: Pop; Chanson; soft rock Singer

Celine Dion is the top selling Canadian recording artist in history, and she also ranks among the top 20 best sellers worldwide.

Born near Montreal, the youngest of 14 children, at age 13 she made her recording debut in French. For the rest of the '80s, she experienced modest success in French-speaking Quebec, but in 1990 she released her first English language records. Her breakthrough came in 1991 with the title track from the Disney animated film *Beauty and the Beast*. She followed that up in 1992 with the LP *Celine Dion* and, a year later, with *The Color of My Love*, which sold 20 million copies and featured her first signature tune, "The Power of Love." Gaining fame internationally, she refused to turn her back on her French Canadian roots and, in 1995, released *D'eax (Of Them)*, the best selling French language LP of all time. This was followed in 1996 by *Falling Into You*, her biggest seller ever at 32 million and winner of the coveted Album of the Year Grammy. The album features three key Dion singles, "Because You Loved Me;" "It's All Coming Back to Me Now;" and the Eric Carmen remake, "All By Myself." A year later she was back with *Let's Talk About Love* which has sold over 30 million copies and contains her best-known song, "My Heart will Go On," from the movie blockbuster *Titanic*.

Dion took a hiatus from 1999 to 2002 and, following the birth of a son, released *A New Day Has Come*, yet another worldwide bestseller. Celine also broke ground, beginning in 2003, with her extended residencies at Las Vegas Caesars Palace. These have been called the most successful residencies of all time. In 2008, her outdoor free concert in Quebec City drew nearly half a million people.

Celine Dion is best known for her wide-ranging, soaring voice. She's a technically skilled singer with superb pitch, a pure tone, especially in the upper registers, with great ability to sustain her notes. A great belter, she is sometimes called the "Queen of Power Ballads." She does, however, divide the critics. While some have extolled her immaculate production and emotionally charged vocals, others have heard her as bombastic, lacking in personality, and overly sentimental. Nevertheless, a host of world-class vocalists, from Patti LaBelle to Kelly Clarkson to Barbra Streisand, have sung her praises. Josh Groban, who partnered with her on "The Prayer," had this to say about Celine and her voice, "She's a powerhouse. In this day and age when more and more studio-produced, tiny-tiny voices are being rewarded... she has this extraordinary instrument."

Sadly, Celine, who is only 55, has recently been silenced by a rare neurological disorder. The hope is that she will find a treatment that allows her to resume her career.

Suggested Songs:

Beauty and the Beast (from *Beauty and the Beast*, duet with Peabo Bryson) (1991)
The Power of Love (1993)
Because You Loved Me (1996)
All By Myself (1996)
My Heart Will Go On (Love Theme from *Titanic*) (1997)

#53 Little Richard (1932 - 2020)

Began Recording: 1951
Peak: 1955 - 1958
Genres: Rock & Roll; R&B; Gospel Singer/Songwriter/Pianist)

He was born Richard Penniman in Macon, Georgia, one of 12 children. As a child, he was loud and rambunctious, but he also liked putting on his mother's makeup and was kicked out of his own home at 13 by his father for "being gay," as Richard once told it. Deeply involved in church and gospel music from a young age, Richard was now free to explore the "devil music," R&B, which his family deplored. A chance to sing once with Sister Rosetta Tharpe and hearing a host of Black performers convinced Little Richard, as he now began calling himself, of his life's direction.

Singing blues, gospel, and R&B in bars and clubs, sometimes in drag, he honed his live, uninhibited stage act. Between 1951 and '54, he recorded six records, with two different labels, but they went nowhere. Then, late in 1955, Specialty Records sent him to New Orleans to cut a few tracks. Hesitant and restrained initially, when he began singing a risqué number called "Tutti Frutti" in his live, unfettered fashion, his producer heard the potential; a songwriter was called in to clean up the bawdy lyrics, and little Richard was on his way.

The hits came one after another—"Tutti Frutti," "Long Tall Sally," "Rip It Up," "Lucille," "Jenny Jenny," "Keep A-Knockin'," "Good Golly, Miss Molly." With his strident, gospel-informed, singing-shouting style, punctuated by his trademark falsetto "woooo," he sounded fresh and vital; half standing, half sitting, pounding out his piano triplets, mixing jump blues and boogie-woogie, this was rock & roll, though Richard later commented that it was "just rhythm and blues played fast." All this was accented, of course, with his 6-inch pompadour, eyeliner and makeup, colorful capes and puffy shirts. He was a sensation, appealing to both Black and white audiences, helping to shatter racial barriers in the process. Not just Americans bought in; he was a smash in Britain as well.

Then, just as suddenly as he had struck, he threw it all away, quitting the business in late 1957, announcing that he was going into the ministry; and he did for a while, even cutting gospel records praised by Mahalia Jackson and Quincy Jones. But he couldn't stay away from rock & roll, and soon the up-and-coming Beatles were opening for him onstage. He never regained the success found in the late '50s, but he is known today as the "Architect of rock & roll," and he's been praised and paid homage to by all the greats— Elvis, James Brown, Bob Dylan, the Beatles, Mick Jagger, David Bowie—the list is too long to spell out.

He died in 2020, after a tortured, contradictory life, having finally accepted his dual mission, to bring rock & roll and the Christian gospel to the world.

Suggested Songs:

Tutti Frutti (1955)
Long Tall Sally (1956)
Keep A-Knockin' (1957)
Good Golly, Miss Molly (1958)
Do Lord Remember Me (1961)

#52 Adele (1988 - present)

Began Recording: 2007
Peak: 2011 - 2023
Genres: Soul; Pop Singer/Songwriter

It has been described as a once in a generation voice, like Streisand's or Houston's. Amanda Petrusich of the *New Yorker* heard it as "a gust of wind that has picked up some grit." Her range may not be quite as broad as Mariah's or Celine's, but it doesn't matter. It's the "emotive timbre," as Jon Pareles put it. Ryan Reed called it "a raspy, aged-beyond-its-years thing of full-throated beauty."

Born Adele Laurie Blue Adkins and raised by her mother in working-class London, she was drawn to singing from an early age. Attending the renowned BRIT School for Performing Arts and Technology, Adele was inspired to pick up the guitar by fellow alumna Amy Winehouse and she began closely studying other vocalists such as Etta James. She was discovered after a friend posted a demo on Myspace.

Adele's first album, the soulful *19*, named for her age and featuring mostly her own compositions, was released in 2008 and reached #1 in the U.K. and the Netherlands. Standout tracks include the striking "Chasing Pavements" and a piano-backed Bob Dylan cover, "Make You Feel My Love." In 2011, she was back with her second LP, *21*, which she and others have termed her break-up record. Aside from the expected soul elements, people have heard bits of folk, country, gospel, and blues. With sales of 31 million and three #1 hits, it is the best selling album of the 21st Century. Adele scooped up six Grammys, including the coveted Album, Record, and Song of the Year, the latter two for the raging "Rolling in the Deep." Since the time of its release, *21* has appeared on many lists of all-time greatest albums.

No surprise, of course, that her next two LPs, 2015's *25* and 2021's *30*, have also been worldwide #1 hits. Adele referred to *25* as her "make-up record;" people have also cited themes of motherhood and notes of regret. The pain of letting go comes through in *30*; in the giant hit "Easy on Me"

Adele is heard expressing her vulnerability and her limitations, asking an ex-lover or her son to be gentle with her.

Indeed, vulnerability is a word that comes up often when critics and fans are discussing Adele, as are words like powerful yet fragile, confessional and brave; the word, though, that is perhaps most fitting, is emotive. Not just a technically exceptional vocalist, Adele also communicates the full range of emotions, particularly pain, but also yearning, fury, sadness, and triumph in a way that only the great singers do; and, of course, she is still a young woman.

Suggested Songs:

Make You Feel My Love (2008)
Rolling in the Deep (2010)
Someone Like You (2011)
Hello (2015)
Easy on Me (2021)

#51 Billy Joel (1949 - present)

Began Recording: 1967 (w. The Hassles); 1971 (solo)
Peak: 1977 - 1993
Genres: Pop Rock Singer/Songwriter/Pianist

Billy Joel was a Jewish suburban "baby boomer" who attended Catholic Church as a boy and took piano lessons because his mom pushed him. He had a "gentle upbringing," by his own account, though his parents divorced when he was eight. The Beatles ignited his passion for music and by his late teens he was playing in bands, even cutting a few records that went nowhere.

Fighting his way through depression, a suicide attempt, and treatment at a psychiatric facility, in 1971 he signed an ill-advised record deal with a small time label and cut his first solo LP, *Cold Spring Harbor*. The album went nowhere, and Joel moved to L.A., taking up residence at a Wilshire Boulevard piano bar. Meanwhile, an underground recording of "Captain Jack," a "dreary song," says Joel, about an angsty teenager whose dad commits suicide, was getting airplay in the northeast. This led to Columbia Records buying out Joel's old contract; Joel then parlayed his piano bar experience into the celebrated story song "Piano Man," which has become his signature.

1977's *The Stranger* was the real breakthrough, however, that catapulted Joel to the highest levels of superstardom. "Just the Way You Are" became a massive radio hit, while "Scenes from an Italian Restaurant," though not a single, is one of his best-loved songs. "Scenes..." is a masterful cinematic suite, moving from melodic piano ballad placing us in the present moment in the restaurant, then switches to a jaunty, New Orleans jazz-inflected remembrance of youthful escapades, to a rocking retelling of how the song's couple is now divorced, and finally the song segues back to the present with our red and white wines in the Italian restaurant.

Joel continued to enjoy success for the next 16 years—33 Top 40 hits in all. His 1978 album, *52nd Street,* won the Album of the Year Grammy while his *Greatest Hits* is among the all-time best sellers. Still, Joel has not always been treated kindly by the critics. Dave Marsh once called his work, "self-dramatizing kitsch," while Robert Christgau described his music as "a force of nature and bad taste." Joel, himself, has responded by saying that one can dislike a piece of music without it necessarily being bad. John Landau has said of Joel, "We've been proven wrong."

If the public has the final say, Landau is correct, for though Billy has released no new songs since 1993, he has enjoyed a monthly Madison Square Garden residency since 2014 and it always sells out. "I'm competent," says Joel. "I know how to write. I know how to play. I know how to sing in key… This is a Peter Pan kinda job."

Suggested Songs:

Piano Man (1973)
New York State of Mind (1976)
Scenes from an Italian Restaurant (1977)
She's Always a Woman (1977)
My Life (1978)

#50 AC/DC

Began Recording: 1974
Peak: 1979 - 1982; 1990 - 1991; 2008 - 2010
Genres: Hard Rock; Heavy Metal; blues-rock Band

Famed music producer Rick Rubin called them "the best rock band in the world, of all time." They've also been dismissed by many critics as "simplistic," "minimalistic," and "misogynistic," but what is beyond dispute is that they are one of the top-selling bands ever.

They are AC/DC, the brainchild of two Scottish born brothers, Malcolm and Angus Young. Formed in Australia in 1973, they began as a glam outfit but quickly switched to hard rock. With flashy Angus as the lead guitar frontman, duck walking across the stage in his schoolboy uniform, and steady, quiet Malcolm, the band's anchor, on his power rhythm guitar, there have been a number of other mates through the years. Hard-living Bon Scott handled the vocals 'til 1980. They'd been steadily gaining exposure and fans through a succession of album releases and relentless touring around the world. Then, in 1979, their 7th studio LP, *Highway to Hell,* made them bona fide stars.

As they were beginning work on a follow-up album, Scott, age 33, suddenly died, a victim of "acute alcohol poisoning." After a bit of hesitation, the band decided to hire a new lead singer, settling on Brian Johnson, an R&B-style rocker once praised by Scott himself. In July 1980, AC/DC released their Scott tribute album, *Back In Black.* With Johnson wailing over Phil Rudd's drumming, Cliff Williams' bass, and the driving Young guitars, the tempos may vary, but there is a unified, unstoppable, energetic, hard-edged life force that roars out of the speakers on such numbers as "Shoot to Thrill," "You Shook Me All Night Long," and the title track. Critics may be divided, but fans were and are not. With reported sales of over 50 million copies, it is said to be the second-best-selling album of all time, trailing only Michael Jackson's *Thriller.*

You may think you don't know their music, but AC/DC is everywhere—in countless films, from *The Avengers* to *School of Rock* to *Bridesmaids*; in video games, from *Rock Band* to *Madden NFL*; in commercials, from *NASCAR* to *Dodge* to *Coca Cola*. Hell, "Back In Black" has become the Iowa Hawkeye football theme song. What to say about their music? Is it heavy metal or is it hard rock? People have been known to fight over how to classify them. Loud, clean, headbanging, basic, tight, and consistent are the words that come up the most—and popular. Watching and listening to a stadium full of AC/DC fans leaping and screaming along with "Thunderstruck" is a sight and a sound to behold!

Suggested Songs:

What's Next to the Moon (1978)
Highway to Hell (1979)
Back In Black (1980)
You Shook Me All Night Long (1980)
Thunderstruck (1990)

#49 Chuck Berry (1926 - 2017)

Began Recording: 1954 (w. group); 1955 (solo)
Peak: 1955 - 1959
Genres: Rock & Roll Singer/Songwriter/Guitarist

Little Richard has been called the "Architect" and Elvis, the "King;" just as surely, Chuck Berry has earned the sobriquet "Father of Rock & Roll." Mixing a twangy country sound to the blues he listened to as a boy, Berry produced a distinctive guitar-driven style married to his storytelling lyrics, usually focused on "sex, cars, music, and trouble" as *Rolling Stone* put it. John Lennon once said, "If you were to give rock & roll another name, you might call it Chuck Berry."

As a youth, he was drawn to blues, poetry, and the guitar. Playing in various St. Louis bands in the late '40s and early '50s, he developed his hybrid style. A 1955 meeting with Muddy Waters put him in contact with Chess Records where he cut his breakout single "Maybellene," a reworking of an old uptempo western folk song. Propelled by a steady drumbeat, lively piano fills, and his raucous guitar, Berry unveils the humorous tale of trying to chase and catch his unfaithful Maybellene on the highway. The song reached #5 on *Billboard's* Hot 100 and is now recognized as one of the most influential records of all time. Berry's enunciation is so clear and accent neutral, many listeners, at the time, prejudicially mistook him for a white man.

"Maybellene" was followed by a string of similar sounding rock & roll classics, each with Berry's trademark guitar riffs and narrative wit. "Roll Over Beethoven" urges the old masters to make room for the red-hot, rockin' new style; "Rock and Roll Music" celebrates its powerhouse beat and danceability; "Johnny B. Goode" is his semi-autobiographical classic about a poor boy who lived for playing his guitar and, encouraged by his mom, dreams of one day reaching the big-time. Indeed, by 1959, Berry had had 10 Top 40 hits; he was investing his money wisely and appeared unstoppable. Then, he was arrested for violating the Mann Act, transporting an underage girl over state lines for sexual purposes. He claimed she was working as a hatcheck girl in his club, and that he had nothing to do with her sideline activities, but he was nonetheless jailed for 20 months. Emerging from prison in '64, he discovered that his music was being played by the likes of the Beach Boys, the Beatles, and the Stones.

Berry had a few more hits in 1964 and 1972, but mostly he came to be seen as an early rock & roll father figure. In and out of trouble and notoriously difficult to work with, he seemed to soften toward the end, feted by all the greats who followed in his footsteps. At his death, Bruce Springsteen called him "Rock's greatest practitioner, guitarist, and the greatest pure rock 'n' roll writer who ever lived."

Suggested Songs:

Maybellene (1955)
Roll Over Beethoven (1956)
Rock and Roll Music (1957)
Johnny B. Goode (1958)
No Particular Place to Go (1964)

#48 Neil Young (1945 - present)

Began Recording: 1966 (w. Buffalo Springfield); 1969 (solo)
Peak: 1970 - 1979; 1989 - 1995
Genres: Rock; folk rock; country rock Singer/Songwriter/Guitarist

Canada has seen its share of great recording artists—Leonard Cohen and Joni Mitchell, to name two. Neil Young, like both Cohen and Mitchell, is one of the great songwriter-poets of the last 50 years and has to be added to that list.

By high school, Neil had set himself on a musical trajectory. A chance meeting on L.A.'s Sunset Boulevard led to the formation in 1966 of the groundbreaking country-rock band Buffalo Springfield and, though it lasted but two years, gave Neil his first taste of success. In 1968, Neil began his solo career and, a year later, joined the on again-off again "supergroup" Crosby, Stills, and Nash, adding his name to the band. Neil had played with Stephen Stills in Buffalo Springfield.

Crosby, Stills, Nash & Young had a #1 album in *Deja Vu* and the Young composition, "Ohio," was an arresting, politically charged lament for the students shot at Kent State, but it is with his solo releases and sometime work with the backing band Crazy Horse that Neil has left his biggest musical mark the past half century. His second, third, and fourth LPs are considered among his best. 1969's *Everybody Knows This Is Nowhere*, featuring Crazy Horse, contains three electric guitar heavy classics, "Cinnamon Girl" and the extended epics, "Down by the River" and "Cowgirl in the Sand." 1970's *After the Gold Rush* appears on many all-time great lists and has a more wistful, folk country feel of lost and yearning love, punctuated by the burning rock indictment of racism and slavery, "Southern Man." 1972's *Harvest* was his top-selling album, has a decidedly country rock feel, and contains two masterpieces—"Old Man," which posits that the needs of the young and the old are not so different and "The Needle and the Damage Done," a stark acoustic lament about a heroin addicted friend. "Heart of Gold," the biggest single of Neil's career, also appears on the LP.

Young's career has had its ups and downs, and the fiercely independent musician has experimented with a wide range of styles, some with more success than others; he was once sued by his own label for releasing "unrepresentative" Neil Young music. *Rust Never Sleeps*, *Freedom*, *Ragged Glory*, and *Harvest Moon* have all been deemed career highlights.

One has to mention the voice. It has been described variously as high pitched, plaintive, as a natural falsetto, quavering, as world weary, and vulnerable. Love it or not, his voice is distinctive, and coupled with his ferocious lead guitar playing, his hippie-punk-grunge sensibility, and his evocative songwriting, Neil Young is a true original.

Suggested Songs:

Cowgirl in the Sand (1969)
Heart of Gold (1971)
Old Man (1972)
Powderfinger (1979)
Rockin' in the Free World (1989)

#47 Marvin Gaye (1939 - 1984)

Began Recording: 1957 (backing vocals); 1961 (featured artist)
Peak: 1968 - 1977; 1982 - 1983
Genres: R&B; Soul; Progressive Soul; jazz Singer/Songwriter/Instrumentalist

An established '60s R&B star out of the Motown hits factory, Marvin Gaye remade himself in 1970 and left the world one of the most compelling LPs of all time.

A product of the D.C. housing projects, Marvin, as a youngster, suffered years of harsh physical abuse at the hands of his preacher father, even as he grew up singing in his church. After a brief stint in the Air Force, Marvin began singing doo-wop before signing with Berry Gordy's Tamla label in 1960. He added an "e" to his last name and began writing for the likes of the Marvelettes, playing drums behind the Miracles, and trying to break through as a jazz-style vocalist.

With his versatile voice, he began to growl and rasp his way to R&B success beginning in 1962 with a series of hits: "Stubborn Kind of Fellow," "Pride and Joy," and more. Not quite a Motown A-lister like the Supremes or the Temptations, he was, nonetheless, consistently on the charts. His version of "I Heard It Through the Grapevine" brought him his first *Billboard* #1, but, in 1970, he was devastated by the loss of his sometime singing partner Tammi Terrell to brain cancer.

Marvin decided to move in a completely different direction. Touched by his brother Frankie's tour in Vietnam and inspired by an incident of police brutality witnessed by co-writer Obie Benson, he recorded "What's Going On," a poignant, stream-of-consciousness meditation and plea to all the mothers, siblings, perhaps his own father, as well as to the greater, troubled society for reconciliation, understanding, and peace. Berry refused to release it, calling it too political. Gaye went on strike until Berry relented; the song shot to #2 in 1971. Marvin returned to the studio determined to build an album around the single and handle the production himself, something unheard of in *Motown*. The resulting album, *What's Going On*, plays like an extended suite touching on themes of police brutality, the futility of war, heroin addiction, the child as innocent victim, ecological degradation, systemic racism, urban poverty, and redemption through community, spirituality, and love.

Two years later, Gaye scored again with *Let's Get It On*, an album of intense carnal and romantic yearning that wowed the critics and reached near the top of the charts. Gaye appeared to be riding high in the early '80s with the Grammy winning smash "Sexual Healing" when headlines screamed in 1984 that Marvin Gaye had been shot and killed by his own father. The lurid details threatened to override his legacy, but not quite, for Marvin's masterpiece, *What's Going On*, has only grown in stature, as Britain's *NME*, *The Guardian*, and *Rolling Stone* all voted this landmark record the greatest album of all time.

Suggested Songs:

Ain't No Mountain High Enough (w. Tammi Terrell) (1967)
I Heard It Through the Grapevine (1968)
What's Going On (1971)
Mercy Mercy Me (The Ecology) (1971)
Let's Get It On (1973)

#46 The Beach Boys
Began Recording: 1961
Peak: 1963 - 1967
Genres: Rock; surf; pop; psychedelia Band

They hailed from Hawthorne, one of countless L.A. suburbs, three teenage brothers, a cousin, and a school friend. In the early '60s, blending the rock & roll sounds of Chuck Berry with the harmonies of the Four Freshmen, they sang of the endless California summertime fantasy of sun, sand, surf, girls, and cars, catching the wave to musical stardom with a couple of hit singles, "Surfin' U.S.A.," "Fun, Fun, Fun," and "I Get Around." Soon, the Beach Boys were the most popular American band.

The Beach Boys, though, were not your run of the mill surf-pop outfit. Mike Love, the cousin, was a natural frontman, with a rock & roll voice, a love of doo-wop, and the ability to help write songs. Al Jardine, the classmate, played rhythm guitar and helped sing. The Wilson brothers were baby Carl, just 14 when they first recorded; he played lead guitar and had an underrated voice. Middle brother Dennis was the drummer. Then there was Brian, the natural leader, a self taught composer, arranger, bass and keyboard player, singer, and, as it turned out, musical genius.

1964, however, brought the Beatles and the "British Invasion" wave of English rock bands to American shores. Homegrown acts disappeared overnight; could the Beach Boys compete and survive? In 1966, the Beach Boys answered that question for all time. With the 23-year-old Brian at the production controls and utilizing arresting melodies; unusual chord combinations; thoughtful, introspective lyrics; their trademark sophisticated falsetto tinged harmonies; and driven by a Phil Spector-like "wall of sound," the Beach Boys produced their masterpiece, *Pet Sounds*, which has been praised by artists as diverse as Philip Glass and Paul McCartney. The latter claimed it spurred him to respond with *Sgt. Pepper*. A *Mojo* Magazine music panel in 1995 voted it the greatest record ever, while *Rolling Stone* listed it as the second greatest LP of all time. Individual tracks, "Wouldn't It Be Nice," "Sloop John B," and "God Only Knows" are each considered masterworks.

Later that year, perhaps their most revolutionary single, "Good Vibrations," appeared. With its stunning shifts in key, mood, and tempo, its blend of song fragments and unusual instruments, it still sounds unique. Soon, Wilson was back in the studio, working up another magnum opus; it was to be called *Smile*, but it was never finished. Brian was starting to slip deeper into the schizoaffective disorder that he lives with to this very day. Brother Carl was fighting the draft, and the beginnings of years of legal wrangling left *Smile* the great unfinished rumor.

They would produce more excellent music, but their moment had passed. Dennis, the only actual surfer in the group, drowned in 1983; Carl succumbed to cancer. Mike Love carries on with the Beach Boys name and an oldies act, while Brian and Al perform as part of a trio, but, for a time, the Beach Boys challenged the Beatles.

Suggested Songs:

Fun, Fun, Fun (1964)
Wouldn't It Be Nice (1966)
God Only Knows (1966)
Good Vibrations (1966)
Heroes and Villains (1967)

#45 Rihanna (1988 - present)
Began Recording: 2005
Peak: 2007 - 2016
Genres: Pop; R&B; Dance-Pop; EDM Singer

Robyn Rihanna Fenty was born in the eastern Caribbean island nation of Barbados. She suffered debilitating headaches as a child—caught, as she was, between a mother and father's abusive marriage. Drawn to reggae, rock, and R&B, she was singing with two friends when she was discovered by vacationing American music producer Evan Rogers. Flown at the age of 15 to the U.S. to cut a demo, she was signed by JAY-Z of Def Jam Records.

Her debut single, "Pon de Replay," was released when she was just 17. The infectious dance-pop number invoked her island roots and broke through in the U.S., Britain, and New Zealand. The following year she scored her first #1 hit, "SOS," but it was her edgier third LP, *Good Girl Gone Bad*, that propelled her to superstardom.

In the decade and a half since her first recordings dropped, she has become one of the top 10 best-selling artists of all time. With 14 #1 singles, she is in Beatles, Elvis, Mariah Carey, Madonna territory.

In 2009, en route to the Grammy awards show, she was violently assaulted by her then-boyfriend, R&B singer Chris Brown, who was subsequently charged and convicted. Her follow-up album, *Rated R*, had a darker tone, and many listeners thought they heard allusions to the Brown incident.

Rihanna has cited Bob Marley as her first musical hero and Madonna and Mariah Carey as major influences. Often underrated as a vocalist, she is equally at home with up-tempo dance pop like "We Found Love," mid-tempo numbers like "Umbrella," or honest, soulful ballads like "Stay." Her last album, 2016's *Anti,* may actually be her best, say many critics; one can hear her reaching back to the '50s, as well as taking inspiration from the incomparable Amy Winehouse, in what might well be a new signature song, "Love on the Brain." A prolific collaborator, she has worked with artists as diverse as Justin Timberlake, Eminem, Kendrick Lamar, Shakira, Drake, and Paul McCartney.

Rihanna, just 35, is already a billionaire, having also become a hugely successful entrepreneur with her Fenty Beauty brand, which has been praised for bringing skin care products to people of all skin tones. She also has had a huge charitable footprint in the fields of education and disaster preparedness and relief. Barbados named her an ambassador in 2018 and, in 2021, a "National Hero." It seems likely her stature will grow as one of music's all-time greats.

Suggested Songs:

SOS (2006)
Love the Way You Lie- Part II (w. Eminem) (2010)
Stay (2012)
FourFiveSeconds (w. Ye & P. McCartney) (2015)
Love on the Brain (2016)

#44 Tina Turner (1939 - 2023)

Began Recording: 1958 (w. Ike Turner); 1974 (solo)
Peak: 1984 - 1994
Genres: Rock; R&B; pop Singer

She was a survivor. All she ever really wanted was respect. A two-time inductee into the Rock and Roll Hall of Fame, she had two great careers in music.

She was born Anna Mae Bullock in rural Tennessee. Abandoned by both parents, she was raised by grandparents, later reuniting with her mother in St. Louis. While still in high school, she heard Ike Turner and his Kings of Rhythm performing in a local club. When Ike heard *her* sing, he asked her to join the band. She cut her first single with Ike in 1958 under the name of Little Ann. By 1960, she was the star of the show; Ike, ever in charge, renamed her Tina Turner and his band the Ike & Tina Turner Revue.

The Revue was a moderately successful recording act. "A Fool in Love," in 1960, reached #27 on the *Billboard* Hot 100 (#2 on the R&B chart). The Phil Spector produced "River Deep-Mountain High" flopped but is today considered a "wall-of-sound" classic. Their biggest hit was a cover of CCR's "Proud Mary" in 1971, but they were considered a sensational R&B touring band.

Tina shared that she and Ike began as platonic friends, and she grew to love him. By 1962, they were living as husband and wife. The first beating was with a wooden shoe stretcher; it was usually an object, as Ike was careful to protect his guitar-playing hands. In 1968, Tina attempted suicide for the first and only time; in 1976, mid-tour, she decided to break away with just $0.36 in her pocket. Her divorce was finalized in 1978. For several years, she was in debt, on food stamps, and taking whatever small gigs she could get.

Then, in 1983, she had a modest hit with a cover of Al Green's "Let's Stay Together." Capitol Records okayed a new LP and Tina responded with *Private Dancer*, which remade her as an international rock star, selling more than 10 million copies, winning three Grammys, and giving her a career defining hit, "What's Love Got to Do with It." Initially reluctant to record the song, one can't help but hear Tina's own story in the lyrics. A stadium-filling concert draw, Tina was discovered by millions of new fans, who now dubbed her the "Queen of Rock & Roll." With her high voltage, rough and raspy voice, she at once projected vulnerability and defiance. As her personal story became known, Tina became a feminist icon, though she saw herself more as a survivor. "I had a terrible life," she said. "I just kept going."

Mick Jagger and David Bowie called themselves fans; Beyoncé was an admirer. Tina, though, retired happily, worked sparingly, and claimed not to miss her old life, living quietly in a lakeside Swiss chalet with a devoted husband. After years of struggling with assorted health issues, she passed away in 2023.

Suggested Songs:

River Deep-Mountain High (w. Ike Turner) (1969)
Proud Mary (w. Ike Turner) (1971)
What's Love Got to Do with It (1984)
Private Dancer (1984)
We Don't Need Another Hero (Thunderdome) (1985)

#43 The Who
Began Recording: 1964
Peak: 1969 - 1976
Genres: Rock Band

The Beatles and the Stones certainly got the lion's share of the attention, but there was a third great group to emerge from mid-'60s England: The Who.

By 1964, the basic lineup was set—Pete Townshend played the lone guitar, leaping about on stage, power chords emanating from his windmill arm motion, interspersed with his understated lead licks; Pete handled the bulk of the songwriting too; John Entwistle, the stoic, unmoving virtuoso bass player sometimes used his instrument to play lead riffs; wild man Keith Moon, whose elaborate, imaginative, hyperkinetic style once led *Rolling Stone* to call him the best drummer in rock & roll history; and Roger Daltrey, the bare chested, R&B-influenced lead vocalist, swinging his mic about like a lasso, emotionally supercharged whether delivering a tenderly melodic line or belting in his powerhouse rock baritone.

A favorite of the London mods, the Who gained notice, in part, for their performance art penchant for smashing their instruments after a set. With a focus on teenage angst, their early records first caught on in their native England. "I Can't Explain" and "My Generation" became touchstones for the disaffected. In 1969, though, the Who broke through internationally with what was termed the first rock opera, *Tommy*, a strange story of a boy whose trauma renders him, for a time, unable to see, hear, or speak, becoming, in turn, a pinball wizard and, eventually, a religious messiah. Townshend later admitted that there was a painful autobiographical element in Tommy Walker's story. In subsequent years, *Tommy* has gone on to become a play, a movie, and a Broadway musical.

In 1971, the band released *Who's Next*, their best-selling and highly acclaimed LP. Townshend was beginning to explore new themes—with "Won't Get Fooled Again," he questions the efficacy of so-called revolutionary movements. Does anything really change when the old guard is replaced by the new guard? "Baba O'Riley," mistakenly termed "Teenage Wasteland," seems to celebrate stoner culture, but Townshend claims he was decrying it as a waste; in "Behind Blue Eyes," he explores the psyche of the powerful loner. Two years later, the Who released another "opera," *Quadrophenia*, a sensitive and musically arresting exploration of young Jimmy and his struggles to find meaning in an alienating world.

In 1978, on the heels of another strong record, the Who lost their drummer to an accidental drug overdose. Keith Moon was 32 years old; the band soldiered on with replacement drummer Kenny Jones. They've broken up and reformed even after Entwistle's passing in 2002. Pete Townshend, ever the philosopher, reflected in 2019, "My work has been about trying to recover innocence and real beauty... music... in some way served the spiritual needs of the audience."

Suggested Songs:

See Me, Feel Me (1969)
Won't Get Fooled Again (1971)
Baba O'Riley (1971)
Behind Blue Eyes (1971)
Love, Reign O'er Me (1973)

#42 Loretta Lynn (1932 - 2022)

Began Recording: 1960
Peak: 1966 - 1981; 2004 - 2005
Genres: Country; Americana; gospel Singer/Songwriter

Born in the backwoods of Kentucky, the second of eight children, married at 15 to a philandering husband, raising four children by the time she was 20—the odds were not good that, one day, the world would celebrate Loretta Lynn as one of *the* great recording artists. Her husband Mooney bought her a guitar, and, within a few years, she was singing locally in her own country & western band. In 1960, given a chance to cut a record, she and Mooney drove across country promoting the single, "I'm a Honky Tonk Girl," arriving in Nashville with the song #14 on the *Billboard* country chart.

Her talent quickly recognized, Loretta was signed by Decca and soon was best friends with label mate Patsy Cline, who became her mentor. Her first LP shot to #2 on the Hot Country Albums Chart, and, in 1966, she had her first #1 single, "Don't Come Home a Drinkin' (With Lovin' on Your Mind)," followed the next year by the #1 album of the same name. What was starting to become noticed was that here was an artist committed to releasing frank, autobiographical, and often controversial songs. In 1968, she released *Fist City*, making it clear that she would fight for her man. "Rated X" was a song that took note of the problems faced by divorced women, while "The Pill" hilariously recounts a woman's declaration of marital change now that she's got the pill. Lynn herself later quipped, "If I'd had the pill back when I was havin' babies I'd have taken 'em like popcorn." Not all of her songs were welcomed on country stations; in fact, nine were banned at one time or another, but Loretta gained a reputation for passionately representing the needs of working women.

In 1970, she eulogized her dad and proudly detailed her hardscrabble childhood in the hit "Coal Miner's Daughter." Her 1976 memoir of the same name (co-written with George Vecsey) became an Oscar winning vehicle for Sissy Spacek in 1980, putting Loretta's story on the big screen and turning her into a legend.

Besides her brilliant solo career, Loretta found great success in her collaborations. Early on, she worked with Ernest Tubb; then, beginning in 1971, she released a string of #1 hits with Conway Twitty, establishing them as country's favorite duo. In 1993, recording with Dolly Parton and Tammy Wynette, the trio produced the celebrated *Honkey Tonk Angels*. Though she took much of the '90s off to care for her ailing husband of nearly 50 years, in 2004, collaborating with rock guitarist and producer Jack White, she released *Van Lear Rose*, the most acclaimed album of her career.

The first woman honored as the CMA Entertainer of the Year and a Presidential Medal of Freedom recipient, she was the fiercely independent Loretta Lynn.

Suggested Songs:

Don't Come Home a Drinkin' (With Lovin' on Your Mind) (1966)
Coal Miner's Daughter (1970)
One's on the Way (1971)
The Pill (1975)
Who's Gonna Miss Me? (2016)

#41 Eric Clapton (1945 - present)
Began Recording: 1964
Peak: 1967 - 1971; 1974 - 1977; 1992 - 2001
Genres: Rock; Blues Guitarist/Singer/Songwriter

Raised by his grandparents in Surrey, England, Eric Clapton was nine when he learned they were not his parents, and the revelation that his parents had abandoned him seems to have left a painful mark. As a teenager, he threw himself into the blues and learned to play guitar. At 17, he began playing in a variety of local bands, and, in 1963, joined the blues-rock outfit the Yardbirds. He moved on to John Mayall's Bluesbreakers in '65, gaining a reputation around London as an up and coming blues guitar master. When someone scrawled "Clapton is God" on a London tube station wall, the subsequent photo of the graffiti etched his reputation in millions of young minds.

From 1966 to 1968, Clapton collaborated with virtuoso drummer Ginger Baker and star bass player Jack Bruce to form the blues-rock group Cream. They released four albums, each one building on the success of the other. "Sunshine of Your Love" was the breakthrough single, but internal conflict pushed them apart after just 27 months. Now a superstar, Clapton formed a new supergroup with Baker, Steve Winwood, and Ric Grech. Calling themselves Blind Faith, they disbanded after less than a year.

Clapton, inspired by the ensemble nature of The Band, decided to pull back from the guitar wizard mantle and try to be just one member of a group, joining, for a time, Delaney & Bonnie and Friends. He also released, in 1970, his most celebrated work, *Layla and Other Assorted Love Songs*, featuring his classic of pleading, unrequited love, "Layla." Recorded under the band name of Derek and the Dominos, the recording sessions married Clapton with fellow guitar legend Duane Allman. By this time, though, Clapton was spiraling into an addiction to heroin; he was able to pull himself out after a few years, only to succumb to a horrific descent into alcoholism.

Sober since 1987, he has devoted time and resources to establishing treatment centers for those with substance abuse problems.

In 1991, a tragic accident took the life of his 4-year-old son; partly as a way of dealing with his grief, he co-wrote and recorded the moving "Tears in Heaven." It was later included on his 1992 live *Unplugged* LP, which became the biggest seller of his career and earned him a total of six Grammys the following year, including album, song, and record of the year.

Inspired originally by bluesmen like Robert Johnson and Muddy Waters, Clapton's own influence on guitarists these past 50 years is incalculable. The only three-time inductee in the Rock & Roll Hall of Fame (with the Yardbirds, Cream, and as a solo artist), he is regularly listed among the all-time greats. Perhaps Eddie Van Halen said it best, "His solos were melodic and memorable… that blues-based sound is still the core of modern rock guitar."

Suggested Songs:

Crossroads (Cream) (1968)
Bell Bottom Blues (Derek & the Dominos) (1971)
Layla (Derek & the Dominos) (1971)
Tears in Heaven (1992)
Nobody Knows You When You're Down and Out (1992)

#40 Paul McCartney (1942 - present)

Began Recording: 1962 (w. The Beatles); 1970 (solo career)
Peak: 1970 - 1976
Genres: Rock; Pop Singer/Songwriter/Instrumentalist

When the dust has settled and, 200 years hence, the history of recorded music for this past century is rewritten, arguably the name at the very top will be James Paul McCartney. The early years are well known. Paul was born in wartime Liverpool, his dad was a part-time musician, and he lost his mom when he was 14. The following year, he met John Lennon, and the two went on to form the most successful songwriting partnership in music history as co-leaders of the Beatles.

The Beatles, however, were over in 1970, before McCartney was even out of his 20s. Since that time, Paul, as a solo artist and working with various backing bands and musicians, has gone on to add to his legacy as one of the most revered and beloved songwriters and performers of all time.

McCartney was the first of the Beatles to release a successful solo album, and he was unfairly branded, initially, as the one who broke up the band. Critics were not kind to his first LP, *McCartney*, calling it slight and lightweight. Playing all the instruments himself, the featured song is "Maybe I'm Amazed," heard today as worthy of standing alongside his Beatles' work. *Ram* came next and brought him his first chart topping single, the Beatlesque "Uncle Albert/Admiral Halsey," a surreal ode to his uncle, weaving together song snippets and replete with thunder and rain sound effects. However, it was 1973's *Band on the Run* that won over critics and his ex-mates. Recorded in Nigeria under the moniker Paul McCartney and Wings, it was really just Paul, his wife Linda, and ex-Moody Bluesman Denny Laine. The compelling title track, a musical suite with hints at imprisonment, escape, and the burden of Beatles fame, remains a McCartney high point.

The knock on McCartney, as author Tom Doyle has pointed out, is that he is a "Bambi eyed soft balladeer" and that he has never, since leaving the Beatles, reached those creative heights; but the criticism seems so unfair since the Beatles were a once in a lifetime, synergistic, lightning in a bottle melding of four very distinctive musical and personality giants, and McCartney is but one artist; yet, as a solo artist, he has sold millions of records, remains vital and inventive even at 81, still fills arenas, still produces fresh new music, and still cheerfully sings his songs, be they "Hey Jude" with fellow legends Elton John, Sting, and Clapton or "Ebony and Ivory" with Stevie Wonder. Perhaps "Yesterday" and "Eleanor Rigby" are immortal, but, when Paul breaks into "Every Night," "Just Another Day," "Live and Let Die," or "Silly Love Songs," the stadiums erupt with thousands of voices singing joyfully along; they know the words. He's the legendary Paul McCartney, after all.

Suggested Songs:

Maybe I'm Amazed (1970)
Uncle Albert/Admiral Halsey (1971)
Another Day (1971)
Band on the Run (1974)
Jenny Wren (2005)

#39 Eagles

Began Recording: 1972
Peak: 1974 - 1977
Genres: Country Rock; Soft Rock; Rock Band

In the 1970s, no other American band so captured the zeitgeist as did the Eagles. They took a narrow genre, country rock, and made it mainstream, transforming country music itself in the process. Along the way, they released two of the most iconic, best-selling albums of all time.

Originally, they were four separate musicians who had migrated to L.A.; they came together to back Linda Ronstadt and formed a band, signing with David Geffen's Asylum. Glen Frey, rhythm guitarist, and Don Henley, drummer, wrote most of the songs and handled most of the lead vocals. Bernie Leadon played guitar and brought a country sensibility while Randy Meisner added bass. Their 1972 debut featured "Take It Easy," which put them on the musical map. Their second LP was not a major hit but contained the title track "Desperado," which has grown into a classic, showing up on several all-time lists.

Don Felder joined the band in '74, bringing his considerable guitar skills to the mix, and, the following year, the Eagles broke through with *One of These Nights*, which featured three Top 10 hits. Leadon soon departed over creative and personal differences, to be replaced by the harder-rocking Joe Walsh. In early '76, they released *Their Greatest Hits (1971-1975)*, and the album surprised the world, leaping off the shelves and continuing to sell for years, eventually vying with Michael Jackson's *Thriller* for the title of all-time U.S. bestseller. Later that year, they released their fifth LP, the superlative *Hotel California*. The title track has become mythic, with its lyrical exploration of the underbelly of the American Dream, its iconic intro, and its Walsh-Felder dual lead guitar outro, which was deemed by *Guitarist* magazine the finest guitar solo in history. "New Kid in Town," with its sweet melody and precision harmonies, explored the heart-stopping moment when a lover (or a band) realizes that they are no longer the favorite. "Life in the Fast Lane" served to underline the fact that Joe Walsh had helped move the Eagles in a harder direction.

Through much of the '70s, the Eagles gave rock fans who were uncomfortable with the glam of Bowie, the metal of Zeppelin, and the disco of the clubs somewhere to go musically, but, as the decade waned, punk and new wave emerged. Perhaps the Eagles could have dominated the charts for decades, perhaps not, but internal conflicts were pulling the band apart. By 1980, each member was pursuing his own projects, and, for 14 years, there was no Eagles. Henley once quipped they'd reunite when "Hell freezes over." Sure enough, in 1994, back together, they released the LP *Hell Freezes Over* and resumed touring. In 2016, co-leader Frey died; there have been other lineup changes, including the 2023 passing of Meisner, but, as of this writing, the Eagles carry on.

Suggested Songs:

Desperado (1973)
One of These Nights (1975)
The Last Resort (1976)
New Kid in Town (1976)
Hotel California (1977)

#38 Hank Williams (1923 - 1953)

Began Recording: 1947
Peak: 1949 - 1953
Genres: Country & Western; honky-tonk; rockabilly; Gospel Singer/
Songwriter

He's been called country music's first superstar and the "Hillbilly Shakespeare." He was dead before the age of 30 and has passed into myth, as much for his sad demise as for his music, but it is the music that continues to resonate and inspire.

Hiram Williams was born in rural Alabama, saw little of his father growing up, and learned to play guitar while still a child from Rufus Payne, a Black bluesman who played on the street. At 13, Williams, now going by Hank, was playing and hosting a weekly local radio show and soon dropped out of school to form a band, the Drifting Cowboys, that played around the state. His mom got the gigs and drove for the band. When World War II intervened, the band members were all drafted save Williams, who had been thrown from a bull, aggravating an already delicate back caused by spina bifida occulta.

In 1944, Hank, working in a shipyard, married an aspiring singer, Audrey Mae Sheppard, who encouraged Williams in his musical ambitions. The publication of a notebook full of Williams' original songs led to an opportunity to record with a local label. His songs got just enough attention that MGM Records offered a contract. 1947 brought Hank his first recorded success, "Move It On Over," an early rockabilly or even rock & roll number. In 1949, his cover of "Lovesick Blues" became a huge smash. Suddenly, the Grand Ole Opry opened their doors to him, and Williams became the first singer ever to receive six encores there.

For the next three years, Williams dominated the country & western charts with "I'm So Lonesome I Could Cry," "Cold, Cold Heart," "Hey Good Lookin'," "Jambalaya," and more. He had become a huge star, touring with the likes of Bob Hope and singing on *The Perry Como* TV show;

but Williams, a heavy drinker since his youth, had begun to go into a tail-spin by late '51. He'd taken a nasty fall, aggravating his bad back; tried an unsuccessful medical procedure to address the problem; and then turned to morphine and other painkillers on top of the alcohol to numb the pain. He began missing shows or turning up too drunk to perform; his marriage crumbled, and his career pressures intensified.

On December 30, 1952, he got in the back seat of his powder blue Cadillac to drive to a couple of shows. Coping with his pain, he was drinking and using chloral hydrate and morphine. Before dawn on January 1, his 18-year-old driver realized Hank was dead—his heart had simply given out. A sad and lonely death, no doubt, but his famous family (his son and grandson have since had successful country careers) insists he was a devout, fun-loving man who deeply loved his family and simply could not quite get over the success he'd found with his honest, heartfelt songs—songs that continue to resonate to this day.

Suggested Songs:

Lovesick Blues (1949)
I'm So Lonesome I Could Cry (1949)
I Can't Help It (If I'm Still in Love with You) (1951)
Jambalaya (On the Bayou) (1952)
Your Cheatin' Heart (1953)

#37 Joni Mitchell (1943 - present)
Began Recording: 1968
Peak: 1970 - 1977
Genres: Folk; Rock; Jazz; Pop Singer/Songwriter/Instrumentalist

She never sold records like Madonna, never scooped up Grammys by the armload like Beyoncé, but she has been called the most important female recording artist of the latter 20th century and the first singer/songwriter to be taken as seriously as her male peers.

Roberta Joan Anderson was a Saskatchewan prairie girl, forced, by her own admission, to slow down, become self-reliant and reflective due to a serious bout with polio at the age of nine. Drawn to painting, poetry, and music, she started with a ukulele, because she couldn't afford a guitar, but, by the mid-'60s, she'd been married and divorced (she kept the name) and was writing and playing her own folk-style songs, attracting the attention of Tom Rush, Buffy Sainte-Marie, and others. Judy Collins had a hit with Mitchell's "Both Sides Now" in 1968, and Joni released her first record that same year.

Her third LP, *Ladies of the Canyon*, was a moderate hit and found her adding pop and rock elements to her acoustic folk sound. "Big Yellow Taxi," an environmental protest that doubles as a lover's lament, brought her Top 40 airplay, while "Woodstock" became a celebratory anthem of the festival and her generation.

However, it is her follow up album *Blue*, inspired in part by a journey through Europe and relationship highs and lows that has become a cultural touchstone for generations of listeners. Entirely written and produced by Mitchell, the instrumentation is spare, mostly featuring Joni on guitar, piano, or dulcimer. The songs are confessional, almost like a poet's diary; her voice immediate and vulnerable, singing of conflicting desires and longing for home ("California"), infatuation and romance ("Carey"), the heart's overflowing ("A Case of You"), loss and heartbreak ("River," a Christmas song for sad people, as Mitchell rightly points out), human fragility and dangerous desires ("Blue"), and resignation and cynicism ("The Last Time I Saw Richard"). The album was chosen by NPR as the #1 LP ever created by a woman. It was #3 on *Rolling Stone*'s list of the best of all time, while *The New York Times* called it "one of the turning points and pinnacles of 20th Century popular music."

Joni would go on to record for another 36 years. She would reach her commercial peak in 1974 with *Court and Spark,* a pop-rock masterpiece with jazz notes. Over time, Mitchell would move even further away from her folk roots and deeper into jazz. In recent years, ill health and years of smoking have taken away her bell-like soprano voice and left her a contralto who rarely sings, though she surprised the world in 2022 and '23 with a couple of shows, perhaps signaling that she is back.

Her music and influence is heard everywhere, from Bjork to Taylor Swift, from Herbie Hancock to Lorde, to her friend Brandi Carlile. In recent years, the honors have poured in—from the Kennedy Center to the Gershwin Prize. Joni once put it simply, "Truth and beauty, that's what I hope to deliver."

Suggested Songs:

Both Sides Now (1969 version) and (2000 version)
River (1971)
Blue (1971)
Down to You (1974)
Coyote (1977)

#36 Jimi Hendrix (1942 - 1970)

Began Recording: 1964 (Sideman); 1966 (Lead Artist)
Peak: 1967 - 1969
Genres: Rock; hard & psychedelic rock; Blues; R&B Guitarist/ Singer/ Songwriter

The Rock & Roll Hall of Fame called him "the most gifted instrumental- ist of all time." Like a meteor blazing through the musical firmament, Jimi Hendrix was gone before we really got to know him. His childhood, spent mostly in Seattle, was chaotic, unstable, insecure, and lonely. With a frac- tious home life, the young boy took refuge in music, carrying a broom as his pretend guitar. At 14, he found a one-string ukulele in the garbage; he practiced it diligently, graduating to a $5 guitar the next year and his first electric at 16. A yearlong stint in the army earned him a general discharge, but he soon found his musical direction.

Drawing inspiration from Elvis and the blues masters, Hendrix began playing guitar on the "Chitlin' Circuit" of Black venues throughout the American south, as well as in the mideast, and east coast. In time, he was backing the Isley Brothers and Little Richard, but a 1966 trip to London with ex-Animals' bassist Chas Chandler turned him into an overnight sensa- tion in England, playing for and blowing away the likes of the Beatles, Pete Townshend, and Eric Clapton. Nine months later, the Monterey Pop Festival brought him widespread attention in the U.S. Teaming with English bassist Noel Redding and drummer Mitch Mitchell, the Jimi Hendrix Experience was formed. In their brief time together, they released three studio albums, 1967's *Are You Experienced* and *Axis: Bold as Love*, and 1968's *Electric Ladyland*. All three were best sellers, and each is considered a classic, with such iconic songs as "Hey Joe," "Purple Haze," "Foxy Lady," "Little Wing," and the stunning reimagining of Dylan's "All Along the Watchtower".

Jimi once noted, "Technically, I'm not a guitar player. All I play is truth and emotion." John Frusciante said, "I don't think there's a better guitar player in history," and countless publications, musicologists, and guitarists agree. Hendrix was technically brilliant, expert at melding lead and rhythm guitar parts; he used unusual chord combinations, the bending of notes, stunning arpeggio embellishments, and electronic technology in new and creative ways—his distortion and feedback could simulate the guns and bombs of warfare (most famously, his "Star Spangled Banner" at Woodstock) or the howling cries of a soul in pain.

Jimi, variously described as shy, humble, sweet, kind, and naive, seemed to be a soul in pain, and he died, tragically, at the age of 27, due to complications of alcohol and barbiturate abuse. His death was declared an open verdict by the coroner, and speculation persists as to its exact cause. Mick Jagger, though, put him into perspective as "the most exciting... performer I have ever seen."

Suggested Songs:

Hey Joe (1966)
Purple Haze (1967)
All Along the Watchtower (1968)
Voodoo Child (Slight Return) (1968)
Star Spangled Banner (Live at Woodstock) (1969)

#35 Miles Davis (1926 - 1991)
Began Recording: 1945 (sideman); 1947 (leader)
Peak: 1955 - 1970
Genres: Jazz Trumpeter/Composer/Bandleader

He's been called the most innovative and influential jazz musician of the post-World War II era. Miles Davis was fond of upending the stereotypical assumption that he was born poor in some slum. In fact, his parents were successful professionals, and he studied three semesters at Juilliard before dropping out to play trumpet full-time.

He idolized saxophonist Charlie Parker and, by the mid-'40s, was playing in his quintet. By the latter part of the decade, Miles was leading various bands and moving toward a more relaxed, understated, cool jazz style; for Davis, one key element involved his lack of trumpet vibrato and the attempt to have his instrument sing like a human voice.

Initially, though he was playing and touring, he was also poor, depressed, and struggling with a heroin addiction. However, upon locking himself up on his grandfather's horse farm, he kicked his habit and was primed for his breakthrough. The 1955 Newport Jazz Festival brought him recognition, and the same year saw him form his first great quintet with John Coltrane on tenor sax, Red Garland on piano, Paul Chambers on bass, and Philly Joe Jones on drums. In 1959, he released his masterpiece, *Kind of Blue*. Cannonball Adderly had joined the group on alto sax; there was also a new pianist and drummer. *Kind of Blue*, perhaps the best-selling jazz record ever, is noted for its modal style, which is based more on non-standard scales than on particular chords. It has been called pensive, atmospheric, and impressionistic; it has also been deemed, by many jazz critics and fans, the greatest jazz record ever made, and has been honored by the U.S. House of Representatives, the Library of Congress, and countless music publications.

Never one to stand still, Miles moved on, forming his second great quintet, featuring Wayne Shorter (saxophone) and Herbie Hancock (piano), in the mid-'60s, creating a freer style, with blues and avant-garde elements.

E.S.P. is one celebrated LP from this time. By the late '60s, Miles, now listening to rock artists like Sly Stone and Jimi Hendrix, began creating jazz-rock fusion, releasing *In a Silent Way* in 1969 and *Bitches Brew* in 1970. Many critics and jazz purists were less than enamored at the time; there were cries that Miles had sold out. Today, the work is heard by many as groundbreaking.

Years of hard living took their toll, however. From 1975 to 1980, Miles dropped out of music altogether. Though he returned to recording and touring from 1980 to 1991, critics have not been kind to his last decade of work. He died at age 65, his vitality entirely spent. Davis' own words sum up what he was about: "The world has always been about change. People who don't change will find themselves like folk musicians, playing in museums..."

Suggested Songs:

'Round Midnight (1957)
So What (1959)
All Blues (1959)
Seven Steps to Heaven (1963)
Spanish Key (1970)

#34 Ye (aka Kanye West) (1977 - present)
Began Recording: 2002
Peak: 2004 - 2016
Genres: Hip-Hop; progressive pop, soul, rock Rapper/Songwriter/Producer

Among the artists who have risen to prominence in the 21st century, perhaps none are more acclaimed than Ye. Born Kanye Omari West in 1977, he grew up as an artistic child in Chicago, his interests in poetry, music, and art encouraged by his university English professor (and eventually departmental chair) mother, Donda. Dropping out of college to pursue his musical dreams, Kanye first gained acclaim in the mid and late '90s for his work as a hip-hop producer for the likes of JAY-Z and Alicia Keys. Desperate to gain a record deal as a rapper, he used his near fatal 2002 car accident as a springboard to record the autobiographical "Through the Wire," and his debut LP, *The College Dropout*, was released by Roc-a-Fella in 2004. The album caused a sensation with its "chipmunk soul" sped-up sounds, its use of strings and choirs, and its socially conscious themes of religion, family, consumerism, and education.

Follow-up LPs *Late Registration, Graduation, 808s and Heartbreak*, and, especially, *My Beautiful Dark Twisted Fantasy* made him not only the most celebrated rapper of his era, but also had critics enraptured, citing his use of orchestration and constant shifts in style, along with sublime production values, comparing him to such artistic giants as Brian Wilson of the Beach Boys, the Beatles, Johnny Cash, and Bob Marley. West himself seemed to yearn for a bigger platform, touring the world with U2, then the biggest band on earth. West was modest about his rapping skills and sought to compensate with his rich, wide ranging, decidedly reflective lyrics, pleasing melodies, and elements drawn from such diverse genres as soul, rock, gospel, and punk.

Yet, Kanye West seems to have a genius, as well, for controversy and self-sabotage, making himself one of the most embattled artists of his generation. In 2004, he stormed out of an award show for failing to win as Best

New Artist. His 2009 interruption of a Taylor Swift video award acceptance speech in favor of Beyoncé earned him even less sympathy. When he came out in support of Donald Trump, sporting a MAGA cap, his stock sank still lower. In 2020, he followed through on a pledge to run for President, gaining around 70,000 votes across the country. When he and celebrity wife Kim Kardashian split and he started to attack her new boyfriend publicly, that seemed to signal a new low, but recent months have seen a spate of anti-Semitic tweets and statements. For background, a devastated West lost his beloved mother unexpectedly in 2007, and he has been quite open about his struggles with mental health—citing a variety of disorders; still, there is no question that his stock has fallen precipitously due to the barrage of recent controversies.

In 2021, citing personal religious reasons, Kanye West legally changed his name to Ye. Through highs and lows, he has continued to make fiercely original music, influencing such artists as Drake, Kendrick Lamar, Nicki Minaj, and the Arctic Monkeys.

Suggested Songs:

Diamonds from Sierra Leone (2005)
Flashing Lights (2007)
Runaway (2010)
Power (2010)
I Am a God (2013)

#33 Willie Nelson (1933 - present)
Began Recording: 1957
Peak: 1975 - 1989
Genres: Country; jazz; rockabilly; folk; pop; gospel Singer/ Songwriter/ Guitarist

The voice is instantly recognizable: at once laid back, sweetly nasal, slightly off beat, inflected with jazz phrasing—and, whether singing one of his own compositions or a cover, he always makes the song his own.

Born in Depression-era Texas to teenage parents who abandoned him, Willie Nelson was raised by his grandparents, learned guitar at six, and was making money playing in local bands by 13, partly as a way to avoid having to pick cotton. Trying to make a career in country music, Willie did brief stints in college and the Air Force and worked a variety of jobs: trimming trees, dishwashing, and selling catalog goods door-to-door. A sometime DJ, he kept playing live gigs and honed his songwriting skills before relocating to Nashville.

His mid-'50s self-recorded singles went nowhere, but his musical connection to Ray Price began to get his simple, ruminative songs noticed; soon, he was a recognized writer of hits for others, most famously Patsy Cline's "Crazy." Though offered a recording contract with Liberty Records in 1961, and despite gaining an insiders' reputation as a major talent, his own recordings produced only minor hits.

In 1970, sick of the Nashville music scene, he returned to Texas, shed the coat and tie, and grew out his bright red hair. He changed record labels twice and, in 1975, released the musically spare LP *Red Headed Stranger*. It rose to #1 on *Billboard*'s Country chart and featured his first #1 single, "Blue Eyes Crying in the Rain." Critics began to talk of a new anti-Nashville sound, a grittier, rockabilly, folk Texas sound they dubbed outlaw country. When the sub-genre's two premier performers, Willie and fellow Texan Waylon Jennings, teamed up on *Wanted! The Outlaws* in 1976 and *Waylon & Willie* in 1978, Nelson had reached his commercial peak, but then he turned and went in a completely different direction by releasing an album of traditional pop and jazz standards, *Stardust*. Despite his label's misgivings, the album became one of his biggest sellers and is today a recognized classic.

The '80s saw Nelson release five more #1 country albums and such classics as "On the Road Again," "Always on My Mind," "Pancho and Lefty," and "Forgiving You Was Easy." In 1985, Willie teamed with Jennings and friends Johnny Cash and Kris Kristofferson to form country's first supergroup, the Highwaymen, who went on to release three albums.

A founding member and fixture in the Farm Aid movement, Willie has raised millions to help family farmers; he has also been a leading voice in advocating the legalization of marijuana. Most of all, the quiet, charismatic Nelson loves to play music and, at 90, he continues to do so, often with his sons playing by his side.

Suggested Songs:

Crazy (1962)
Someone to Watch Over Me (1978)
On the Road Again (1980)
You Were Always on My Mind (1982)
Pancho and Lefty (with Merle Haggard) (1983)

#32 JAY-Z (1969- present)
Began Recording: 1995
Peak: 1996 - 2017
Genres: Hip-Hop Rapper/Songwriter

There seems little doubt that hip-hop has overtaken rock as the dominant genre of popular music in the United States, perhaps in the world. The question then follows: who is the greatest rapper of all-time? Certainly, JAY-Z figures in any serious discussion.

Born Shawn Carter in the depressed Brooklyn projects, he and his siblings were raised largely by his mother. A high school drop out, Shawn became a petty criminal, selling crack cocaine for a while, and narrowly escaping the jail or early death fates of too many of his peers. Shawn, however, had a potential out: a talent and a love for rapping, nurtured from a young age. Working with artists such as Jaz-O (from whom he took his name JAY-Z) and Big Daddy Kane, initially JAY-Z sold CDs out of a car, but, scraping together a little money with two friends, in 1995 they formed Roc-A-Fella Records with Jay as the artist.

His 1996 debut album, *Reasonable Doubt,* told the story of Carter's challenging past with a mix of bravado, humor, arrogance, and regret. Today a recognized classic, it features the standout track, "Dead Presidents II." Celebrated for his flowing rap style, JAY-Z's approach has been described as silky-smooth, with arresting, engaging, visual lyrics. Nas, a longtime rival, once commented that, "Hip-hop has to thank God for JAY-Z."

In all, JAY-Z has released 13 solo studio albums, the last 11 of which reached #1 status on the *Billboard* 200. Besides his esteemed debut, three others have also been deemed classics: 1998's *Vol. 2… Hard Knock Life,* which featured his first international hit single "Hard Knock Life (Ghetto Anthem)," with its clever sample from Broadway's *Annie*; 2001's *The Blueprint,* which is heavily reliant on soul music samples; and 2003's *The Black Album,* featuring JAY-Z's "double-time stutter" on "My First Song," a Barack Obama favorite.

With 24 Grammy wins, JAY-Z is tied with Ye for the most of any rapper, and he ranks 3rd in hip-hop records sold behind Eminem and Ye; however, JAY-Z has arguably left as big a footprint as an entrepreneur. In 2004, he took over Def Jam Recordings while retaining control of Roc-A-Fella. He also has expanded into clothing, sports bars, technology ventures, and numerous other fields. Married to R&B superstar Beyoncé since 2008, they are arguably the wealthiest, most celebrated, and powerful couple in entertainment today. The first rapper in the Songwriters Hall of Fame and the first living solo rapper in the Rock Hall, JAY-Z's style and subjects have continued to evolve, as heard most clearly on his recorded love letter to his wife, *4:44*. That he has left an indelible mark on popular music is simply beyond dispute.

Suggested Songs:

Where I'm From (1997)
Hard Knock Life (Ghetto Anthem) (1998)
My 1st Song (2004)
Empire State of Mind (with Alicia Keys) (2009)
4:44 (2017)

#31 Eminem (1972 - present)
Began Recording: 1996
Peak: 1999 - 2005; 2009 - 2017
Genres: Hip-Hop Rapper/Songwriter

He's been cited for "screwing up America" and as one of the great artists of his time. There is no argument that he is the best-selling rapper ever and the man who shattered hip-hop's color barrier and brought it to middle America.

Marshall Mathers, by all accounts, had a turbulent youth: economically unstable, raised by his mom, shuttling from home to home until landing in Detroit, forced to fight or take beatings from neighborhood and school bullies. A high school dropout, he escaped into comic books and hip-hop. Early on, he called himself M&M, which morphed into Eminem. His first solo recording with a local label went nowhere; he was told repeatedly that rap was a Black man's game and he should go into rock & roll.

A 2nd place finish at the 1997 L.A. Rap Olympics got his EP into the hands of N.W.A's Dr. Dre, however, who quickly got him signed and became his mentor. Between 1999 and 2003, Eminem rocketed to the top of the rap and entertainment world: LPs *The Slim Shady LP*, *The Marshall Mathers LP*, and *The Eminem Show* became musical and cultural phenomena, teeming with outrageous, complex rhymes that were "obscenity-strewn, gleefully violent, spastic, hilarious and demented" (*Rolling Stone* Magazine's characterization); then, he became a movie star in 2002 with the semi-autobiographical *8 Mile*, featuring "Lose Yourself," the inspiring bootstraps track that brought hip-hop a moment of mainstream acceptance never before attained and brought Eminem a standing ovation from Hollywood A-listers.

Still, there's no denying the people Eminem has offended along the way. His songs' targets have included Christina Aguilera, George W. Bush, and Will Smith. He's been called a nihilist, a homophobe (though he counts Elton John as a close friend), an advocate for domestic violence; hell, his own mother sued him for slander. Mathers himself has said, "My thoughts are so fucking evil when I'm writing shit...It's not how I feel in general, it's how I feel in the moment." His use of alter ego Slim Shady to express his over the top sex and violent fantasies has been extolled as a healthy defense mechanism and metaphorical device, a pressure valve for a wounded soul and a wounded society; he's also been condemned as being "unnecessarily hurtful and deeply disrespectful," or, to put it rather more bluntly, as journalist Bob Herbert does, "No image is too vile. In Eminem's world all women are 'whores' and he is eager to rape and murder them."

To be fair, Eminem apologized on record to his mom; he successfully raised his daughter to adulthood and the two are close. Dangerous libertine and poster boy for all that's wrong with contemporary society or the greatest lyricist since Bob Dylan, what do you hear as *you* listen?

Suggested Songs:

My Name Is (1999)
The Way I Am (2000)
Stan (2000)
Lose Yourself (2002)
Sing for the Moment (2003)

#30 Ray Charles (1930 - 2004)
Began Recording: 1949
Peak: 1959 - 1964; 1966 - 1967
Genres: R&B/Soul- blues, jazz, gospel; Country; Pop Singer/Songwriter/
Pianist/Bandleader

Born in Albany, Georgia, and moved in infancy to a poor, rural town in northern Florida, Ray Charles Robinson was playing piano by age five and had completely lost his sight by seven. At a school for the deaf and blind, he learned to read music using Braille and to play classical piano. When he lost his beloved mother at 14, he quit school and began to make a meager living as an itinerant pianist.

In Seattle, he met his lifelong friend and "brother," Quincy Jones, and teamed with two others to make a few jazz and blues records for a small label. Moving to L.A. in 1950, Ray, who had dropped the Robinson from his name, had his contract taken over by Atlantic Records. Soon, he was producing a powerful amalgam of blues, jazz, and gospel known as soul music. "I've Got a Woman" was his first R&B hit, and, in 1959, he was in the national spotlight with "What'd I Say," a gospel inspired holler with "devil's words," as critics complained, the song heard by some as too sexual. For Ray, it was just doing his music, naturally.

When he jumped labels in 1959, Charles produced his signature classic, the soulful pop oriented Grammy winner "Georgia on My Mind," followed up by the driving R&B track "Hit the Road Jack." When he suddenly shifted gears and told ABC Records that he wanted to do country & western, they were aghast, but Ray pulled it off with *Modern Sounds in Country Music* and *Modern Sounds in Country Music Volume Two*, which reached numbers 1 and 2 on the *Billboard* 200 chart and contained the biggest hit of his career, "I Can't Stop Loving You."

Ray, variously known as the "Genius" and the "Father of Soul," is truly unclassifiable for the unique ways in which he mixed genres to produce his own readily identifiable music. Nobody sounds like Ray Charles, playing early Nat Cole-inspired jazz piano, fused with the gospel rhythms of his childhood Baptist church, mixed with the slow or barreling blues of the sui generis "Chitlin' Circuit," and married to the unique country-crying, ancient-timbred, wailing, hollering, grunting, soulful, bluesy baritone of his inimitable, instantly recognizable voice.

He healed from a 17-year heroin addiction, helped break down the nation's color barriers, and even co-piloted his private planes. He claimed to be unbothered by the loss of his sight. "I've known some people who have all five senses and they're pretty pathetic to me," he once quipped. His impact on modern music cannot be overstated. From Jones to Stevie Wonder, Van Morrison to Billy Joel, Aretha Franklin to Greg Allman, Ray Charles was a mentor and an inspiration.

Suggested Songs:

What'd I Say, Parts I & II (1959)
Georgia on My Mind (1960)
Hit the Road Jack (1961)
I Can't Stop Loving You (1962)
You Don't Know Me (1962)

#29 Garth Brooks (1962 - present)
Began Recording: 1989
Peak: 1990 - 2001; 2014 - 2020
Genres: Country; country pop & country rock Singer/Songwriter

Journalist Michael Corcoran once wrote, "Garth Brooks is country music for people who hate country music. He's also for those who love country." The RIAA puts him above Elvis and 2nd only to the Beatles among certified best-selling album artists in the United States; certainly he's the #1 best selling country artist ever.

By his own admission, Brooks is no sex symbol: a bit plump; balding; a good, not great, singing voice... Yet, even after a lengthy hiatus from the music business to concentrate on raising his daughters, he remains an industry force.

His late mother had a brief career in country music in the '50s, and Garth, the overprotected baby of the family, became an athlete. In college, drawn increasingly to music, he looked to James Taylor, Dan Fogelberg, George Jones, and George Strait for inspiration. Married and relocated to Nashville, in 1989, he released *Garth Brooks*, which became a country hit. Two songs, he claims, launched him into the stratosphere: 1990's "The Dance," a Brooks' favorite, which can be heard as a love song or a reflection on dying without regret, and the iconic follow-up, "Friends in Low Places," a blue-collar anthem that skewers the snobby rich.

No Fences (1990) and its 1991 successor, *Ropin' the Wind*, became the biggest sellers of his career, and, coupled with his rock-style stage shows (bounding across the stage, a la Bruce Springsteen, wearing a wireless headset mic like Madonna might use, and borrowing from the likes of Elton John and KISS), Brooks brought American country to the suburbs and the rest of the world.

His regular guy, humble image is no act, say those who know him. He has followed through on a promise to his initial studio recording musicians, the G-Men, to continue using them throughout his career. He supports a wide range of charities, such as *Habitat for Humanity*. In song, he extols the virtues of lasting love, a good conscience and a good time, and tolerance. His support for gay rights in song and word and his decision to play at Joe Biden's inauguration might have hurt a lesser country artist's career.

Though Garth often co-writes his songs, many of his biggest hits were written by others: Billy Joel's "Shameless" in 1991; "To Make You Feel My Love," Bob Dylan's standard that was successfully covered by Adele and countless others; and Lady Gaga's movie hit, "Shallow." When he was awarded the Library of Congress Gershwin Prize for Popular Song in 2020, he became the youngest performer ever so honored. As of this writing, he's playing at Caesars, Las Vegas.

Suggested Songs:

The Dance (1990)
Friends in Low Places (1990)
To Make You Feel My Love (1998)
More Than a Memory (2007)
Shallow (with Tricia Yearwood) (2020)

#28 James Brown (1933 - 2006)
Began Recording: 1956
Peak: 1963 - 1974
Genres: Funk; R&B; Soul Singer/Songwriter/bandleader

"The hardest working man in show business," his long time emcee would intone before "Soul Brother Number One" would take the stage and proceed to live up to his intro. Toward the show's end, the star would invariably collapse, exhausted, whereupon the emcee would emerge with a cape, helping the singer stagger off stage—before miraculously springing back to life, rejuvenated, and continuing the show, the audience wild with glee.

This was James Brown, of course, the artist who almost single-handedly invented funk. Deeply poor as a child, raised by an aunt in Georgia, he learned music from his neighbors and church. At 16, he went to juvenile prison for breaking into cars, serving three years. While incarcerated, he began singing gospel and, upon release, joined a gospel turned R&B group that later took the name the Flames.

Discovered by Little Richard, in 1956 James Brown and the Famous Flames released their first record, "Please, Please, Please." It reached #6 on *Billboard*'s R&B chart. His career built slowly, but, in 1963, his label reluctantly released *Live at the Apollo*, thinking there was little demand for a live recording. The LP was instead a smash, reaching #2 on the *Billboard* Top LPs, and James Brown was a star. It was followed by his first real hits, "Prisoner of Love" (1963), "Papa's Got a Brand New Bag" (1965), and "It's a Man's, Man's, Man's World" (1966).

Then, in 1967, Brown changed musical direction: the new style, known as funk, was less melodic and featured rhythmic, staccato beats driven by strong bass and percussion. "Cold Sweat" introduced the style and was followed by a series of hits in a similar vein: "Say It Loud—I'm Black and I'm Proud" (1968), "Get Up (I Feel Like Being A) Sex Machine" (1970), and "Get on the Good Foot" (1972).

Brown had become a giant, a musical symbol of the budding Black Pride movement who met presidents and was asked by politicians to help quell riots. But beneath the ermine coats, velvet jumpsuits, and gold jewelry, all was not well. Brown, married four times, was a serial domestic abuser against the women in his life; though he had a strict no drugs/no alcohol policy for members of his band, he, increasingly, became unhinged by his use of PCP, cocaine, and other substances. A 1988 incident involving a shotgun, threats, and a wild police chase landed him back in jail for 18 months.

Upon his release, though, he was back in front of huge, adoring, international crowds. Why? He was an amazing entertainer, one of the great live artists of all-time, possessed of a voice that was raspy, biting, and powerful—ecstatic or coarse, depending on your taste—and there was simply no one who could dance like James Brown. With his leaps, splits, and gravity defying footwork, nobody did it better. As though living an authored life, he died of heart failure on Christmas Day; speculation persists that he was murdered.

Suggested Songs:

I Got You (I Feel Good) (1965)
Papa's Got a Brand New Bag (1965)
It's a Man's, Man's, Man's World (1966)
Cold Sweat- Part 1 (1967)
Say It Loud- I'm Black and I'm Proud - Part 1 (1968)

#27 Bob Marley (1945 - 1981)

Began Recording: 1962
Peak: 1973 - 1981
Genres: Reggae, ska, rocksteady, rock Singer/Songwriter

Bob Marley was perhaps the first recording artist who hailed from a so-called developing country to gain worldwide acclaim. More importantly, he is still, today, more than 40 years after his untimely death, recognized internationally as a bearer of peace.

Born in rural Jamaica to a white, largely absent, father and a Black mother, by the age of 12, he was living in a West Kingston slum known as Trench Town. Along with his half brother Neville Livingston, later known as Bunny Wailer, he was early on drawn to American artists such as Fats Domino and Ricky Nelson, and to Jamaican ska, a mix of island folk, calypso, and American jazz and R&B. While still a youngster, he teamed with Bunny and a third boy, Peter Tosh, forming a vocal group, calling themselves the Teenagers and, later, the Wailers.

Marley's initial solo recording sessions in 1962 failed to break through, but, in 1964, the Wailers scored a #1 hit in their native Jamaica with their first single, "Simmer Down," an uptempo ska number urging an end to local gang violence. Still, it would take another decade before Marley and the Wailers would become superstars. Indeed, with money tight, for a time in the mid-'60s Bob migrated with his new wife Rita to Delaware, taking jobs as a parking attendant, lab assistant, and forklift operator, all the while working on his music.

After returning to Jamaica, Marley, raised a Catholic, converted to Rastafari, a Jamaican religion that combines elements of both Old and New Testament Christianity with mysticism, and incorporates a pan-African focus that acknowledges many African descendants "downpressed" in diasporic exile throughout the world.

Jamaican music was also changing in the late '60s. Ska, primarily a dance form, had morphed into rocksteady, which had a slower tempo and booming bass lines, and rocksteady was now turning into reggae, with its still slower, laid back feel and syncopated beats. Toots and the Maytals, an island band, first used the term in a 1968 recording, and into this fertile, evolving musical mix stepped Marley, Wailer, and Tosh.

Incorporating the socially conscious lyrics that would become a hallmark of reggae, 1973's *Catch a Fire* was the LP that introduced what was previously a niche genre to a global audience. Considered one of the great albums of all time, its success also helped light the fuse that broke up the Wailers. Jealousy and legitimate differences over which directions the band should pursue caused the split the following year, with each pursuing solo careers. Before the break, however, one final album, *Burnin'* (1973), produced Marley's iconic social justice anthem, "Get Up, Stand Up," and a second track, "I Shot the Sheriff," which rocketed to #1 when covered by Eric Clapton. Bob continued recording under the moniker Bob Marley and the Wailers, but there were now new backing musicians.

Marley's fame and influence continued to grow. In late 1976, he was asked to sing a song at a Smile Jamaica concert in the midst of a tense political campaign. Marley's "yes" was seen by the incumbent's political opponent as a tacit endorsement of the prime minister. On December 3, Marley was ambushed at his house by seven armed assailants. He was shot in the chest and arm, his wife shot in the head, and two others were also wounded. All survived, and, two days later, Marley sang for 90 minutes at the concert, reportedly remarking, "The people who are trying to make the world worse aren't taking a day off. How can I?"

Marley continued to make vibrant; popular; socially, politically, and religiously conscious music for another five years. In 1978, he was awarded a U.N. medal for peace and, increasingly, was recognized for incorporating elements of tolerance, understanding, and peace into the world's musical lexicon, but a melanoma growth discovered under a toenail metastasized throughout his body, and he died in a Miami hospital in 1981. He was 36 years old. An estimated 100,000 Jamaicans filed past his casket, and he was given a state funeral in his beloved Jamaica.

Suggested songs:

Get Up, Stand Up (as The Wailers) (1973)
I Shot the Sheriff (as Bob Marley and the Wailers) (1973)
No Woman, No Cry (as Bob Marley and the Wailers) (1974)
One Love/People Get Ready (as Bob Marley and the Wailers) (1977)
Three Little Birds (as Bob Marley and the Wailers) (1977)

#26 Dolly Parton (1946 - present)
Began Recording: 1959
Peak: 1973 - 1987
Genres: Country; Country-Pop; gospel; bluegrass Singer/ Songwriter/ Instrumentalist

Dolly Parton is one of the best-loved singers in America. Born "dirt poor" in rural Tennessee, she learned music from her mother and aunt. She began guitar at age 7; at 13, she recorded her first single, "Puppy Love," and made a guest appearance at the Grand Ole Opry. She graduated high school and moved immediately to Nashville where she had some initial success as a songwriter. An invitation to be on TV's *The Porter Wagoner Show* in 1967 proved to be the break she needed. Though not accepted immediately by the country music establishment, her partnership with Wagoner, coupled with her persistent, upbeat demeanor, helped make her a star.

"Joshua," in 1970, was her breakthrough country hit; three years later, she scored again with "Jolene," a plea to a beautiful rival to leave her man alone. Parton says the song was written about a redheaded bank teller who had eyes for her husband (with whom she's stayed married for 57 years). The following year, she split from Wagoner, determined to forge her own path; she penned and recorded the immortal "I Will Always Love You" as her farewell. In 1977, she made a calculated decision to reach a larger audience with two country-pop crossover albums, *New Harvest... First Gathering* and *Here You Come Again*, which brought Dolly her first mainstream success.

In 1980, she co-starred in *9 to 5*, a comedy that shined a spotlight on workplace discrimination against women. A single of the same name became one of her biggest hits. Three years later, she scored another crossover smash with "Islands in the Stream," a duet with Kenny Rogers.

Perhaps the most celebrated woman in country music history, Dolly has always pushed the boundaries—by foraying into pop, then later into gospel and bluegrass; by eschewing the expected modest country lady image in favor of a "town tramp" look she consciously adopted in homage to a prostitute whose looks she'd admired as a child; by fiercely taking and keeping control of her music catalog; and by opening the wildly successful theme park Dollywood, against the advice of her business handlers.

Parton plays six instruments, has an instantly recognizable soprano voice once deemed unsuitable for country, and has sold over 100 million records. Though she prefers not to use the label feminist, she has opened doors for women throughout the industry and has penned a number of empowerment anthems (e.g., "Eagle When She Flies"). Humble to a fault ("I've always said I've had more guts than I've got talent"), she has yet to slow down, releasing her 48th solo LP, *Run, Rose, Run* in March, 2022, with a new one, a rock release, scheduled for late 2023. She's a member of both the Country and Rock Halls of Fame.

Suggested Songs:

Jolene (1973)
I Will Always Love You (1974)
Here You Come Again (1977)
9 to 5 (1980)
Islands in the Stream (with Kenny Rogers) (1983)

#25 Pink Floyd
Began Recording: 1967
Peak: 1973 - 1980
Genres: Progressive Rock; psychedelic and space rock Band

In the late '60s and early '70s, a new subgenre of rock began to emerge, known as progressive or prog rock. Seen as a logical outgrowth of the Beatles' *Sgt. Pepper's*, the idea was that rock music could transcend simple chords, melodic structures and lyrics and aspire to high art, something akin to classical composition. This led to the use of new sonic textures; long, virtuoso instrumental solos; and, often, fantastical lyrics, stories, stage sets, and costumes. Some prog groups, Yes, for example, met with success; critics, however, often found much of the genre to be overblown and pretentious. Undoubtedly, though, the most celebrated and successful of the prog era was the band Pink Floyd.

Named for two American bluesmen, Pink Floyd was formed by a couple of London architecture students, Roger Waters and Nick Mason, who teamed with two others, Syd Barrett and Richard Wright, in 1964. Originally, they played R&B, but, soon, they began to experiment with extended solos, unusual sounds, and lighting. They became pioneers in what was coming to be known as psychedelia. Barrett composed, played lead guitar, and sang, and so became the leader. They played parties and local clubs with Waters on bass, Mason on drums, and Wright on keyboards. Some found them arresting; others termed them "noise."

They found a manager and a sponsor and were offered a modest contract with EMI, the Beatles' label. Initial efforts met with mild success in the UK, but Barrett, reliant on LSD and struggling with severe mental health issues, began to break down. Once a gregarious sort, he became increasingly depressed, withdrawn, and erratic. In one concert, he stood onstage untuning his guitar; at times, he appeared catatonic. In late 1967, the band invited a Barrett classmate and friend, David Gilmour, to join them on guitar, hoping that Barrett could continue as a studio member. By

1968, Syd's continued presence in the group was seen as untenable, and he was dropped.

Without their leader, Pink Floyd struggled for the next four years to find their way, releasing a series of six mildly successful albums. Waters had emerged as the new leader, setting the group's thematic direction and writing the band's brooding lyrics. In 1973, they released *The Dark Side of the Moon*, recognized today by critics and much of the public as one of the great LPs of all time. With a focus on social pressures felt by the band, the album, whose title refers to lunacy and not astronomy, tackles such issues as greed, the inexorable weight of time, mental illness, and death. The album is purportedly the 3rd highest seller worldwide; it spent a staggering 18+ years on the *Billboard* album charts. It has also been honored by inclusion in the *National Recording Registry* of the Library of Congress.

With *Dark Side*, Pink Floyd's legacy would be ensured, but this was followed up by two more best selling masterworks, 1975's *Wish You Were Here* (more than 20 million in sales), a tribute to Barrett who had showed up unannounced at the final mixing of "Shine On You Crazy Diamond," and 1979's *The Wall*, a 2-disc rock opera centered on Pink, an alienated rock star increasingly walled off from others; the LP went on to sell 30 million copies.

Pioneers, too, in massive, elaborate stage shows, sadly, at their peak, the band began to wall themselves off from one another. Wright was fired in '79 for "non-contribution;" in 1984, frustrated with his mates, Waters left the group. A fractured Pink Floyd carried on, but the glory days were over. In 2005, Waters reunited with Gilmour, Mason, and Wright for a one-off benefit concert, but within a few years Syd Barrett and Richard Wright were dead of cancer.

There has never been a band quite like Pink Floyd. With their superb musicianship, Gilmour's soaring guitar, haunting melodies, the odd bits of random, nearly subliminal voices, and Waters' philosophical lyrics that touched on "truth and illusion, life and death, time and space, causality and chance, compassion and indifference," as O'Neill Surber put it; and with songs that "seem to unfurl in slow motion" (Sanneh), of course they were the first band whose music was played in outer space.

Suggested Songs:

Money (1973)
Us and Them (1973)
Wish You Were Here (1975)
Another Brick in the Wall (Part II) (1979)
Comfortably Numb (1979)

#24 Duke Ellington (1899 - 1974)
Began Recording: 1924
Peak: 1931 - 1942
Genres: Jazz Composer/Bandleader/Pianist

Edward "Duke" Ellington has been cited as one of America's great composers. Percy Grainger went further, placing him alongside J.S. Bach as one of the greatest who ever lived. Categorized as a Black jazz composer and musician by critics and historians, Duke bristled at this reductionist labeling, preferring to see himself as an artist who wrote American music, "beyond category," for *all* people.

He grew up in a decidedly middle-class household in segregated Washington, D.C.; both parents played piano, and Edward began lessons at the age of seven. A boyhood friend nicknamed him Duke, and he grew into the sobriquet over time, evincing a relaxed, suave bearing and an elegant sartorial style.

Influenced by the then-popular piano styles of ragtime and stride, with their syncopated rhythms, he wrote his first song at 15, and, by his late teens, an odd-jobbing Duke was forming bands and playing at D.C. dances and parties for both Black and white audiences. In 1923, he made his first foray into New York City, and though it was slow going initially, by 1924 he was working steadily, playing in and forming various bands and beginning to record under such names as The Harlem Footwarmers and the Jungle Band.

Initially working with six or seven players (piano, string bass, banjo, sax, trumpet, drum), soon, Duke was fronting his bands and adding additional musicians: 10 by 1925, 14 or 15 by 1928 (five on reeds, four trumpets, three trombones, drum, bass, and the Duke conducting from the piano). His big break came in 1927 when he was offered an opportunity to take over as the house band at Harlem's Cotton Club, which catered to a rich, all-white clientele. Duke and his band began to get radio exposure and hit records such as "Creole Love Call." Influenced by his sensational "wa-wa" style trumpeter, Bubber Miley, Duke's sound began to morph (and not for the last time) from a sweet, romantic tone to a hotter, stomping style with multiple key changes and textures known as the "Jungle Sound." "East St. Louis Toodle-Oo" is a prime example from this era.

Though Ellington was an accomplished pianist himself, he is remembered also as a remarkable bandleader who seemed to bring out the best in other musicians. Johnny Hodges, called by Benny Goodman "the greatest man on alto sax that I ever heard," played with Duke on and off for nearly 40 years. Jimmy Blanton, who played double bass as a solo instrument, and Ben Webster, who brought a tenor sax to the mix, were two other world-class artists who thrived for a time with Ellington.

It is, however, as a composer that Duke has reached immortal status. By the mid-'30s the acknowledged master of the three-minute jazz piece, Ellington was a visionary who longed to work in long-form classical structures as well. In 1939, he began collaborating with Billy "Swee' Pea" Strayhorn, a classically trained composer and pianist who worked with the Duke as co-composer, arranger, and fill-in pianist and bandleader until Strayhorn died in 1967. The two worked so closely, though the father figure Ellington was clearly the public face of their partnership, that it is difficult today to delineate just who contributed what to their compositions ("Take the 'A' Train," Ellington's signature tune, was written by Strayhorn). In 1943, at Carnegie Hall, Ellington presented his innovative extended jazz work, *Black, Brown, and Beige*, with its ambitious theme of depicting African-American history.

Ellington fell out of favor, for a time, but experienced a comeback beginning in 1956 at the Newport Jazz Festival and remained relevant, fresh, and popular in jazz circles 'til his death in 1974, having collaborated with such luminaries as Count Basie, John Coltrane, Louis Armstrong, and Frank Sinatra. Still composing and performing to the very end, his passing was marked by a huge New York City funeral attended by thousands. Fittingly, Judy Collins, Charles Mingus, and Stevie Wonder each honored him with original songs.

Suggested Songs:

East St. Louis Toodle-Oo (1927)
Mood Indigo (1931)
Caravan (1936)
Take the "A" Train (1941)
My Little Brown Book - with John Coltrane (1963)

#23 Whitney Houston (1963 - 2012)
Began Recording: 1984
Peak: 1985 - 2000
Genres: R&B; Pop; dance Singer

A troubled and iconic figure in the tapestry of pop, Whitney Houston was born in a middle-class neighborhood in Newark into a family of music royalty: her aunt was famed vocalist Dionne Warwick; her cousin, opera singer Leontyne Price; while her mother, Cissy Houston, had had a successful career singing background for the likes of Elvis and Aretha Franklin before going solo.

Cissy taught her to sing, and, by 11, Whitney was a soloist at church. She attended a prestigious, all-girls Catholic high school, and, before graduation, she was already singing background on several R&B albums; joining her mom, from time to time, onstage; and working as one of the most sought after teenage models in the country.

At the age of 19, she signed with music legend Clive Davis of Arista Records. Tony Bennett reportedly commented to him, "You finally found the greatest singer I've ever heard in my life." Davis launched her gradually, beginning with a Teddy Pendergrass duet in 1984, but, the following year, *Whitney Houston*, her debut LP, dropped, and, buoyed by four hit singles, "You Give Good Love," "Saving All My Love," "How Will I Know," and "Greatest Love of All" (the last three of which rose to #1 on the *Billboard* Hot 100), hit the top of the *Billboard* albums chart, remaining there for 14 weeks. Her 1987 follow up album, *Whitney*, sold 20 million copies and produced four more #1 singles giving her seven in a row at the top, breaking a mark held by the Beatles.

She was an international sensation, a huge concert draw, scooping up honors and awards from all corners. When criticized for being too poppy, she moved toward a more rhythm and dance oriented direction with her next album, *I'm Your Baby Tonight*. 1992's *The Bodyguard* made her a movie star when she appeared alongside Kevin Costner in the wildly popular film, but it was Whitney's soundtrack recording that became the best-selling soundtrack in history, brought her a Best Album Grammy, and gave her a signature song, Dolly Parton's "I Will Always Love You," the best-selling single by any female artist ever. She played at the White House and sang before 200,000 in South Africa to honor Nelson Mandela; she was among the most famous people on the planet.

But there was another side. The pop princess with the soaring voice and superstar status was wounded when *Time* unfairly called her "the prom queen of soul" and was betrayed when she was booed and called "whitey" by hecklers at a *Soul Train* award show. She may well have been bisexual, in a relationship with her dear friend Robyn Crawford, but there was no way she could express that publicly. Kelefa Sanneh quotes her mother, "Maybe she got tired of that middle-class, church going, good-girl image." In 1992, she married rapper and singer Bobby Brown and, a year later, birthed her only child, Bobbi Kristina Brown. By 1999-2000, friends, family, colleagues, and, soon, the public noticed the changes. She was losing weight, canceling or failing to show for appearances, and giving erratic interviews. Unfortunately, Whitney was seen more in the tabloids than on stage. In 2003, Brown was arrested for assaulting her; they divorced a few years later. Her voice was a shell of what it once was. There were several comebacks, but suddenly, tragically, she was gone, found drowned in a Beverly Hills hotel bathtub; a tox screen noted the presence of several drugs in her system, but her death was ruled accidental. Perhaps cruelest of all, her 22-year-old daughter died in similar circumstances three years later.

Yet, it is "the Voice" that will be remembered: the perfect vibrato; the pure, powerful tone; the 4-octave range; the control and precision; the command of knowing when to use melisma and when not to. Singer Faith Evans perhaps summed it up best, "She was a true musician. Her voice was an instrument and she knew how to use it. With the same complexity as someone who has mastered the violin or the piano, Whitney mastered the use of her voice."

Suggested Songs:

Saving All My Love (1985)

Greatest Love of All (1986)

I Wanna Dance with Somebody (Who Loves Me) (1987)

I Will Always Love You (1992)

I Have Nothing (1992)

#22 Barbra Streisand (1942 - present)
Began Recording: 1962
Peak: 1963 - 1999
Genres: Traditional Pop; Show Tunes Singer

She was the lonely little girl with no father and the good voice. Raised in poverty in Brooklyn, by age seven, she was already yearning to escape and dreamed of becoming an actress. As she grew toward adolescence, Barbara's singing began to get noticed by her neighbors and the PTA. Her mother, though, who also possessed a lovely voice, was mostly critical and actively discouraged Barbara's dreams, pointing out that her "homely" looks would keep the doors to showbiz closed.

After graduating from high school, she moved, alone, to Manhattan, working menial jobs, sleeping where she could, desperately wanting to be close to the theater. At age 18, she landed a gig singing in a gay club in the Village. She continued to hear that she didn't have the looks, but her voice kept attracting attention. She dropped an "a" from her first name, becoming Barbra; moved to a more upscale nightspot; began listening to and learning from other female singers' records; and got invited to do a couple of songs on TV. She turned 19 and was asked to audition for a new Broadway play, *I Can Get It For You Wholesale.* She got the part, received rave reviews, and continued to appear with Johnny Carson and others on TV. She was becoming a sensation.

At 21, Barbra Streisand was being compared to Elvis for all the excitement she was generating; she signed a recording contract with Columbia, taking less money than was offered in exchange for her keeping creative control. That year, 1963, *The Barbra Streisand Album* was released. The LP garnered the Album of the Year Grammy. Over a 19-month-period, she released four albums that flirted with the top of the charts and landed the lead role in a new Broadway musical, *Funny Girl*, which gave her two early signature songs, "Don't Rain on My Parade" and "People." By the end of the decade, Barbra Streisand had already won a Tony (Star of the Decade), an

Oscar (Best Actress, *Funny Girl*), and several Emmys and Grammys—and she was not yet out of her 20s.

More than anything, it was the voice. "One of the natural wonders of the age, an instrument of infinite diversity and timbral resource," said esteemed pianist Glenn Gould. Classical music critic Anthony Tommasini noted, "She had a way of reaching the peak of a phrase and sustaining a pitch with such focused vibrato and pulsing tone that she seemed to be soaring effortlessly." Yet she was completely untrained. She took only one voice lesson, rarely warmed-up, found singing exercises boring. She called it intuitive. Singing, she said, was an extension of acting. It was all about mechanics and willpower. She hit and held certain notes through sheer determination. Her voice is instantly recognizable with a pure tone, phenomenal control, a bit of a Brooklyn nasal quality—very dramatic and emotive. Tommasini points out that she "sings as if she's speaking to you." Her fans have included some of the greats, Judy Garland, Aretha Franklin, Diana Ross, Lady Gaga, and Adele. She has lost some of her upper register in recent years, but she has learned to make the new depth work for her.

She was the all-time bestselling female artist for decades, but she has lost that title to Madonna. Streisand is, however, still the only recording artist to have at least one #1 album on the *Billboard* 200 in six consecutive decades. Primarily a balladeer of traditional pop and show tunes, she has forayed into disco (with Donna Summer) and even rock (*Stoney End*). Notoriously reluctant to perform in concert (she has cited stage fright, intense self-criticism, and a hatred of dress fittings as reasons), she went 27 years between tours, though she has relented and done five since 1993. Still supremely in control of her creative output, Streisand has been unfairly criticized all her life for being bossy and difficult, but there's no denying that the vulnerable little girl who so missed her father has achieved genius results.

Suggested Songs:

People (1964)
He Touched Me (1965)
The Way We Were (1974)
You Don't Bring Me Flowers (w. Neil Diamond) (1978)
Memory (1982)

#21 Prince (1958 - 2016)
Began Recording: 1978
Peak: 1982 - 1991
Genres: R&B; Rock; Pop; Soul; Funk Singer/Songwriter/Multi-Instrumentalist

"The greatest recording artist of all-time," said the *Daily Beast* at the time of his death. Nik Cohn, a well-known British music critic, called him "rock's greatest ever natural talent." He was known by his first name, Prince, though, for a time, in the mid-'90s, he went by an unpronounceable "love symbol" and was also dubbed "The Artist Formerly Known as Prince." He wrote, arranged, sang, produced, and played all 27 instruments on his first album, when he was but 19 years old.

Born into a Minneapolis musical family, his father was a pianist, composer, and bandleader, his mother a singer. When his parents divorced, Prince bounced back and forth between households before exiting to live in a friend's basement. In high school, he was an excellent basketball player; a ballet dancer; and a musician who could play guitar, bass, drums, and keyboards.

Success did not come overnight; in fact, in 1981, he was booed off stage by Rolling Stones fans as he attempted to open the show for them, but, by 1982, his LP *1999*, and its eponymous single were making waves. In 1983, his provocative, double entendre single, "Little Red Corvette," was following Michael Jackson through the color barrier on MTV. Then came 1984's *Purple Rain*, Prince's semi-autobiographical film, starring himself. That year, he simultaneously had the #1 movie, album (*Purple Rain* sold over 13 million copies in the U.S. alone), and single, a feat never before accomplished by a single artist. "When Doves Cry" reached #1, as did "Let's Go Crazy," while the title track peaked at #2. The album also contained the song "Darling Nikki," with its explicit sexual references, which was the catalyst for Tipper Gore's crusade to slap Parental Advisory Stickers on albums with questionable content.

Certainly Prince has often sung about sex, seduction, and eroticism, often eschewing a euphemistic approach in favor of a more direct depiction. In fact, he projected a highly charged, sexually androgynous image and style in his manner of dress, performance, and off stage behavior. Some saw it as a fearless commitment to freedom and a desire to tear down gender norms and traditional sexual roles. He was not the first artist to walk this road. Little Richard in the '50s and David Bowie in the '70s were, in some sense, precursors. Still, it is the sheer musical talent for which he is best remembered. He was a brilliant singer, a natural tenor who could easily switch from an airy falsetto to a rich baritone and infuse it all with emotive squeaks and screams. Musically, he drew from such diverse artists as James Brown, Sly Stone, and Stevie Wonder, whom he viewed as something of a role model, but also from Carlos Santana, Fleetwood Mac, and Joni Mitchell, and he created a dynamic hybrid of hard or psychedelic rock married to a funky, soulful R&B. His multi-instrumental prowess was legendary (perhaps only Stevie Wonder can touch him), and several publications called him the greatest guitarist of them all. He was revered by musicians as diverse as Miles Davis and Justin Timberlake. His influence on the likes of Beyoncé, Bruno Mars, Rihanna, Alicia Keys, Lady Gaga, and Beck was profound.

The term may be overused, but there are a number of live Prince performances considered legendary: his 2004 Rock Hall performance of George Harrison's, "While My Guitar Gently Weeps" still elicits awe, and the 2007 Super Bowl Halftime show, delivered in the pouring purple rain, is still considered the best ever.

His death at 57 from an accidental opioid overdose shocked the world, for the man who brought so much joy to millions died senselessly in seclusion in an elevator at his sprawling Paisley Park complex. That lonely end is part of his legacy, but so too is the assessment of musician Lenny Kravitz: "He's right there with Mozart, Miles Davis, Jimi Hendrix. He's right there with the best that ever lived."

Suggested Songs:

1999 (1982)
Little Red Corvette (1983)
Purple Rain (1984)
When Doves Cry (1984)
Sign O' the Times (1987)

#20 Queen
Began Recording: 1973
Peak: 1975 - 1982; 1985 - 1986
Genres: Rock (hard, art, pop) Band

What kind of a band is this? They are four highly educated men: one, Roger Taylor, has a degree in biology, is the group's drummer, but can slide over to lead or bass guitar if need be; John Deacon graduated with honors in the field of electronics, became the band's bass player and sometimes rhythm guitarist; Brian May studied math and physics and today is a PhD astrophysicist, a university researcher, author, and sometimes chancellor when he's not playing world class lead guitar for one of the best selling bands in history; the fourth member was a Tanzanian-born, Indian-reared, London-educated graphic designer and illustrator, Farrokh Bulsara, better known as Freddie Mercury, pianist and lead singer. They drew inspiration from across the musical spectrum, from Jimi Hendrix to Liza Minnelli, from John Lennon to classical opera. Though they created some of the most musically complex and arresting works of their era, they were, for a time, largely dismissed by critics for their lack of originality and for their bombastic style. Of course, I am speaking of Queen.

Queen self-funded their initial recording in 1973, a hard, metal-tinged album, out of Trident Studios in London. After three mildly successful LPs and a hit single, "Killer Queen," they were still broke but beginning to make an international name for themselves. In 1975, backed by EMI Studios, Queen recorded *A Night at the Opera*, at the time the most expensive album ever produced. Working with 24-track tape, Queen was uniquely collaborative (all four members contributed songs). Mercury, May, Taylor sang, multi-tracked, over and over until they sounded like a celestial choir. May, using his homemade "Red Special" guitar in conjunction with Deacon's home built amp, produced layered guitar mixes that created a symphonic feel. Queen took great pride in the fact that no synthesizers were used in their early works. Today, recognized as their finest, the album was a mix of styles: hard and progressive rock, pop ballads, and the mini-opera master-piece, "Bohemian Rhapsody."

A Mercury composition, the song begins with an a cappella multi-voice intro then morphs into a spine-tingling, piano-backed ballad by Mercury. As the ballad builds, adding drums and guitar, it abruptly cuts, leaving quiet staccato piano chords introducing the opera section with its multi-voice overdubs, quick changing rhythms, and lyrics that hint at a supernatural struggle over the narrator's soul. A hard rock guitar solo accompanied by Mercury's impassioned vocal, looking for escape, follows, before Freddie's piano breaks in again, taking us back to the intro melody to conclude with Mercury's resigned denouement and a climaxing gong, Loved or hated, profound or nonsense, the song, which was nearly nixed by record execs, has been a sensation since its release. It is the most streamed song recorded in the 20th century.

Freddie Mercury's voice, in fact, has been one of the most studied in history. Analyzed by scientists and called the best by such diverse artists as Roger Daltry of the Who and opera soprano Montserrat Caballe, Freddie is famed for his expressive, four-octave range and for his confident, self-possessed, charismatic command of the stage. Queen's 1985 appearance at the Live Aid fundraiser, before 72,000 live and 1.9 billion watching on TV, has often been cited as the greatest rock performance of all-time.

Sadly, Freddie Mercury succumbed to AIDS-related pneumonia in 1991. Devastated by the loss, John Deacon retired from the band a few years later. May and Taylor continue to play as Queen with Adam Lambert handling lead vocals. The music of Queen, rich, broad, and self-effacing, continues to delight listeners on all continents, and artists as diverse as Faith Hill, Metallica, Katy Perry, Nirvana, Lady Gaga, Radiohead, and George Michael have testified to the influence that Queen has had on their own music and lives.

Suggested Songs:

Bohemian Rhapsody (1975)
Somebody to Love (1976)
Save Me (1980)
Under Pressure (with David Bowie) (1981)
Radio Ga Ga (1984)

#19 Beyoncé (1981- present)
Began Recording: 1997 (w. Destiny's Child); 2002 (solo)
Peak: 2003 - 2023
Genres: R&B; Pop, hip-hop Singer/Songwriter

Beyoncé Giselle Knowles, known professionally as Beyoncé, grew up singing, rapping, and dancing in Houston. At the age of eight, she became a member of a local vocal group, Girl's Tyme, which eventually became the highly successful recording quartet (later trio) Destiny's Child. With Beyoncé singing lead, and managed by her father Mathew Knowles, between 1997 and 2004, Destiny's Child released five studio albums and sold over 60 million records.

During a two-year hiatus, Beyoncé and her singing partners, Michelle Williams and Kelly Rowland, each released successful solo albums, and, after reuniting in 2004 for one final LP, each went amicably her own way. Beyoncé's solo debut LP, *Dangerously in Love*, featured the single "Crazy in Love" with rapper JAY-Z and shot to #1 on the *Billboard* 200 album chart. In fact, all seven Beyoncé studio albums have rocketed to the top of the charts upon their release, a feat never before accomplished by a solo artist. Besides taking her place among the world's best-selling musicians, Beyoncé, in her still relatively short career, has already become one of the most awarded and honored female recording artists in history; in fact, her 32 Grammys (the first three with Destiny's Child) tops all artists.

While her voice is not as celebrated as Whitney's or Aretha's, Beyoncé's mezzo-soprano contains plenty of power and can range well beyond three octaves. Jon Pareles of *The New York Times* wrote that her voice is "Velvety yet tart, with an insistent flutter and reserves of soul belting." She has popularized a staccato rap-singing style and influenced a host of great performers from Rihanna to Ariana Grande to Adele, who once commented that, "My artist of my life is Beyoncé." Even Paul McCartney and Garth Brooks say they have learned from her live performance style.

Beyoncé has released some of the most iconic, best-selling singles of the 21st century, including her moving "If I were a Boy," which makes all too clear that we still live in a world of gender inequality; the female empowerment number "Single Ladies (Put a Ring on It);" the power love ballad "Halo;" and the R&B celebration of Black culture "Formation." Beyoncé has never shied away from honest expression, chronicling her feelings of betrayal in her 2016 masterwork, *Lemonade*, after husband JAY-Z strayed from his marriage vows. Reconciled, the ultimate music industry power couple has been together now for 21 years and married for 15.

In July of 2022, Beyoncé released the dance flavored LP *Renaissance*, preceded by the exuberant, defiant anthem "Break My Soul," insisting over and over that that wouldn't happen. Beyoncé has also had a strong presence in a number of films, notably 2006's *Dreamgirls*, where some saw echoes of Diana Ross, and 2008's *Cadillac Records*, portraying the brilliant but troubled Etta James. Beyoncé calls herself a "modern-day feminist" and has spoken out unapologetically in favor of gun control, LGBTQ+ rights, and the Black Lives Matter movement. Jody Rosen of *The New Yorker* called "Queen Bey" "the most important and compelling musician of the twenty-first century," while Kelefa Sanneh opined that she has gone "from mere pop star to... a cross between a folk hero, a cult leader, and a royal eminence."

Suggested Songs:

Crazy in Love (with JAY-Z) (2003)
If I Were a Boy" (2008)
Halo (2009)
Love on Top (2011)
Formation (2016)

#18 Johnny Cash (1932 - 2003)
Began Recording: 1955
Peak: 1963 - 1965; 1968 - 1972
Genres: Country; gospel; blues; folk Singer/Songwriter

He was known as the Man in Black. Though he once quipped it was easier to keep such outfits clean while on the road, he also wrote a song explaining why he dressed head to toe in black: to represent and honor society's discarded and forgotten.

Johnny Cash clearly had an affinity for the downtrodden, as he demonstrated all his life. He was born J.R. into a poor sharecropper family in rural Arkansas and worked the cotton fields as a boy. At 12, he lost his beloved brother Jack to a freak accident; committed to Jesus; and took up the guitar, mixing gospel, folk, and country & western. During a 4-year stint in the Air Force, he met his first wife, Vivian, and began singing in taverns.

Settling in Memphis after leaving the service, "John" sold appliances and worked on his music. In 1955, he and two friends auditioned for Sam Phillips, who had discovered the young Elvis the year before. Passing on the trio's gospel numbers, Sam agreed to record the country flavored "Cry, Cry, Cry" by Johnny Cash and the Tennessee Two. He got a $2.41 royalty check, a new first name, and a chance to tour with Presley.

Johnny had his first #1 on *Billboard*'s Hot Country Songs chart a year later, the signature tune, "I Walk the Line." As his success grew, Cash decided to sign with a more established label, Columbia. The country hits kept coming, and Johnny stayed on the road, fueling his frenetic pace with alcohol and pills. Nurturing an outlaw image, overdosing, getting busted several times, and growing estranged from his wife, Johnny was out of control. In 1966, Vivian divorced him. Cash, who had grown close to the musically famed Carter family, turned to them and back to the Church in a desperate effort to get clean. In 1968, Johnny married one of the Carters, singer June. At the same time, his career was rebounding with the release of two career-defining LPs, *Johnny Cash at Folsom Prison* and *Johnny Cash at San Quentin.* Though Cash himself had only spent a couple of nights in jail, his struggles with addiction seemed to give him a natural empathy for and credibility with the inmates. One San Quentin prisoner was a young Merle Haggard, who later expressed that seeing and hearing Cash in that setting turned his life around and that Johnny was instrumental in getting him to tell his own story.

Cash was an iconoclast. Music critic Kelefa Sanneh wrote, "Johnny Cash… made unpredictable country hits for decades while remaining somehow unclassifiable; no one ever had more success in country music while taking the industry less seriously." In 1964, having recently scored a #1 single, "Ring of Fire," and a #1 album, *I Walk the Line,* he decided to record an album that spotlighted the systemic oppression of Native Americans. The blowback from his record label and the country music industry was fierce; still, he persisted, releasing the LP *Bitter Tears: Ballads of the American Indian.* It reached #2 on the *Top Country Albums* chart, and Johnny remained committed to Native causes. Between 1969 and 1971, *The Johnny Cash Show* aired on TV from country music capital Nashville, yet Johnny regularly featured such non-country artists as Neil Diamond, Louis Armstrong, Joni Mitchell, and friend Bob Dylan. In 1972, when Cash met President Nixon in the White House to promote prison reform, Nixon asked him to sing the conservative Haggard anthem, "Okie from Muskogee;" Johnny responded by singing "What Is Truth?," "The Man in Black," and "The Ballad of Ira Hayes" from his *Bitter Tears* album.

In his last two decades, Johnny's health continually failed him, yet he toured, recorded, and grew bigger than the world of music. His friend Kris Kristofferson might have said it best, "He went from being this guy who was as wild as Hank Williams to being almost as respected as one of the fathers of our country."

Suggested Songs:

I Walk the Line (1956)
Ring of Fire (1963)
Folsom Prison Blues (1968)
Man in Black (1971)
Hurt (2002)

#17 U2

Began Recording: 1979
Peak: 1985 - 2006
Genres: Rock; alternative rock; pop rock Band

It's 1976 and 14-year-old Larry Mullen Jr. tacks up a notice on his school bulletin board, hoping to find mates to start a rock band. He gets a few takers and a couple days later they meet to practice. Among the attendees are David and Dik Evans, Adam Clayton, and Paul Hewson. Dik, who is older than the rest, eventually drops, but the world now knows David as the Edge and Paul as Bono. By 1978, having won a local talent show, they begin to call themselves U2. Touring their native Ireland, they gain exposure and soon a record deal. They slowly acquire a following and a reputation for dynamic live shows. By 1987, they have the best selling and most celebrated album in the world, *The Joshua Tree*, both a paean to the ideals and beauty of the United States and a critique of its foreign policy, and noted *L.A. Times* music critic Robert Hilburn writes that this "confirms on record what the band has been slowly asserting for three years now on stage: U2 is what the Rolling Stones ceased being years ago—the greatest rock and roll band in the world." For the next three and a half decades, no band anywhere is bigger.

Six of their albums have sold ten million or more copies; twice, their LPs have taken home the Grammy for Album of the Year (*The Joshua Tree* and *How to Dismantle an Atomic Bomb*); in fact, no band has won more than their 22 Grammys. Yet U2 is not blessed with the kind of virtuoso musicians found in a Led Zeppelin. Their music has been described as simple, anthemic, muscular, and passionate. Originally coming out of a post-punk tradition, they have, in time, evolved into a power rock, even a pop rock, arena-style outfit. The Edge's chiming guitar, with its echo, distortion, and delay, is central to their sound. The rhythm guys, Clayton on bass and Mullen on drums, are efficient and generally stay out of the spotlight. Bono is the larger than life character recognizable for his emotional, passionate vocal delivery. All four members supply ideas for the music, while Bono writes the majority of the lyrics, which often focus on social, political, personal, and spiritual themes. There are those who assert that U2 is really a Christian band in disguise. Songs like "With or Without You," "I Still Haven't Found What I'm Looking For," "Until the End of the World," and "Ultra Violet (Light My Way)" take on a different meaning when heard with a Christian ear.

It's interesting to note that U2 has been one of the most polarizing acts in rock history. Millions, of course, have bought their records, attended their shows, and count themselves devoted fans, celebrating not only their stadium-filling energy but also their commitment to peace and a more hopeful future. They have, without a doubt, influenced scores of contemporary artists, from Coldplay to Ed Sheeran. Yet their detractors are legion. Their music has been called, by some, droning, insistent, overwrought, and repetitive. In 2014, when U2 cut a deal with Apple and their latest LP, *Songs of Innocence*, just showed up on millions of iTunes subscribers' playlists uninvited, many were aghast. *The Washington Post* quipped that this was "rock-and-roll as dystopian junk mail." Much of the vitriol, though, seems to be aimed at Bono, who is frequently disparaged as preachy, a do-gooder, or holier than thou. What really is the offense? The fact is, U2 has consistently been, from the beginning, both collectively and individually, involved in trying to make our world a better place. Whether it was playing concerts to raise money to fight hunger (Band Aid and Live Aid), working to promote peace and human rights (Amnesty International tour and Northern Ireland peace efforts), or pressing politicians on debt relief, it is undeniable that few music stars have been more visible in such efforts than Bono and U2.

Suggested Songs:

Sunday Bloody Sunday (1983)
With or Without You (1987)
I Still Haven't Found What I'm Looking For (1987)
One (1992)
Walk On (2001)

#16 Taylor Swift (1989 - present)
Began Recording: 2006
Peak: 2008 - 2023
Genres: Country; Pop; alternative rock Singer/Songwriter

In 2006, the 16-year-old released her first record, the self-titled LP *Taylor Swift*; it peaked at #5 on the *Billboard* 200 chart. Her next nine studio albums all climbed to #1, as did three rerecorded ones. At 34, she is already among the 15 best selling artists of all-time. Billy Joel likened her to the Beatles. Paul McCartney celebrates her work ethic, while Ringo simply says, "I love her."

Born in West Reading, Pennsylvania, to parents successful in finance, at a young age Taylor was doing local musical theater and taking acting and voice lessons. She says that Shania Twain records got her interested in country music, and, by age 11, she had already submitted a demo tape to Nashville. With single-minded determination, the family moved there when Taylor was 14, and Swift began working with a songwriters' group after school. At 15, she signed with an independent record label and, within a year, released the single "Tim McGraw" and the aforementioned first album. *The New York Times* noticed, calling the album "a small masterpiece of pop-minded country."

Her 2008 sophomore release, *Fearless*, became the best selling album of the following year and spawned the hits "Love Story" and "You Belong with Me." While still recognized as primarily a country artist, Taylor clearly had huge crossover appeal and *Fearless* captured the prestigious Grammy for Album of the Year, making Taylor Swift the youngest artist to ever accomplish that feat. At an MTV Video Awards show, Kanye West complained from stage that Beyoncé was more deserving of a particular honor, but the incident largely brought increased recognition and sympathy to Swift.

Her 2010 release, *Speak Now*, again hit the top and was supported by a huge tour; like clockwork, 2012 saw her release *Red,* which is today seen as a crossover record with some country flavoring, but veering more toward pop. While "We Are Never Getting Back Together" became her first #1

U.S. single (*Billboard* Hot 100*)*, the track that ultimately has gained the most recognition is "All Too Well." Critics across the board have praised the song for its brilliant songwriting (Liz Rose collaborated, but she assures that the song is all Taylor and that she, Liz, was there to help her edit a 10 or 12 minute story down to a manageable four and a half; Taylor's 10 minute 2021 rerecording of the song displaced "American Pie" as the longest single ever to reach #1), for its attention to detail, and for its emotional heft. It is, fundamentally, a break up song, something Taylor is famous for, but it is also honest, heartbreaking, angry, and triumphant. Two years later, with the release of *1989*, and another best album Grammy, her full transition to pop was complete. *Reputation, Lover, Folklore, Evermore*, and *Midnights* added to her streak of #1's, dipping with the two penultimate releases into the world of mellow alternative rock.

Taylor Swift has been a critical darling from the start, but not everyone is a fan. Her songwriting has been criticized, by some, for being too self-referential (Taylor writing mostly about Taylor, though she insists she often writes about other characters). Some have commented that her voice is just average and not world class like her contemporaries, Ariana Grande or Adele. Then, too, her every move—who she is dating, who are her friends and her perceived enemies—has been scrutinized ad-nauseam by the tabloids and social media.

Taylor has also impacted the music business and the culture, positively, in ways that are undeniable. When she called out a DJ who had groped her (even going to court), she was applauded for speaking up against rampant misogyny in the industry. When she pulled her music (temporarily) from Spotify and iTunes in an effort to get fair compensation, the industry took notice; when she decided to re-record her early albums so that she could retain creative control of her music, she struck a blow against traditional industry dynamics.

When *Folklore* won her a third best album Grammy in 2021, she became the first woman to ever achieve that feat. Taylor Swift is clearly not finished. She has, in fact, been shattering records left and right of late: besting Barbra Streisand as the woman with the most *Billboard* 200 #1 albums in history, while her current Eras Tour is on pace to go down as the highest grossing ever. With legions of passionate, devoted fans, it would seem that Swift has entered that rarified air of popular acclaim only tasted previously by Elvis, the Beatles, and Michael Jackson.

Suggested Songs:

Love Story (2008)
Shake It Off (2014)
Tolerate It (2020)
No Body, No Crime (2020)
All Too Well (Taylor's Version) (2021)

#15 Bing Crosby (1903 - 1977)
Began Recording: 1926 (w. A. Rinker & D. Clark); 1931 (solo)
Peak: 1931 - 1954
Genres: Pop; jazz Singer

His name and his music is no longer known to countless young music fans. Yet, it is indisputable that Harry "Bing" Crosby was the most popular recording artist of the first half of the 20th century. Though accurate figures are hard to come by, it is believed by many that only the Beatles, Elvis, and Michael Jackson have sold more records. With 41 #1 singles, he still holds that record. He was a giant in three distinct areas of entertainment: recordings (with 1600 songs, nobody ever recorded more); broadcasting (he made a huge mark in both radio and television); movies (he starred in 55 feature films and even won an Oscar for Best Actor).

Harry grew up in the state of Washington and, as a child, was already known as Bing. Though he studied law, he chose instead to go into entertainment, hoping to parlay his singing and drumming skills into a career. In 1925, he and a friend, Al Rinker, drove to Los Angeles and soon were traveling up and down the west coast on the vaudeville circuit. A year later, prominent bandleader Paul Whiteman signed the duo, added a third member, and soon they were singing and recording as the Rhythm Boys.

In 1928, the Rhythm Boys had a #1 hit, a jazz-inflected version of "Ol' Man River." By this time, it was apparent that Crosby was the star, and, in 1931, he decided to go solo. That year, he was introduced to radio audiences, had three #1 records, and, within a year, began making movies. His 1932 recording of "Brother, Can You Spare a Dime?" became something of a Depression-era anthem.

One of the most prominent artists Bing worked with was the jazz great Louis Armstrong. Both were on the cusp of stardom when they met, and there was a mutual admiration, on and off collaboration, and a lasting friendship that developed. Crosby said he learned from Armstrong to incorporate jazz elements into his singing, while Armstrong heard Crosby as a genius singer and borrowed from his style. Over the years, Armstrong appeared on Crosby's *Kraft Music Hall* radio program, they collaborated on record, and made several movies together. Crosby fought to assure that Armstrong got equal billing, and Louis later remarked how appreciative he was of his friend's racially progressive views and actions.

Bing's singing style has been described as intimate; he is perhaps the consummate "crooner." Really, what that means is that he didn't need to belt out a song's lyrics to be heard in the back of an auditorium. He learned how to use the microphone to communicate nuance and subtlety, to sing in a conversational style. Jazz influenced his phrasing, especially early in his career, and he was said to be emotionally honest. Frank Sinatra adored him.

As the '30s turned into the '40s, Bing's popularity soared. At one point it was estimated that half of radio's musical airtime was taken up by Bing Crosby. As the United States entered World War II in 1941, Crosby threw himself into serving America's soldiers with personal appearances and concerts here and abroad. He corresponded with thousands of soldiers and their families and raised money for war bonds. After the war, a poll said that nobody had done more for GI morale than Crosby.

Crosby had a hand in saving the record industry twice, once by pushing for lower retail costs for discs in exchange for artists receiving royalties per records sold, and a few years later for helping to pioneer new recording technology with the use of magnetic tape. Crosby slowed down in later years. His last TV appearance featured the odd pairing of Bing with a young David Bowie singing a Christmas duet. A few days after the program aired, Bing Crosby died of a massive heart attack. The song he is most remembered for today? "White Christmas," with its 50 million copies sold, still the best seller of all-time.

Suggested Songs:

Brother, Can You Spare a Dime? (1932)
Pennies From Heaven (1936)
Remember Me? (1937)
White Christmas (1942)
Swinging on a Star (1944)

#14 Led Zeppelin

Began Recording: 1969
Peak: 1969 - 1979
Genres: Hard Rock/Heavy Metal; Blues Rock Band

In 2007, a band that had broken up 27 years earlier agreed to a one-off concert in London. They'd done a couple of reunion shows before to disastrous results; their original drummer was gone, and his son would be filling in. There were 20 million requests for tickets! Led Zeppelin is the defining band in the categories of hard rock and heavy metal. Musical artists as diverse as Black Sabbath, Queen, Nirvana, and Madonna have felt their influence. Who are they?

They were four uniquely talented English musicians: Jimmy Page, former member of the '60s rock band the Yardbirds, played a blues oriented lead guitar, sometimes aggressive, occasionally distorted, at times sweetly melodic, occasionally even using a cello bow to droning effect. Robert Plant was the band's singer, noted for his powerful, soaring vocal histrionics and long, flowing blonde locks. He has frequently been dubbed the greatest vocal front man in rock history. John Paul Jones was the quiet, brilliant bassist and keyboardist; and John Bonham, the powerful, propulsive anchor behind the drums, is today recognized as perhaps the greatest of all-time.

Formed in late 1968, two members of a rival band, the Who, joked that they'd go over like a lead balloon. When Page and the New Yardbirds were ordered for legal reasons to change their name, they settled on Led Zeppelin with its oxymoronic connotations of light and heavy. Success came quickly. Two albums, *Led Zeppelin* and *Led Zeppelin II*, released in 1969, climbed to #6 and #1, respectively, on Britain's Official Albums Chart. Such well-known tracks as "Dazed and Confused" and "Whole Lotta Love" come from these discs. *Led Zeppelin III*, with the classic "Immigrant Song," followed in 1970 and again topped the charts on both sides of the Atlantic. Still, critics were not yet impressed. The band then decided to release their next album with no identifying words whatsoever on the cover. Today widely known as *Led Zeppelin IV*, it has sold over 37 million copies and is one of the best selling LPs of all-time. The album's best-loved track is "Stairway to Heaven," which is famous for its slow build, mid-song drum arrival, and blazing guitar denouement, coupled with Plant's frenzied finishing falsetto. "Stairway to Heaven," though never released as a single (the band fiercely resisted releasing singles), became the most requested and popular song of the 1970s, by *any* artist.

As Led Zeppelin became a recording phenomenon, they also became the most popular live act of their day, ushering in the age of stadium rock. They were outdrawing even such giants as the Rolling Stones and became renowned for the brilliant musicianship and power of their shows. The critics came around. At the same time, they developed a reputation for controversial offstage behavior. Stories of drug excess and young groupies abound. In addition, there were whispered tales of occult practices that have become part of their legacy. It's difficult to sort it all out, but there is no evidence any of them made a rumored blood pact with the devil, though Jimmy Page did develop an obsessive fixation on British black magic occultist Aleister Crowley, going so far as buying his old, supposedly haunted, house on the shores of Loch Ness.

In 1980, while rehearsing for their next tour, drummer John Bonham was found dead in his bed. An autopsy revealed that he had the equivalent of 40 shots of vodka in his system. He also had been taking an antipsychotic and an antidepressant, though, crucially, the coroner found no evidence that the mix was toxic. It was ruled an accidental death. Led Zeppelin canceled the upcoming tour and soon after chose to disband. Despite the occasional reunion project, there was never a reconstituting of the band.

How are they remembered today? As various music critics and millions of fans would attest, not only were they the most popular hard rock band, they were also the best.

Suggested Sings:

Whole Lotta Love (1969)
Going to California (1971)
Stairway to Heaven (1971)
Trampled Under Foot (1975)
Kashmir (1975)

#13 Louis Armstrong (1901 - 1971)

Began Recording: 1923
Peak: 1925 - 1964
Genres: Jazz; traditional pop Trumpeter/Singer/Songwriter

His beginnings were not auspicious, yet noted literary critic Harold Bloom cited him and Walt Whitman as the two Americans who made the greatest artistic contributions to world culture.

Louis Armstrong was born and raised in poverty in the infamous New Orleans neighborhood known as "the Battlefield." As a child, he bounced between his mother, his grandmother, a local Jewish immigrant family, and his father. He ran the streets, did odd jobs, and sang for change. At seven, he bought a cornet with money given him by the Jewish Kornoffsky family, but he didn't really learn to play until he was locked up in a segregated reform school for firing his dad's pistol on New Year's Eve. He was 11 years old and spent a year and a half in the spartan environment, but music teacher Peter Davis taught him to play. Upon his release, he returned to hauling coal, collecting junk, and selling newspapers, but, mostly, he looked for opportunities to play the emerging New Orleans blues and ragtime mix known as *jazz*.

Joe "King" Oliver became his mentor. Soon, Louis was playing on Mississippi riverboats. He learned to read music. By the early 1920s, he was getting noticed for his daring solos and for his singing. Oliver had moved to Chicago, and he invited Louis to join his band. In 1923, he did his first recordings with "King" Oliver's jazz band; acoustic style, the band huddled together around the open end of a funnel to record. A year later, Louis moved to New York to join the Fletcher Henderson Orchestra, the top Black band in the U.S. Louis' impact on them was profound, turning them into America's first major jazz band.

Armstrong's second wife, Lil Hardin, saw bigger things for him, however, and pushed a reluctant Louis back to Chicago where he formed Louis Armstrong and His Hot Five (later the Hot Seven). Between 1925 and 1928, Louis and his bandmates made music history with such jazz classics as "Heebie Jeebies" (with its early use of scat singing) and "Potato Head Blues." The jazz masterworks "Weather Bird" and "West End Blues" also date from this time.

Armstrong's popularity exploded. In the 1930s, Satchmo (from the probable childhood nickname *Satchelmouth*), as he was now affectionately known, was a fixture on radio, on records, and, increasingly, in film. He had, however, gotten wrong with several mobsters, and, after years of intense pressure on his lips, the two issues forced him to lay low for a bit. By the late '30s and into the '40s, though, his career was back in full gear. His film, concert, recording, and travel schedule was busier than ever. By the last two decades of his life, Armstrong was something of a cultural goodwill ambassador for the United States. He was one of the few African Americans who could straddle both white and Black society, although he once remarked that only white folks called him Louie while he knew himself as Louis. To his friends he was Pops.

By the 1950s, there was a serious divide between many younger jazz artists and Louis. Miles Davis summed it up succinctly: "I loved the way Louis played trumpet, man, but I hated the way he had to grin to get over with some tired white folks."

There is, however, no denying his impact on music. He was a virtuoso trumpet player whose improvisational skill and sublime solos totally transformed jazz. Duke Ellington called him a "master." His singing style was also hugely impactful. Billie Holiday and Ella Fitzgerald were both inspired by his vocals. Friend and colleague Bing Crosby called him "the greatest pop singer in the world that ever was and ever will be."

In 1964, he had his biggest hit, the surprising "Hello Dolly," which pushed the Beatles (he liked to listen to them on his personal mixtapes along with Miles Davis, Al Jolson, Latin, African, classical music, and more) out of the #1 spot. The last 12 years of his life, his health gave out repeatedly. He died in his sleep a month before turning 70. Among his honorary pallbearers were Bing Crosby, Ella Fitzgerald, Dizzy Gillespie, and Count Basie.

Suggested Songs:

Hotter Than That (1926)
Potato Head Blues (1927)
Ain't Misbehavin' (1929)
On the Sunny Side of the Street (1947)
What a Wonderful World (1967)

#12 Aretha Franklin (1942 - 2018)

Began Recording: 1956
Peak: 1967 - 1973; 1985 - 1987
Genres: R&B/Soul; gospel Singer/Songwriter/Pianist

The BBC said she was the "Greatest singer in U.S. history." *Rolling Stone* Magazine simply called her the greatest singer of all time. Though she sold millions of records in a 60-year career, except for a brief few years, she never dominated the charts the way Madonna, Celine Dion, or Mariah Carey did. Little doubt, though, she was born to sing.

Raised in the Baptist Church by her celebrity preacher father, she was a naturally gifted pianist and vocalist, already on the road singing gospel, with her father as manager, before she reached her teenage years. She knew Sam Cooke; learned technique from the King of Gospel, James Cleveland; broke bread with Dr. King; and, at 14, cut her first record. If there was early promise, there was also surely unspeakable pain and trauma. By 14, she had been pregnant and given birth, twice. Before she was out of her teens, she was married to a man who physically abused her.

When she turned 18, Aretha moved to New York to pursue a career in popular music, but her first major record label, Columbia, failed to adequately showcase her talent, and she moved over to Atlantic Records in 1967. She quickly broke through with "I Never Loved a Man (The Way I Love You)" from the LP of the same name, but, later that year, her version of an Otis Redding composition, "Respect," shot to the top of the charts. Redding, when he heard her version, reportedly commented, "I just lost my song. That girl took it away from me." The song became Aretha's signature. Over the years it has gained stature as a feminist and Civil Rights anthem. In fact, in 2021, *Rolling Stone* named it the #1 song of all-time, displacing Bob Dylan's "Like a Rolling Stone." In 1968, Aretha scored with two more hit albums, *Lady Soul* and *Aretha Now*. The airways were flooded with her music: "Chain of Fools," "Ain't No Way," "(Sweet Sweet Baby) Since You've Been Gone," "Think," and "I Say a Little Prayer."

In 1971, she released the celebrated *Aretha Live at Fillmore West*, and, in 1972, her live church gospel LP, *Amazing Grace*, continued her wondrous run of groundbreaking music. She never again, though, found the formula for topping the popular charts, save one 1987 corroboration with British singer George Michael, "I Knew You were Waiting (For Me)." Still, she continued making remarkable music, winning 18 Grammy awards along the way. She periodically astounded with sensational live performances, such as at the 1998 Grammys, when she was given 20 minutes to prepare to fill in for her ailing friend Luciano Pavarotti in singing the classic opera piece "Nessun dorma," which she delivered in breathtaking style, or when she brought tears to President Obama and obvious joy to honoree Carole King at the 2015 Kennedy Center Honors with her stirring rendition of King's "(You Make Me Feel Like) A Natural Woman."

What was it about that mezzo-soprano voice? Vocal coach Beth Roars says it's a combination of ease, warmth, confidence, and honesty that always comes through. "It's like she's speaking to you, even when belting." Others have noted her sense of immediacy, being fully in the moment. Still others point not simply to her obvious power, but also her ability to shade, to vary her dynamics and her tempo. Mary J. Blige called her, "a gift from God... there is no one who can touch her." Freddie Mercury said, "I wish I could sing like her. She sings like a dream." Alicia Keys and Whitney Houston both pointed to her uncanny ability to make us feel. Mariah Carey, finally, summed her up, "When Aretha sings, you don't stand there and try to compete...You revere her."

She gave to the very end. Before her death from pancreatic cancer, she was in touch with her friend Jennifer Hudson about the upcoming Aretha biopic, while, with Stevie Wonder, she was preparing to record a track called "The Future."

Suggested Songs:

I Never Loved a Man (The Way I Love You) (1967)
Respect (1967)
Ain't No Way (1968)
I Say a Little Prayer (1968)
How I Got Over (1972)

#11 Elton John (1947 - present)

Began Recording: 1968
Peak: 1970 - 1976
Genres: Rock & Pop Singer/Songwriter/Pianist

Reginald Dwight was a most unlikely pop star. Shy, pudgy, bookish in appearance and deportment, if his dad had had his way, Reg might have become a banker. But the parents brought music into the post-war London home, dad with his trumpet, mom with her records: Elvis, Little Richard, Bill Haley. At age three or four, the boy was already teaching himself to play piano; at seven, he was taking formal lessons, and, by age 11, he had a scholarship to the Royal Academy of Music. At 17, he dropped out of school and bounced around the starving artist scene for more than half a decade. Soon, he was calling himself Elton John, based on the first names of two band mates.

In 1967, answering an ad in a music magazine, Elton was quite fortuitously teamed with a young, unknown lyricist, Bernie Taupin. Bernie would quickly pen the words for a packet of songs and pass them on to Elton, who would just as quickly compose the music to the ones he felt drawn to, discarding the others. It is a partnership that has endured to this day. The two don't work in the same room, but, according to John, they've never argued or fought, professionally or personally, in over 50 years. Together, they have collaborated on over 30 albums.

Initially, Elton and Bernie wrote for others, though with little success. Encouraged by a music publisher to write songs for Elton to sing and play, his initial recordings in 1968 and '69 flopped. Then, in 1970, his second LP, titled *Elton John*, broke through following a critically acclaimed appearance at a West Hollywood nightclub, the Troubadour. With a tiny audience filled with the likes of Neil Diamond, Linda Ronstadt, and John's hero Leon Russell, Elton kicked away his piano bench, a la Jerry Lee Lewis, while pounding the keys, Little Richard style. When the B-side single "Your Song," with its earnest, halting lyrics and sweet melody, began to climb in the pop charts soon after, Elton John, new superstar, was born.

To say that Elton John dominated record sales between 1970 and 1976 is to understate the case. Indeed, from 1972, with the release of *Honky Chateau,* to 1975's *Rock of the Westies*, John had an amazing seven consecutive #1 albums, including his acknowledged double album masterpiece, *Goodbye Yellow Brick Road*. Transitioning easily between exquisite ballads ("Daniel") and piano pounding, guitar slashing rock ("Saturday Night's Alright for Fighting"), many of John's most memorable and best-selling songs come from this six-year period: "Tiny Dancer," which celebrates Bernie Taupin's new wife; "Rocket Man," which competes with Bowie's "Space Oddity" in the metaphoric use of astronaut as working-class dreamer; "Crocodile Rock," with its retro rock & roll feel; "Bennie and the Jets," with its signature syncopated piano run; and the melodramatic, autobiographical, "Someone Saved My Life Tonight."

His superb piano playing, seamlessly blending classical, gospel, and rock elements, with his pleasing vocals, memorable melodies, and often cinematic lyrics made John a huge star, among the five best-selling recording artists of all time; his stage shows, with their imaginative costuming, grew to legendary proportions, but, off-stage, John was struggling with substance abuse and a closeted sexuality. John, in time, chose to come out of the closet, and he credits meeting the young AIDS patient Ryan White with giving him the impetus to get sober.

In 1994, John's corroboration with lyricist Tim Rice on Disney's *The Lion King* reached #1 status; then, in 1997, when his friend Princess Diana died, he sang and re-recorded an earlier tribute song to Marilyn Monroe, "Candle in the Wind," with new lyrics as "Goodbye England's Rose." The new version is thought to be the 2nd best selling single of all time behind Bing Crosby's immortal "White Christmas." His Farewell Yellow Brick Road tour, which ended in the summer of 2023, finished as the highest-grossing tour of all time.

Suggested Songs:

Your Song (1970)
Tiny Dancer (1972)
Mona Lisas and Mad Hatters (1972)
All the Girls Love Alice (1973)
Candle in the Wind 1997 (1997)

#10 Stevie Wonder (1950 - present)

Began Recording: 1962
Peak: 1972 - 1977; 1980 - 1986
Genres: R&B; Pop; Soul; Funk Singer/Songwriter/Instrumentalist

He was born Stevland Judkins, six weeks premature, in Saginaw, Michigan, and lost his eyesight as he struggled for life in those first few hours and days in an incubator. His mom changed his surname to Morris after a divorce and moved the family to the suburbs of Detroit. Naturally protective of her sightless child, he was kept largely inside where he developed a prodigious talent for music. By the time he was 11, he was playing piano, drums, and harmonica; singing in a church choir; and, with a friend, performing at parties. When a member of the R&B vocal group the Miracles heard him, an audition with Berry Gordy Jr., founder of Motown, was arranged. It was the harmonica playing that really sold Berry, and the prodigy was signed. Dubbed Little Stevie Wonder, his contract stipulated that he would be given a stipend of $2.50 per week, a tutor when performing on the road, and that his royalties would be held in trust until he turned 21.

His first couple of records, released at the age of 12, flopped, but, in the summer of 1963, both his newest LP, *Recorded Live: The 12 Year Old Genius*, and the album's single, "Fingertips-Part 2," rose to #1 on the charts. Wonder was the youngest performer to reach this rarefied perch. It didn't last; with his voice changing, the next two years brought little success, and there was talk of dropping the youngster from the record label. When he struck pay dirt again late in 1965 with "Uptight (Everything's Alright)," the "Little" was dropped from his name, and he was soon a fixture on *Billboard*'s Hot 100 and R&B charts.

Upon turning 21, Stevie was owed his back royalties, and he was in a position to demand a much more favorable contract from Motown, which he duly received just in time for what's been called by academic Jack Hamilton and others the "greatest creative run in the history of popular music." Often referred to as Wonder's "classic period," between 1972 and

1976 he released four of the most celebrated albums of all time: *Talking Book* (1972), *Innervisions* (1973), *Fulfillingness' First Finale* (1974), and *Songs in the Key of Life* (1976); the final three each won the Grammy for Album of the Year, something never before and never since achieved by the same artist. Even more remarkably, Wonder not only wrote and sang the songs on these albums but also produced them and played most of the instruments. Some of the unforgettable tracks from these LPs include "Superstition," "You Are the Sunshine of My Life," "Living for the City," " All in Love Is Fair," "Higher Ground," and "Sir Duke." Wonder blends R&B, rock, folk, Latin, reggae, even jazz and classical elements, touching on themes of drug abuse, systemic racism, love, loss, political despotism, and more.

What is less well known is that Stevie Wonder has been one of music's great humanitarians, involved in causes as diverse as international advocacy for the disabled to stumping tirelessly for an MLK national holiday; in 2009, the U.N. designated him a Messenger of Peace.

His impact on the music industry itself has been profound. The new contract he signed with Motown in 1971 set a new, higher standard for artist compensation; he also helped open the door to greater creative control for recording artists over their own work. In addition, he helped introduce a range of new musical technology to the mainstream, from the expanded use of synthesizers to new digital recording methods.

What do other artists say about Stevie Wonder? Paul Simon called him "the composer of his generation." Marvin Gaye said, "He had twice the energy of all of us combined." Luciano Pavarotti opined, "We enjoy his music because we are in front of a great, a great genius of music." Finally, Elton John added, "*Songs in the Key of Life*. For me, it's the best album ever made… His message, I think, is about love."

Suggested Songs:

Superstition (1972)
All in Love Is Fair (1973)
Living for the City (1973)
Don't You Worry 'bout a Thing (1974)
Sir Duke (1977)

#9 Frank Sinatra (1915 - 1998)

Began Recording: 1939
Peak: 1941- 1947; 1955 - 1970
Genres: Traditional Pop; light jazz Singer

Francis Albert Sinatra, born in 1915 in Hoboken, New Jersey, in the shadow of New York City, the only son of working-class Sicilian immigrants, rose to become "the greatest singer of the 20th-century," according to esteemed music critic Robert Christgau.

As a teenager, Sinatra was inspired to sing as he listened to his idol Bing Crosby. Winning an *Amateur Hour* radio contest at the age of 19 provided Frank with his first break. His initial recordings were with the Harry James band in 1939, but he failed to chart. Leaving James a year later for the Tommy Dorsey band, Sinatra was inspired by Dorsey's superb breath control on his trombone and worked to incorporate that into his singing. By 1942, Sinatra had become so popular that he left his father figure, Dorsey, much to the latter's bitter chagrin. "Sinatramania," much like "Elvismania" in the '50s and "Beatlemania" in the '60s, had begun. Screaming, teenaged, female fans greeted Sinatra with near-riotous adulation. "All or Nothing at All" was a breakthrough hit for "Frankie Boy," as he was known. For several years, he was America's most popular crooner; his first album, *The Voice of Frank Sinatra*, soared to #1 on the *Billboard* charts, but a spate of bad publicity, highlighting his connections to organized crime figures and the collapse of his marriage, caused his popularity to plummet. In 1952, Columbia Records dropped his contract. At one Chicago concert, only 150 patrons showed up to see him.

Curiously, Sinatra's first big comeback came through Hollywood. He won an Oscar in 1954 for his non-singing role in *From Here to Eternity*. He went on to find even more acting success in 1955's *The Man with the Golden Arm* and 1962's *The Manchurian Candidate*. In 1953, Sinatra signed a new recording contract with Capitol Records; began recording with a host of new collaborators, most notably with arranger Nelson Riddle; and, over the next seven years, produced some of his most celebrated work. These include two early "concept albums" focused on a particular theme or mood, *In the Wee Small Hours* and *Songs for Swingin' Lovers!* Classic songs from this era include "You Make Me Feel So Young" and "I've Got You Under My Skin."

By the 1960s, Sinatra had become a cultural icon. He was a fixture in Las Vegas, along with Dean Martin and Sammy Davis Jr., as the lead member of the so-called "Rat Pack," with their image of hard-drinking, hard-gambling, hard-loving jetsetters. Though musical tastes in the broader culture were turning toward rock & roll, Sinatra continued to enjoy success with such indelible releases as "Strangers in the Night," "That's Life," and what became his signature song, "My Way." Still, more and more, Sinatra felt marginalized by changing musical tastes, and he announced his retirement in 1971. Two years later, however, "Ol' Blues Eyes" was back. He had one more iconic hit left in him, the "Theme from New York, New York."

Near the end of his life, he produced two popular albums of duets (*Duets* and *Duets II*), featuring vocal collaborations with such musical giants as Barbra Streisand, Aretha Franklin, Tony Bennett, and Willie Nelson. His voice a dry, grainy husk of what it once was, Sinatra gave his last concert in 1995 and died of a heart attack in 1998.

Sinatra was one of the best-selling recording artists of all-time. Nelson Riddle said he sang with the "warm timbre of a cello." He had an uncanny way with phrasing and, though untrained musically, was highly respected for his musical ear, dedication to his craft, and his ferocious drive toward perfection. He could deliver uptempo jazz numbers and emotional ballads with conversational intimacy, astonishing honesty, and resonance. Today, he is recognized by multiple generations as one of the very greatest singers of the past century.

Suggested Songs:

All or Nothing at All (1943)
I've Got You Under My Skin (1956)
You Make Me Feel So Young (1956)
My Way (1969)
Theme from New York, New York (1980)

#8 Madonna (1958 - present)

Began Recording: 1982
Peak: 1984 - 2005
Genres: Pop; Dance-Pop Singer/Songwriter

Madonna Louise Ciccone was born into a large Italian family in Michigan; lost her mother at age 5; and was a straight-A, if rather exuberant, Catholic school student who dropped out of college and moved to New York City in 1978 to pursue her dream of dancing professionally. Sexually assaulted at knifepoint soon after arriving, she turned by 1979 to music and soon was shopping around her demo. In 1982, she signed her first recording contract and released the dance-pop single "Everybody," which got some play on the dance-club circuit. Not yet a star, Madonna, drawing on a steely resolve that some speculate may have come from her early tragedies, was on her way.

Coming on the national music scene at the same time as Cindi Lauper, there were the inevitable comparisons and critics who predicted that Lauper would have real staying power while Madonna would fade. Interestingly, it is Madonna who has gone on to become the best-selling female artist of all-time and, though precise numbers cannot be calculated, one of the five best-selling recording artists, mentioned regularly just behind the Beatles, Elvis Presley, and Michael Jackson.

1984 was Madonna's breakout year, as she released her #1 selling album *Like a Virgin*, which featured top-selling singles "Material Girl" and the provocative "Like a Virgin," which garnered uproarious national attention when she performed the song on an MTV Video Awards show dressed in a wedding gown atop a giant cake and wound up rolling around on the stage. In some ways, the song was a template for her career, for, if anything, Madonna has proved polarizing and controversial.

"Papa Don't Preach" was criticized by those who felt it encouraged teen-age sex, while others commended the song for its protagonist's avowal to keep an unexpected child. "Like a Prayer" played with ambivalent lyrics: was she singing about prayer or about a sexual relationship? The music video, however, took the controversy to another level as it featured Madonna with the stigmata, dancing before burning crosses, kissing a black plaster saint who comes to life, all the while the music building with a celebratory Black gospel choir. Critics and much of the public loved it, but the video, especially, drew harsh condemnation, even from the Vatican.

In all, Madonna has seen nine of her albums go to the top of the charts, but she is clearly much more than the "Queen of Pop." *Rolling Stone* called her the "most important female voice in the history of modern music." Not a particularly strong vocalist, she has, like David Bowie who was an early influence, shown an uncanny ability to change not simply her voice but, indeed, her entire image. She is also remarkable for the unique control she has exerted from the very beginning over every aspect of her career. In what is an industry dominated by men, Madonna became an absolute force and has opened doors for all the women who have followed. Music critic Steven Hyden wrote of her that "Madonna has been primarily defined not by her music but by her ambition and her ability to present herself in visually interesting and ever-changing guises." Academic Camille Paglia called her less a pop star than a "global cultural icon," even an "historical figure." Ann Powers wrote that Madonna is a "secular goddess" and that she embodies sex, capitalism, and celebrity. Certainly an icon, an icon of ambition; of fashion; of discipline and physicality; of sexual liberation; of fierce, independent feminism; and, yes, of popular music—controversial, to be sure, drawing equal amounts of praise and condemnation, but quite simply the most famous woman in the world. As both Susan Sarandon and *Billboard* put it, in pop music, there is before and after Madonna.

Suggested Songs:

Like a Virgin (1984)
Papa Don't Preach (1986)
Like a Prayer (1989)
Don't Cry for Me Argentina (1996)
Hung Up (2005)

#7 David Bowie (1947 - 2016)

Began Recording: 1964
Peak: 1972 - 1984
Genres: Rock; electronic & experimental pop Singer/Songwriter

Musical success did not come quick or easy for David Jones. As a child, he was enamored of Little Richard and Elvis; took up saxophone and guitar; and dreamed of a life in music, theater, or art. His early stabs at rock & roll, blues, folk, even an Anthony Newley/music hall/vaudeville pastiche failed to catch on. He tried Buddhist monasticism, mime, and changed his last name to Bowie, since another Davy Jones was rising with the prefab band the Monkees. He gained and lost several recording contracts; then came Apollo 11 and "Space Oddity" in the summer of 1969, and Bowie had his first hit.

The success didn't last, but, soon, a new cast of characters entered David's life: Angela Barnett, who would become his hard-driving first wife and arguably gave the shy young artist the needed push to step into the outrageous; Tony Visconti, who would produce and work with David to the very end; Mick Ronson, whose virtuoso guitar work and arranging would help the new Bowie soar; and Tony Defries, the hard-bitten manager who presented to the world the superstar Bowie before he really was one.

His career languishing, in early 1972, Bowie told a *Melody Maker* journalist, "I'm gay and I always have been," at a time when it was strictly taboo to be out of the closet. At the same time, Bowie introduced to British audiences the redheaded, androgynous alien rocker Ziggy Stardust, who was bringing to our endangered earth both a warning and a message of hope. It may or may not be a stretch to say that Bowie/Ziggy was a John the Baptist character paving the way for the "Starman." Bowie's performance of "Starman" on the popular British TV program *Top of the Pops* propelled him to stardom. He took the character to the United States and became a minor sensation. Bowie later admitted that he created various characters to present his songs with their recurring themes of loneliness, alienation, and the outsider looking for connection. In time, Bowie, who feared mental illness because of its pronounced presence in his family, felt the Ziggy character was taking him over, and he made the decision to kill him off which he did in a July 1973 concert in London. To this day, though, *The Rise and Fall of Ziggy Stardust and the Spiders from Mars* remains Bowie's most loved, celebrated, and iconic work.

More characters, major shifts in musical styles, and unforgettable records followed: *Aladdin Sane*, best seen, perhaps, as Ziggy's harder-edged American cousin, gave us "The Jean Genie." With *Diamond Dogs*, Bowie took on Orwell's *1984* and gave us glam rock's last gasp with "Rebel Rebel." Bowie next morphed into a "plastic soul" singer, producing *Young Americans* and his first U.S. #1 single, "Fame." Then came the cold, steely, fascistic Thin White Duke with the classics "Station to Station" and "Golden Years." By the late '70s, cognizant that cocaine was causing him to lose his grip on sanity, Bowie returned to Europe and produced his three so-called Berlin albums, mixing rock, ambient pop, world music, and electronic avant-garde to confounding and creative effect. His signature anthem, "'Heroes'," comes from this era. After the brilliant confessional "Ashes to Ashes" and the Freddie Mercury duet, "Under Pressure," Bowie stepped, ever so briefly, into the mainstream in 1983 with his biggest seller, the disco oriented *Let's Dance*. Commercial and artistic ups and downs would follow for the rest of his storied career. Following a 10-year hiatus after an emergency angioplasty, Bowie reappeared in 2013 with the raucous, acclaimed *Next Day*. Three years later, on his 69th birthday, Bowie surprised the world with *Blackstar*, a jazz-infused exploration of death and dying. Two days later, Bowie shocked the world for the last time, perishing quietly due to liver cancer. Few knew he was even sick, but "the Starman" was gone. *Rolling Stone* summed him up: the "greatest rock star ever."

Suggested songs:

Space Oddity (1969)
Life On Mars (1971)
"Heroes" (1977)
Ashes to Ashes (1980)
Lazarus (2016)

#6 Bruce Springsteen (1949 - present)
Began Recording: 1973
Peak: 1975 - 1991
Genres: Rock Singer/Songwriter/Guitarist/bandleader

In 1974, a music journalist wrote, "I saw rock and roll future, and its name is Bruce Springsteen." Within months, the journalist, John Landau, quit his job and began helping Springsteen complete his masterpiece breakthrough album, *Born to Run.*

Born on the Jersey Shore to a working class family, Bruce Springsteen bounced around in the area, playing guitar, singing, and composing in a series of local bands. In 1972, up and coming manager Mike Appel signed him and introduced him to John Hammond, who had signed Bob Dylan a decade earlier. Springsteen inked a deal with Columbia and cut two critically acclaimed albums in 1973. Hailed as the next Dylan for his dense, free-associating story telling lyrics, the two LPs flopped. Under the gun at Columbia, Springsteen, a notorious perfectionist and tough taskmaster as leader of his E Street Band, spent 14 grueling months working on his third go-round. Going for a Phil Spector-like "wall of sound," Springsteen recorded eight tracks layered with strings, brass, saxophones, guitars, booming drums and bass, various keyboards with piano high in the mix, voices, and even a glockenspiel. When *Born to Run* was released in August of 1975, it was a triumph. *Time* and *Newsweek*, the nation's two leading newsweeklies, simultaneously featured Bruce on their covers. The supercharged, anthemic LP, with its traditional themes of heroic, romantic on-the-road escape; freedom in the face of doubt and fear; reaching for one's dream; perseverance; betrayal; friendship; and love, struck a chord deep in the American psyche. "Thunder Road," "Jungleland," "Born to Run," classics, all.

A legal dispute with Mike Appel kept Springsteen out of the studio for two years, but, when he returned, a second masterwork emerged, *Darkness on the Edge of Town. Darkness* was harder than its predecessor, and it also featured his first sustained foray into recurring themes of working class pain and struggle.

Springsteen, with his dynamic E Street Band, featuring the peerless keyboardist Roy Bittan, his brilliant co-lead guitarist and sometime co-producer Steven Van Zandt, and the gentle giant Clarence Clemons on sax, was emerging as one of the great live acts in rock music history. His shows were akin to religious revivals, extending for two and a half, three, even four hours, as Bruce would leap, swagger, cajole, testify, and sing in his harsh, gravelly baritone his high energy story-songs of conflict, misery, hope, and triumph. His fans were like disciples— once initiated, true believers in the gospel of "the Boss, " his take on the American dream.

Bruce just kept getting bigger. 1980's *The River* lept to #1 with its title track weaving the sad tale of a youthful, economically burdened marriage gone cold and "Hungry Heart," his biggest single to date. Then, after an acoustic foray into the shadowy world of drifters, outsiders, criminals, and murderers on the highly praised *Nebraska*, Springsteen reached his commercial peak in 1984 with the epic *Born in the U.S.A.* The title track, with its booming, seemingly celebratory chorus repeated over and over, seemed to obscure the obvious message of the verses, which told a tale of returning Vietnam vets, bitter and alienated back home. This did not prevent politicians like President Reagan from trying to use it as a flag-waving anthem for their own neoconservative causes. In many ways, Reagan's actions seemed to awaken a new political consciousness in Bruce that has ever since aligned itself with a whole host of progressive causes.

Springsteen, never much of a singles artist, has continued to make best selling albums to this day. Nine of his LPs have reached the top of the charts; he has written a remarkably honest autobiography, detailing his struggles with depression. He has even scored with a stunning one-man Broadway show featuring his trademark storytelling and songs—as always, passionately challenging us to reach for our dreams.

Suggested Songs:

Born to Run (1975)
The River (1980)
Born in the U.S.A. (1984)
Dancing in the Dark (1984)
I Wish I Were Blind (1992)

#5 The Rolling Stones
Began Recording: 1963
Peak: 1965 - 1972; 1978 - 1982
Genres: Rock; Blues; rock & roll; pop Band

They began their musical life as a Chicago blues and rock & roll cover band in 1962 London. Multi-instrumentalist Brian Jones saw an old Muddy Waters record and named them the Rollin' Stones; two years later, they added the "g." The myth is that there was bad blood between the Stones and the rival Beatles, but it was Lennon-McCartney who gave them their second song, "I Wanna Be Your Man," to record, wanting to help out their friends. Their '60's teenage manager/producer Andrew Loog Oldham saw that they'd have more commercial and staying power if they wrote their own material, and so childhood friends Mick Jagger (lead singer) and Keith Richards (lead and rhythm guitars) began to compose and took over leadership of the band from Jones; Bill Wyman on bass and Charlie Watts, drummer, rounded out the original five.

In early 1965, with a self-penned composition, "The Last Time," the Rolling Stones hit the top of the British charts. It did wonders for their confidence. Oldham, meanwhile, had decided to accent the contrasts between the Beatles and the Rolling Stones. If the Beatles were seen as clean-cut, uniformed, charming lads one could bring home to mom and dad, then the Rolling Stones would be unkempt, with long, straggly hair, and rebellious, even threatening in demeanor; thus, they became the "bad boys" of rock & roll. When "(I Can't Get No) Satisfaction" broke through as the biggest international hit of 1965, the Rolling Stones had arrived as a force.

They've never really gone away. There have, however, been some major speed bumps along the way for the "greatest rock & roll band in the world," as they are routinely introduced. Brian Jones became increasingly alienated from his mates in the late '60s as Jagger and Richards took greater control. Jones's paranoia, drug problems, and all-around boorish behavior further exacerbated the falling out and he was fired from the band. Three weeks later, he was dead, an apparent drowning victim under still-suspicious circumstances. Mick Taylor stepped in to replace Jones on guitar for six years before departing to be replaced by Ron Wood, who remains a member. In the mid-1980s animosity, principally between Jagger and Richards, nearly derailed the Stones, but they soldiered on. In 1992, Bill Wyman retired and was replaced by Darryl Jones for live shows, while self-effacing Charlie Watts passed away at the age of 80 in 2021.

Many critics agree that the Rolling Stones, while an impressive live act to this very day, made their most interesting, groundbreaking, even revolutionary music between 1965 and 1972. The albums from this era are iconic: *Beggar's Banquet, Let It Bleed, Sticky Fingers, Exile on Main Street.* This is the era of "Satisfaction," of course, but also of "Paint It Black," with its ominous sitar; the hard rocking "Jumpin' Jack Flash;" "Sympathy for the Devil," with its ironic plea for recognition of a world full of atrocities; "Street Fighting Man," with its nod to political action; "Wild Horses," perhaps their greatest love ballad; and the incomparable "Gimme Shelter," which Jagger referred to as an "end-of-the-world song." Though they would produce best-selling and vital music again, such as 1978's "Miss You," the Rolling Stones, once the counterculture outsiders, had become the ultimate insiders. There is no doubt that they are one of the greatest concert draws of all-time; in fact, three of the largest concert tours in history featured the Rolling Stones. That they are among the best-selling artists ever is indisputable; they may even truly be the "greatest rock & roll band in the world, " but there are others that also want to lay claim to that title.

Suggested Songs:

(I Can't Get No) Satisfaction (1965)
Sympathy for the Devil (1969)
Gimme Shelter (1969)
Wild Horses (1971)
Miss You (1978)

#4 Elvis Presley (1935 - 1977)

Began Recording: 1954
Peak: 1956 - 1963; 1968 - 1970
Genres: Rock & Roll; rockabilly; pop; country; gospel Singer

Elvis Aaron Presley was born in a two-room Mississippi house deep in the segregated south to a father who had difficulty holding a job and a mother whom he adored who introduced him to church and gospel music and bought him his first guitar. The young loner moved with his family into public housing in Memphis, Tennessee, when he was 13. The bullied mama's boy began playing guitar and listening to a mix of country music, especially Hank Snow, and so-called "race records:" black spirituals, blues, and R&B. By the time he graduated from high school, he had won a talent contest and had dreams of making a living with music.

Sam Phillips owned a small, local studio, Sun Records, and dreamed of getting rich, according to his secretary, by finding a white singer who could sing black music. Elvis and Sam found each other. Elvis's first single, "That's All Right," failed to chart, but it got him noticed. The following year, a middle-aged hustler, Colonel Tom Parker, found his way into Presley's circle and negotiated a deal with RCA Victor to buy out Elvis's contract. The ex-carnival barker would, in time, become Presley's all-controlling manager.

1956 was a watershed year for Elvis Presley. He broke through with his first #1 singles, "Heartbreak Hotel," "Don't Be Cruel"/"Hound Dog," and "Love Me Tender." In addition, he was all over TV, appearing first with Milton Berle; next with Steve Allen who sought to ridicule and put him in his place; and finally with Ed Sullivan. The Sullivan appearances, especially, brought Presley and rock & roll to a much wider audience. From the beginning, though, Presley, though wildly popular with youth, had his detractors. With his swiveling hips, Presley was seen as too sexually provocative, referred to sneeringly as "Elvis the Pelvis." It was said that he was inspiring a generation of juvenile delinquents and was, no doubt, singing the devil's music. J. Edgar Hoover called him, "A definite danger to the security of the

U.S." One major objection to Presley, no doubt, revolved around race. He was singing rockabilly music, a hybrid of white country with black R&B. He wasn't the only one, of course, but he was the face of this new, "integrated" music. In no time, rockabilly mutated into rock & roll, with its choral background singing, more amplified guitar work, and tougher edge. Though not originally credited as such, Elvis could sing. He had a high baritone, sometimes tenor, voice and he was emotionally expressive. In addition, he had a humble, yet confident, winning demeanor and Hollywood looks, which he immediately parlayed into a 7-year movie deal.

Despite a two-year stint in the U.S. Army from 1958-'60, Elvis dominated the record charts for seven years, and he would go on to sell more records than any solo artist in history. How many of the greats who followed in his path, from John Lennon to Bob Dylan to Jimi Hendrix, would have even bothered to pick up a guitar were it not for Presley's breathtaking breakthrough? Yet, by 1964, with the rise of The Beatles, the Rolling Stones, and Dylan, Elvis, the "King of Rock 'n Roll," was no longer seen as a musical or cultural trailblazer. His songs no longer resonated; he was a purveyor of light, disposable, semi-comedic Hollywood fluff films. In 1968, he launched his comeback with a brilliant TV special; this was followed in 1969 with his last #1 single, "Suspicious Minds." In the '70s, Elvis toured throughout North America and became a fixture in Las Vegas, but, from 1973 onward, his health rapidly deteriorated. He overindulged in junk foods, struggled through his shows, developed a severe addiction to prescription pills, and grew increasingly reclusive and erratic. He died of a massive heart attack in his Memphis mansion, Graceland, in 1977, his body riddled with drug-induced maladies. He was 42 years old.

Suggested Songs:

Heartbreak Hotel (1956)
Hound Dog (1956)
Can't Help Falling in Love (1961)
Suspicious Minds (1969)
An American Trilogy (1972)

#3 Michael Jackson (1958 - 2009)
Began Recording: 1968 (w. Jackson 5); 1971 (solo)
Peak: 1979 - 1993
Genres: R&B; Pop, soul, funk Singer/Songwriter

Before he was even in his teens, Michael Jackson was an internationally known recording star. The lead singer of his family vocal quintet, the Jackson 5, Michael was recognized early on as a musical prodigy. While still a member of the Jackson 5, Michael released his first solo effort for Motown Records at the age of 13. Seven years later, signed now to Epic Records and nominally still a part of the Jacksons, Michael released *Off the Wall*, a masterpiece album that has sold over 20,000,000 copies and produced such signature songs as "Don't Stop 'Til You Get Enough," "Rock With You," and the heartbreak ballad, "She's Out of My Life," in which Michael reportedly broke down in tears while recording.

While the Jackson 5 produced mostly light, upbeat, R&B-oriented pop fare, with *Off the Wall*, Jackson, now working with renowned arranger Quincy Jones, experimented with light jazz, synths, complex R&B-disco hybrids, and new vocal phrasing and mannerisms. Three years later, the 24-year-old released the LP that would launch him into a musical strato- sphere only reached by a select few artists, *Thriller*. With sales of over 70,000,000 copies, it is still the best-selling album, worldwide, in history. The singles—"Beat It," with its unabashed rock riff, and "Billie Jean," with its R&B funky dance groove—helped Jackson sweep the Grammys, while the 1983 Motown TV special featured the debut of Michael's now celebrated "moonwalk" dance. Michael Jackson had become a worldwide phenome- non, in the mold of the 1950's Elvis and the 1960's Beatles.

Jackson's next two albums, *Bad* and *Dangerous*, both generated world- wide sales of over 30,000,000 copies, producing more classics, such as "Man in the Mirror," "Smooth Criminal," and "Black and White." He helped write and perform the USA for Africa theme song, "We Are the World" and was feted by presidents. Behind the scenes and in the tabloids, however, things were beginning to crumble. Jackson's skin disease, vitiligo, in which sufferers lose pigmentation, coupled with plastic surgery, caused at first gradual then rapid changes in his facial appearance; reports that he was traveling with a pet chimpanzee and that he was sleeping in an oxygen chamber led to the derogatory nickname "Wacko Jacko." There was more: a quick marriage and then divorce with the daughter of Elvis Presley, dangling his son from a 4th floor hotel balcony, then a series of child sexual abuse charges, followed by a 2005 child molestation trial in which he pleaded not guilty (and was subsequently found not guilty), which left Jackson broken. He moved, for a while, to Bahrain before announcing a comeback tour in 2009. While rehearsing in Los Angeles for his upcoming shows, Jackson died of cardiac arrest, a victim of a propofol (an anesthetic and sedative usually given to surgery patients) overdose, a drug given him by his physician, who was subsequently charged with involuntary manslaughter and sentenced to four years in prison.

How should Michael Jackson be viewed today? What is his legacy? Unquestionably, he is one of the greatest recording artists of all time, probably third (behind the Beatles and Elvis) in total records sold; he was a brilliant singer who produced music of stunning quality and a breathtaking live entertainer who captivated an entire world while donating millions to charity. However, controversy and credible allegations persist even 14 years after his death. Child sexual abuse charges continue to be leveled against Jackson, and polls show that many Americans believe the charges. Perhaps we have to live with the ambiguity— as these mini biographies show time and again, very flawed human beings can produce great art. The question for each listener is how to bridge aesthetic appreciation and their own values—where to draw the line.

Suggested Songs:

She's Out of My Life (1980)
Beat It (1983)
Billie Jean (1983)
Man In the Mirror (1988)
Smooth Criminal (1988)

#2 Bob Dylan (1941 - present)
Began Recording: 1962
Peak: 1963 - 1969; 1974 - 1976; 1997 - 2006
Genres: Rock; Folk; Blues; country; gospel Singer/Songwriter

In January 1961, a scruffy Minnesota college dropout made his way to the wintery streets of Greenwich Village, New York. Sleeping on borrowed couches and rifling through his hosts' album and book collections, the 19-year-old Robert Zimmerman, who had begun calling himself Bob Dylan, began to hit the local coffee bars and clubs, Cafe Wha? and Gerde's Folk City on Hootenanny and open-mic nights, singing mostly Woody Guthrie and traditional folk tunes. Joan Baez later put it into song, "You burst on the scene already a legend... " Not quite, but, by year's end, Dylan was headlining at Gerde's, had received a glowing review in *The New York Times*, and was signed by legendary talent scout John Hammond to Columbia Records.

Dylan's 1962 recording debut was inauspicious enough, a collection of mostly folk covers that failed to sell, but, by 1963, he was being hailed as the king of modern folk and a songwriting genius. *The Freewheelin' Bob Dylan*, with its iconic cover photo of Bob and girlfriend Suze arm in arm in the Village, features at least five genuine classics: "Blowin' in the Wind," perhaps Dylan's most famous composition, covered hundreds of times, most famously by Peter, Paul, and Mary, who sang it at the 1963 March on Washington; "A Hard Rain's A-Gonna Fall," repeatedly linked to the Cuban Missile Crisis, though it was written before; "Masters of War," with its timeless, no-holds-barred attack on the nameless politicians and industrialists who profit from war; "Don't Think Twice, It's All Right," a bittersweet breakup lament; and the timeless love ballad, "Girl from the North Country."

It was, however, in 1965-1966, in the space of 15 months, when Dylan recorded and released his unrivaled trio of classic rock and blues albums, with their surreal, poetic pyrotechnics, that he became a genuine recording superstar, the epitome of the hip New York artist and cultural/generational leader, admired and emulated even by the Beatles. "Like a Rolling Stone," which "sounded like somebody'd kicked open the door to your mind," said Bruce Springsteen; "Subterranean Homesick Blues," in many ways a prototype rap; "Mister Tambourine Man," with its poetic exploration of drug-induced or musically stimulated consciousness; "Desolation Row," Dylan's urban emulation of Eliot's *The Waste Land*; the joyful longing of " I Want You;" "Just Like a Woman," with its painful sense of lost love—these, and so many other celebrated songs, come from this fertile period.

Though Dylan would never again quite reach these heights of musical and social influence (though many would argue that 1975's *Blood on the Tracks* was also a career defining moment), his career would, nevertheless, feature astonishing, shape-shifting experiments with new genres, such as country ("Lay, Lady, Lay"), gospel ("I Believe in You"), and even vaudeville ("Po' Boy"). Left for dead, artistically and commercially, time and again, he has had a knack for remarkably resurrecting both his art and his career. Though he is lauded as a songwriter, his singing and performing styles have always been controversial. Dylan haters growled about the "dog with his leg caught in barbed wire" vocal sound (folk singer Mitch Jayne), and his live shows drive some attendees crazy for the way he fails to sound like his records. Still, there are others who praise his emotional vocal range and honesty and who appreciate the constant reinvention of his creations.

Finally, it is probably safe to say that no other recording artist has been so honored this past century. In a few short decades, Dylan has gone from being hounded by *Newsweek* to being taught in universities from Stanford to Harvard and having his lyrics quoted by Supreme Court Justices. Dylan has had *two* Broadway plays utilizing his music; he has won Grammys, an Oscar, a Pulitzer, a Presidential Medal of Freedom, equivalent French and Spanish honors, even the prestigious Nobel Prize for Literature. Academics now speak his name in the same breath with Shakespeare and Virgil, but Dylan himself would be the first to say not to take anybody else's word for it—go and listen for yourself.

Suggested Songs:

Blowin' in the Wind (1963)
Like a Rolling Stone (1965)
Desolation Row (1965)
Tangled Up in Blue (1975)
Mississippi (2001)

#1 The Beatles

Began Recording: 1961 (w. Tony Sheridan); 1962 (as The Beatles)
Peak: 1963 - 1970
Genres: Rock; Pop Band

Their story is the stuff of legend: in the late 1950s, three post-war British teenagers, John Lennon, Paul McCartney, and George Harrison, from the Northwest English seaport of Liverpool, inspired by the likes of American rock & rollers, Little Richard, Elvis Presley, and the Everly Brothers, decide to form a skiffle band. They finally find a drummer, Pete Best, in 1960, and, after trying on various monikers—the Quarrymen, Johnny and the Moondogs—finally settle on *the Beatles* and depart for Hamburg, Germany's red-light district, where they hone their musical chops over the next two years. While playing in a Liverpool cellar club, they are discovered one night by a local record-store owner, Brian Epstein, who helps them, after several false starts, sign a recording contract with George Martin, a producer of comedy records for EMI Parlophone. On the eve of their first recording session with Martin, they swap out drummers, replacing Best with the more experienced Ringo Starr. Their second single with George Martin, "Please, Please Me," shoots to #1 in the UK in early 1963, and "Beatlemania," the intense, almost hysterical reaction of their screaming fans, is underway.

In the United States, people were reeling from the recent assassination of President Kennedy; so, when radio stations began playing "I Want to Hold Your Hand" as the New Year broke in 1964, there was an explosive, cathartic response from the nation's youth. In February, the Beatles arrived in New York City and played the first of three live shows on the popular Sunday evening program *The Ed Sullivan Show*. The appearance drew a record TV audience, but the age divide was stark. The Beatles were a youth phenomenon, while adult reaction was largely critical.

Still, one cannot overstate the Beatles' importance in the history of recorded music. Though it is impossible to get accurate figures (extreme high end estimates of combined singles and album sales are close to three billion worldwide), it is almost universally acknowledged that they are the best selling recording artists of all time. 20 of their singles reached #1 in the U.S. in the brief time they were together. Eventually, the Beatles won over the music critics and many adults as well, drawing comparisons to artists as diverse as Beethoven and Picasso. Their impact on both popular music and on culture is simply incalculable. Musically, they were restless experimenters in the studio, pushing the limits of recording technology, trying out new instruments and sounds, creating sonic masterpieces like the albums *Revolver, Sgt. Pepper's Lonely Hearts Club Band, The Beatles* (aka *The White Album*), and *Abbey Road*. Changes in hair and clothing styles, in recreational drug use and meditation, the rise in teenage idealism and the '60's counter-culture, not to mention the legitimization of popular music as an art form, can all be traced, in some fashion, back to the Beatles.

The songwriting duo of Lennon-McCartney, with their memorable melodies and witty lyrics that run the gamut from boy meets girl ("I Feel Fine") to heart tugging slice-of-life ("She's Leaving Home") to downright surreal ("I Am the Walrus"), is still recognized as the most successful in history; their brilliant songs, combined with their bright harmonies and innovative playing and studio work, made the Beatles an unstoppable (if short-lived) force. Internal tensions caused then to split apart in 1970, never to reunite. Sadly, John Lennon was murdered in 1980, and George Harrison succumbed to cancer in 2001. Nevertheless, they were the best-selling musical artists of the first 15 years of the new millennium, decades after they ceased recording—they were the Beatles.

Suggested Songs:

I Want to Hold Your Hand (1964)
Nowhere Man (1965)
Here, There, and Everywhere (1966)
A Day in the Life (1967)
While My Guitar Gently Weeps (1968)

AFTERWORD

Now that I have completed my task, I am left with several thoughts and feelings. One, this was an impossible job. Having given two full years of my life to bring this book to completion, I realize that, despite my hubris, this is not a definitive list—it cannot be; nobody could make such a list definitive. Yes, I had my categories and my rubric, and, yes, I tried to be as objective as I possibly could in following that rubric, but, really, there were scores of judgment calls to make, particularly in assigning points for musical and cultural influence. Of course I read and researched extensively, but, here and elsewhere, it often came down to my human, fallible judgment. As mentioned in the introduction, other readers, listeners, researchers, and writers would, no doubt, have listed and profiled a number of different artists.

I have agonized over who is and who is not included on the list. I have run my numbers half a dozen times (without exaggeration) to account for new developments in the recording world, to be as up to date as I could be, and to make room for new discoveries on my part; still, it pains me to leave certain artists off the list. In fact, no sooner did I finish that I was compiling the list of the next 250 artists, and wondering who would be #501.

So, this was a thankless task in many ways, yet I feel proud for having taken it on and, at least, furthering the *conversation* about who the recording artists are that really have been most consequential these past 100 years. To reiterate, in no way does this list or this ranking purport to say who are the *best* or finest musicians over the past century! That would be a completely different discussion. I have had friends question the inclusion of several artists, commenting that they don't belong because their music isn't very good. To repeat—that's not what this study is about. That would be a whole different book, a *critical* analysis. This book, on the other hand, used three factors, imperfectly calculated, no doubt, but calculated nonetheless—popularity, influence, and honors—to arrive at a compendium of the *greatest* or most consequential musical artists of the past 100 years. Again, if this work furthers discussion, and, more importantly, if it leads to more listening, especially across genres, then it was a worthwhile exercise.

Part of me rebels against the very idea of ranking artists, and, at several points, I considered dropping that aspect of my study, but I was encouraged to include it with the argument that it would generate more interest in the book, that it would engage more readers and listeners, because we all love to share our opinions and offer contrasting points of view. I want to state, though, as clearly and unequivocally as I can, that, to me, all of these artists are deserving of inclusion because all of them have made music that has stirred and moved listeners deeply (as have thousands of other artists not found in this book!). In the end, what I wanted to do was explore a variety of musical styles and genres, to open wider my own ears and heart, to hear what others have heard from artists I never before gave the time of day to. So, I ask you, too, dear reader, please listen and reread with an open heart. It's All Music, and music is one of the greatest gifts we enjoy as we sojourn through the ages here on Mother Earth. And if you are a purist, inclined to dismiss all but your favorites, I humbly ask you to try and put that aside, and listen with new ears and a new heart to what might be for you *new* music. I am amazed at how often and how deeply I was moved by what was for me new music.

Finally, I would like to briefly address two thorny issues that arose for me in researching and writing this book. One is the matter of race. As the great American historian and filmmaker Ken Burns has shown time and again in his work, it is simply impossible to deal honestly with big topics in American history without grappling with race. In this study, time and again, we read of "race records," of segregated venues, of white artists finding hits with music originally created by Black artists. Indeed, many of the most popular genres discussed in this book—blues, jazz, R&B, early rock & roll, hip-hop—have their roots in Black communities. As I am not a sociologist, I have nothing more to add to the discussion. I do, however, admire those artists that managed, in some way, to transcend the color barriers that ultimately wound us all.

Second, it is clear that many of these artists struggled as human beings. We've read of substance abuse, artists charged with heinous behaviors, sometimes, criminal conduct. It's been my intention, throughout, to present relevant information as honestly and objectively as possible, without glossing over a person's history, however troubling, and without editorializing. I am not an expert on these issues, and it is beyond the scope of this work, given the constraints I had in presenting 250 brief narratives. As a lifelong struggling musician, God knows I have nothing but the utmost respect for every single artist— as an artist— discussed in these pages. That is not in any way to condone the misdeeds of any of these flawed human beings, which is an altogether separate matter. God knows, I doubt that I could stand up to close *personal* scrutiny. But I do know what it takes to create and share of oneself through music and to touch and move others. In my mind, each of these musicians, as an artist, is a giant, a legend— a music titan.

ACKNOWLEDGMENTS

There are many people I would like to thank for helping me bring this book to fruition. From my childhood, I'd like to acknowledge my parents and my siblings for I was blessed with a steady stream of music—via radios, records, and TV—which, from an early age, nurtured this passion; I particularly want to mention my brother Bob with whom I made lists as a child after listening for many hours together. Thanks, also, to my oldest friend, Paul, who turned me on to music I might never have bothered to explore and with whom I joined my first band. I'm grateful to Eric and Ben and a host of other musical collaborators; thanks, as well, to Danny, Don, Pia, and to my nephew Tim (of the Tim Williams Band) for their welcome feedback and support; to Stephen, whose honest criticism, keen eyes, and encouragement kept me moving forward; to Savannah for her time, expertise, and red pen; to Peter and Kevin and Sally for reading, caring, and responding; and to the good people at BookBaby for their professional assistance. Above all, though, I want to thank my best friend and partner, my lovely wife, Rosy, who patiently and enthusiastically read every entry as I wrote it, giving her candid and insightful feedback on a daily basis. Without her this book would never have seen the light of day.Finally, I would be remiss if I didn't mention the countless artists whose music has brought so much joy and life to me and light to a world that sorely needs what they have to share.

SELECTED BIBLIOGRAPHY

Every effort was made to use multiple sources in creating this manuscript. The following is not an exhaustive list of every source consulted, but it is a large and fair representative sample. Therefore, I want to thank all those listed below because this project would have been impossible were it not for—

Music

Spotify

I used the Spotify digital music service, as well as discs, to listen for countless hours to the music of all the artists discussed in this book. Neil Young and Joni Mitchell removed their music from the streaming service in January 2022, but I was already very familiar with the music of both artists, and both can still be found on YouTube and, of course, on disc. In addition, I used Spotify to compile a personal playlist based on my "Suggested Songs."

Video

YouTube

For each artist, I watched and listened to music videos, performance footage, interviews, analysis, and mini-biographies.

In addition, the following long-form films and videos were viewed and considered:

Biggie: I Got a Story to Tell (2021). Emmett Malloy, director. An Original Netflix Documentary

Brian Wilson: Long Promised Road (2021). Brent Wilson, director. Ley Line Entertainment. Distributed by Universal Pictures

The Carter Family - Will the Circle Be Unbroken (2005). Kathy Conkwright, director. Produced by Nashville Public Television, Inc. for *American Experience*

Ella Fitzgerald. Just One of Those Things (2019). Leslie Woodhead, director. Produced and distributed by Eagle Rock and MultiScreen. Streamed on Netflix

Hallelujah: Leonard Cohen, A Journey, A Song (2021). Dan Geller and Dayna Goldfine, directors, producers. Sony Pictures Classics. Streamed on Netflix

Hip-Hop Evolution (2016). Directed by Darby Wheeler, Sam Dunn, Scot McFadyen. Banger Films (4 Seasons, 16 episodes). Streamed on Netflix

James Pankow, Musicians Hall of Fame Backstage, Chicago (with Joe Chambers) (2021). Musicians Hall of Fame & Museum

Karen Carpenter "Too Young to Die" (2019). A Film by Jobst Knigge. Broadview TV. Streamed on YouTube

The Kate Bush Story: Running Up That Hill (2014). Adrian Sibley, director. A BBC Documentary; from the Videodrome Discotheque Vault. Streamed on YouTube

Linda Ronstadt: The Sound of My Voice (2019). Rob Epstein & Jeffrey Friedman, directors. CNN Films and Greenwich Entertainment

Miss Americana (2020). Lana Wilson, director. Tremolo Productions. Distributed by Netflix

Pink Floyd - The Making of the Dark Side of the Moon (2003). Matthew Longfellow, director. From Classic Albums series. Eagle Rock Entertainment. Streamed on Prime Video

Ray Charles-The Genius of Soul (1991). Yvonne Smith, writer, director. Kirk D'Amico, Toby Byron, producers. VPI-Videfilm Producers International, Ltd. part of Masters of American Music Series

To Bop or Not To Be: A Jazz Life (1990). Jan Horne, director. nrk. Streamed on YouTube

The Trailblazing Peggy Lee (2022 broadcast). Story produced by John D'Amelio. *CBS Sunday Morning*/CBS News

Travelin'Band: Creedence Clearwater Revival at the Royal Albert Hall (2022). Bob Smeaton, director. Streamed on Netflix

The Two Killings of Sam Cooke (2019). Kelly Duane, director. Distributed by Netflix

Understanding Trent Reznor. (2018). a Lie Likes Music video on Patreon. Streamed on YouTube

What Happened, Miss Simone? (2015). Liz Garbus, director. Streamed by Netflix

When You're Strange (2009). Tom DiCillo, director. distributed by Rhino Entertainment

Whitney (2018). Kevin Macdonald, director. Simon Chinn; Jonathan Chinn; Lisa Erspamer, producers. Distributed by Miramax, Altitude Film Distribution, Roadside Attractions

The Who: The Making of Tommy (2013). Martin Smith, director. Streamed on Prime Video

Books

Blake, Mark (2008). *Comfortably Numb. The Inside Story of Pink Floyd.* Cambridge, MA: Da Capo Press

Bradley, Adam (2017). *Book of Rhymes. The Poetics of Hip Hop.* New York: Basic Civitas

Buck, Kevin W. (2018). *A Concise History of Rock 'n' Roll.* Year of the Book

Byrne, David (2017). *How Music Works.* New York: Three Rivers Press

Dalton, David (2012). *Who Is That Man? In Search of the Real Bob Dylan.* Hachette Books

Davies, Hunter (1968). *The Beatles* (Revised 2009 ed.). N.Y. & London: W.W. Norton

Duncan, Dayton (2019). *Country Music* (Based on a documentary film by Ken Burns). New York: Alfred A. Knopf

Emerick, Geoff; Massey, Howard (2006). *Here, There and Everywhere: My Life Recording the Music of* The Beatles. New York: Gotham

Garofalo, Reebee (2002). *Rockin' Out - Popular Music in the USA.* Upper Saddle River: Prentice Hall

Gioia, Ted (2019). *Music - A Subversive History.* New York: Basic Books

Goldberg, Bernard (2005). *100 People Who Are Screwing Up America.* Harper

Gray, Michael (2000). *Song and Dance Man III: The Art of Bob Dylan.* London: Continuum International

Heatley, Michael (gen. editor) (2007). *The Definitive Illustrated Encyclopedia of Rock.* London: Star Fire Publishing

Hoskyns, Barney (2007). *Hotel California: The True Life Adventures of Crosby, Stills, Nash, Young, Mitchell, Browne, Ronstadt, Geffen, the Eagles, and Their Many Friends.* Wiley

Hyden, Steven (2016). *Your Favorite Band Is Killing Me.* New York: Little, Brown and Company

Jones, Dylan (2017). *David Bowie: A Life.* Crown Archetype

Joyner, David Lee (2009). *American Popular Music*. New York: McGraw-Hill

Kingsbury, Paul (1995). *The Grand Ole Opry, History of Country Music*. New York: Villard Books

Klosterman, Chuck (2009). *Eating the Dinosaur*. N.Y.: Scribner

Lawrence, Sharon (2005). *Jimi Hendrix - The Man, The Magic, The Truth*. New York: Harper Collins

McDonough, Jimmy (2002). *Shakey: Neil Young's Biography*. N.Y.C.: Random House.

Meacham, Jon, McGraw, Tim (2019). *Songs of America*. New York: Random House

Pegg, Nicholas (2006). *The Complete David Bowie*. Reynolds & Hearn

Questlove with Greenman, Ben (2021). *Music Is History*. New York: Abrams Image

Ribowsky, Mark (2020). *The Big Life of Little Richard*. Diversion Books

Ritz, David (1986). *Divided Soul: The Life of Marvin Gaye*. Cambridge, MA: Da Capo Press

Rosenthal, Elizabeth (2001). *His Song: The Musical Journey of Elton John*. New York: Billboard Books

Sanneh, Kelefa (2021). *Major Labels. A History of Popular Music in Seven Genres*. New York: Penguin Press

Springsteen, Bruce (2016). *Born to Run*. Simon & Schuster

Stanley, Bob (2022). *Let's Do It*. New York: Pegasus Books

Stanley, Bob (2014). *Yeah! Yeah! Yeah!: the Story of Pop Music from Bill Haley to Beyoncé*. New York: W.W. Norton & Company, Inc.

Thomas, Richard F. (2017). *Why Bob Dylan Matters.* New
York: HarperCollins

Ward, Geoffrey C. and Burns, Ken (2000). *Jazz, A History of America's
Music.* Alfred A. Knopf

Wenner, Jann S. (2022). *Like a Rolling Stone. A Memoir.* New York: Little,
Brown and Company Hachette Book Group

Williamson, Nigel (2002). *Neil Young - Stories Behind the Songs.* London:
Carlton Books Limited.

Online Sources

https://www.123helpme.com
https://aaep1600.osu.edu
https://www.abc.net.au
https://www.theabsolutesound.com
https://achievement.org
https://www.thealabamaband.com
http://albumlinernotes.com/The_Piano_Rolls.html
https://www.allmusic.com
https://www.americanbluesscene.com
https://americansongwriter.com
https://www.arts.gov
http://www.theassociation.net/txt-music5.html
https://www.theatlantic.com
https://www.atlanticrecords.com
https://theaudiophileman.com
https://thebasie.org
https://www.bbc.com
https://www.thebeatles.com
https://www.becomesingers.com
https://beegeesfanfever.blogspot.com
https://www.bet.com

https://www.bethroars.com

https://www.billboard.com

https://billhaley.com

https://billieholiday.com

https://www.biography.com

https://www.blackpast.org

https://www.bobdylan.com

https://www.bostonherald.com

https://theboot.com

https://www.britannica.com

https://brucespringsteen.net

https://www.bryanadams.com

https://www.buzzfeednews.com

https://www.caroleking.com

https://case.edu

https://www.cbc.ca

www.cbsnews.com

https://chartmasters.org

https://chicago.suntimes.com

https://www.chicagotribune.com

https://www.classicfm.com

https://www.classicrockhistory.com

https://www.cmt.com

https://www.cnn.com

https://www.colorado.edu

https://www.complex.com

https://concord.com

https://consequence.net

https://theconversation.com

https://www.coolaccidents.com

https://coronadoexplorer.com

https://www.countryliving.com

https://countrymusichalloffame.org

https://www.countrythangdaily.com

https://www.cracked.com

https://criticofmusic.com

https://www.culturesonar.com

https://theculturetrip.com

https://www.thecurrent.org

https://www.curtismayfield.com

https://www.thedailybeast.com

https://detroithistorical.org

https://www.discogs.com

http://www.divadevotee.com

https://www.the-dowsers

https://www.earthwindandfire.com

https://www.ellafitzgerald.com

https://www.elle.com

https://www.elsewhere.co.nz

https://www.eltonjohn.com

https://www.encyclopedia.com

https://www.entertainmentbreakdown.com

https://www.ericclapton.com

https://www.esquire.com

https://www.estheticlens.com

https://www.express.co.uk

https://www.thefamouspeople.com

https://faroutmagazine.co.uk

https://www.fatsdominoofficial.com

https://www.forbes.com

https://fordhamobserver.com

https://forums.stevehoffman.tv

https://genius.com

https://glennmillerorchestra.com

https://www.globalcitizen.org

https://sites.google.com/site/pittsburghmusichistory/
pittsburgh-music-story/jazz/jazz---early-years/lena-horne

https://gospelmusichalloffame.org

https://www.gq-magazine.co.uk

https://www.graceland.com

https://www.grammy.com

https://grammymuseum.org

www.grobanarchives.com

https://growlermag.com

https://www.grunge.com

https://www.theguardian.com

https://www.guitarworld.com

https://halfhearteddude.com

http://www.henrymancini.com

https://www.highbrowmagazine.com

https://hiphopgoldenage.com

https://www.hiphopscriptures.com

https://www.history.com

https://www.hotnewhiphop.com

https://www.huffpost.com

https://www.icelandtravel.is

https://www.iheart.com

https://www.independent.co.uk

https://inews.co.uk

https://www.infoplease.com

https://www.irishnews.com

https://jazzfuel.com

https://www.jazzstandards.com

https://jazztimes.com

https://www.jazzwise.com

https://www.johncoltrane.com

https://johndenver.com

https://johnnymathis.com

https://junkee.com/

https://www.keepinspiring.me/music-quotes

https://www.kerrang.com

https://www.kexp.org

https://www.kixcountry.com.au
https://www.last.fm
https://www.latimes.com
https://www.latintimes.com
https://ledgernote.com/blog/interesting/best-selling-artists-of-all-time
https://www.thelist.com
https://literatureessaysamples.com
https://www.literarymatters.org
http://www.livingstoriescollective.com
https://www.loc.gov
https://www.loudersound.com
https://loudwire.com
https://themaneater.com
https://www.masterclass.com
https://meaww.com
https://www.andmeetings.com
https://www.mentalfloss.com
https://www.mercurynews.com
https://www.metallica.com
https://www.metalsucks.net
https://metro.co.uk
https://michaelrm.com
https://michiganrockandrolllegends.com
https://millersmusic.co.uk
http://www.modachicago.org
https://www.mswritersandmusicians.com
https://music.si.edu
https://www.musical-u.com
https://musicgoat.com
https://musicianguide.com
https://www.natfinn.com
https://ndsmcobserver.com
https://www.newworldencyclopedia.org
https://www.newyorker.com

https://www.ninasimone.com
https://nitinbharadwaj.medium.com
https://nmaahc.si.edu
https://www.nme.com
https://www.notablebiographies.com
https://npg.si.edu
https://www.npr.org
https://www.nytimes.com
https://observer.com
https://oneweekoneband.tumblr.com
https://ontheaside.com
https://www.openculture.com
https://outsider.com
https://www.pastemagazine.com
https://www.pbs.org
https://www.peggylee.com
https://www.peoplesworld.org
https://www.theperspective.com
https://www.pghcitypaper.com
https://philipglass.com
https://pitchfork.com
https://playback.fm
https://www.politico.com
https://www.popmatters.com
https://www.psu.edu
https://www.reviewjournal.com
https://www.theringer.com
https://www.rockhall.com
https://rockthebells.com
https://www.rollingstone.com
https://www.salon.com
https://screenrant.com
http://www.session-player.co.uk
https://datebook.sfchronicle.com

https://www.sfgate.com

http://www.sinatra.com

https://slate.com

https://www.smithsonianmag.com

https://www.smoothradio.com

https://www.songfacts.com

https://www.songhall.org

https://www.songwriteruniverse.com

https://sonicdictionary.duke.edu

https://www.soundpasta.com

https://www.spaceagepop.com

https://www.splicetoday.com

https://www.spokesman.com

https://www.standard.co.uk

https://www.startribune.com

https://www.statista.com/statistics/271174/
top-selling-artists-in-the-united-states

http://stevenlewis.info

http://www.steviewonder.org.

https://www.straitstimes.com

https://www.sun-sentinel.com

https://www.sundayobserver.lk

https://www.sundaypost.com

https://www.texasmonthly.com

http://www.thisdayincountrymusic.com

https://time.com

https://www.today.com

https://www.townandcountrymag.com

https://www.udiscovermusic.com

https://ultimateclassicrock.com

https://umusic.co.nz

https://www.un.org

https://www.usatoday.com

https://www.vanityfair.com

https://variety.com
https://www.vibe.com
https://www.vice.com
https://www.villagevoice.com
https://explore.lib.virginia.edu
https://vocalgroup.org
https://www.vogue.com
https://www.voicesinc.org
https://www.vulture.com
https://www.washingtonexaminer.com
https://www.washingtonpost.com
https://www.wideopencountry.com
https://en.wikipedia.org
https://thewire.in
https://woodyguthriecenter.org
https://wordpress.clarku.edu
https://woub.org
https://www.wsj.com
https://www.yahoo.com/entertainment
https://hub.yamaha.com
https://yonamariemusic.com
https://zerotodrum.com

INDEX

Blind Faith- 427

Blondie- **121-122**

Bloom, Harold- 492

bluegrass- 69, 73, 99, 175, 365, 458

blues- 6, 9, 13, 17, 27, 29, 35, 49, 57, 77, 143,
    159, 177, 179, 229, 239, 251, 279, 281,
    285, 299, 300, 303, 307, 308, 309, 321,
    325, 343, 357, 363, 364, 365, 372, 375,
    389, 403, 405, 411, 427, 428, 439, 449,
    450, 460, 479, 489, 492, 508, 514, 520

blues rock- 143, 145, 159, 281, 299, 322, 343,
    363, 375, 395, 409, 427, 489

Blues Hall of Fame- 5, 6, 27, 49, 240, 279,
    300, 304, 308, 364

Bob Marley and the Wailers- see
    Marley, Bob

Bon Jovi- **241-242**

Bon Jovi, Jon (Bongiovi, Jon)- 241

Bonham, John- 489, 490

Bono- 237, 282, 482, 483

Bono, Sonny- see Sonny & Cher

boogie-woogie- 95, 221, 245, 403

Booker T. and the M.G.'s- 251

Boone, Pat- 5, 95

Boston Pops Orchestra- 350

Boswell, Connee- 387

Boulanger, Nadia- 53, 71

Bowie, David- 29, 53, 75, 87, 97, 109, 121,
    165, 291, 315, 355, 380, 404, 422, 432,
    473, 476, 488, 507, **508-510**

Box Tops, The- 17

Boyz II Men- 83, 168, 391

Brandy- 15

Braun, Scooter- 267

Brennan, Kathleen- 9

Brooks, Garth- 369, **451-452**, 477

Brothers, Kerry- 301

Brown, Bobby- 467

Brown, Chris- **45-46**, 419

Brown, David- 285

Brown, James- 183, 305, 404, **453-454**, 473

Browne, Jackson- **93-94**

Brubeck, Dave- **157-158**

Brubeck, Iola- 157

Bruce, Jack- 427

Bruce, Michael- 151

Bryan, David- 241

Bryson, Peabo- 402

bubblegum music- 115, 163

Buck, Peter- 311

Buckingham, Lindsey- 375, 376

Buckland, Johnny- 317

Buffalo Springfield- 125, 413

Burke, Clem- 121

Burke, Sonny- 35, 59

Burton, Cliff- 383

Bush, Kate- **81-82**, 131

Butler, Geezer- 343, 344

Butler, Jerry- 201

Buxton, Glen- 151

Bynum, Taylor Ho- 131

Byrds, The- 13, 93, 125, **135-136**, 311,
    313, 354

Byrne, David- 119

C

CBGB- 163, 181

CCR- see Creedence Clearwater Revival

Caballe, Montserrat- 476

Cadence Records- 117

Cain, Jonathan- 139

Cale, John- 291

Callas, Maria- 393

Calloway, Cab- 51, 336

Campbell, Glen- 13, 69, **333-334**

Campbell, Mike- 313

Capitol Records- 91, 143, 171, 421, 503

Carabello, Michael- 285

Carey, Mariah- 115, 127, **391-392**, 405, 419,
    495, 496

Carlile, Brandi- 436

Carmen, Eric- 401

Carnegie Hall- 293, 297, 385, 388, 389, 464

Carpenter, Karen- 31

Carpenter, Richard- 31

gospel- 6, 13, 29, 61, 63, 69, 138, 153, 173, 201, 221, 223, 249, 251, 263, 275, 281, 287, 302, 308, 363, 372, 381, 385, 386, 403, 404, 405, 425, 433, 441, 443, 449, 450, 453, 458, 479, 495, 496, 499, 507, 516, 520, 521

Gospelaires, The- 61

Gossard, Stone- 169

Gould, Glenn- 470

Graham, Johnny- 371

Graham, Larry- 223

Grainger, Percy- 463

Grammy Awards- 2, 5, 6, 9, 11, 17, 19, 23, 31, 33, 35, 39, 41, 43, 45, 51, 59, 62, 63, 69, 71, 75, 77, 79, 91, 105, 113, 127, 129, 133, 141, 143, 154, 158, 165, 175, 179, 184, 185, 189, 203, 207, 211, 213, 215, 217, 236, 253, 267, 275, 279, 285, 294, 301, 302, 305, 317, 318, 324, 328, 333, 337, 350, 353, 358, 361, 371, 374, 379, 382, 388, 390, 391, 394, 396, 397, 399, 401, 405, 407, 416, 419, 421, 428, 435, 446, 449, 467, 469, 470, 477, 482, 484, 485, 496, 502, 521

Grand Ole Opry- 69, 347, 433, 458

Grande, Ariana- **115-116**, 477, 485

Grandmaster Flash- 195

Granz, Norman- 387

Grateful Dead- 343, **365-366**

Great American Songbook- 39, 357, 387, 394

Grech, Ric- 427

Green, Al- 119, **249-250**, 421

Green Day- 163, **203-204**, 234

Green, Peter- 375

Greenwood, Colin- 337

Greenwood, Jonny- 337

Groban, Josh- 402

Grohl, Dave- 91, 359

grunge music- 91, 169, 359, 360, 414

Guardian, The- 43, 173, 416

Guitarist (magazine)- 431

Guns N' Roses- 234, **273-274**, 396

Guthrie, Woody- 155, 199, 263, **329-330**, 520

H

Hackett, Steve-57

Hagar, Sammy- 227

Haggard, Merle- 73, 153, 265, **341-342**, 369, 444, 480

Haley, Bill- **103-104**, 187, 498

Hambitzer, Charles- 283

Hamilton, Jack- 501

Hamilton, Tom- 395

Hammett, Kirk- 383

Hammond, John- 279, 297, 389, 390, 511, 520

Hampton, Lionel- 298

Hanan, Stephen- 335

Hancock, Herbie- 436, 439

hard bop- see bebop

hard rock- 6, 91, 145, 151, 227, 229, 241, 273, 339, 359, 383, 395, 409, 410, 473, 475, 476, 489, 490

Hardin, Lil- 492

Harris, Emmylou- 263

Harris, Steve- 67

Harrison, George- 197, 473, 523, 524

Harrison, Jerry- 119

Harrison, Nigel- 121

Harry, Debbie- 121

Hart, Mickey- 366

Hathaway, Donny- 354

Hawkins, Coleman- 52

Hawkins, Ronnie- 269

Hawkins, Screamin' Jay- 29

Hawkins, Taylor- 91, 92

Headon, Nicky- 255

heavy metal- 6, 67, 87, 145, 149, 151, 205, 227, 229, 241, 273, 327, 359, 383, 384, 395, 409, 410, 432, 475, 489

Helm, Levon- 269

Henderson, Fletcher- 297, 298, 492

P

Price, Leontyne- 294, 466

Price, Ray- 137, 443

Prince- 15, 82, 165, 224, 259, 305, 339,
  472-474

Prince, Wesley- 355

Prine, John- **19-20**, 143

Product G&B, The- 286

Professor Griff- 289

progressive pop music- 81, 441

progressive rap music- 63

progressive rock music- 6, 57, 81, 139, 145,
  441, 460, 476

progressive soul music- 415, 441

psychedelic music- 57, 63, 135, 247, 277,
  285, 321, 333, 343, 365, 417, 460, 473

Public Enemy- 255, 271, **289-290**

Pulitzer Prize- 5, 71, 316, 521

punk- 6, 77, 87, 91, 119, 121, 131, 149, 161,
  163, 181, 203, 205, 233, 255, 291, 327,
  359, 414, 432, 441

Q

Quaife, Pete- 149

Queen- 203, 259, 359, **475-476**, 489

R

RCA Records (RCA Victor)- 73, 127, 235,
  257, 263, 307, 516

R.E.M.- 136, 291, **311-312**

RIAA (Recording Industry Association of
  America)- 3, 5, 17, 39, 147, 169, 245,
  361, 390, 397, 451

R&B (rhythm & blues)- 6,11, 13, 15, 25, 27,
  33, 37, 43, 45, 49, 61, 79, 83, 95, 101,
  103, 111, 115, 127, 143, 147, 159, 165,
  167, 173, 177, 179, 183, 185, 193, 201,
  207, 217, 221, 223, 249, 250, 251, 253,
  255, 261, 267, 269, 275, 277, 281, 287,
  295, 299, 301, 305, 339, 353, 355, 357,
  363, 371, 377, 391, 392, 397, 403, 409,
  415, 419, 421, 423, 446, 449, 453, 455,

460, 466, 472, 473, 477, 495, 501, 502,
  517, 518

R&B Music Hall of Fame- 5, 6, 25, 29, 62,
  148, 278, 390

Radiohead- 312, **337-338**, 476

ragtime music- 2, 463, 492

Rainey, Ma- 303

Raitt, Bonnie- 19, **143-144**

Ramones- **163-164**, 203, 255, 359

rap- see hip-hop

rap rock- 205, 271, 327

Red Hot Chili Peppers- **327-328**

Redding, Noel- 437

Redding, Otis- **251-252**, 377, 495

Redman- 127

Reed, Lou- 291

Reed, Ryan- 405

reggae- 6, 63, 121, 161, 181, 225, 255, 305,
  381, 455, 456, 502

reggae rock- 225, 305

Replacements, The- 203

Reprise Records- 203

Reznor, Trent- 87

Rhodes, Nick- 107

Rhythm Boys, The- see Crosby, Bing

Rice, Tim- 499

Rich, Frank- 387

Richards, Keith- 240, 514, 515

Richardson, Kevin- 83

Richie, Lionel- **185-186**, 193, 247

Riddle, Nelson- 393, 503, 504

Ridgeley, Andrew- 275

Riggs, Jonathan- 361

Righteous Brothers, The- 354

Rihanna- 45, 318, **419-420**, 473, 477

Rimes, LeAnn- 348

Roach, Max- 189

Roars, Beth- 496

Robertson, Robbie- 269

Robinson, Cynthia- 223

Robinson, Smokey- **33-34**, 147, 193, 277,
  287, 295

Roc-A-Fella Records- 441, 445, 446

Townshend, Pete- 423, 424, 437
Traveling Wilburys, The- 197, 198, 313
Travolta, John- 141, 142, 378
Trucks, Butch- 159
Tubb, Ernest- 426
Tucker, C. Delores- 195
Tucker, Moe- 291
Turner, Ike- 27, 421, 422
Turner, Tina- **421-422**
Twain, Shania- 75, **367-368**, 484
Twitty, Conway- 426
Tyler, Steven- 395

U

U2- 291, 441, **482-483**
Ulrich, Lars- 383, 384
Ulvaeus, Bjorn- 345
Underwood, Carrie- **153-154**, 368, 378
Union Station- 175, 176
Universal-International- 133
Usher- 45, **165-166**, 267, 301

V

Valens, Richie- 187, 231
Valentine, Gary- 121
Valory, Ross- 139
Van Halen- 197, **227-228**, 344, 396
Van Halen, Alex- 227
Van Halen, Eddie- 227, 428
Van Zandt, Steven- 512
vaudeville- 279, 335, 487, 521
Vaughan, Sarah- **59-60**
Vecsey, George- 425
Vedder, Eddie- 169
Vee, Bobby- 353
Velvet Underground, The- **291-292**
Vicious, Sid- 233, 234
Victor Company- see RCA Records
Virgin Records- 43
Visconti, Tony- 508
vocal duo- 117, 373
Vocal Group Hall of Fame- 25, 117, 129, 296

Vogue- 171

W

Wagner, Richard- 349
Wagoner, Porter- 458
Wailer, Bunny- 455, 456
Wailers, The- 455, 456, 457
Waitts, Tom- **9-10**,
Walker, T-Bone- 363
Waller, Fats- 279
Walsh, Joe- 431, 432
Ward, Bill- 343
Warhol, Andy- 291
Warner Bros. Records (Warner Records)- 227, 371
Warnes, Jennifer- 17, 18
Warwick, Dee Dee- 61
Warwick, Dionne- **61-62**, 371, 466
Was, Don- 143
Washington Post, The- 483
Waters, Muddy- 27, **299-300**, 411, 428, 514
Waters, Roger- 19, 460, 461, 462
Watts, Charlie- 514, 515
Weavers, The- 199, 200
Webb, Chick- 387
Webb, Jimmy- 253, 333, 334
Webster, Ben- 464
Webster, Paul- 59
Weeknd, The- 43
Weir, Bob- 366
Welborn, Larry- 187
Wells, Dicky- 279
Wells, Mary- 33,
West, Dottie- 348
West, Kanye- see Ye
western music- 333
western swing- 103, 369
Wexler, Jerry- 287
Weymouth, Tina- 119
Wham!- 275, 276
White, Bukka- 363
White, Jack- 426

ABOUT THE AUTHOR

Amateur musician, teacher, and historian, Steve Williams has been playing his guitar and singing for decades—on street corners, in sundry bar gigs, even in church, while making his living as a longtime, award-winning classroom schoolteacher across seven different states. Drawing on his lifetime love of music and history, this is Steve's first published book. He and his wife make their home in Maui.

Dear Reader

I am grateful that you took the time to read my book. If you enjoyed it, tell your friends and family and please consider writing an honest review (e.g., on Amazon, Goodreads, BookBaby, or any platform you are comfortable with), for that is how indie authors, like myself, gain exposure. Thank you.